Validating Holistic Scoring for Writing Assessment: Theoretical and Empirical Foundations

WRITTEN LANGUAGE
S E R I E S

(Marcia Farr, editor)

Validating Holistic Scoring for Writing Assessment: Theoretical and Empirical Foundations

Editors

Michael M. Williamson
Indiana University of Pennsylvania

Brian A. Huot
University of Louisville

HAMPTON PRESS, INC.
CRESSKILL, NEW JERSEY

Printed in the United States of America

Library of Congress Cataloging-in-Publication Data

Validating holistic scoring for writing assessment: theoretical and
    empirical foundations/ Michael M. Williamson and Brian A. Huot,
    editors.
        p. cm. — (Written language)
    Includes bibliographical references and index.
    ISBN 1-881303-94-2 (cloth). — vii
ISBN 1-881303-95-0 (paper)
        1. English language—Composition and exercises—Study and
    teaching. 2. English language—Rhetoric—Study and teaching.
    3. English language—Ability testing. 4. Examinations—Validity.
    5. School prose—Evaluation. 6. College prose—Evaluation.
    I. Williamson, Michael M. II. Huot, Brian A. III. Series.
    LB1631.V35 1992
    808'.042'076—dc20   92-37934
                                                                    CIP

Hampton Press, Inc.
23 Broadway
Cresskill, NJ 07626

Contents

Series Preface

Marcia Farr, series editor
University of Illinois at Chicago

This new series examines the characteristics of *writing* in the human world. Volumes in the series present scholarly work on written language in its various contexts. Across time and space, human beings use various forms of written language—or writing systems—to fulfill a range of social, cultural, and personal functions, and this diversity can be studied from a variety of perspectives within both the social sciences and the humanities, including those of linguistics, anthropology, psychology, education, rhetoric, literary criticism, philosophy, and history. Although writing is not often used apart from oral language, or without aspects of reading, and thus many volumes in this series include other facets of language and communication, writing itself receives primary emphasis.

In this volume, issues surrounding the assessment of writing are addressed. As Williamson and Huot point out, the burgeoning of research on writing processes and on the contexts in which writing occurs has not been matched with studies of assessment. Even more crucially, theoretical issues in the assessment of writing have been, by and large, neglected, in spite of the centrality of these issues to the entire field. Assessment, after all, raises fundamental questions about how to define the model, or set of standards, by which we judge particular pieces of writing. In other words, the assessment of writing necessarily entails a shared understanding about that elusive set of qualities we call "good writing," or perhaps about an equally elusive set of processes that we believe are involved in producing "good writing." This volume contributes significantly to our theoretical understanding of writing assessment, and it is intended to stimulate further work in this area.

While the study of writing is absorbing in its own right, it is an increasingly important social issue as well, as demographic movements occur around the world and as language and ethnicity accrue more intensely political meanings. Writing, and literacy more generally, is central to education, and education in turn is central to occupational and social mobility. Manuscripts that present either the results of empirical research, both qualitative and quantitative, or theoretical treatments of relevant issues are encouraged for submission.

Preface

Assessment has been one of the most controversial aspects of the study of writing. Unlike the study of writing itself, positions on writing assessment have become entrenched and inflexible. Part of the answer lies in the amount of money spent by school districts and colleges on assessment each year. We believe that the greater the risk, under these circumstances, the less likely individuals are to take risks. Furthermore, the testing industry has been heavily invested in a particular approach to writing assessment. Most of their energy has been directed toward defending their position, as opposed to developing new ideas. Although, to be fair, most of the current developments in writing assessment, including the most radical, have involved staff researchers and test developers at the Educational Testing Service. At the same time, the study of writing has undergone radical transformation in the last 30 years. Researchers and theorists have developed new insights that represent a considerable elaboration of our understanding of writing and the teaching of writing, since 1963 when Richard Braddock, Richard Lloyd-Jones, and Lowell Schorer wrote in *Research on Written Composition*, "Today's research in composition, taken as a whole, may be compared to chemical research as it emerged from the period of alchemy . . . the field as a whole is laced with dreams, prejudices, and makeshift operations" (NCTE Press, p. 5).

While an individual's tendency toward optimism or pessimism may determine whether the field is seen as having grown to any extent since that time, there is no denying, however, that powerful new explanatory concepts have emerged in the literature. The value of such concepts as cognitive processes and social construction for a theory of writing remains under discussion. The suggested research methodologies espoused by Braddock et al. have been refined and challenged during that time, indicating a field in development.

Writing assessment, on the other hand, has not experienced a similarly rich development. In 1977, Charles R. Cooper and Lee Odell edited a book published by NCTE Press, *Assessing Writing: Measuring, Describing, Judging.* Representing the state of the art, it contained chapters on holistic scoring and primary trait scoring, among others. There was no chapter on indirect assessment, the technique which dominated in assessment and evaluation practices at the time. In 1985, Ed White consolidated what we know about writing assessment and in 1986, Karen L. Greenberg, Harvey S. Weiner, and Richard A. Donovan published another edited collection, *Writing Assessment: Issues and Strategies*. The value of this book lay primarily in the historical perspective on writing assessment developed by some of the authors and the practical advice of others. There was little development or elaboration of a theory of writing assessment in the decade between the two books. Notably, there was considerable challenge to direct assessment, suggesting that the controversy had become more powerful during that time.

As we worked on this book, we were encouraged by the changes that we began to see in approaches to writing assessment. While developments in the practice of writing assessment have not been as profound as those in the teaching of writing, we were pleasantly surprised by the work of researchers such as Bill Smith, Sandy Murphy, and Leo Ruth reported here. A single new concept, contextualization, summarizes what we believe will be the basis for a radical change in approaches to assessing writing in the future.

Chapter One is intended to make this development explicit through both a longish introduction to the book and an attempt to explain current developments. It provides as comprehensive an introduction as time and space allowed.

Our efforts have been aided by too many people to be mentioned here, although there are some we must now mention. We want to thank Bill Smith for the many hours he invested in talking with us, even before we has the idea for the book. He has been an informal mentor to many of us in the profession over the years. His contribution to innumerable careers can never be acknowledged adequately. We also want to thank Barbara Bernstein of Hampton Press for her patience, encouragement, and skill.

Finally, we want to thank Sarah, Caitlin, Meghan, and Emily for the thousands of hugs that make the daily struggle worthwhile. We wish this book was as interesting as *Where the Wild Things Are*.

MMW   Indiana, PA
BAH   Jeffersonville, IN

REFERENCES

Braddock, R., Lloyd-Jones, R., & Schorer, L. (1963). *Research in written composition*. Urbana, IL: National Council of Teachers of English.

Cooper, C. R., & Odell, L. (1977). *Evaluating writing: Describing, measuring, judging*. Urbana, IL: National Council of Teachers of English.

Greenberg, K. L., Weiner, H. S., & Donovan, R. A. (Eds.). (1986). *Writing assessment: Issues and strategies*. New York: Longman.

White, E. M. (1985). *Teaching and assessing writing*. San Francisco: Jossey-Bass.

1

An Introduction to Holistic Scoring: The Social, Historical, and Theoretical Context for Writing Assessment

 **Michael M. Williamson**
Indiana University of Pennsylvania

INTRODUCTION

Judging writing ability on the basis of written texts is probably as old as written language itself; and, the subjectivity of these judgments is well documented (Britton, Martin, & Rosen, 1966; Cast, 1939, 1940; Diederich, 1974; Diederich, French, & Carlton, 1961; Finlawson, 1951; Hartog & Rhodes, 1936; Hillegas, 1915; Hinton, 1940; McColly, 1970; Noyes, 1963; Willing, 1918; Wiseman, 1949). Multiple choice, machine-scored tests of writing, deemed objective because they provided consistent estimates of students' writing ability, were one response to this subjectivity. Formal procedures for judging student writing, intended to mirror the objectivity of multiple choice tests by helping teachers to make consistent judgments about student writing, were a second response.

This latter response, *direct writing assessment,* is a continuation of the historical use of writing as an assessment tool in all disciplines (Britton, Martin, & Rosen, 1966; Diederich, 1974; Hillegas, 1915; Hartog & Rhodes, 1936), as well as an application of recent developments in the study of writing. However, the assessment theory used in direct assessment, holistic scoring in particular, is an alternate application of the same empirical methodologies of educational and psychological measurement used in developing machine-scored *indirect writing assessment.*

The relative merits of direct and indirect writing assessment pro-

1

cedures have been argued at considerable length and are well documented (Breland, Camp, Jones, Morris, & Rock, 1987; C. Cooper, 1977;
P. Cooper, 1984; Godshalk, Swineford, & Coffman, 1966; Huot, 1990;
Spandel & Stiggins, 1980). Missing, however, has been an examination of
the context for writing assessment in American education—the context
for the debate between proponents of both approaches. While this
context sheds light on the practical and theoretical controversy over the
two approaches to assessing writing, it is more important for
understanding the future of writing assessment and the validity of direct
assessment (see Camp, this volume). Since holistic scoring is the most
popular and widely used form of direct assessment (Charney, 1984; Gere,
1980; Huot, 1990), we chose to focus our efforts in this book on that
approach alone.

This first chapter is intended (a) to provide a historical, social, and
theoretical context for understanding the various theoretical and
empirical studies of the validity of holistic scoring reported in the
following chapters, and (b) to raise some basic problems with the validity
of holistic scoring that have yet to be addressed in any validation research.

Written Texts and Writing Ability

The context for validation research on holistic scoring begins with an
understanding of the distinction between written texts and writing ability.
This dichotomy emerged from the intellectual tradition of Western
European philosophy and a science, rooted in the influence of Kant on
modern American psychology (Peters, 1962), and based on explaining
behavior or inferring mental structure from its manifestations in human
behavior. Thus, because writing assessment emerged from measurement
theory in education and psychology, understanding the conflict over
writing assessment involves understanding the differing perspectives on
the theoretical meaning of written texts and the conflicting theories of
writing ability proposed to explain written language. R. D. Cherry
(personal communication, March 1989) suggests that the most important
problem with writing assessment tools has been that writing ability, as a
mental phenomenon, is conceived as involving a very broad set of mental
and social structures (also see Camp, this volume). In his view, the validity
of assessment techniques has not been established because explicit,
coherent models of writing do not exist to provide evaluation criteria for
validation research.

Basic Theoretical Differences between Direct and Indirect Assessment

Three important theoretical differences emerge in the dispute over direct
versus indirect assessment. First, proponents of indirect assessment view
reading as the extraction of meaning from a text and writing as

communication of ideas through written language. Proponents of direct assessment view both reading and writing as the construction of meaning. These two conflicting views reflect different beliefs about the structure of the human mind and written language, emerging from different epistemological frameworks (Camp, this volume). Second, proponents of each view cite different key texts (White, this volume) and advocate different measurement devices. Finally, each model has grown out of different views of American education and, as will be shown in this chapter, they have profoundly different impacts on teachers and students in writing classrooms.

Several general criticisms of multiple choice tests emerged with the very first proposals to replace writing as an assessment tool with multiple choice tests. These objections can be summarized as follows: (a) multiple choice items, because they have a single correct answer, involve convergent thinking (Camp, this volume); (b) convergent thinking is the easiest to measure objectively since it usually involves a simple conception of correct and incorrect responses by students, but it is often the least important aspect of any curricula (Popham, 1988); (c) the use of convergent evaluation tools tends to focus teachers' efforts away from a balance between convergent and divergent thinking because curricula are driven by assessment (Popham, 1988); and therefore, (d) assessment must be planned around curricular goals, including the most and least objectively assessed outcomes (Popham, 1988).

Furthermore, many educators also continue to believe that writing promotes a synthetic view of their disciplines and they have shown a continuing concern that, as assessment moves away from the use of writing, writing has little place in curricula (Emig, 1977).

While criticizing the model of language underlying objective tests of writing, English teachers responded to the development of indirect assessment with an important counter-assertion; direct assessment is more valid than indirect assessment because it involves performance of the behavior being assessed (Eley, 1955). Unfortunately, the logical and theoretical limits of this tautology have occupied the energy and focus of proponents of direct assessment ever since. This stance toward indirect assessment has also prevented a critical examination of the limits of various approaches to direct assessment.

Implicit in the tautological defense of direct assessment are two beliefs shared by all the authors in this volume. These beliefs provide the basis for developing a theory of writing assessment out of a theory of writing. First, writing is a constructive mental process more complicated than the various types of knowledge which are its component parts; and second, a more recent belief that writing is a highly contextualized process that cannot be segmented from the social, linguistic, and situational context in which it occurs (Camp, this volume).

Unfortunately, proponents of direct assessment have apparently not looked beyond the tautology cited above to examine the limits of holistic scoring in terms of the recent developments in the study of writing. Typically, they have only stated their argument in terms of the tautology itself by claiming that they judge multiple choice tests to involve a view of writing too limited to be considered valid. This argument employs the psychometric concept of *content validity* to refute the use of indirect procedures. Content validity is defined in psychological measurement theory as the judgment of experts about the adequacy of the content of a test and the testing procedures themselves to measure the phenomenon of interest (Anastasi, 1976). This argument also clearly exposes the use of psychometric theory to justify holistic scoring procedures, among other forms of direct assessment.

White (this volume) provides a window on the early problems faced by writing specialists as they attempted to have their views taken seriously by assessment specialists. Reading his chapter, I could not help but think that most writing specialists were treated as uninformed children, as he suggests, because their theories of writing were often too incomplete to provide a solid foundation for counter-proposals to indirect assessment. Furthermore, their arguments began to take on a religious character at times. The apparently uninformed, childlike character of their presentations was, no doubt, reinforced by their imprecise interpretation of concepts from psychometrics as they were not trained in psychometric theory. Thus, the interpretation of the meaning of content validity suggested in the tautology I cited above probably led psychometricians to reject the argument out of hand.

Furthermore, psychometricians have been less concerned with content validity, a process used in the construction of an assessment procedure, and have pointed to empirically established limits in the measurement properties of direct assessment, most importantly the limited statistical reliability of judgments of writing samples. As White (this volume), who is a strong proponent of holistic scoring suggests, lack of reliability implies an unfair and illogical basis for assessment. From the perspective of psychometrics, then, indirect assessment has been viewed as more valid because validity is both a logical and statistical function of the reliability of a test (see Cherry & Meyer, this volume). Moreover, proponents of indirect assessment can point to their own experts who can provide content validity judgments counter to the claims of proponents of direct assessment.

The problem for the authors in this book has been to break free of the stasis in writing assessment imposed by the continuing debate. We all seem to accept the notion that holistic scoring has been one of the best solutions to the problem of direct assessment so far. However, we also believe that the future of writing assessment must begin with a critical look at what we have achieved since the first codifications of holistic scoring procedures (Conlon, 1976; Cooper, 1977; Diederich, 1974).

Organization of This Chapter

In the second section of this chapter, I will continue to develop a context for writing assessment through sketches of the theoretical and historical development of educational and psychological measurement. In the third section, I will trace the social functions of assessment in American schools. As they are relevant, I will show how each of the subsequent chapters in this book provide an important basis for continuing developments in writing assessment. In the fourth and final section of this chapter, I will sketch the social issues that seem likely to confront future developments in writing assessment, issues beyond the scope of the other chapters in this book.

EDUCATIONAL AND PSYCHOLOGICAL MEASUREMENT: THEORY

The general goal of American behaviorist psychology, the body of scientific theory that gave birth to psychometrics, has been to create a science based in the empirical discovery of laws governing behavior (Hebb, 1949; Hull, 1943; Skinner, 1938; Thorndike, 1932; Tolman, 1932; Watson, 1930). Science, in this definition, was explicitly modeled on the positivist empiricism of the natural sciences (Guilford, 1954, Lord & Novick, 1968; Skinner, 1956). Thus, the goal of psychological assessment originated in an emulation of the positivist foundation of measurement in natural science, as did the behaviorist psychology that it was developed to assist.

As in natural science, empirical research in American behaviorist psychology was expected to yield generalized, a priori laws of behavior applicable to both humans and animals (Skinner, 1957). Furthermore, in the explicit emulation of the natural sciences, mathematics was conceived as the formal modeling tool for the language of psychological measurement (Spearman, 1937; also cited in Guilford, 1954), with Guilford (1954) suggesting that the maturity of a science could be estimated by the sophistication of its mathematical procedures.

The theoretical functions of measurement or assessment tools in psychometrics parallel the functions of measurement in the natural sciences. Instruments are designed to sample empirical phenomena—to gather data—such as observable human behavior in psychology, or the movement of the stars in astronomy. These empirical data form the basis

for testing hypotheses about the nature of laws governing the phenomenon. Of course, all complex scientific instruments are subject to
measurement error resulting from internal processes in the measuring
device itself or from external errors due to the operator/observer. Thus,
instrumental reliability is important for the validity of theories based
upon data gathered by instruments because errors in empirical
observation alter the truth of the phenomenon, leading to incorrect
statements of the laws governing empirical phenomena.

This view of science maintains that both the data collected by
instruments and the explanation of that data exist independently of the
observer. Theory is discovered by the scientist; the truth of theory is
independent of the temporal and cultural limits of that person. Because
theory is held to be unaltered by its historical and temporal context, as
well as the social and cultural context of the observer, this view of science
has been labeled "context-free" (Guba, 1990). Psychological instruments,
and the behavioral laws they were designed to discover, were also held to
be context-free (Guilford, 1954; Skinner, 1956). In radical behaviorism,
laws of behavior were expected to generalize directly from animals to
humans. For instance, Skinner (1957) saw language as an instance of
more general laws governing all learning processes in all species.

It is important to note that some disagreement existed among
behaviorists about the use of mediating concepts such as the mind in a
theory of human behavior. As psychology emerged from the intuitionist,
clinical applications of psychoanalysis and developed into an empirical
science, psychologists believed it important to demystify intuitive
methodologies and to build a science on research methodologies that
could be described explicitly. They also questioned the value of theoretical
constructs, such as the mind, which were used to explain behavior, but
could not be observed directly. Radical behaviorism, proposed initially by
Watson, and matured with Skinner, was based upon a denial of any entity
that could not be observed directly through empirical techniques. Current
developments in cognitive psychology have shifted the focus of
psychological inquiry from a discovery of laws of behavior to an
explanation of the structure of the human mind. This shift represents a
return to some of the earlier goals of psychology, and a rejection of the
extreme positivist empiricism of radical behaviorism (Gardner, 1987).

Unfortunately, psychometrics has developed an independent life
through its applications in educational tests and clinical assessment.
These applications have not kept pace with developments in cognitive
psychology and associated research methodologies, such as protocol
analysis. Thus, applications of protocol analysis are common in basic
research on writing while the earlier developments of psychometrics,
based in a behaviorist psychology, continue to dominate writing

assessment practices. I will attempt to make explicit some of the reasons for this apparent fossilization of theory in the next section of this chapter.

Foundations of Measurement Theory in Psychology and Education

The primary concern of the measurement scientist is to overcome the physical and temporal limits of the human senses by designing instruments that measure and record data with sufficient precision and accuracy to insure a valid basis for hypothesis testing about the laws governing the phenomenon of interest. This validity criterion provides the objectivity that, in turn, validates the context-free assumption of measurement in science. If instruments are independent of the limits of human perception, then they provide an objective record of the events they measure. Further-more, the objective record can be consulted for regularities which reflect the existence of a priori laws that govern the phenomenon. As I have been suggesting, such laws of behavior have been the goal of behaviorist psychology.

All scientific instruments, however, provide an indirect view of the phenomena they measure. From a common sense framework, this statement seems less true of a telescope, for instance, than a psychological test because the telescope appears to directly extend the limits of one of the human senses. In fact, a telescope magnifies the light or radio waves reflected or emitted by cosmic bodies and does not result in direct observation at all. All theoretical descriptions of astronomical bodies are based on interpretation of the meaning of such waves in terms of a theory of the relationship between the data provided by a telescope and the hypothesized structures of cosmic bodies developed in advance of the collection of data. Thus, the theory itself determines how the observer will collect and evaluate data.

A mental illness, such as schizophrenia, is observed as a cluster of behavioral symptoms. In theory, the symptoms result from some root cause in the human mind. Since mind is an abstraction, it cannot be observed directly. Therefore, schizophrenia, an abstract, theoretical explanation of a particular set of symptoms, cannot be measured directly. Thus, the clinical psychologist may depend upon an instrument to provide an independent measure of the extent of the mental illness as part of the diagnostic process. This observational process is modeled on the observational process in natural sciences. The patient's behavior is sampled and interpreted in terms of a theory of mind and its manifestations in behavior. Thus, the theory of mind itself determines how data will be sampled and understood.

However, a patient's symptoms, like the light or radio waves reflected by a planet, could be explained from a variety of theoretical perspectives.

Even if the scientist believes that data exist prior to his/her measurement, those data could reflect a variety of events, some of which might not be contained in any theory. Thus, the accuracy or validity of scientific instruments in both the natural and social sciences would seem more important than their instrumental precision (the reliability of instruments), because what instruments measure and what observers see, depends upon their initial theoretical assumptions. Validation research requires that these assumptions be stated explicitly and the validity of instruments be evaluated against the claims of the theory.

Consistent with the common sense view that social sciences are not as rigorously empirical as natural sciences, Lord and Novick (1968) suggest that measurements in the physical sciences are inherently more reliable than in psychometrics, and that the physical scientist has greater control over the variables under examination than the mental scientist. Of course, this view is founded upon a positivist empiricism that maintains that the laws of science and the phenomena that they explain exist prior to their discovery. Science is the act of discovering and describing them. Furthermore, citing Torgerson (1958), Lord and Novick argue, "The concepts of theoretical interest (in psychology) tend to lack empirical meaning, whereas the corresponding concepts with precise empirical meaning often lack theoretical import . . ." (Torgerson, 1958, p. 8)

In other words, important mental events cannot be clearly defined in empirical terms and empirically precise (reliable) mental measurements are rarely of any theoretical importance (lack validity). It seems unnecessary for me to suggest that this criticism of psychometrics by psychometricians summarizes the current dilemma facing writing assessment.

Thus, reliability as the ground for the debate over writing assessment is curious, if not counterintuitive. Since data (behaviors related to writing) are one step removed from the phenomenon under study (the mental structures involved with writing), a concern for the validity of measurement techniques would seem to increase. But, the psychometric criticism of direct assessment procedures has focused primarily on reliability, not validity. Thus, in the long run, indirect measures, with their emphasis on reliability, are a victim of the criticism raised within the field that provided an assessment framework for developing them. They lack "theoretical import." Unfortunately, direct measures do not have demonstrable validity either, because their proponents only assert that they are more valid than indirect measures. Again, the circularity of the logic involved with defending direct measures has made their proponents a victim of their own argument because they cannot point to any significant body of research—quantitative, qualitative, or theoretical— that addresses the problems raised about both their validity and reliability (Charney, 1984; Gere, 1980; Huot, 1990). Certainly, techniques have been developed to insure reliable judgments (Cooper, 1977; Myers,

1980). However, what techniques have been developed to insure that the whole measurement process is a reliable assessment of a writer's ability (Cherry & Meyer, this volume)? Students often perform with very differential results on different topics within a single discourse mode because their familiarity with a topic determines how articulately they are able to write about it (Faigley, Cherry, Jolliffe, & Skinner, 1985). The current theoretical solution to the problem of writing assessment provided by proponents of indirect approaches—segmentation of knowledge of writing from knowledge of topic—is clearly too artificial (Camp, this volume). While the bulk of research on writing confirms the accuracy of this criticism, there is no evidence either that direct assessments have been designed that account for the implications of this problem. Furthermore, to the extent that direct assessment is built upon context-free assumptions about measurement, assessment techniques conflict with the basic notion that writing is a highly contextualized act (Camp, this volume; Murphy & Ruth, this volume).

A Theory of Writing Consistent with Psychometric Theory

Halloran (1990) outlines a theory of writing consistent with psychometric approaches to assessment: (a) Writing involves a stable form of knowledge about language that can be passed directly from teacher to students; (b) this knowledge is primarily about linguistic forms and discourse formats; and (c) writing is only a vessel for communication of ideas. Since thinking and writing are individual sets of knowledge which must be evaluated separately, declarative knowledge about writing is a reflection of an individual's writing ability. Halloran suggests that these beliefs emerged in the late nineteenth century when rhetoricians expected to base a theory of writing on empiricist principles. It also connected them to the logical positivism emerging in science at the time.

Writing and psychometrics find a common ground here because multiple choice items are best at capturing declarative, decontextualized knowledge. On the other hand, contemporary theories of writing stress the need to account for the context of language use. This principle grows directly out of the application of linguistics to the study of writing, discourse analysis, and sociolinguistics in particular. If indirect assessment has failed to account for the influence of context in writing, a theory of holistic scoring emulating the qualities of indirect assessment and based in the context-free assumptions of psychometrics diverges radically from the current mainstream in the study of writing. Again, the emulation of properties of indirect assessment underscores the foundations of holistic scoring procedures in educational and psychological measurement.

An independent, language-based theory of assessment (Huot & Williamson, 1990) would have to begin with an examination of the foundations for assessment as they emerge from theories of writing, as opposed to the cognate disciplines. However, this examination, like much of the research on writing, may examine cognate disciplines, such as psychometrics, for critiques of particular proposals for assessment.

Unfortunately the debate over direct and indirect assessment has emphasized only the operational limits of each approach, leading to an increasing polarization of the two camps, with both sides merely defending their ground instead of moving forward to examine the theoretical validity of their assumptions about writing and the methodological and practical implications of those assumptions. Despite this stasis, and due to recent developments in the study of writing, writing researchers and teachers clearly believe that direct assessment is the most productive approach to writing assessment in the long run (Camp, this volume). This view is shared by all of the authors in this book. This premise provides an important context for understanding our interest in undertaking studies of the validity of holistic scoring, in spite of the criticisms of direct assessment and the current limitations of holistic scoring procedures. Explaining and overcoming these limitations is, precisely, the challenge for studies of the validity of holistic scoring.

Consequently, the tautology, "writing is the best measure of writing," has to be rejected as an argument in its own right because it does not provide solutions to the problem of assessing writing, a multifaceted mental act profoundly influenced by the social contexts of its use. The demand for objectivity as a criterion for effective writing assessment techniques, in the sense that emerged in early psychometric theory, does not seem reasonable either.

The Two Definitions of Validity

Referring to Greenberg, Weiner, and Donovan's (1986) preface to their edited collection on direct writing assessment, Bizzell (1987, p. 587) suggests that validity has a "colloquial sense," a usage not part of the specialized vocabulary of a discipline. She is referring to their use of the content validation argument, in which they claim a consensus among writing specialists that direct assessment is the only valid way to measure writing ability and identifying validity as the most reasonable and logical of the measurement procedures. But, reason and logic, like objectivity, are terms that need to have their assumptions foregrounded. Clearly, Greenberg, Weiner, and Donovan meant the assumptions about writing implicit in the content validity tautology which I have outlined. Also implicit is the belief that validity necessarily involves an understanding of the function of writing assessment in educational settings in terms of its effects on students, teachers, curricula, and pedagogy (Camp, this volume). Thus, to understand the validity of a particular writing assessment technique, we need to know that the structure and functions of writing assessment reflect those functions we desire for writing in the schools (Camp, this volume).

Proponents of indirect assessment, because they believe their approach is context free, do not admit that the structure of indirect approaches has an influence on the functions of writing in school. They also point to other forms of validity to justify their use of indirect approaches. Educational and psychological measurement theory poses three types of validation procedures for mental measurements:

1. Content validity, the judgment of experts about the efficacy of the content and procedures of an assessment technique for measuring the phenomenon of interest;
2. Criterion-related validity, the prediction of performance on some task or in some setting (predictive validity) and the relationship between a measure and other similar measures of the same or similar phenomena (concurrent validity); and
3. Construct validity the conformity of a measure with a model or theory of the phenomenon of interest (Anastasi, 1976).

Authorities disagree, of course, over exact definitions with some proposing slightly different formulations (Anastasi, 1976; Cronbach, 1970, 1971; Jensen, 1980; Lord & Novick, 1968). However, Anastasi's definitions provide adequate breadth and are sufficiently pluralistic for my purposes in this chapter.

Criterion-related validity, and in particular predictive validity, is an important but rarely discussed aspect of validity in writing assessment. One very common use of writing assessment procedures is to determine student placement into different levels of a writing curriculum. Smith's (this volume) study of placement testing procedures focuses on the use of holistic scoring to place college-aged students into writing courses at the University of Pittsburgh. The complexity of the research he reports is an indication of the effort necessary to insure valid prediction of student success in a writing curriculum. Of course, the context-free assumptions of psychometric theory were not applied in his study because the assessment was designed to place students in the curriculum at the University of Pittsburgh. Thus, psychometric assessment, as a cognate discipline for writing, provides a potentially important source of critiques. In this case, separating the notion of predictive validity from its context-free assumptions and restating it as "adequacy of placement" in the University of Pittsburgh writing curriculum led to an important research program validating one use of holistic scoring. Smith (this volume) uses the term "adequacy of placement" as a way of separating the concern for the validity of decisions made on the basis of the Pitt placement testing techniques from the problematic theoretical aspects of psychometrics. Particularly important here is the fact that writing assessment procedures are highly contextualized.

On the other hand, simplistic applications of psychometric concepts have caused a great deal of the current stasis in writing assessment. One general criticism of direct assessment procedures which have emerged from an overly simplistic definition of objectivity is that procedures like Smith's "do not travel," meaning that writing tasks and holistic reading procedures cannot be utilized in multiple contexts. This notion of objectivity demands the decontextualization of assessment which implies that every curriculum in every school or university is or should be the same. As Smith's study suggests, only the teachers in the writing courses at Pitt are able to place students into the courses because they share important contextual knowledge about the student population, the writing curriculum, and the functions of writing in the university. In effect, these teachers do not judge students' texts; they infer the teachability of the students in their courses on the basis of the texts they read (Smith, this volume). This predictive view of writing ability is narrow because it is highly contextualized and creates a new dimension to reliability that cannot be evaluated through interrater agreement indices alone (see Cherry & Meyer, this volume; Murphy & Ruth, this volume, for further discussion).

Furthermore, Murphy and Ruth (this volume) suggest that the prompts or topics used in direct assessment procedures are also subject to contextual effects. Topics developed in one school produce very different results in other schools because students read them in very different academic, historical, social, and temporal contexts. The influence of topic knowledge as well as geographic and temporal context on writing performance is well documented (Langer, 1986; Murphy & Ruth, this volume). Indirect assessments are considered objective because they do not show such contextual bias. They are also considered cheaper and more efficient because they can be purchased ready-made "off the shelf" from test manufacturers and can be machine scored. The technology for machine scoring is now available to anyone with an inexpensive microcomputer.

There is no evidence for the predictive validity of indirect measures. The research on indirect assessment involves concurrent validity, the other type of criterion-related validity. Indirect measures are validated against direct measures of writing (Breland et al., 1987; Breland & Gaynor, 1979; Godshalk, Swineford, & Coffman, 1966). Thus, the use of indirect measures is a doubly indirect view of the potential performance of students in writing curricula. Tests predict how well students would perform on a concurrent set of writing tasks which, in turn, predicts their placement into writing courses. Unfortunately, all writing curricula are not the same. Thus, the relationship between students' hypothesized performance on the criterion tasks in the study and their performance in the courses in a particular curriculum cannot be known without further study. Thus, off-the-shelf assessment, both direct and indirect, requires further research to discover the appropriate level of performance for assignment to individual courses (in this volume see, Huot; Janopoulos; Murphy & Ruth; Pula & Huot; Smith). Furthermore, the types of writing tasks used in a concurrent validation study of an indirect measure may not reflect the variety of discourse modes and types taught in courses in particular writing curricula. Thus, the assignment of students to courses through indirect measures, without a validation study as thorough as that reported by Smith (this volume), is a haphazard affair. Thus, the relative efficiency and cost effectiveness of indirect measures disappears since inappropriate placement is an expensive proposition for both individual students and for writing programs as a whole (Smith, this volume). Furthermore, continual assessment of the effectiveness of a measure is necessary due to changes in student populations entering curricula and changes to curricula.

Validity also has different meanings for both those who do the assessing and those who are assessed. Validity ultimately requires that all parties to the decision being made on the basis of the assessment understand the nature of the assessment and the process of decision making. In the case of college and university writing course placement testing, parents, students, and teachers must understand how the test works and be assured that the test does not place students incorrectly. For example, Smith (this volume) discovered that a certain percentage of students, when tested at a later time, placed into a different course. He then took steps to reduce that percentage while making the procedures a matter of public knowledge for teachers and students. Explicitness about the process of decision making through testing is, perhaps, the only basis for validity in a postmodern, postpositivist world.

Anastasi (1976) has suggested that face validity, or the appearance that an assessment technique measures the phenomenon of interest, is of little concern. However, this assumption is only valid if measurement is context free and does not have an impact on the functions of writing in the schools. Few writing specialists believe either proposition. Further, face validity becomes problematic when the construct validity of a measure has not been established, as is the case to date with both direct and indirect assessment.

Of the three types of psychometric validity, construct validity is the most important for validation research on holistic scoring because it involves examining the extent to which an assessment tool conforms to a theory of writing. Again, it is possible to segment a concern for the relationship between an assessment procedure and a theory of the phenomenon it is intended to measure from the context-free assumptions of psychometrics. In one sense, this notion is a purely intuitive test of the validity of a procedure for assessing writing.

Construct validation requires that effort be given to the study of validity, defined as a model or theory of the construct. To say a consensus exists among writing specialists that direct assessment is the most valid approach to writing assessment focuses away from important concerns about the current limits of direct assessment tools and the need to continue refining them. Of course, the claim for consensus has to be understood in the context in which it was made. The immediate need for writing assessment demanded the development of assessments constructed within the limitations of current theory and within the fiscal limitations imposed by specific educational institutions. At that stage, there was little time for further study and only time for standing one's ground and insisting on the limits of the other argument. However, both psychometricians and writing specialists would probably agree that the conformity of writing assessment procedures with a theory of writing is the most important aspect of their validity.

As a study of predictive validity, Smith's (this volume) placement process is an example of the development of a demonstrably valid application of holistic scoring. No single strand of the complex research program would have been adequate. Instead, the research program summarized in Smith's chapter represents both a continuing skepticism about the meaning of the procedures and a continuing commitment to holistic scoring as the best solution in the long run. While we might see problems with the scheme at various stages and while it needs further study, there is little doubt that continuing research has moved the scheme dramatically toward convergence with our understanding of the complexity of writing. Exact theoretical conformity between assessment and theory in a field is not a reasonable or logical criterion. Theory changes as a field grows (Popkewitz, 1990), and Smith (personal communication, April 1988) is the first to affirm this fact. Furthermore, developments in assessment can help theory take a broader view of the field. Smith can claim validity for his assessment procedure because he has a body of research that demonstrates its meaning for placing students into writing courses at the University of Pittsburgh. The continuing critical study and refinement of the measurement procedures he describes provides sufficient warrant for claims for their validity.

Janopoulos (this volume) describes an initial construct validation study of holistic scoring for non-native speakers of English. The strength of his work lies in his elaboration of a construct based in the research literature on proficiency and communicative competence in the speaking and writing of English as a second language. From this model a set of criteria emerge for the adequacy of writing assessment for this group of students. His study is a test of holistic scoring procedures against those assumptions. As he suggests, his conclusions are tentative and will require the kind of continuing examination that is seen in Smith's (this volume) work and Murphy and Ruth's (this volume) work.

Validity and Context

Validity, as I have defined it so far, has one important meaning for writing assessment. We should be able to point to an existing body of research demonstrating the validity of procedures for the particular contexts in which they are used. This criterion is, in fact, required of all psychological tests (Anastasi, 1986; Camp, this volume; Messick, 1989; Murphy & Ruth, this volume). Equally important, contextual validation involves how reasonable and logical assessment procedures appear when viewed from a particular theoretical framework. Different beliefs about the nature of writing lead to differing views of the reasonableness or logic of procedures as I have suggested. Unfortunately, the need to provide validation for current practices in writing assessment has grown quietly as the basic assumptions of a positivist, context-free psychometrics have been challenged from within. The positivist pictures of both psychometrics and the natural sciences that I painted earlier represent a set of assumptions that are now being challenged. The social sciences, in particular, are involved in a dispute over the context-free assumptions of positivist science and the apparent need for contextualizing theory (Guba, 1990). Furthermore, writing assessment specialists are often not experts in psychometrics and are not conversant with the emerging challenges to context-free assessment. Thus, they may often continue to operate with simplistic and dated views of psychometrics.

One further implication of both the view that writing assessment has to be understood from within its own context and that validity has a variety of forms has to do with the applications of holistic scoring in various settings. Four chapters in this volume—White, Smith, Cherry and Meyer, and Huot—make the point that holistic scoring has been applied in a variety of ways. One application is in program placement and exit testing, the primary emphasis of most of the validation research in this volume. However, holistic scoring has been used to rank order students' texts in basic research on writing, as well as for large scale evaluation projects. The authors in this book, with the exception of White, all believe that validity has to be viewed differently in each of these assessment contexts.

In addition to the less formalistic definition I have suggested above, validity has had another meaning in psychometrics, one requiring that an assessment conform to an abstract standard of "truthfulness" insured by the use of validation methodologies. This objective standard for validity can be understood in an explication of the psychometric term *true score* which is defined as the score that an individual would receive on a measure if he or she took the test a theoretically infinite number of times (Lord & Novick, 1968). In this context, objectivity is achieved by statistical procedures that estimate a person's true score from the single score that results when he/she actually takes the test. Validity is determined by the accuracy of the prediction of a person's true score from his/her observed score. Recognizing that error is inherent in predicting what a student knows about writing on the basis of a test, valid writing assessment in this context is that which minimizes the difference between true and observed scores. From this framework, accuracy of prediction of true score is sufficient for objectivity and no particular approach to measurement is logically necessary to achieve an accurate prediction. Particular approaches to placement, however, must be judged by their ability to achieve accurate prediction in a particular context. Smith (this volume) chose "accuracy of placement" to describe the goal of his research precisely because he wanted to avoid the positivist implications of true score in describing his search for a valid writing placement measure for students entering the University of Pittsburgh.

The application of the statistical definitions of true score have resulted in some questionable solutions to problems in assessing writing. To increase statistical indices of predictive validity as judged by quantitative criteria, holistic scoring procedures have often been scaled such that more score points are used to judge writing than the actual decisions that have to be made about the placement of the students who wrote the texts. For instance, in the studies reported by Huot (this volume) and Pula and Huot (this volume) only one decision is actually made—whether to place students into a beginning college writing course or a basic writing course at Indiana University of Pennsylvania. The holistic scoring procedures, however, called for raters to make judgments on a scale of 1 to 4. From a statistical perspective, this larger scale range has the effect of increasing the variance among the scores, resulting in an increase in their statistical reliability. This result is artifactual, because the greater the statistical variance in the formula used to compute reliability, the greater the reliability. Similarly, the predictive validity of the tests is increased because the validity coefficient is enhanced by a boost in the reliability of the measure (Cherry & Meyer, this volume). This manipulation is routinely used in holistic scoring sessions. It seems, however, to obfuscate the real validity issue here, which is not a statistical question, but rather are students being fairly and accurately assigned to courses? Thus, the concern for reliability clouds the basic issue and a simplistic application of psychometrics has led writing assessment in directions far away it.

Holistic procedures that make raters focus on score points rather than actual placement decisions force them away from the real decision they have to make—assigning students to one of two courses—and focuses them on some possibly irrelevant qualities of the text in order to create a score distribution. In fact, Huot (this volume) suggests that raters in holistic training sessions conspire to undermine the rubric in an attempt to make their actual placement decisions easier. Reliability and validity in a more complex sense than statistical procedures for estimating true score are sacrificed for the immediate demonstration of statistical reliability because this statistical repair procedure for holistic scoring does not focus upon the strength of trained, experienced teachers and their expertise in judging the ability of students from the texts they produce. Knowledge of students and their abilities are precisely the expertise of trained, experienced teachers in any discipline. This knowledge grows out of their experience with a wide variety of data, including their observation of students' processes, self-reports, and texts. Expert teachers require considerably less data than novice teachers to form opinions of students' abilities. The role of expertise in helping practitioners to focus upon relevant data and to exclude irrelevant data in decisions about clients is documented in many fields (Huot, this volume; Pula & Huot, this volume; Shulman, 1987; Smith, this volume). Thus, we would expect that more experienced teachers would agree with one another more readily, on the basis of more limited data, when they are asked to decide how to place a student in specific writing courses than when they are asked to judge written texts on the basis of abstract categories typically enumerated in a holistic scoring rubric.

In fact, Huot (this volume) and Pula and Huot (this volume) in their studies found that the raters disregarded the rubric and used reasonably common criteria for rating essays, regardless of their expertise with holistic scoring. Similarly, Smith's (this volume) procedures blur the statistical reliability of his measure but increase, immeasurably, its conceptual reliability by reducing the rater's decision to placing students in a single course in the curriculum, the course in which raters have the most recent teaching expertise.

Objectivity, Validity, and Reliability

Since reliability is an important aspect of validity, from a statistical viewpoint, the strength of indirect measures is that they have very high internal and external reliability (see Cherry & Meyer, this volume). Further, this reliability would lead to very consistent assignment of students to specific writing classes. For a direct measure to be reliable, in this sense, we would expect holistic raters to give the same piece of writing the same score every time they read it and for every rater to give a piece of writing the same score. In terms of true score, one might imagine that it is the score an essay would get if it were rated an infinite number of times. This criterion seems to be what White (this volume) means by a reliable and fair test. However, the same reader will respond to a text in a reliably different way (Smith, this volume) if he/she reads it in a second and different context. Thus, the meaning of a true score for a written text, as it represents an individual's writing ability, is problematic.

The statistical definition of true score was proposed in response to an understanding that all measurement in psychology involves error. Since true score, as a platonistic idea, could never be known, Lord and Novick (1968), following the dictates of classical test theory, rejected the concept of true score as an absolute. The mathematical theory of true and error score they proposed is consistent with other writers of the time. It represents a mathematical fix for the ultimately unknowable true score. This particular theoretical turn also makes it clear that the notion of an individual's true score is constructed on a probabilistic model. The observed score distribution is used to estimate the true score distribution and from that, an individual's true score can be estimated. However, I would argue that a statistical true score is as inconceivable as a platonistic one because a statistically estimated true score can never be known. Psychometric theory has developed to a point where test reliabilities for indirect measures are nearly perfect (approach 1.00) in statistical terms. However, the meaning of reliability in postpositivist social science research is not clear because every act with social implications has a different temporal context and, consequently, a different social context. Thus, the reading of a text in different contexts produces a different assessment of the individual.

Reliability is important in psychometrics in a limited sense, both mathematically and logically (Cherry & Meyer, this volume). Mathematically, the reliability of a measure determines how precisely a true score can be estimated from an observed score. Logically, if the true score is constant and the observed score is not perfectly reliable, then estimations of a true score lack reliability by an amount that can only be estimated. Such estimation errors are held to be mathematically random (Lord & Novick, 1968).

How accurate is this conception of true score when it is applied to writing ability? If writing ability is a complex set of cognitive functions, then the fact that particular writing tasks may not be comparable is not necessarily problematic. Furthermore, if writing is a highly contextualized skill, the criticism that holistic procedures do not travel is not damaging because no measure of writing ability can ever be context free. On the other hand, from the psychometric perspective on reliability and validity, the unreliability of holistic ratings seems an insurmountable obstacle for validation research, particularly when reading is a subjective and highly contextualized act. In fact, this inherent subjectivity would seem to validate the statistical criterion of true score (see White, 1985, for a similar discussion). The true score of a text might be the average of ratings given by a very large number of readers. Thus, a true score can be estimated for a text by using the ratings of two or more readers from a statistical perspective. However, the validity of a global estimation of an individual's ability to write from such a score remains problematic.

Although White's (this volume) discussion of holistic scoring continues to demonstrate an affiliation with this definition of true score for written texts, the definition is essentially meaningless because texts are written for a particular reader or set of readers within the social structures of a particular discourse community. This set is theoretically both finite and enumerable. Thus, the use of random mathematical models for estimating the error of measurement is not appropriate. Members of that community will make judgments about the text based upon their prior knowledge of the community as much as on the basis of what appears in the text itself. The problem for placement and exit testing is not to score a text, but to understand what that text means for student writers participating in an academic discourse community. Thus, holistic raters making course placement or exit decisions, for example, reflects a judgment about the individual's writing ability within a specific writing curriculum and within a specific educational institution. Since an infinite number of people would probably derive a very diverse set of scores based upon an infinite number of responses to a text, it seems safer to rely on the agreement observed among groups of writing teachers who work together (Myers, 1980) and limit their decision to a highly contextualized one (Smith, this volume).

The Problem of Validation Research

It would be unfair and inaccurate, however, to claim that psychometric theory is not intensely concerned with validity. Construct validation requires a theoretical statement of the phenomena of interest to permit the construction of a measure to study it. However, constructs cannot be verified empirically without a measure. Thus, a mental trait has to be bootstrapped, that is, constructed from an initial theoretical statement and refined through the constant interplay between increasingly sophisticated construct definitions and measures. Given the complexity of this process, there is little wonder that Lord and Novick (1968) subscribe to the notion that reliable measures often do not have adequate validity, and valid measures often lack rigor. Indirect measures of writing typically begin with a theoretical statement about the nature of writing. Then, the relevant knowledge is defined and items are constructed to measure an individual's possession of that knowledge. Experts are asked to judge the content validity of the items and the procedures. Norming samples are used to determine internal consistency and test-retest reliability, as well as to develop some sense of the relative performance levels of different groups in the population of interest.

The chief criticism of these procedures has been that the instruments they have produced emphasize limited aspects of writing. Note, however, that the procedures themselves were not the cause of this limited view. In theory, the procedures should allow an instrument to test any knowledge. The chief problem is the limited criterion definition of the initial construct itself, as opposed to the actual procedures employed, since the procedures for psychological measurement depend on the construct definition. For instance, reducing writing to declarative knowledge of structural aspects of standard written English authorizes the use of one set of measurement methodologies, the recognition task used in indirect measures. However, if language is defined as a creative act, involving a variety of mental structures (Chomsky, 1957, 1965, 1982), then the measurement procedures used to study language learning have to be more complex, requiring active production of language as a part of the test.

Importantly, refinement of measurement procedures through statistical methodologies used in test and item analysis do not appear to assist in further refinement of the initial criterion definition. Item analysis procedures, some of the most developed aspects of psychometric research methodology, provide assurances about the statistical reliability of an instrument because they homogenize the individual items on a measure. Note that items of real theoretical import, in terms of the construct definition as confirmed by content validation procedures, could be removed in the statistical process of item analysis that follow from a pilot administration of the measure. Thus, only the study of writing can provide this kind of knowledge. But, the study of writing, when approached from an empirical framework, is dependent upon the existence of valid measures of writing.

THE VALIDITY OF HOLISTIC SCORING
AND CONTEXTS FOR HOLISTIC SCORING

Some studies of holistic scoring reported in this book are largely limited to examinations of the predictive validity of placement testing procedures. Huot (1988, 1990, this volume) has suggested that researchers need to recognize that holistic scoring is used for a variety of purposes, including placement and exit testing, as well as quality rankings for basic research on writing. He claims that each of these purposes involve different decisions by raters and require different validation studies.

The studies by Huot (this volume), Pula and Huot (this volume), and Smith (this volume) are primarily about the validation of placement procedures. On the other hand, criterion related validation has been the main approach to validating indirect measures of writing. In these types of studies, an indirect measure of writing is compared to either another indirect measure or to a direct measure. Godshalk, Swineford, and Coffmann (1966) used such an approach to demonstrate the validity of indirect measures. They concluded that "the most efficient predictor of a reliable direct measure of writing ability is one which includes essay questions or interlinear exercises in combination with objective questions" (p. 41). More recently, a second study of writing assessment was sponsored by the Educational Testing Service and the College Entrance Examination Board (Breland et al., 1987). This comprehensive and thorough, by any standard, evaluation of the problems of direct and indirect writing assessment suggests that the safest approach to large group writing assessment is to combine the sampling reliability of indirect assessment with the performance sampling of a direct measure. The approach to validity in this study was similarly based on a comparison of concurrent measures.

Mirroring the results of the earlier study by Godshalk, Swineford and Coffman (also ETS staff researchers), the results of this study seem to strike a compromise about the nature of writing assessment. Furthermore, the criterion definition of validity is as rigorous as the limits of time and financial support could ever allow. While the first study utilized five 20-minute essays, the second study utilized six 45-minute essays across three discourse modes: narration, exposition, and persuasion.

The earlier study served as one historical basis for the emerging use of indirect assessment. It provided sufficient evidence for ETS to drop the use of a writing sample from the English Composition Test in the SAT battery. However, the inadequacy of the criterion definition in the Godshalk, Swineford and Coffman study, the length of time for writing the essays, and the limitation of the writing sample to persuasive and expository modes, is apparent today. Variety of discourse modes is addressed in the Breland et al. (1987) study with the use of "portfolios" of writing. However, as I suggested earlier, the predictive validity of the dual measure of writing advocated by Breland et al. is not established if the measures they developed are used for placement in a particular school or university writing curriculum. Furthermore, the goal of both research projects was to define a global measure of writing ability. Research on writing, however, continues to suggest that writing is not a single, global ability. The ability to write narration may be quite independent of the ability to write persuasion. Thus, the global estimation of writing ability is not a proper goal for writing assessment. Moreover, placement or exit decisions are highly contextualized, embedded in the institution in which the placement or exit decision is made.

Researchers' desire to define a global measure of writing ability seems to have two origins. In the first place, a global measure of writing ability is based in the belief that each person has such an ability and that the best way to estimate a person's true ability is to estimate his/her true score on some measure or battery of measures. Second, the historical and social factors surrounding the development of psychometric theory gave rise to this view of mental traits. It is to this context for the development of psychometric theory that I will now turn.

EDUCATIONAL AND PSYCHOLOGICAL MEASUREMENT: HISTORY

A number of pragmatic issues emerge in the application of psychological theories of measurement to education. Tests of writing ability differ from personality assessments, such as an inventory of schizophrenia, in one important sense. Ability tests are conceived as maximum performance tests. The purpose of the test is to demonstrate the maximal extent of an individual's knowledge. Personality tests are typical performance tests, intended to show an individual's usual emotional reaction. In practice, multiple choice ability tests examine convergent knowledge because items on the tests have a single correct answer. Tests that do not have a single correct answer measure divergent knowledge. A direct measure of writing is an example of a divergent measure. Unfortunately, divergent measures can be very difficult to score, while convergent measures can usually be scored by a computer. The total score on an educational test, convergent or divergent, is held to represent how much the person knows about a topic. Typical performance or personality tests, in practice, do not have a single correct answer. How a person answers an item is an indication of one of several ways in which he/she might be functioning in daily life.

In the United States the use of educational assessment, based in psychometric theory, emerged from the rapid changes in the nature and character of public education after World War I. It was also in this context that the notion of maximal performance emerged. It was the war itself, however, that developed the technology for mass educational assessment and motivated the changes in the schools that ultimately led to the importance of testing as an aspect of schooling.

During the end of the nineteenth century, Alfred Binet and his colleague Henri Simon developed a scale for identifying French school children who would be unable to profit from instruction in school without special help. Essentially, the scale was a standardized interview intended for use by a trained examiner to help identify mentally retarded children. Separate learning intervention strategies were developed to assist the children identified by the interviewer as needing help (Anastasi, 1976; Ryan, 1972).

The use of the label "intelligence" in the title of these early tests means only that the tests predict school performance. Thus, IQ (Intelligence Quotient) is not a measure of an abstract human ability, but a highly contextualized assessment predicting a child's performance in school. A notable measurement property of the Binet-Simon Scale (Binet & Simon, 1908) was that the Scale was administered to only a single child at a time by a single adult. The resulting distribution of children's scores on the test was dichotomous in a practical sense. One group of students attended regular school while the others were sent to special schools intended to address their particular needs. Anyone who has administered an individualized interview can attest to the special role of the examiner in individual tests of intelligence. In the first place, unlike paper and pencil intelligence tests, many items in interview tests do not have a single correct answer. An examiner gives a student credit for a correct response if it conveys the concept in a general way or is synonymous with the correct answer. Second, the examiner has a responsibility to probe ambiguous responses. Thus, the examinee also gets feedback about the test during the testing process, as well as interaction with a live human being. In addition, the examiner is expected to provide the student with some form of encouragement. Finally, incidental evidence about the student's performance is gathered to help determine the cause and nature of the difficulties that were referred for assessment. Some students, for instance, may exhibit evidence of learning difficulties due to social adjustment problems with school, as opposed to mental retardation or other organic learning disabilities. Even a cursory reading of the early American texts on IQ tests (e.g., Terman, 1916) is sufficient to demonstrate that intelligence was viewed as a global intellectual trait and that it was used as a uniform explanation across a variety of social contexts even when other intervening social factors such as dialect or socioeconomic differences might be involved.

It is worth noting, however, that both standardized interviews and paper and pencil intelligence tests are heavily loaded with items that encourage convergent, as opposed to divergent thinking. There is always an implied correct answer or a limited set of correct answers for an item. Creativity, which involves divergent thinking, is not really encouraged by either type of test. The primary difference in this regard is that a skilled examiner using an interview can evaluate a student's responses for evidence that wrong answers may show a strong ability for divergent thinking, one characteristic of a highly intelligent person. Since convergent thinking is rewarded in school and divergent thinking is discouraged, the examiner may ultimately recommend some sort of intervention strategy. However, these strategies are different than those used to address organic problems. Multiple choice tests do not provide sufficient information to distinguish between these two types of students. Thus, an interview test is necessary when the results of written tests imply that a student might have serious difficulties with school.

The need for efficiency promoted the use of paper and pencil tests in assessment situations in both education and psychology. At the time the United States entered World War I, large numbers of recruits selected through the draft had to be sorted and trained quickly to fight in Europe. By that time, Louis Terman of Stanford University had imported the Binet-Simon methodology and published an American version that came to be known as the Stanford-Binet (Terman, 1916). One of his students at Stanford, Arthur Otis, developed an intelligence test based on a multiple choice format. Based on that multiple choice format, psychologists working for the United States Army developed two large group tests, known as the Army Alpha and Beta tests. These tests were quite efficient for sorting out the top end of the score distribution to determine potential officer candidates as well as candidates for specialized work. Thus, the technology for large scale assessment of ability that has become a part of American education was developed. In the years following the war, the new objective tests became part of assessment in all levels of schooling, resulting in the sorting devices used today to track children from birth until the move into graduate school. In some fields, mass testing is also used as a sorting device for promotion within organizations. Most government agencies (excluding political appointments) and some private organizations use some form of mass testing in hiring and promotion processes.

To a large degree, psychometric theories of assessment owe the extent of their development to the attention and funding that they received in American public education and in the wars fought by Americans in this century. The belief that they provide objective data about an individual has also helped their spread into government and business. In government service, charges of graft and patronage in handing out civil service jobs after elections provided an important motivation for the use of independent measures to assess a person's ability to perform. Scores on tests became a way to assign government jobs in response to fears of graft and nepotism rampant in the early part of this century. Similarly, the need for a technology to help sort students in the face of mass public secondary education, a movement growing out of John Dewey's theories of education, was no less important than the immediate need of the federal government in organizing to fight a war. The war provided the sudden need that jump-started the burgeoning use of psychometric assessment. The growth of public schooling and the positivist sense that technology could solve educational and other problems helped to spread its use into other settings, such as educational and occupational assessment.

In both psychology and education, mistrust of the judgments of professionals about their clients fueled the drive toward widespread use of paper and pencil tests. The subjectivity of human judgment was suspect and was therefore replaced with the objectivity of instrumentation. This change represents the victory of positivism over the earlier intuitionism of Freudian psychoanalysis on the one hand and the use of written examinations in all disciplines in education on the other.

An important factor contributing to the dominance of psychological theories of assessment in American education was the fact that most teachers did not have even a rudimentary theory of assessment, even though they knew and used practical approaches to pupil assessment and evaluation. In the same way that psychological theories and research methods provided theoretical and methodological grounding for the study of learning and curriculum and instruction, psychometric theories and research methodologies provided the basis for pupil assessment. The variability of teachers' grades and their highly contextualized nature were seen as important weaknesses. Grades were considered subjective, contaminated by teachers' positive and negative prejudices about students, as well as subject to the variability of teachers' length of service and quality of training. In contrast, objectivity and reliability, considered the primary strengths of psychometric testing, were believed to have the potential to lift American education up and out of the one-room school house with its quaint, but antique, orientation toward teaching and learning. Thus, a primary criticism of these early pupil evaluation methods was that they lacked the empirical, scientific foundation of the emergent technologies.

EDUCATIONAL AND PSYCHOLOGICAL MEASUREMENT: SOCIAL FUNCTIONS

The social aspects of American education at this time were another important motivation for the adaptation of psychometric methods in the schools. Gutek (1972) suggests that between 1880 and 1920 the structure of American society and economy was predominantly rural and agrarian. Secondary schooling was primarily intended as college preparation. This period corresponds with the development of college entrance examination requirements, based upon published lists of literary works (Applebee, 1974). However, Gutek and Applebee both note that the essence of school curricula changed as the focus of American public education moved to an urban setting after World War I, with corresponding demographic shifts from country to city and accompanying changes in the American economy. The basic intention of secondary education was bifurcated during this period. College preparation continues as a curriculum goal to this day for some students. At the same time, Dewey's "common school" notions (1916) and Spenser's "social Darwinism" (1851), coupled with some basic changes in the psychology of learning, produced a sense of the need for secondary education for all students (Applebee, 1974).

Two conditions in particular supported the development of objective educational assessment methods beyond those typically used by teachers. As before, those students capable of college preparatory work had to be sorted from those who were not. Previously, those unable to continue schooling were channeled into the workforce. With the advent of common schooling, these pupils were channeled into vocational curricula that also emphasized subjects intended to help them become better citizens as well as better workers. As the number of students increased, the sorting task became more difficult and subject to challenge by those who felt wronged by the decision. Thus, school administrators and teachers had to be able to defend the objectivity and fairness of the procedures that they used. Efficiency was also a necessity since the task became greater as the American population grew.

Halloran (1990) also notes the growing sense in American society around 1900 that socioeconomic mobility was a matter of ability as opposed to birthright. Thus, tests being used in the schools had to support the middle-class belief that an individual is able to achieve success as a measure of his/her ability, and this surely continues to this today. Objectivity for any educational test lies in the belief that it validly measures an individual's ability to succeed in school coupled with the belief that success in school is the key to moving up the socioeconomic ladder. Admitting that reading is an inherently subjective act complicates this need for objectivity because it suggests that the rules of the game are not simple and that they cannot ever be entirely fair. But, this admission also damages the simple connection between ability and achievement because it suggests that successful writing is a socially determined process, a function of a writer's knowledge of specific contexts rather than knowledge of rules of language structure.

Developments in psychometric assessment in education provided the second condition that supported the formal introduction of assessment techniques into American education. Since some form of schooling for all American citizens became a reality, some sorting of pupils was deemed necessary. The basic assumption, mirrored in the mathematical models of psychometrics, was that not all students could profit from continuing instruction. That is, students were expected to drop out or fail in increasing numbers as they progressed through schooling because they would not have the aptitude (intelligence) to benefit from the increasing complexity of instruction in various subjects. This assumption about schooling mirrored the belief that, while all people are created equal in a political sense, some will achieve more than others in a socioeconomic sense due to inherent ability or energetic activity. This romantic notion of genius or giftedness continues to be a common-sense explanation for the differential achievements of individuals (Blair, 1783/1965).

The same types of intelligence tests that provided the basis for sorting soldiers into job classifications during wartime were utilized to sort pupils, to predict the likelihood of their success at higher levels of schooling and to place them into tracks that would guide them to an appropriate level of schooling. The distributional assumption behind this belief is important here. Since resources at each successively higher level of school are increasingly more limited, an increasingly limited number of students have to be selected to continue schooling. This selection is based on their rank within the distribution of students taking the test. Thus, individuals who start school at the top of the distribution receive differential instruction intended to help prepare them for the increasing complexity of the advanced levels. Further down the distribution, students are prepared for different treatments at advanced levels, treatments intended to prepare them to leave school and enter the workforce. Thus, the different types of curricula help to create the self-fulfilling prophecy of the initial assessment device.

The mathematical model used to represent this distribution is the normal curve, the same mathematical model for error in estimating true score from observed scores. The model assumes that both errors in observation and mental traits are randomly distributed in populations. Thus, approximately 70% of children tested will possess an average amount of that ability (between one standard deviation above and below the mean), and approximately 24 (between 2 and 3 standard deviations above and below the mean) will possess an unusual amount or have an unusual deficit. Approximately 5 (beyond 3 standard deviations above or below the mean) will possess an exceptional ability or will be so deficient that they cannot be expected to function at all. The 2-1/2% of children above the third standard deviation above the mean are those with a gift for the ability. These distributional assumptions would not be pernicious if school curricula were not tailored to maximize the differ-ences between the various groups described by the distribution.

In this context, assessment functions as a determinant of socio-economic class since amount of education is loosely correlated with class and status distinctions in America. In the school setting, this function does not mirror the original purposes of Binet's approach which was to identify children who need extra help to succeed in normal instruction.

The concern for the unreliability of teachers' grades as indicators of students' achievement, another predictor of future educational success, led to the use of standardized tests for pupil assessment. Teachers assign grades based on a number of criteria. Grades may indicate either growth of a pupil's knowledge or the extent of a pupil's mastery of knowledge. Further, teachers often use grades as rewards or punishments for social behavior in class that has nothing to do with the extent of a pupil's learning. Thus, teachers' grades are highly contextualized statements. They are difficult to interpret whether one is looking for national trends in American public education or even whether a particular seventh grade writer can handle the demands of writing in eighth grade English. When educating the American public after World War I began to take on national dimensions, educators began to feel the need for context-free assessments of pupil progress for both sorting and comparative purposes. Psychometric approaches to measurement were present with an emerging theory and a developing body of research techniques.

Beyond the problem of grades as highly contextualized summaries of student performance, educational phenomena also seem to be subject to the basic reliability and validity problems of the behavioral sciences. If one conceptualizes teachers as observers and their tests as instruments, then how reliable are their judgments of pupils' achievements? As Diederich (1974; based on a study by Diederich, French, & Carlton, 1961) rather convincingly suggested, judging writing in some contexts is not very reliable. The raters in their study—readers from very divergent backgrounds including education, business, and government—gave papers in the rating sample every grade on the scale. They also disagreed widely with their own previous ratings when the material was reread at a later time. Of course, this problem had been recognized for some time (Hopkins, 1921). Due to this demonstrated unreliability, standardized, indirect writing tests became the basis for predicting student achievement in writing, the basis for comparison of student achievement in writing between different educational settings, and the basis for assessing individual student achievement.

The comparison of social and educational functions of testing in Binet's original testing model with modern ability/achievement testing models suggest profound differences in their use. Essentially, Binet's model was built on the assumption that most children can be successful in school if they are given the appropriate assistance. Bloom (1964; Bloom, Hastings, & Madaus, 1971) has extended this view in his theory of mastery learning which postulates that most children, excluding the small number with organic disfunctions, can be expected to master most learning taught in the schools if they are given sufficient time and individualized assistance. In this model, assessment in the schools should focus on elaborating children's needs. Bloom's view is in contrast to the current assumption underlying the use of the normal curve equivalent in contemporary educational and psychological measurement in which proportions of students are expected to perform at particular achievement levels based on the assumption that psychological data conform to a mathematical model of randomness.

Clearly teachers of writing who believe that some students are talented will believe that their task is to discover those children and help them. They will also never expect the weakest students to be achievers and will sentence average students to pedestrian mediocrity for their lack of talent.

THE COLLISION OF THE STUDY OF WRITING AND PSYCHOLOGICAL MEASUREMENT IN WRITING ASSESSMENT

Few writing specialists have ever been thoroughly cross-trained in educational and psychological measurement theory or understand the context-free assumptions of psychometric assessment which support both direct and indirect writing assessment. This lack of training and the positivist origins of psychometrics combine to prevent any real interest among younger writing researchers. Cherry and Meyer (this volume) claim that writing researchers and program evaluators have shown little sophistication when using writing assessment techniques in their research, suggesting that the principles of educational and psychological measurement and the methods of their application in writing assessment seem virtually unknown. For instance, researchers often fail to specify their methodology in a holistic scoring session in sufficient detail for reasonable comparison among studies or for replication of studies. Further, Cherry and Meyer also claim that researchers using holistic scoring procedures calculate reliability coefficients in unusual or meaningless ways. Similarly, Gere (1980), among others, argues that direct writing assessment lacks a theoretical grounding. However, holistic scoring procedures have always involved the use of psychometric statistical procedures to evaluate the reliability of holistic scoring sessions.

Historically, early empirical composition researchers were trained primarily in English teacher education, including curriculum and instruction. Typically, their training also included some introduction to educational research and measurement. From the early empirical research, they developed a sketchy construct definition of writing and designed ap-proaches to writing assessment built upon their knowledge of both writ-ing and psychometrics. They developed holistic scoring procedures to use experts, that is, teachers of writing, to provide objective judgments on the relative merits of written texts. Other experts, such as White (this volume), were trained in literary criticism and brought a background rich in the study of written language to the task of developing approaches to writing assessment. White's chapter in this volume is a chronicle of the zeal of early proponents of writing as they challenged psychometric approaches to writing assessment with their intuitions about the nature of writing.

An Examination of Context-Free Holistic Scoring Procedures and Comparison with Context-Dependent Holistic Scoring Procedures

Freedman (1984) found that English teachers' judgments of texts by professional writers when compared to their judgments of texts produced by student writers showed significantly greater variability. In the rating session, the teachers were not told that some of the texts were by professional writers. Consequently, their judgments about the texts were based partly on how appropriately the texts conformed to status and role expectations dictated by the register of school writing. Some of the professional authors in the study rebelled at the context provided by the school sponsored topics. This rebellion led them to violate the customary status and role relationships for school writing, leading no doubt to the variability in the teachers' judgments. This variability would mean a very low reliability. Thus, English teachers who rate texts with a typical scoring rubric, in the absence of other explicit instructions, expect the texts to conform to social functions of school writing, thus reinforcing the status and role distinctions between teachers and students, important aspects of writing in academic settings.

Three studies in this volume speak directly to the importance of context in validation research on holistic scoring. Huot (this volume) and Pula (this volume) are two complementary studies that provide an excellent view of the variety of contexts that can be utilized by holistic raters. Perhaps, most importantly, they provide a window into the mental processing of holistic scorers that suggests that one of the most important aspects of the judgment lies in the nature of the judgment itself. Janopoulos (this volume) provides an elaboration of how experienced teachers of English as a second language respond to written English composed by non-native speakers of English.

Huot's (1988; this volume) study, in particular, demonstrates that when holistic raters read essays for placement decisions, they consciously dismiss some aspects of their responses to a text in the process of arriving at a decision. Furthermore, his study suggests that training in and experience with holistic scoring frees up raters' attention to the text, permitting them to respond to writing in personal terms while simultaneously making a placement decision about a particular essay. The inexperienced raters, on the other hand, were at the mercy of their reading strategies as teachers, which forced them to process all aspects of a text, leaving no mental processing resources for personal response to the writer's message. Thus, the way in which the context for the rating is communicated to essay raters can have a profound effect on the manner in which they view the texts they are reading.

Pula and Huot's (this volume; Pula, 1990) study suggests that various rater background variables, such as teaching experience and training, form an important aspect of the way that raters process student texts in a holistic rating session. They use the concept of discourse community to explain the function of background variables in the process of holistic rating for writing course placement. Individual raters belong to a variety of discourse communities, each defined by different aspects of a rater's background. One important community for a rater is provided by the theoretical assumptions about writing that they acquired during their training and continued growth in the profession of teaching English. The other teachers that a rater works among are also an important discourse community because they provide an important resource to help the individual teacher develop as a reader of student writing. Further, prior experiences with holistic scoring and with the group of holistic raters in a particular session provide another additional important context for raters' performances.

The raters in Huot's and in Pula and Huot's studies were all English teachers enrolled in graduate English teacher training programs. As a result of their graduate training, they had fairly explicit models of writing, the teaching of writing, and responding to student writing. However, it is common practice in many school and university settings to employ essay readers with little training or experience in teaching writing. What background characteristics affect the way that these individuals respond to texts? What features of texts do they attend to in the process of making rating decisions about particular texts? Until the Huot (this volume) and the Pula and Huot (this volume) studies, we could only guess that the rubric used in training holistic raters, while apparently a significant tool in achieving rater agreement, was not a significant tool in giving raters clues about relevant features of student texts for placement decisions. Until Pula and Huot extended this last finding, we did not know that rating placement decisions were mediated through an extensive and complex web of background variables, including personal response.

This final aspect of rating underlines the function of writing in schools, for English studies at least. When English teachers typically read writing, they seem to ignore its communicative aspects and attend only to its structural aspects, as did the untrained raters in Huot's study. The more focused decision by the trained raters allowed them to take a broader view of the text. In many instances, the transcripts of think-aloud protocols in Huot's (this volume) and Pula and Huot's (this volume) studies of the same rating group provide a window into raters whose judgment of the communicative value of a paper is quite divergent from their judgment of whether the student needs remediation. Janopoulos's (this volume) work is a study of the extent to which teachers of English as a second language are able to use communicative competence as a standard for ratings in holistic scoring. Their judgments then reflect non-native speakers' ability to communicate in written English as opposed to a

more limited knowledge of the structure of English. But, it is teachers'
models of writing ability in English for non-native speakers that prepares
them to evaluate how effectively the message is being communicated.
English teachers without training and experience in working with these
students often find themselves bogged down in problems with linguistic
and stylistic conventions. Consequently, they are unable to make an
informed placement decision. This last supposition is also supported by
Smith's (this volume) research with placement testing.

In addition, different rating decisions about texts—placement,
competency, and rank ordering—provide different contexts for readers
(Huot, 1988, 1990, this volume). How does the nature of the judgment
made by the raters in the ETS studies (Breland et al., 1987; Godshalk,
Swineford, & Coffman, 1966), when ranking texts in terms of their
quality, differ from the nature of the placement decisions made by raters
in the Huot (this volume), Pula and Huot (this volume), and Smith (this
volume) studies?

If, as the Huot (this volume), Pula and Huot (this volume), and
Freedman (1984) studies suggest, English teachers read texts within a
context that involves a concern for structural knowledge and within the
conventions of a special register, then the absence of a pragmatic
decision about the student writer should force them to depend more
heavily in their rating upon the conformity of texts to that register.
Further, since the focus in the ETS studies is on the quality of the texts
and on the "teachability" of the writer in the Smith study, lesser details of
structure take on greater importance in sorting the texts in the ETS study
as the goal is to produce a ranked list. All characteristics of a text come
into play in the process of making decisions about rankings, while only a
limited number of features, those more likely to reflect the presence or
absence of larger knowledge structures on the part of the writer, are
involved in a decision to place students in one course or another. In
further support of this conclusion is the difficulty that placement raters
have when asked to score students on a scale with more score points
rather than on pragmatic decisions that actually have to be made about
the student who wrote the text (Huot, this volume; Pula & Huot, this
volume). Those raters with actual teaching experience in the curriculum
found it easier to make a decision than those who did not have such
experience. However, as a local discourse community developed among
the raters, they shared this knowledge, undermining the rubric with
which they were trained. Thus, expertise as an holistic placement rater is
both highly individual, emerging in the personal responses to texts and
the ability to make teachability decisions, and highly contextualized,
emerging from a variety of contexts, both local and discipline-based.

In light of these findings, it is not surprising that holistically scored
essays, where the goal is to produce a rank-ordered list of examinees,

correlate highly with indirect measures. If both the prompts used in holistic scoring procedures and the rating procedures themselves have to be contextualized (Camp, this volume; Murphy & Ruth this volume; Smith, this volume), we would expect some difference in the process of the rating itself. As I stated earlier, this contextualization led Huot (1990) to suggest that holistic scoring procedures will differ according to the particular use—course placement, course exit, and research—and will require separate validation research programs.

The distributional assumption for the mathematical model of reliability and criterion-related validity, analysis of variance [ANOVA], in the Breland et al., (1987) study is that the data conform in a general way to a normal distribution. A well-established artifact regarding any ratings that humans make is their tendency to pick the middle category of an odd-numbered set (Oppenheim, 1966), producing very narrowly distributed data sets. Holistic scoring procedures have attempted to undermine this effect by using an even number of categories, such as the 1 to 4 scale (Huot, this volume; Pula & Huot, this volume) or the 1 to 6 scale (Breland et al., 1987). This type of metric forces rates to use both sides of the distribution and tends to help them spread their ratings out in a distribution that conforms more nearly to the mathematical randomness of the normal curve. Of course, as I mentioned previously, this distribution is a theoretical and mathematical assumption of psychometrics. *The assumption also specifies that writing ability is normally (randomly) distributed within the population of student writers.*

Assuming that writing ability, like all human mental traits, is normally distributed, also assumes that an individual's writing ability can be ranked on a numerical scale with interval properties. On the other hand, Chomsky (1957; 1965) and others (Newmeyer, 1983; Steinberg, 1982) have pointed out that the human language capacity does not demonstrate this type of variation. These linguists, as well as many researchers and theorists in writing, believe that all humans without clear physical deficits are capable of mastering the structural complexities of language, suggesting that both oral and written language acquisition mirrors the learning theory proposed by Bloom (1964).

Matching the notion that ability in school is a stable trait of the individual that can be predicted by early tests, the notion that skill in writing is a gift suggests that teaching writing to those without the gift is of little profit (Willinsky, 1987). However, many researchers studying the acquisition of written language in young children have demonstrated that learning to write is as natural a process as learning to speak. What is required for acquisition of written and oral language is an environment that supports both the acquisition of linguistic knowledge and the acquisition of models for the use of that knowledge, that is, an understanding of the functions of writing and speaking.

These two views of writing and of assessment are clearly incompatible. More important, they have serious pragmatic consequences for students. Teachers of composition probably act very differently toward their students if they believe that a few students are gifted but that 50% of them are destined to fall below the mean, despite their best instructional efforts.

On the other hand, if teachers believe that language ability is relatively independent of other aspects of cognition, and acquisition of linguistic structure is independent of intelligence, then they will assume that written language as it is used in everyday life, like spoken language, is within the grasp of all normal persons. Thus, while relatively few students may ever write texts that will become canonized for study by professional readers of literature, most of them can learn to write reasonably well for everyday purposes in their work and private lives.

UNSOLVED PROBLEMS FOR WRITING ASSESSMENT: THE SOCIAL FUNCTIONS OF LANGUAGE

The research reported in this book represents several important new directions for writing assessment. However, one important direction remains unexplored to a large extent. Camp (this volume) implies that particular approaches to writing assessment may disadvantage speakers of dialects outside of the cultural mainstream.

The function of language for establishing and maintaining membership in discourse communities will have an important role in the future of writing assessment. Simon (1980) has suggested that the "decline of English" is reflected in the fact that the language is undergoing radical changes. Furthermore, Bloom (1987) and Hirsch (1987) have linked these changes to a general decline in American culture. From another perspective, however, these changes represent an increasing cultural pluralism. American culture can no longer be understood as representing only white, middle-class American male values and norms. The white, middle-class male varieties of spoken and written English that have dominated our culture are now subject to challenge as a diversity of other ethnic groups continue to struggle with the dilemma of assimilation on the one hand, and preservation of their unique cultural heritage on the other. These heritages are embodied in large part in the languages and dialects of their home communities.

Both sides in this struggle demonstrate the functions of language in creating a sense of unity among members of a group as their common language creates a discourse or speech community (Hymes, 1968). The dominance of varieties of English spoken by white, middle-class Americans reflects their dominance in American cultural, political, and economic life. Thus, when writing assessment focuses on conformity of student writing to a standard of correctness emerging from this cultural framework, it functions to reinforce the dominance of those cultural norms. This situation reflects the continuing difficulty that English teachers have experienced in defining their own functions within American education, a reflection of the broader dispute over the nature of language and culture in America. On the one hand, some legislators are proposing that English should be maintained as the only legally sanctioned language in America. At the same time, large numbers of new immigrants are changing the cultural and linguistic background in many places. As with earlier immigrant populations in America, they have to struggle with maintaining their cultural heritage versus entering the mainstream culture.

Writing assessment that serves to enforce the norms of a particular dialect of English certainly equates success with mastery of that dialect and with joining the cultural group for whom the use of that dialect is the norm. On the other hand, changing writing assessment to allow for a diversity of usage involves changing the rules for people who have previously enjoyed success. Testing that changes previously established rules involves basic validation issues for examinees because they no longer have a sense that the test is fair. From their point of view, changes in the rules that allow people whom they perceive to be different to succeed, creates an illogical and unreasonable test.

Again, face validity, the perceptions of an examinee or test user about the validity of a psychological or educational test, is relevant. Certainly, when a person taking a test feels that it is unfair, the test lacks face validity. Typically, face validity has not been an important concern in the development of assessments. I think, however, that validity in this nontechnical and colloquial sense is what is truly at issue here. Ultimately, the debate over direct and indirect assessment represents a debate between opposing academic views on the nature of written language and a debate over the reasonableness of requiring children to conform to the linguistic standards of a particular cultural group. If English teachers and researchers are divided about this issue, clearly the broader culture is divided. The stasis in writing assessment is fairly easy to understand from this perspective.

Unfortunately, only one of the chapters in this book has addressed this problem directly (Janopoulos, this volume) and only one refers to it obliquely (Camp, this volume). Janopoulos's study reflects the dominant view in teaching English to speakers of other languages that the most important aspect of learning English is communicative competence. Mastery of linguistic form is not the goal of instruction, so much as students' ability to communicate to meet their particular needs. Communicative competence is a measure of non-native speakers' ability to communicate within particular contexts. Implicit in this measure is the assumption that communication is fairly robust with respect to violations of particular linguistic norms. Also implicit in this measure is the assumption that the ability to communicate in specific contexts—about business dealings, for instance—may be the only necessary context for an individual's needs. Once the person has that ability, he/she may find the time and effort required to achieve native-like fluency in English prohibitive; at the same time the need which would provide the motivation no longer exists.

Camp's view of the need to develop writing assessment procedures sensitive to the language and dialect differences increasingly present in American schools is less developed. Her position reflects the current inability of writing teachers to come to terms with this issue. Clearly, professional organizations such as the Conference on College Composition and Communication of the National Council of Teachers of English (Butler et al., 1974) have taken a position on students' rights to their home dialects and languages. In practical terms, this position is opposed by those who would mandate standard written English and certain oral dialects as the norm for schools. More important is the fact that these dialects *are* the norm in American schools today.

It is not within the scope of this book to settle this issue. To conclude this chapter, I would like to point to some of the key issues involved in settling this dispute over the function of language in American society versus how schools function to give students' an understanding of language and its role in our culture. This dispute is, ultimately, the largest framework for understanding the validity of individual assessment procedures and far more important for the future of writing assessment than the theoretical disputes within the measurement community. However, the academic dispute is rooted in this larger dispute.

THE FUNCTIONS OF WRITING
AND THE FUNCTIONS OF ASSESSMENT

Because psychologically based theories of measurement have dominated writing assessment, there has been little systematic consideration of the role of linguistic function in planning approaches to the measurement of writing. Indirect assessment proposals are explicit about the importance of the prestige dialect, standard written English. Declarative knowledge about linguistic structure is the primary target of writing assessment, and conformity to the norms of standard written English is the primary goal of writing instruction. Recent developments in direct assessment suggest that the goals of assessment should be broader. Proposals for portfolio assessment have suggested that writing assessment should consider a broad range of goals, including communicative and expressive ones, through a broad range of discourse modes, including narration and description in addition to persuasion and exposition (see Camp's and White's chapters, this volume). Implied in these proposals is the notion that writing assessment must consider both academic and nonacademic uses of written language.

However, assessment procedures such as Smith's (this volume) have demonstrated reliability and validity precisely because they are highly contextualized and limit the nature of the decisions made by raters. Advocates of holistic scoring have been troubled by very high correlations between holistic scores and formal text variables such as length, handwriting, and correctness. It seems likely that holistic raters, in the absence of other salient criteria emerging from the context, would pay more attention to linguistic forms. Furthermore, these correlations would explain the very high correlation between holistic scoring and multiple-choice tests.

The broad approaches to assessment suggested by White (this volume) and critiqued by Camp (this volume) seem to be at odds with the strengths of Smith's scheme (this volume). The purposes for Smith's assessment are local and derive directly from the curriculum that the assessment serves. Smith is quite explicit about the purposes of the curriculum because the validity of the assessment derives from the goals of the curriculum itself. Those curricular goals are local and related to specific functions of writing that the English faculty wish to sponsor.

Behind the new theoretical basis for writing assessment proposed by Camp (this volume) and the future for holistic scoring proposed by White (this volume) is an implicit call for redirecting the functions of writing in the schools. Ultimately, the functions of both written and spoken language in schools are the real contexts for future developments in writing assessment. Clearly, their suggestions that portfolio assessment, using some form of holistic scoring, seems to be the most likely direction for the future of writing assessment implies that school-sponsored writing should involve a variety of communicative purposes, as opposed to the transactional function of language to communicate learning that currently dominates in student writing in academic settings (Applebee, 1981; Britton, Burgess, Martin, McCleod, & Rosen 1975).

CONCLUSION

If schools are going to serve an integrative function and take a broad, culturally pluralistic view, what is the role for writing and what would be the future of writing assessment in this setting? Clearly, private, expressive uses of writing should play an important role. If expressive writing serves as a tool for self-directed learning (Emig, 1977; Fulwiler, 1982) and public writing serves as a tool for learning to participate in an academic discourse community (Bartholomae, 1985; Bizzell, 1987; Phillips, 1990; Smith, forthcoming; Williamson, 1988), then we have to seek a balance between the two uses of literacy. Furthermore, we have to insure that academic literacy is not presented as a matter of making a choice between alternatives, leading to rejection of one or the other. It has to be seen as part of broadening the identity of individual students. Beyond that, we have to recognize that the linguistic norms for academic discourse are simply that, norms. These norms, like any normative behavior, are subject to change over time as a result of the changing environment and makeup of a society. We can choose to reconstruct those norms in a more democratic fashion, one that allows for the diversity of cultures in the broader society outside of schools and universities.

In writing assessment the need for gatekeeping will then disappear. Currently, this function dominates all assessment in the schools. I am not certain that we can see a need for assessment as we have conceived it to date in such a setting. I am equally certain that I will be accused of overly idealistic and utopian thinking. However, without such thinking, we will remain mired in the real controversy behind writing assessment—the controversy over which forms and functions of language will dominate in academic settings and in our society as a whole. Clearly, some presently unimagined resolution to the debate over the functions of language in our society has to emerge at some point if we are to become a truly pluralistic society.

Ultimately, the problem for the future of writing assessment is much more complicated than tearing itself loose from the theoretical foundations of psychometric theory and establishing itself with a foundation based in a theory of writing. Since all assessment in schools serves both educational and cultural functions, a much broader constituency than assessment or writing specialists has to make important decisions about the social functions of assessment in American schools. More important, American society will have to come to terms with the function of language in both society-at-large and in the school. Speaking and writing "correctly" reflect gatekeeping functions for assessment. Unfortunately, none of us can really yet imagine functions for assessment that depend on a culture that does not yet exist. As with the theory building process that got us to this point, assessment will continue to evolve through trial and error as we refine and develop a theory of writing and as American society evolves new functions for language in and out of schools. Only by making these constructs explicit and using them to judge our continuing development of writing assessment techniques will we establish claims for the validity of those techniques.

REFERENCES

Anastasi, A. (1986). Evolving concepts of test validation. *Annual Review of Psychology, 37,* 1–15.

Anastasi, A. (1976). *Psychological testing* (4th ed.). New York: Macmillan.

Applebee, A. N. (1974). *Tradition and reform in the teaching of English.* Urbana, IL: National Council of Teachers of English.

Applebee, A. N. (1981). *Writing in the secondary school: English and the content areas.* Urbana, IL: National Council of Teachers of English.

Bartholomae, D. (1985). Inventing the university. In M. Rose (Ed.), *When a writer can't write* (pp. 134-165). New York: Guilford.

Binet, A., & Simon, T. (1908). Le development de l'intelligence chez les enfants. *Annee psychologique, 14,* 1-94.

Bizzell, P. (1987). Review: What can we know, what must we do, what may we hope: Writing assessment. *College English, 49,* 575-584.

Blair, H. (1965). In H. F. Harding (Ed.), *Lectures on rhetoric and belles lettres.* Carbondale, IL: Southern Illinois University Press. (Original work published in 1783).

Bloom, A. (1987). *The closing of the American mind.* New York: Simon and Schuster.

Bloom, B. S. (1964). *Stability and change in human characteristics.* New York: Wiley and Sons.

Bloom, B. S., Hastings, J. T., & Madaus, G. F. (1971). *Handbook on summative and formative evaluation of student learning.* New York: McGraw-Hill.

Breland, H. M., Camp, R., Jones, R. J., Morris, M. M., & Rock, D. A. (1987). *Assessing writing skill: College Entrance Examination Board research monograph no. 11.* New York: The College Entrance Examination Board.

Breland, H. M., & Gaynor, J. L. (1979). A comparison of direct and indirect assessment of writing skill. *Journal of Educational Measurement, 15,* 119-128.

Britton, J. (1963). Experimental markings of English compositions written by fifteen-year-olds. *Educational Review, 16,* 17-23.

Britton, J., Burgess, T., Martin, N., McCleod, A., & Rosen, H. (1975) *The development of writing abilities (11-18).* London: Macmillan Education.

Britton, J. N., Martin, N. C., & Rosen, H. (1966). *Multiple marking of compositions.* London: Her Majesty's Stationery Office.

Butler, Melvin A. and members of the Committee on CCC Language Cast, B. M. D. (1939). The efficiency of different methods of marking English composition, Part I. *British Journal of Educational Psychology, 9,* 257-209.

Cast, B. M. D. (1940). The efficiency of different methods of marking

English composition, Part II. *British Journal of Educational Psychology,* *10,* 49-60.

Charney, D. (1984). The validity of using holistic scoring to evaluate Chomsky, N. (1957). *Syntactic structures.* The Hague: Mouton & Company.

Chomsky, N. (1965). *Aspects of a theory of syntax.* Cambridge MA: Massachussetts Institute of Technology.

Chomsky, N. (1982). *Some concepts and consequences of the theory of government and binding: Linguistic inquiry monograph six.* Cambridge, MA: Massachussetts Institute of Technology.

Conlon, G. (1976). *How the College Entrance Examination Board English Test is scored.* Princeton, NJ: Educational Testing Service.

Cooper, C. R. (1977). Holistic evaluation of writing. In C. R. Cooper & L. Odell (Eds.), *Evaluating writing: Measuring, describing, judging* (pp. 3-32). Urbana, IL: National Council of Teachers of English.

Cooper, P. L. (1984). *The assessment of writing ability: A review of research: Educational Testing Research Report 84-12 (Graduate Record Examination Research Rep. GREB No. 82-15R).* Princeton, NJ: Educational Testing Service.

Cronbach, L. J. (1970). *Essentials of psychological testing* (3rd ed.). New York: Harper & Row.

Cronbach, L. J. (1971). Test validation. In R. L. Thorndike (Ed.), *Educational measurement* (2nd ed., pp. 443-507). Washington, DC: American Council on Education.

Dewey, J. (1916). *Democracy and education* (reprinted 1964). New York: MacMillian.

Diederich, P. B. (1974). *Measuring growth in English.* Urbana, IL: National Council of Teachers of English.

Diederich, P. B., French, J. W., & Carlton, S. T. (1961). *Factors in judgments of writing ability* (Research Bulletin 61-15). Princeton, NJ: Educational Testing Service. (ERIC Document Reproduction Service No. ED 002 172)

Eley, E.G. (1955). Should the General Composition Test be continued? The test satisfies an education need. *College Board Review, 25,* 10-13.

Emig, J. (1977). Writing as a mode of learning. *College Composition and Communication, 28,* 122-127.

Faigley, L., Cherry, R. D., Jolliffe, D. A., & Skinner, A. N. (1985). *Assessing writers' knowledge and processes of composing.* Norwood, NJ: Ablex.

Finlawson, D. S. (1951). The reliability of the marking of essays. British *Journal of Educational Psychology, 21,* 126-134.

Freedman, S. W. (1984). The registers of student and professional writing: Influences on teachers responses. In R. Beach & L. S. Bridwell (Eds.), *Research in composing.* New York: Guilford.

Fulwiler, T. (1982). The personal connection: Journal writing across the curriculum. In T. Fulwiler & A. Young (Eds.), *Language connections: Reading and writing across the curriculum* (pp. 15-32). Urbana, IL: National Council of Teachers of English.

Gardner, H. (1987). *The mind's new science: A history of the cognitive revolution.* New York: Basic Books.

Gere, A. R. (1980). Written composition: Toward a theory of evaluation. *College English, 42,* 44-48.

Godshalk, F. I., Swineford, F., & Coffman, W. E. (1966). *The measurement of writing ability: College Entrance Examination Board* (Research Monograph No. 6). New York: The College Entrance Examination Board.

Greenberg, K. L., Weiner, H. S., & Donovan, R. A. (1986). *Writing assessment: Issues and strategies.* New York: Longman.

Guba, E. G. (1990). The alternative paradigm dialog. In E. G. Guba (Ed.), *The paradigm dialog* (pp. 17-27). Newbury Park, CA: Sage.

Guilford, J. P. (1954). *Psychometric methods.* New York: McGraw-Hill.

Gutek, G. L. (1972). *A history of the western educational experience.* Prospect Heights, IL: Waveland Press.

Halloran, S. M. (1990). From Rhetoric to composition: The teaching of writing in America to 1900. In J. J. Murphy (Ed.), *A short history of writing instruction from ancient Greece to twentieth-century America* (pp. 151-182). Davis, CA: Hermagoras Press.

Hartog, Sir P., & Rhodes, E. C. (1936). *The marks of examiners.* London: Macmillian.

Hebb, D. O. (1949). *The organization of behavior.* New York: Wiley.

Hillegas, M. B. (1915). *A scale for the measurement of quality in English compositions by young people.* New York: Teachers College.

Hinton, E. M. (1940). *An analytical study of the qualities of style and rhetoric found in English compositions.* New York: Teachers College.

Hirsch, E. D., Jr. (1987). *Cultural literacy: What every American needs to know.* Boston: Houghton Mifflin.

Hopkins, L. T. (1921). *The marking system of the College Entrance Examination Board: Harvard monographs in education series 1, no. 2.* Cambridge, MA: Harvard University.

Hull, C. L. (1943). *Principles of behavior.* New York: Appleton-Century-Crofts.

Huot, B. (1988). The validity of holistic scoring: A comparison of the talk-aloud protocols of expert and novice holistic raters. *Dissertation Abstracts International, 49,* 2188A (University Microfilms No. 88-17, 872).

Huot, B. (1990). Reliability, validity, and holistic scoring: What we know and what we need to know. *College Composition and Commu-nication, 41,* 201-211.

Huot, B. & Williamson, M. M. (1990). *Toward a language-based theory of writing assessment*. Unpublished manuscript, University of Louisville.

Hymes, D. (1968). The ethnography of speaking. In J. A. Fishman (Ed.), *Readings in the sociology of language* (pp. 99-138). The Hague: Mouton.

Jensen, A. R. (1980). *Bias in mental testing*. New York: The Free Press.

Langer, J. M. (1986). *Children reading and writing: Structures and strategies.* Norwood, NJ: Ablex.

Lord, F. M., & Novick, M. R. (1968). *Statistical theories of mental test scores.* Reading, MA: Addison-Wesley.

Messick, S. (1989). Validity. In R. Linn (Ed.), *Educational measurement* (3rd ed., pp. 13-103). New York: American Council on Education.

McColly, W. (1970). What does educational research say about the judging of writing ability? *The Journal of Educational Research, 49*(4), 148-156.

Myers, M. (1980). *A procedure for writing assessment and holistic scoring.* Urbana, IL: National Council of Teachers of English.

Newmeyer, F. (1983). *Grammatical theory: Its limits and its possibilities.* Chicago: University of Chicago Press.

Noyes, E. S. (1963). Essay and objective tests in English. *College Board Review, 49*(Winter), 7-11.

Oppenheim, A. N. (1966). *Questionnaire design and attitude measurement.* New York: Basic Books.

Peters, R. S. (1962). *Brett's history of psychology* (edited and abridged). Cambridge, MA: MIT Press.

Phillips, D. C. (1990). Postpositivistic science: Myths and realities. In E. G. Guba (Ed.), *The paradigm dialog* (pp. 31-45). Newbury Park, CA: Sage Publications.

Popham, J. W. (1988). *Educational evaluation* (2nd. ed.). Englewood Cliffs, NJ: Prentice Hall.

Popkewitz, T. S. (1990). Whose future? Whose past? Notes on critical theory and methodology. In E. G. Guba (Ed.), *The paradigm dialog* (pp. 46-66). Newbury Park, CA: Sage Publications.

Pula, J. J. (1990). *The function of personal background, professional training, and work experience on rater performance in holistic scoring sessions: A study of the disciplinary enculturation and placement context.* Unpublished doctoral dissertation, Indiana University of Pennsylvania.

Ryan, J. (1972). IQ-The illusion of objectivity. In K. Richardson & D. Spears (Eds.), *Race and intelligence: The fallacies behind the race-IQ controversy* (pp. 36-55). Baltimore, MD: Penguin.

Shulman, L. S. (1987). Knowledge and teaching: Foundations of the new reform. *Harvard Educational Review, 57*, 1-22.

Simon, J. (1980). *Paradigms lost: Reflections on literacy and its decline.* New York: Potter.

Skinner, B. F. (1938). *The behavior of organisms.* New York: Appleton-Century.

Skinner, B. F. (1956). A case history in scientific method. *American Psychologist, 2*, 221-233.

Skinner, B. F. (1957). *Verbal behavior.* New York: Appleton-Century-Crofts.

Smith, A. (forthcoming). *Writing in a doctoral program in rhetoric.* Doctoral dissertation in progress, Indiana University of Pennsylvania (1991).

Spandel, V. & Stiggins, R. J. (1980) *Direct measures of writing skill: Issues and applications.* Portland, OR: Northwest Regional Educational Development Laboratory.

Spearman, C. (1937). *Psychology down the ages.* New York: Macmillian.

Spenser, H. L. (1851). *Social statistics.*

Steinberg, D. D. (1982). *Psycholinguistics.* New York: Longman.

Terman, L. M. (1916). *The measurement of intelligence: An explanation of and a complete guide for the use of the Stanford revision and extension of the Binet-Simon Intelligence Scale.* New York: Houghton Mifflin

Thorndike, E. L. (1932). *Fundamentals of learning.* New York: Teachers College.

Tolman, E. C. (1932). *Purposive behavior in animals and men.* New York: Appleton-Century.

Torgerson, W. S. (1958). *Theory and methods of scaling.* London: The Institute of Physics.

Watson, J. B. (1930). *Behaviorism* (rev. ed.). New York: Norton.

White, E. (1985). *Teaching and assessing writing.* San Francisco: Jossey-Bass.

Williamson, M. M. (1988). A model for investigating the functions of written language in different disciplines. In D. A. Jolliffe (Ed.), *Writing in academic disciplines, Advances in writing research Volume Two* (pp. 89-132). Norwood, NJ: Ablex.

Willing, M. H. (1918). The measurement of written composition in grades IV-VIII. *English Journal, 7*, 193-202.

Willinsky, J. M. (1987). The seldom-spoken roots of the curriculum: Romanticism and the new literacy. *Curriculum Inquiry, 17*, 268-91.

Wiseman, S. (1949). The marking of English composition in grammar school selection. *British Journal of Educational Psychology, 19*, 200-209.

2

Changing the Model for the Direct Assessment of Writing*

Roberta Camp
Educational Testing Service

INTRODUCTION

Research and practice in writing and writing instruction have led us in recent years to look at writing as a rich and multifaceted activity deeply immersed in the context that surrounds it. As a community of educators and researchers interested in writing, we understand more thoroughly than we once did that the tasks of writing vary with purpose, audience, and context (Hairston, 1982). We think of writing, like reading, as a meaning-making activity requiring the orchestration of skills and strategies, and we see that each mode or purpose for writing draws on different skills and strategies, and different linguistic abilities and cognitive operations (Applebee, 1986; Durst, 1987; Freedman & Pringle, 1981; Langer & Applebee, 1987; Odell, 1981; Penrose, 1989; Pringle & Freedman, 1985).

In addition, we now see that this meaning-making activity occurs over time and involves processes that are recursive, that are used differently by different writers, and that vary with knowledge of the topic, the context

*The author would like to thank Drew Gitomer, Pamela Moss, and Sandra Murphy for their reviews of earlier versions of this chapter. The views expressed are those of the author.

for writing, and personal and cultural history (Applebee, 1986; Flower & Hayes, 1981; O'Conner, 1989). We know now, too, that writers switch among processes and strategies as they generate text, depending on their perception of goals for the writing and their plans for addressing them, and that writers' awareness of the strategies they use is important to their performance in writing (Bereiter & Scardamalia, 1987; Flower & Hayes, 1980; Thompson, 1985). Further, we recognize that many of the processes and strategies for writing involve interaction with texts—and therefore the skills and strategies of reading—and with a social and communicative context (Bruffee, 1986; Carter, 1990; Faigley, 1986; Freedman, Dyson, Flower, & Chafe, 1987; Johnston, 1987; Macrorie, 1976; Moffett, 1968; Smith, 1982; Valencia, McGinley, & Pearson, 1990).

This complex view of writing is not easily reconciled with traditional approaches to assessment. The magnitude of the differences in perspective are prefigured in the conflicts about writing assessment in recent decades, especially in the long-standing controversies surrounding the two most common forms of writing assessment—multiple-choice tests and holistically scored writing samples. Although workable compromises have frequently been found for dealing with the issues behind these controversies, the issues have never been resolved to the complete satisfaction of all parties concerned. With the development of more complex views of writing, there is reason to expect that the issues driving the earlier controversies will resurface in terms that are far more challenging (see Johnston, 1987).

To set out more clearly the issues to be confronted in writing assessment and the possible resolutions of those issues, this chapter will first present a historical and theoretical perspective. The discussion will begin with a reflection on the history of writing assessment in recent decades, then go on to examine the current status of existing models for writing assessment. It will next outline recent shifts in measurement theory that indicate the need for assessments compatible with our new and more complex views of writing. The final section of the chapter will present a description of resources that can help to guide us in the development of new models for writing assessment. The chapter will close with a summary of characteristics likely to be incorporated in such models.

TRADITIONAL FORMATS FOR WRITING ASSESSMENT

The prevailing formats for large-scale writing assessments in the last decades, at least until very recently, have been the multiple-choice test and the impromptu writing sample, and in many cases a combination of the two. The combination in particular has represented for many, including developers of smaller-scale assessments, a compromise accommodating both traditional psychometric expectations for reliability and the concern for validity expressed by teachers of writing and others convinced that judgments about writing ability should be based on writing performance (Breland, Camp, Jones, Morris, & Rock, 1987; Coffman, 1971; Conlon, 1986; Diederich, 1974; Spandel & Stiggins, 1980; White, 1986). It seems worthwhile here to examine the issues that lie behind that compromise.

The History: Balancing the Requirements of Reliability and Validity

The multiple-choice test, with its machine-scorable items, provides evidence taken from multiple data points representing relatively discrete components of the writing task each measured separately. The number and the discreteness of the items yield high test reliability and make possible the construction of multiple versions of the test that are parallel in difficulty and in the characteristics of the tasks presented. Although human judgment is involved in the development and selection of test items, the multiple-choice test is unaffected by the subjectivity of human scoring. It has been seen as reliable, efficient, and economical.

From the perspective of traditional psychometrics, in which high test reliability is a prerequisite for validity, the multiple-choice writing test has also been seen as a valid measure. The claims for its validity have rested on its coverage of skills necessary to writing and on correlations between test scores and course grades—or, more recently, between test scores and performance on samples of writing, including writing generated under classroom conditions (Breland et al., 1987; Breland & Gaynor, 1979; Godshalk, Swineford, & Coffman, 1966). By and large these claims have been more convincing to statistically oriented members of the measurement community than to teachers of writing, who have pointed to the limitations of testing component skills separately and to the narrowness of the range of skills that can be tested in multiple-choice format (see Faigley, Cherry, Jolliffe, & Skinner, 1985).

The claims for the validity of using multiple-choice tests to determine writing competence are not entirely without foundation. Most students who do well on carefully designed and relatively comprehensive multiple-choice tests of grammar, sentence structure, and usage are likely to perform well in response to well-designed prompts for writing, as the correlational studies indicate. It may be that students who have relatively good control over such aspects of writing as mechanics, usage, grammar, and syntax can more easily generate text within relatively short periods of time (Bereiter & Scardamalia, 1987; Scardamalia & Bereiter, 1985). Or perhaps the breadth and depth of experience with reading and writing that help students to recognize conventional expectations for language use also provide them in most instances with the more global skills they need to generate good prose. Whatever the explanation, under most circumstances and for most test takers, performance on a series of independent multiple-choice questions corresponds fairly well with performance on a writing sample (Breland & Gaynor, 1979).

Yet the validity of the multiple-choice test as a measure of writing ability has never been completely certain. Although Breland and Gaynor (1979) felt they had demonstrated, on the basis of correlational studies, that indirect, multiple-choice measures of writing tap skills similar to those called for by writing samples, later studies reflecting greater sensitivity to cognitive processes have come to different conclusions. Ward, Frederiksen, and Carlson (1980), looking at free-response and machine-scorable versions of items testing the ability to generate hypotheses, pointed out that multiple-choice items which depend on the test takers' ability to recognize possible solutions may be a sufficient basis for predicting performance in actually generating solutions, as indicated by correlational studies, but they do not necessarily measure constructs identical with those measured by open-ended, free-response formats. Similarly, and more to the point here, a study of direct and indirect measures of writing for first- and second-language users of English, while finding the expected correlations between performance on indirect and direct assessments of writing, found in the factor analyses that the two formats were not measuring identical skills (Carlson, Bridgeman, Camp, & Waanders, 1985).

In addition, theoretical considerations suggest limitations in the validity of multiple-choice tests of writing. As concepts of writing ability began to focus on performance beyond the sentence level, it became increasingly clear that multiple-choice tests do not sample the full range of knowledge and skills involved in writing (Cooper, 1977; Gere, 1980; Lloyd-Jones, 1977; Odell, 1981). Nor do they sample writing skills in a manner that is consistent with either the theoretical constructs for writing—what we currently understand writing to be—or with practices to be encouraged in the teaching of writing (Odell, 1981).

Furthermore, increased awareness of the differences in the operational grammars of working-class and middle-class children and of speakers of black English and standard English (Cole & Moss, 1989, citing Bernstein, 1975, Heath, 1982, and M. D. Linn, 1975) and of basic writers (Bartholomae, 1980; Beaugrande, 1982; Shaughnessy, 1977) suggests that the cognitive tasks presented by multiple-choice items may be substantially different for nontraditional students and for students familiar with the standard dialect. If this difference proves to be more than theoretical for students whose language experience lies outside the cultural mainstream, the multiple-choice test may be less valid as an indicator of writing ability for such students than it is for mainstream students. To the extent that multiple-choice tests emphasize grammar and usage, they may also be less valid as measures of these students' writing ability than assessments tapping a more comprehensive range of writing skills and abilities.

In many respects, the holistically scored writing sample fares better than the multiple-choice test with respect to validity. As a performance measure drawing on the broader range of skills and strategies necessary for actually generating a piece of writing, the writing sample has frequently been seen as a more valid form of assessment. It allows students to demonstrate skills not tapped by the multiple-choice test and more compatible with the current theoretical construct for writing and with desirable practice in writing instruction. It has therefore been seen by some writing assessment practitioners as a stand-alone format for more valid assessment, especially when more than one writing sample is used, and by others as essential to the validity of writing assessments based on the combination of multiple-choice tests and writing samples.

However, concerns about the relatively low reliability of the writing sample have persisted, especially in the measurement community (Breland et al., 1987; Conlon, 1986), and with some justification. Some of the factors contributing to this low reliability arise from the complex and generative nature of the task of writing. Performance in response to a single prompt for writing, which involves the complexities of understanding and interpreting a task and generating text in response to it, varies far more from one occasion to another and from one prompt to another than does performance on a multiple-choice test made up of a relatively large number of discrete tasks, each of which typically requires little more than recognizing errors or choosing among alternative phrasings. Awareness of these sources of variation in the test taker's performance and of similar sources of variation in raters' perceptions of writing has led even strong advocates of direct assessment to recognize the limits of a single sample of writing (Cooper, 1977; Greenberg & Witte, 1988; Odell, 1981). Even with the high interrater reliabilities now possible in well-run holistic scoring sessions drawing on the expertise of experienced raters, the estimated test reliability for a single essay scored twice is insufficient to fully justify the use of a single essay as the sole basis for important judgments about students' academic careers (see Breland et al., 1987, Table 5.4, p. 27).

Thus the compromise has persisted. Multiple-choice tests of writing offer reliability, efficiency, economy, some contribution to validity, and a convenient basis for statistical comparisons from one test to another, even though they measure only a limited number of subskills for writing, and measure them only indirectly. The impromptu writing sample provides a demonstration of the writer's handling of both subskills for writing and the larger-order skills involved in actually composing text: generating and developing ideas, organizing, establishing connections within the text, and finding a tone and rhetorical stance appropriate to the topic and audience. In addition, use of the writing sample in assessment sends a clear message that writing performance is important, and that grammar and usage are not sufficient proxies for actual writing (Conlon, 1986).

What We Have Learned from Our Experience with Direct Assessment

In the last decades, our collective experience with writing assessments based on the combination of the multiple-choice test and impromptu writing sample has led to genuine advances in knowledge and practice. In recent years, as we have become increasingly aware of the complexities of performance in writing and increasingly skeptical of multiple-choice formats, we have focused proportionally greater attention on direct assessment based on the writing sample. The efforts of researchers and test designers have brought increased awareness of the procedures necessary to enhance the reliability and validity of direct assessment (Lucas & Carlson, 1989). They have also enhanced our understanding of the performance required of writers not only in assessments but in other, more typical situations for academic writing (Faigley et al., 1985; Ruth & Murphy, 1988).

We can estimate how much we have learned from our experience with writing assessment, particularly direct assessment based on the writing sample, by looking at the sizable and rapidly growing bibliography on writing assessment. Within that bibliography we find, in addition to the early formulations of issues for direct assessment (Cooper, 1981; Cooper & Odell, 1977), works that describe and examine the practices and procedures of prompt design and holistic evaluation (i.e., Brossell, 1983; Freedman, 1981; Hoetker, 1982; Ruth & Murphy, 1988; White, 1985), increasingly sophisticated treatments of the history and issues of writing assessment (i.e., Greenberg, Weiner, & Donovan, 1986), and historical retrospectives looking at the last decades as a basis for future directions in writing assessment (i.e., Faigley et al., 1985; Keech-Lucas, 1988a, 1988b). Some of these efforts, especially those focusing on the cognitive processes of writers responding to topics and of raters evaluating writers' performance, have contributed to our reconceptualizations of the skills and strategies involved in writing in both test and nontest situations.

We have also made a number of changes in assessment practice for the purpose of improving the measurement properties of holistically scored writing samples. We attempt to minimize or compensate for those factors most likely to create variation in writing performance from one occasion to another. We try to present prompts that are immediately accessible to all test takers—whatever their individual interests, knowledge, or cultural experience—and that can be dealt with in the limited time available for writing. We avoid topics that are likely to evoke emotional responses on the part of the writer or the rater of the paper. We ask that test takers all write under comparable conditions, with the same time allotment and in an environment free of distraction or interruption.

In the interest of reliable and equitable assessment, we have in effect streamlined the writing experience and removed from it the particulars of context in which it typically occurs. We have created within the constraints of the testing situation the circumstances for a limited performance in writing that we expect will correspond to other writing experiences—a simulated, universalized performance that we use to predict performance on a number of other occasions and in a variety of other circumstances for writing.

We have further increased the reliability of the writing sample and the usefulness of the information it provides by attending to the ways in which we conduct evaluation sessions and report the results. We use controlled procedures in the evaluation of writing samples; we develop shared sets of standards for the scoring of papers; and we ask that papers be scored anonymously and independently by individuals with broad experience of student writing and few eccentricities in judging its quality. We publish examples of writing accompanied by analyses that make public—for teachers, students, and the community—the criteria that inform the raters' holistic judgments.

Altogether, we have made significant changes, in both research and practice. Yet in many respects we have not, until recently, recognized the assumptions about writing implied in the traditional model for assessment—indeed, in any model that depends on a single impromptu writing sample for much of its validity. As Faigley et al. (1985) have observed in the case of writing assessment in general, "practice has far outrun theory" (p. 205). We are now able to see more clearly the assumptions underlying traditional approaches to writing assessment in part because we are moving away from them. With the clarity of hindsight, we are now able as well to examine their implications.

NEW VIEWS OF WRITING AND THE ASSUMPTIONS BEHIND TRADITIONAL FORMATS FOR ASSESSMENT

From the perspective of our new understanding of writing and writing processes, the assumptions about writing underlying the traditional model for writing assessment become more apparent; so, too, do the model's limitations. Whereas we once regarded a piece of writing in a single mode or for a single purpose to be a sufficient sample, we now see it as insufficient to represent the variety of modes and purposes for writing (Emig, 1982; Greenberg & Witte, 1988). The timed, controlled conditions for writing that once seemed the means to ensure equal opportunity to all test takers now seem unnatural limits that preclude use of the processes, among them interactions with others, that we now understand to be part of most writing (Polin, 1980). The prompts that we so carefully designed for equal accessibility are now seen to cut off the opening explorations of a topic in which writers find a way into it that engages their interests and allows them to use their knowledge and skills to best advantage. Our reluctance to evoke emotional responses even seems at times to have precluded the kind of personal engagement that is at the heart of really good student writing. Ironically, many of the efforts we made to enhance the reliability of the writing sample—especially those aimed at streamlining and universalizing the writing experience—appear now to limit the value of the assessment (Keech-Lucas, 1988b).

Questions About the Validity of the Impromptu Writing Sample

From this perspective, the traditional formats for writing assessment, including the writing sample, seem insufficient. The skills measured by multiple-choice tests of writing seem more remote than ever from the skills required for complex performances in writing. More critically, how-ever, the streamlined performance represented by the single impromptu writing sample, which corresponds to only a small portion of what we now understand to be involved in writing, no longer seems a strong basis for validity. Performance on the writing sample no longer appears to be an adequate representation of the accepted theoretical construct for writing; nor does it seem an adequate representation of students' likely experi-ences with writing, past or future, or with the skills and strategies called upon in those experiences. In addition, the view of writing encouraged by the assessment does not reflect the instructional goals required by our new and more complex views of writing.

The implication, when we take all of these observations into account, is that the changes in our views of writing amount to a shift in the construct to be measured in writing assessment. It is no longer possible to claim that "an adequate essay test of writing ability is valid by defini-tion" (Eley, 1955, p. 11) or to trust in the belief that "good writing is good writing." What we are experiencing, in fact, is a mismatch between the complexities of the conceptual framework for writing that we find in current research and practice and the simpler construct implied by traditional approaches to writing assessment, including the writing sample. Very likely we are also seeing the signs of a growing incompati-bility between our views of writing and the constraints necessary to satisfy the requirements of traditional psychometrics—in particular, of reliability and validity narrowly defined.

Perhaps we can better understand the full extent of our dilemma by seeing it in schematic terms. First, let us go back to the multiple-choice test, the writing sample, and the relationship between them in the traditional model for assessment. As indicated earlier, the multiple-choice test draws on discrete skills required to recognize correct and incorrect or better and worse language use presented in the context of multiple, largely unrelated, and quite brief examples of writing. The inclusion in the multiple-choice test of a relatively large number of such items addressing a variety of skills at the sentence and sometimes intersentence level was once thought a sufficient basis for content validity; in this view, the items were seen as sampling fully if indirectly the universe of skills necessary for writing. With our more complex and enlarged views of writing, however, the domain sampled by the multiple-choice test appears far more constricted. We now see the multiple-choice test as drawing on relatively low-level skills (such as recognition of agreement or lack of agreement between subject and verb or between pronoun and antecedent), which we are now likely to understand as subskills or component skills necessary for writing performance.

From our new perspective, we see the writing sample as drawing on a variety of skills and strategies related to one another, many of them beyond the scope of the multiple-choice test, with any particular writing sample from any particular student drawing on some but not all of the skills tapped by a particular multiple-choice test. For example, a prompt calling for narrative writing based on personal experience may not require the writer to deal with parallelism in sentence structure. Or a particular writer responding to such a prompt may choose a rhetorical strategy that does not involve writing sentences calling for parallelism.

In schematic terms, we might see the domains covered by the writing sample and by the multiple-choice test as circles that are partially overlapping but not concentric (see Figure 1).

Multiple-Choice Test

Writing Sample

Figure 1. Relationship of Domains Covered by the Multiple Choice Test of Writing and the Writing Sample

In earlier views of writing and assessment in which the multiple-choice test and the writing sample were assumed to be measuring the same skills, the circle for the domain sampled in the multiple-choice test might have been seen—if we had examined our assumptions carefully—as more or less congruent with the circle for the writing sample. The two formats would have been understood to be measuring roughly the same construct, defined generally as writing ability. We now see the circles as overlapping but not congruent, and the formats as measuring some but not all of the same skills. Further, we are more aware of the differences in skills required for performance on the two kinds of tests; we make a stronger distinction between the skills required to recognize correct and incorrect language use and those required to generate text in response to a prompt.

Getting the Picture on Validity: The Mismatch Between the Model for Assessment and Current Concepts of Writing

Now let us place this model for assessment within the conceptual framework for literacy suggested by Valencia, McGinley, and Pearson (1990, p. 129) in their discussion of the need for forms of literacy assessment that reflect our current understanding of literacy and learning. In this framework, reading and writing are seen as holistic processes drawing on a number of specific but related subskills, such as decoding or comprehension skills for reading and understanding of grammar or principles of organization for writing. The holistic processes of reading and writing, in turn, are perceived as serving and shaped by particular functions and goals in the life of the individual using them. Thus, for example, if a person writes on one occasion primarily to gain clarity or insight about a difficult issue and on another to communicate what is already known, it is likely that the processes and strategies the person uses will vary across the two occasions (see Figure 2).

The relationship between subskills and holistic processes is represented in the Valencia et al. framework by two concentric circles, the inner circle representing subskills (described as "the infrastructure for reading and writing") and the surrounding circle representing the holistic processes of reading and writing. A third concentric circle surrounds the other two, representing the ways in which context informs holistic processes as they are shaped to serve particular functions in the life of the reader or writer.

If we focus only on writing for the moment (with apologies to Valencia et al.) and superimpose our figure for writing assessment on the framework, we can place the multiple-choice test entirely within the innermost circle of discrete subskills. Without altering the relationship of the writing sample to the multiple-choice test, we can place the writing

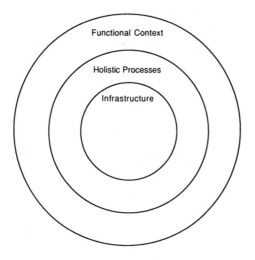

Figure 2. Valencia et al: Dimensions of Reading and Writing

sample within the circle representing holistic processes and overlapping into the innermost circle representing subskills for writing (see Figure 3).

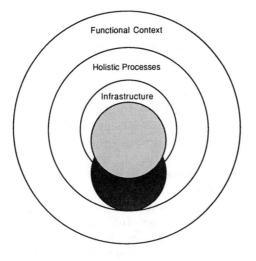

Figure 3. Relationship of Domains Covered by the Multiple-Choice Test of Writing and Writing Sample to Dimensions of Writing

The relationship of the area of the writing sample circle to the area of the two inner circles fits with what we know from research, from discourse theory, and from experience with prompt design and analysis of student writing samples. It reflects our current awareness that the skills and strategies needed in writing for one mode or purpose are not necessarily those needed in writing for another (Greenberg & Witte, 1988; Pringle & Freedman, 1985). It corresponds to what we know about the knowledge of text structure and discourse type required by each mode or purpose for writing—that each mode or purpose requires different knowledge (Pringle & Freedman, 1985; Scardamalia & Bereiter, 1985). It even allows us to see that the skills and strategies required may differ from any one writing task to another, or from one writer to another, depending on how familiar the writer is with content related to the topic and on how the writer redefines the task in the course of writing.

In this respect, the figure is consistent with observations such as those reported by Breland et al. (1987). In the Breland study, in which the same groups of first-year college students wrote on six topics, the writing samples showed evidence of students using different rhetorical strategies and cognitive processes for each of the topics, and even for the same topic. For example, the topic that asked for persuasive writing on an issue involving trends over time called on repeated use of both comparative structures and the vocabulary of comparison, neither of which was evoked to any great extent in the other five topics, and the organizational structure for narrative papers varied with the course of events described. The differences in performance across purposes and topics were observed by researchers and by readers scoring the papers; they were also reflected in the factor analysis (see Breland et al., 1987, pp. 19-22 and 40-47).

We can also see from Figure 3 that even if we focus only on writing independent of reading, the traditional formats for assessment address only a portion of the subskills and strategies represented in our new construct for writing. An assessment addressing all of the construct would be represented by a series of circles (and possibly other shapes) covering the whole of both the subskills and holistic processes circles—or, in nonschematic terms, by a variety of assessments, including multiple samples of writing generated for a variety of modes and purposes and written under both test and nontest conditions.

Whereas we might once have seen the results of performance on the multiple-choice test or the writing sample or both as a basis for generalizing to all other performance in writing, we are now reluctant to do so. The arguments for the predictive validity of these two formats for writing assessment, arguments based on correlations between scores derived from the assessments and statistical indicators of performance in other contexts, now seem beside the point; they do not take into account what we know to be important about writing. Again we see in the figure the disjuncture between the assumptions and methods of the traditional model for assessment and our new concepts of writing.

The limitations of the traditional formats for writing assessment become even more striking if we look in Figure 3 at the relationship of the circles representing the multiple-choice test and the writing sample to the third and outermost of the concentric circles from the Valencia et al. framework, the one representing processes related to the communicative contexts for writing. If we understand this outermost circle to include ways in which contexts for writing enrich and inform the processes for writing, we see represented in it the most substantial of the challenges to traditional views of assessment. We can see in this graphic representation what we have lost by streamlining and universalizing writing performance to fit the constraints of test conditions. We discover that we have excluded from the assessment many of the experiences and resources that motivate and shape writing (see Johnston, 1985), especially for novice writers and for writers who do not easily see themselves as participants in the academic discourse community.

The figure tells us that by cutting off performance in writing from social and communicative contexts, both multiple-choice test and writing sample formats eliminate the collaborative exploration and problem solving that enable many student writers to engage with issues, to identify their own perspectives, and to discover and shape a topic appropriate to that perspective. These formats also eliminate the opportunity for the writer to draw on private explorations of particular interests and knowledge in personal and expressive writing, unless the topic of the prompt happens to coincide with one the writer has already begun to explore. Also absent from performance in either format are opportunities to try out strategies and reshape ideas orally before committing them finally to paper. The model for assessment represented in the multiple-choice and writing sample formats thus deprives many student writers of the advantages that come with writing for genuine communicative purposes and contexts.

The loss of communicative purpose and context is likely to be most damaging for students who are relatively unfamiliar with the mainstream culture and the discourse of academic settings. We have become increasingly aware in recent years of the discomfort experienced by these students when they are asked to write in settings in which the implicit expectations for discourse are unfamiliar to them (see Heath, 1983; Rafoth & Rubin, 1988; Rose, 1989; Taylor, 1989). With our greater understanding of the interaction between cognitive and social dimensions of expertise in writing, we have also become more attentive to the differences between the strategies used by these writers and those used by writers familiar with academic discourse. If students with less expertise fall back on more general strategies for writing, and if these general strategies are related to cultural expectations for discourse, as seems to be the case (Carter, 1990), then students from nonmainstream cultures may be especially disadvantaged by the lack of social and instructional context in traditional formats and conditions for assessment (see Johnston, 1987).

Yet the figure does not tell the whole story. In addition to the limitations made visible in Figure 3, a further limitation becomes apparent when we match our current concepts of writing with the construct implied in and the information provided by traditional formats for writing assessment. Neither the multiple-choice test nor the impromptu writing sample provides a basis in the assessment for obtaining information about metacognitive aspects of writing, information that is essential to instruction and to the writer's development (Bereiter & Scardamalia, 1987; Campione & Brown, 1990; Scardamalia & Bereiter, 1985). Neither yields information about the ways in which writers monitor the processes and strategies they use in writing performance. The impromptu writing sample draws on only the most constrained of the processes and strategies available to writers in other situations, and it provides no opportunity for writers to demonstrate the ways in which they modify processes and strategies in relation to their understanding of the goals and conditions for writing.

TAKING STOCK: THE CURRENT STATUS OF WRITING ASSESSMENT

Altogether then, the views of writing evident in research and increasingly evident in instruction pose serious challenges to traditional approaches to writing assessment and to the assumptions behind them. The multiple-choice test and the writing sample seem clearly insufficient for measuring writing ability as we now understand it. More significantly, the concept of writing implied in the two formats and in combinations of them no longer approximates the concepts for writing evident in research and forward-looking instruction.

What does this state of affairs mean for writing assessment? Are we to conclude that neither multiple-choice tests nor writing samples can ever be used in a writing assessment without risk to its validity? That what we have learned in the last decades about enhancing the measurement value of direct assessment is somehow worthless? That our careful attention to the characteristics of writing tasks or to the procedures for scoring has been wasted? Not at all. The achievements of writing assessment in recent decades are real. No responsible educator would want to see a return to evaluations of writing based on the private idiosyncrasies of the individual evaluator (see Keech-Lucas, 1988b). Nor would we want to see assessment based on any of the shared, but largely unexamined, assumptions about literacy and learning evident in previous eras of writing assessment (see

Witte, Trachsel, & Walters, 1986). But the advances we have made do not answer the challenges we now face.

There is considerable work to be done. To facilitate that work, we need to develop a conceptual framework for writing assessment that reflects our current understanding of writing. Within that framework we need to examine the limitations of the traditional formats for assessment so that we understand what our assessments can tell us and what they cannot tell us about student ability. If we determine, as we have already in many instances, that our new views of writing are too complex to be served well by any single approach to assessment, then we will need to think about the ways in which different formats for assessment— including some yet to be developed—can provide us with information about different aspects of writers' skills, processes, and strategies. We will then be able to explore possible ways in which the different kinds of information obtained from different formats can be used to serve different assessment purposes. In addition, we will be able to think about ways in which information from different assessments can be combined to create more comprehensive descriptions of writers' knowledge and abilities.

Such a conceptual framework for writing assessment will also help us to estimate the value of new approaches to assessment, to understand which aspects of writers' knowledge and abilities they address, and what kinds of inferences they can be expected to support. As new approaches are developed in both large-scale and classroom-based assessments, they can be placed within the conceptual framework. Their purpose and value in promoting the comprehensive understanding necessary to teaching and learning, as well as to institutional decisions and research, can then be determined. In addition, where aspects of the writer's experience in writing or development as a writer are not addressed by available approaches to assessment, we can identify the need for further information and perhaps the possible means by which we might obtain it.

Thinking about such a conceptual framework for writing assessment and about the approaches to assessment that might fall within it requires a substantial change in our understanding of the issues in educational assessment. If it is true that the limitations of the two most prevalent formats for writing assessment reflect an incompatibility between complex views of writing and the requirements of traditional views of measurement, as has been suggested here, then a new perspective on educational measurement is essential for richer and more comprehensive approaches to writing assessment. In fact, if assessments are to be created that truly reflect our new understanding of writing and writing processes, we will need, in addition to new methodology, nothing less than a redefinition of the very purposes and roles of assessment within our educational institutions.

NEW VIEWS OF THE MEANING
AND FUNCTIONS OF ASSESSMENT

Many of the concerns about the limitations and effects of assessment that are felt by educators and researchers focusing on writing are shared by educators and researchers in other fields, including educational measurement. Indeed, some of the same intellectual and societal concerns are at work across academic disciplines and research communities. In particular, the recent developments in cognitive psychology that have stimulated new perspectives on writing have brought new views of intellectual behavior and learning to all of education, including the field of assessment. Similarly, the emphasis in the educational reform literature of the last decade on students as active learners and on teachers as professionals has affected researchers and practitioners across the entire educational community, including those involved in assessment. In addition, the sense of social responsibility that stimulates our attempts in the field of writing to better understand and serve the needs of minority populations is shared by educators in other academic disciplines and in the assessment community. It may well be time, therefore, to survey the changes in perspective evident in current thinking about assessment and to incorporate these perspectives in our attempts to shape new approaches to the assessment of writing.

New Views of Validity

Within the educational assessment community in recent years, considerable attention has been given to the concept of validity. As a result, validity is now seen as a single, unified concept in which the construct to be measured is central to all other considerations (Cole & Moss, 1989; Cronbach, 1988; Messick, 1989a, 1989b; Moss, in press). At one time the validity of a test might have been discussed in terms of one or more kinds of validity, each seen as independent of and more or less equal in value to the others: content validity, construct validity, criterion-related validity (including predictive and concurrent validity), and face validity. In the last two decades, however, validity has been increasingly seen as taking on a central focus: the inferences about a test taker that are derived from performance on a test. (See Moss, in press, for a comprehensive review and analysis of emerging perspectives on validity.) Investigations of validity involve the ongoing evaluation of such inferences on the basis of evidence derived from multiple considerations. The investigations may draw on the methodologies associated with the earlier approaches to validity, but to be consistent with current views, they must consider validity in integrated and comprehensive terms and always in relation to the theoretical construct—what the assessment is intended to measure. In addition, the evidence for validity must be examined in relation to the social consequences of the inferences made about test takers and the actions taken on the basis of those inferences (Cole & Moss, 1989; Messick, 1989a, 1989b; Moss, in press).

Thus, the investigation of validity is seen as including far more than traditional content validity studies, which were essentially examinations of the coverage of the subject represented by the test's content, and also as more than the comparisons of performances within and across tests that have characterized many studies of predictive validity. Most important, however, is that all evidence for validity is to be interpreted in relation to the theoretical construct, the purpose for the assessment, and therefore the inferences derived from it, and the social consequences.

What this view suggests for writing assessment is that our concerns about validity are legitimate. The mismatch between the current theoretical constructs for writing and the construct implied by traditional formats for assessment casts serious doubt on the validity of traditional approaches to writing assessment. Furthermore, that doubt is not entirely relieved by the familiar arguments for the content validity of the multiple-choice writing test as a broad sampling of writing subskills or for criterion validity as indicated by correlational studies showing a high degree of correspondence between performance on multiple-choice tests and writ-ing samples. In addition, our concerns about the possible deleterious effects of conventional writing assessment formats on students outside the mainstream of academic culture no longer appear peripheral; they are central to validity, especially if those effects derive from misrepresentation of the construct of writing.

Current thinking about validity suggests that problems with a test's validity, especially those likely to be associated with adverse social consequences, be investigated by looking at the ways in which the construct to be measured is represented in the test. In the case of writing, we should think about whether our assessments adequately represent writing as we understand it. If an assessment fails to include important and relevant dimensions or facets of the construct—as we have said traditional writing assessments do—it is said to suffer from "construct underrepresentation." If the assessment is easier or more difficult for some test takers than for others for reasons irrelevant to the construct—as we suspect may be the case with our traditional writing assessment formats—then it is said to exhibit "construct-irrelevant variance" (Messick, 1989a). Similarly, if the information derived from an assessment is more valid for some groups of the test-taking population than for others—if it exhibits "differential validity"—the assessment can be said to show test bias (Cole & Moss, 1989).

These criteria for validity can be quite useful as we investigate traditional formats for writing assessment and search for new ones. What they suggest is that our assessments, and the inferences about writers' abilities we derive from them, must take into account both the current construct for writing in its entirety and the possible distortions in our estimates of writers' abilities that derive from limitations in our formats for assessment.

Also useful to our investigations of existing and experimental formats for assessment is a shift in methods used for construct validation (Messick, 1989a). The historical development associated with emerging views of validity is moving the field away from a primary emphasis on patterns of relationships, such as the correlational studies of predictive validity so often used to justify multiple-choice tests of writing, toward methods more likely to be supportive of complex performances in writing. Studies of predictive validity are still seen as contributing to investigations of construct validity, but there is considerably more interest in insights to be derived from studies of the processes underlying performance on the assessment and studies of test takers' performances over time and across groups and settings.

Following upon the new definitions of validity in which all considerations are related to the construct, the inferences made, and the social consequences of those inferences, a further expansion of the concept of validity has recently become evident—one that has far-reaching implications, especially if we combine it with our emerging sense of the new constructs for writing. Pointing out the unfortunate effects of indirect assessments on teaching and learning, Frederiksen and Collins (1989) suggest that our notions of validity be expanded to include the effects of an assessment on the educational system in which it occurs. For an assessment to demonstrate "systemic validity," they argue, it must support instruction and learning that foster development of the cognitive skills the assessment is intended to measure.

In this view, indirect assessments, despite their purported economy, efficiency, and objectivity, are seen as extracting a high price in terms of such effects on teaching and learning as the emphasis on isolated, low-level skills and the displacement of skills and strategies necessary to higher-order thinking, problem solving, and metacognitive awareness. Direct assessments, however, have the advantage from this perspective of being based on performances that can address the intended cognitive skills directly and incorporate not only the product to be created but the process of creating it. They also provide a basis for developing awareness among teachers and learners of the characteristics important to good performances and products. The processes involved in creating the assessment, especially if they occur within the educational institution they serve, provide opportunities for teachers and learners to become aware of the expectations and criteria for performance.

This expansion of the concept of validity to include systemic effects has a number of implications for writing assessment. It means, first of all, that in many respects the struggle to establish the legitimacy of direct assessment has been won. Thus, the procedures associated with the direct assessment of writing are seen from this perspective as exemplary for assessments in other areas of the curriculum (Frederiksen & Collins, 1989; Linn, Baker, & Dunbar, 1991). The setting of representative tasks, the identification of criteria and standards for judging performance on the tasks, the development of libraries of sample performances illustrating how the scoring criteria have been applied, and the involvement of all parties to the assessment, including classroom teachers and eventually students, have the effect of emphasizing the skills and strategies the assessment is intended to address. In short, the procedures involved in direct assessments of writing are seen as having great potential for enhancing systemic validity.

Moreover, the concept of systemic validity can help us find direction for the writing assessments of the future. If we take from systemic validity the sense of assessment as a set of contextualized experiences and procedures, many of them already familiar to us from direct assessments of writing, and if we combine that sense with our understanding of the recently expanded constructs for writing, we can begin to address the challenges for assessment that we now experience. We can envision richer approaches to writing assessment, approaches that reflect the current construct for writing, that are more closely integrated with instruction, and more immediately useful to teachers and students.

Broader Concepts of Assessments and What They Should Measure

Within the educational assessment research community there have been indications in the last several years of dissatisfaction with the limited perspective on human intelligence underlying traditional standardized tests and implied by the psychometric methods that support them (N. Frederiksen, 1984, 1986). Increased attention to the cognitive processes involved in taking tests has brought increased awareness of the limitations of test and item formats in both multiple-choice and essay tests. Multiple-choice tests are seen as unsuitable for the measurement of higher-order skills, and essay exams as too far removed from those real-life situations in which the test taker will eventually need to use the skills tested. In addition, most test-taking situations, with their controlled, timed, strictly monitored settings and their expectations for "right answers," are seen as restricting the use of cognitive processes because they allow little opportunity to reformulate a problem or develop an original solution and virtually no opportunity to deal with the kinds of ill-structured problems we encounter in real life (N. Frederiksen, 1986).

Clearly, such criticisms of prevailing test formats echo those so often raised for traditional approaches to writing assessment. In fact, much of this argument is consistent with the discussion earlier in this chapter of the limitations of multiple-choice and writing sample formats for writing assessment. Two suggestions associated with this argument seem especially applicable to the current challenges for writing assessment. One such suggestion is that conventional tests be supplemented with simulations of real-life problems that allow for some of the open-endedness characteristic of responses to real-life situations, but "with enough structure and standardization to make data interpretable" (N. Frederiksen, 1986, p. 446). The second is that simulated performances and scoring systems be developed that yield qualitative descriptions of the strategies and processes evident in the test takers' responses rather than a single-score report (N. Frederiksen, 1986).

Cognitive Psychology Perspectives on Measurement

The influence of cognitive psychology is clearly evident in the perspectives on validity and assessment already described. But to fully understand the implications of cognitive psychology for measurement, and for writing assessment in particular, we need to look more directly at its influence on measurement theory.

One of the ways in which cognitive psychology influences educational measurement is through the methods it provides for examining the constructs measured by tests (Snow & Lohman, 1989). Focusing on the skills, processes, and strategies used in responding to assessment tasks, the methods of cognitive psychology aim to identify more precisely what a task or set of tasks measures than do the correlational studies and factor analyses of more traditional psychometrics. They also attempt to make distinctions among the component behaviors that contribute to successful or unsuccessful performance. As suggested earlier in the discussion on new views of validity, the methodology provided by cognitive psychology thus addresses issues of construct validity in ways that are more supportive of rich and complex forms of writing assessment than were earlier methodologies.

Research in cognitive psychology also leads to a more detailed understanding of learning and of the ways in which instruction—and assessment—can promote learning (Snow, 1989). Combined with closer examination of the constructs measured by assessment and increased awareness of the issues of context, this research is beginning to help us identify more precisely the limitations of existing assessments and the likely characteristics of more promising approaches. Particularly relevant to writing assessment are studies using information-processing models to examine performance. Studies investigating how and how well individuals process information, or how they use controlled and automated modes of processing and shift between them, for example, will eventually inform the development of models for assessment, including writing assessment, that are truly helpful to learning and informative to instruction.

Not surprisingly, the perspectives on learning and performance developed by cognitive psychologists have led to increased awareness of the shortcomings of the psychometric models underlying most standardized tests. From a cognitive perspective, conventional psychometric approaches are deficient because they lack a theory of learning (Snow & Lohman, 1989). The result is that tests and test items have no inherent psychological justification in terms of the processes they evoke in the test taker. Purely psychometric models are therefore seen as incapable of addressing the meaning of test performance except in terms of statistical properties. To the extent that conventional psychometric models de facto imply a view of learning, it is learning as the aggregation of discrete skills and knowledge, a view inconsistent with recent research in cognitive psychology (Mislevy, in press; Shepard, 1991; Wolf, Bixby, Glenn, & Gardner, 1991).

A further criticism of conventional test theory from this perspective is that it does not take into account the differences among test takers that affect their performance (see Snow & Lohman, 1989). The individuals taking tests use different strategies on different tests and even on the items within a test, depending, among other things, on ability level, level of expertise with the tasks presented, and test taking or learning style. Yet these differences are not reflected in test scores because they are not captured by psychometric models of the test-taking experience. In this sense, test scores appear to indicate differences among test takers along a single dimension, while the real differences may need to be described in terms of multiple dimensions (Snow & Lohman, 1989). Without some differentiation among these dimensions and an indication of the extent to which each is represented in the score, the meaning of the score cannot be understood in terms that are genuinely useful to learners and to the institutions that serve them.

To address the shortcomings of conventional test theory and create the foundations for new approaches to assessment, a number of researchers in educational measurement have begun to lay the groundwork for a theory of measurement "more suited to the new constructs" (Snow, 1989, p. 8), one that "can provide a theoretical basis for developing new assessment methods" (N. Frederiksen, 1990, p. ix) and can "link testing with the cognitive process of learning" (Mislevy, in press). That theory will support a greater variety of assessment approaches than does traditional test theory, because it will recognize a variety of purposes for assessment, among them the need to provide information directly useful for instruction and learning, and because it will recognize multiple goals for instruction and learning (Snow, 1989). It is likely to be a theory far more supportive of assessment compatible with our current construct for writing than traditional psychometric models have been.

Some researchers keenly aware of the role that processes and strategies play in learning have already begun to develop new models for assessment as well as the research base necessary to support them. One such model, dynamic assessment, focuses on how students actually learn and how well they are able to use resources made available to them (Campione & Brown, 1990). The purpose of this model is to "assess as directly as possible the psychological processes involved in task performance" (p. 142), thereby providing a more accurate basis for predicting future academic performance than standardized tests. The method in dynamic assessment, which combines instruction with assessment, is to provide a small-scale cooperative learning environment in which instructional support is supplied as needed by the learner, and to estimate the learner's potential levels of performance by taking into account the extent and kind of support supplied. This approach appears to be especially useful in estimating the capabilities of students who have not had the advantages of rich environments for learning. The data from the research on this approach indicate that "estimates of [students'] initial response to instruction and of their ability to make use of newly acquired resources are powerful tools" (p. 167) in determining which students are likely to do well and which are likely to experience difficulties.

The Call for Contextualized Assessment

The movement toward new theories of measurement is complemented by a movement within curriculum and school reform toward alternative models for assessment (Berlak et al., 1992; Gardner, 1988; Glaser, 1988; Haney & Madaus, 1989; Mitchell, 1989; Resnick & Resnick, 1985; Stiggins, 1988; Wiggins, 1989). In many of these alternative models, assessment is based on the performance of complex and meaningful tasks that are related to real-world contexts and are themselves valuable to learning (Archbald & Newmann, 1988; Gitomer, in press; Mitchell, 1992; Wiggins, 1989). The performances draw on knowledge and skills integrated within the context of purposeful problem solving, which is accomplished in collaboration with others and within a relatively extended and flexible time frame. The tasks are challenging, but support is provided as needed, enabling all performers to demonstrate some degree of success.

The performances central to these models of assessment are likely to culminate in production of discourse or artifacts that yield evidence of achievement, but the products are not the exclusive focus for evaluation. The evaluation involves informed judgment on the part of knowledgeable witnesses to the performance (teachers, for example) who attend to the essentials of performance, including the strategies and processes used to bring it about. Evaluative judgments are expressed in the form of scoring systems built on multiple indicators of achievement or indicators of achievement described in multiple facets. The criteria informing the judgments are public, shared, and eventually internalized by performers and evaluators alike. The tasks for the assessment are consistent with individual and institutional goals for learning, and the purpose of assessment is to enable learners to discover and demonstrate what they can do and what they might work on in the future.

Possible models for contextualized assessment are being explored, as are the issues involved in their implementation, in discussions and projects extending across academic disciplines and educational institutions. Some of these assessments are built around hands-on, problem-solving projects, as in the science projects developed by the National Assessment of Educational Progress and the Connecticut Assessment of Educational Progress, in the New York science and mathematics assessments, and in the science and mathematics projects in the British Assessment Performance Unit. Others, especially in reading and writing, but also in other areas of the curriculum, involve students in the creation of portfolios. A number of schools, school districts, states, and college writing programs from Juneau, Alaska to Fort Worth, Texas and from California to Vermont are developing portfolio assessments (see Belanoff & Dickson, 1991; Murphy & Smith, 1991; Tierney, Carter, & Desai, 1991; Yancey, 1992).

Such models have strong potential for addressing the limitations of traditional approaches to literacy assessment, including those identified in this chapter. They represent a movement toward assessments that are "ecological" in the ways described by Keech-Lucas (1988a, 1988b): They have a positive effect on the learning environment, they take into account the whole environment of the learner, and they increase the amount, quality, and usefulness of the information provided to teachers and students. These models also point toward assessment which exhibits the qualities that Valencia et al. indicate as necessary for richer forms of literacy assessment—assessment that is "continuous, multi-dimensional, collaborative, knowledge-based, and authentic" (1990, p. 144). Equally important is that the use of such models reflects significant transformations in the expectations for assessment held by the institutions that use them, transformations consistent with current discussions of school reform and restructuring (Berlak et al., 1992; Camp, 1992b; Darling-Hammond & Ascher, 1991; Newmann, 1991).

MOVING TOWARD NEW MODELS
FOR WRITING ASSESSMENT

The challenges involved in developing models of assessment compatible with our new understanding of writing will not be met easily or quickly. Clearly, though, we are not alone in our effort. Educators and designers of assessments in other academic disciplines face many of the same challenges, and researchers in educational measurement are engaged with many of the same issues. It may be helpful to consider briefly the resources we have available to us, both in the research literature on measurement and in our previous experience with writing assessment.

Resources for a New Conceptual Framework for Writing Assessment

The work of several of the researchers already cited in this chapter can provide us with guidelines for new approaches to assessment. Frederiksen and Collins describe several "Principles for the Design of Systemically Valid Testing" (1989, p. 30). Snow identifies three major "Issues for Assessment Development" (1989, pp. 10-11). Archbald and Newmann identify critical issues for alternative assessments (1988, p. vi), as well as criteria for the tasks presented (1988, pp. 2-4). Wiggins describes "Criteria of Authenticity" for contextualized assessment (1989, pp. 711-712). Linn, Baker, and Dunbar (1991) identify a set of criteria to be applied in evaluating complex, performance-based assessments. Valencia et al. indicate "Important Attributes of Classroom and Individual Assessment" (1990, pp. 2-4), and Keech-Lucas describes criteria for ecological validity in writing assessment (1988b, p. 5). Although these various sets of criteria arise out of different perspectives, they are remarkably similar in the issues they address. They constitute the beginnings of a literature to which we can refer in our efforts to shape writing assessments compatible with the construct of writing as we currently understand it.

The principles behind such established psychometric concerns as reliability and validity can also inform us in our design and evaluation of new approaches to assessment, although they need to be understood and applied in new ways. Principles of fairness, equity, and generalizability still pertain to assessments based on complex performance in writing; the challenge now is to apply them in ways that lead far beyond the narrow focus on score reliability and the constricted definitions of validity that characterized earlier discussions of the measurement properties of writing assessments (see Gitomer, in press; Linn, Baker, & Dunbar, 1991; Moss, in press). We will need to think and observe carefully, for example, to determine whether the writing performance required for our new assessments are equally appropriate for students drawing on different cultural and linguistic experiences. Similarly, we will need to consider which kinds of performances are central to students' learning about writing, what kinds of information can legitimately be derived from those performances, and what generalizations about students' ability and development can be made on the basis of the information derived. Although we do not yet have methodologies that tell us how to apply these principles, the principles themselves can help guide us until the methodologies are developed.

A further resource in our attempt to create richer forms of assessment lies in the research that has been done on the processes and strategies involved in writing. The work of researchers such as Flower and Hayes, Beaugrande, and Scardamalia and Bereiter, for example, will help us to develop models for assessment that inform both teachers and student writers about the ways in which the writers' processes and strategies contribute or fail to contribute to the success of the writing performance. In moving toward these assessments, we will be building on and enlarging the scope of research like that of Ruth and Murphy, which has focused on analysis of the demands of writing tasks used in assessments.

Other aspects of our earlier experience with direct assessments of writing are also likely to help us move toward the design and evaluation of more complex performances in writing. Lucas and Carlson (1989), in creating a prototype for alternative assessment strategies, described the procedures of development, evaluation, and analysis familiar from direct assessment as providing "some systematic control," yet permitting writers and evaluators of the writing to accommodate performance on more open-ended tasks (pp. 14-16). These procedures move through several stages drawing on the expertise of individuals experienced in the teaching and assessment of writing. The first stages involve identifying the competencies to be assessed and the expectations for performance, translating them into specifications for the tasks to be presented, and developing the tasks. Later stages involve trying out the tasks, evaluating them, exploring preliminary scoring systems, and further refining tasks and scoring systems. The final stages focus on training readers, scoring the samples resulting from the performances, conducting statistical and qualitative analyses to establish reliability, validity, and generalizability, and examining the assessments' feasibility, cost effectiveness, and social consequences.

Procedures such as these suggest an orderly and responsible approach to developing and trying out new assessments of writing, including assessments that draw on performances considerably more complex than those evoked by traditional approaches. With some adaptation, such procedures can also allow the developers and users of the assessment to focus attention on the skills and strategies addressed as well as the performances themselves. What is more, if the procedures are carried out through activities that involve teachers in the development and refinement of the assessment design, the evaluation of student performances and products, and the examination of the effects of the assessment on teaching and learning, and if they result in the articulation of criteria and standards for performance and the selection of performances illustrating those criteria and standards, then they can also become in themselves a means of promoting the kinds of learning addressed in the assessment (Camp, 1992b). In short, they can help to establish the assessment's systemic validity (see Frederiksen & Collins, 1989).

It is no accident, then, that the procedures associated with the direct assessment of writing are seen as exemplary for models of assessment designed to foster desirable instruction and learning within educational systems. Very likely, these procedures will inform us in our exploration of new approaches to writing assessment, especially if we use what we have learned from them to press beyond the constraints of current forms of assessment.

Probable Characteristics of New Models for Writing Assessment

Attempts to describe a new conceptual framework for writing assessment or the probable new forms for assessment seem premature, as do attempts to describe the range of possibilities for new forms of writing assessment. Nevertheless, if we survey both the needs that lead us to search for new approaches to assessment and the exploratory activity evident in classrooms, schools, school districts, and state departments of education, we can get a sense of some possible approaches and—more to the point—of the qualities we might hope to find in writing assessment compatible with our current understanding of writing and writing instruction.

The most obvious examples of forward-looking writing assessment are provided by assessments using portfolios. In terms of both their potential for accommodating the new constructs for writing and the intensity of current exploration, portfolio approaches to writing assessment seem especially promising. Portfolios can provide evidence of complex and varied performance in writing, of writing generated in a rich instructional and social contexts, of the processes and strategies that students use, and of their awareness of those processes (Camp, 1990, 1992b; Camp & Levine, 1991; Mitchell, 1992; Paulson, Paulson, & Meyer, 1991; Wolf, 1989). The procedures associated with portfolio design, implementation, and evaluation provide valuable opportunities for discussion of the skills and abilities that the portfolios are intended to measure and of the criteria and standards used to evaluate performances; through these opportunities they become a stimulus for teachers' professional development (Belanoff & Elbow, 1986; Camp, 1990, 1992a, 1992b;

Murphy & Smith, 1990). If portfolios are designed to engage students to reflect on their work in writing, they can also help them to learn to evaluate their writing and to assume increased responsibility for their own learning (Camp, 1990, 1992b, in press; Camp & Levine, 1991; Howard, 1990; Paulson et al., 1991; Reif, 1990; Wolf, 1989).

Other assessment approaches closely related and complementary to portfolios are being explored in a number of school assessments, school sites, and research projects. Some of them involve extended classroom projects integrating instruction and assessment and emphasizing the use of writing as a tool for exploring ideas or techniques, or for solving problems (see Levine, in press). A few such projects have already been developed with an explicit connection to writing (Central Park East High School in New York City, Arts PROPEL imaginative writing projects and the Syllabus Examination Program in Pittsburgh, the College Outcomes Examination Program for the New Jersey colleges); they suggest an approach to writing assessment that may be well worth exploring, especially since comparable projects are being developed in other areas of the curriculum (see *Arts PROPEL: An Introductory Handbook*, 1992; Lesh & Lamon, 1992; Mitchell, 1992).

Despite the limitations of our experience with assessments based on alternatives to the traditional formats, some tendencies seem likely on the basis of our collective experience to date, the current constructs for writing, and the current developments in measurement as they have been described in this chapter. These tendencies suggest a number of characteristics we might expect to see in future writing assessments:

- Use of a variety of assessment approaches with different methods and formats serving different purposes and educational contexts
- Samples of writing performances and products generated on multiple occasions, for multiple purposes, and under various circumstances—including circumstances typical for classroom writing and over extended periods of time
- Increased attention to the cognitive processes involved in writing, with awareness of the connections between the processes used and the skills, abilities, and strategies available to the writer
- Opportunities for writers to reflect on the processes and strategies they use in single and multiple pieces of writing and over extended periods of time
- Increased attention to the knowledge required and cognitive processes involved in evaluating writing products and performances
- Increased attention to the procedures involved in developing and conducting writing assessments, with particular interest in the opportunities they provide for teachers' professional development,

for curriculum development, and for examination of institutional goals for learning
- Formats for reporting on writing performance that are more informative to teachers and student writers than are single numerical scores, including profiles and qualitative descriptions about the processes and strategies evident in writing performance
- Ca tion in generalizing from single performances in writing to performances that call for substantially different knowledge, skills, and strategies, that make different resources available to the writer, or that draw on different kinds of linguistic or cultural experience
- Assessments that take into account the evolving abilities of writers and the evolving needs of the educational systems within which assessment occurs.

REFERENCES

Applebee, A. N. (1986). Problems in process approaches: Toward a reconceptualization of process instruction. In A. Petrosky & D. Bartholomae (Eds.), *The teaching of writing. 85th Yearbook of the National Society for the Study of Education* (Part II, pp. 95-113). Chicago: University of Chicago Press.

Archbald, D. A., & Newmann, F. M. (1988). *Beyond standardized testing.* Paper published by the National Center on Effective Secondary Schools, School of Education, University of Wisconsin-Madison.

Arts PROPEL: An Introductory Handbook. (1992). Princeton, NJ: Educational Testing Service.

Bartholomae, D. (1980). The study of error. *College Composition and Communication, 31,* 253-269.

Beaugrande, R. de. (1982). Psychology and composition: Past, present, future. In M. Nystrand (Ed.), *What writers know: The language, process, and structure of written discourse* (pp. 211-267). New York: Academic Press.

Belanoff, P., & Dickson, M. (Eds.). (1991). *Portfolios: Process and product.* Portsmouth, NH: Heinemann Boynton/Cook.

Belanoff, P., & Elbow, P. (1986). Using portfolios to increase collaboration and community in a writing program. *Writing Program Administration, 9,* 27-40.

Bereiter, C., & Scardamalia, M. (1987). *The psychology of written composition.* Hillsdale, NJ: Erlbaum.

Berlak, H., Newmann, F. M., Adams, E., Archbald, D. A., Burgess, T., Raven, J., & Romberg, T. A. (1992). *Toward a new science of educational testing and assessment.* Albany, NY: State University of New York Press.

Breland, H. M., Camp, R., Jones, R. J., Morris, M. M., & Rock, D. A. (1987). *Assessing writing skill* (Research Monograph No. 11). New York: College Entrance Examination Board.

Breland, H. M., & Gaynor, J. L. (1979). A comparison of direct and indirect assessments of writing skill. *Journal of Educational Measurement, 16*, 119-128.

Brossell, G. (1983). Rhetorical specification in essay examination topics. *College English, 45*, 165-173.

Bruffee, K. A. (1986). Social construction, language, and the authority of knowledge: A bibliographical essay. *College English, 48*, 773-790.

Camp, R. (1990). Thinking together about portfolios. *The Quarterly of the National Writing Project and the Center for the Study of Writing, 12*(2), 8-14, 27.

Camp, R. (1992a). Portfolio reflections in middle and secondary school classrooms. In K. Yancey (Ed.), *Portfolios in the writing classroom: An introduction* (pp. 61-79). Urbana, IL: National Council of Teachers of English.

Camp, R. (1992b). Assessment in the context of schools and school change. In H. H. Marshall (Ed.), *Redefining student learning: Roots of educational change* (pp. 241-263). Norwood, NJ: Ablex.

Camp, R. (in press). The place of portfolios in our changing views of writing assessment. In R. Bennett & W. Ward (Eds.), *Construction versus choice in cognitive measurement*. Hillsdale, NJ: Erlbaum.

Camp, R., & Levine, D. (1991). Portfolios evolving: Background and variations in sixth- through twelfth-grade portfolios. In P. Belanoff & M. Dickson (Eds.), *Portfolios: Process and product* (pp. 194-205). Portsmouth, NH: Heinemann Boynton/Cook.

Campione, J. C., & Brown, A. L. (1990). Guided learning and transfer: Implications for approaches to assessment. In N. Frederiksen, R. Glaser, A. Lesgold, & M. G. Shafto (Eds.), *Diagnostic monitoring of skill and knowledge acquisition* (pp. 141-172). Hillsdale, NJ: Erlbaum.

Carlson, S. B., Bridgeman, B., Camp, R., & Waanders, J. (1985). *Relationship of admission test scores to writing performance of native and non-native speakers of English* (TOEFL Research Report No. 19). Princeton, NJ: Educational Testing Service.

Carter, M. (1990). The idea of expertise: An exploration of cognitive and social dimensions of writing. *College Composition and Communication, 41*, 265-286.

Coffman, W. (1971). Essay examinations. In R. L. Thorndike (Ed.), *Educational measurement* (2nd ed., pp. 271-302). Washington, DC: American Council on Education.

Cole, N., & Moss, P. (1989). Bias in test use. In R. Linn (Ed.), *Educational measurement* (3rd ed., pp. 201-219). New York: Macmillan.

Conlon, G. (1986). "Objective" measures of writing ability. In K.

Greenberg, H. S. Weiner, & R. A. Donovan (Eds.), *Writing assessment: Issues and strategies* (pp. 109-125). New York: Longman.

Cooper, C. (1977). Holistic evaluation of writing. In C. Cooper & L. Odell (Eds.), *Evaluating writing: Describing, measuring, judging* (pp. 3-31). Urbana, IL: National Council of Teachers of English.

Cooper, C. (Ed.). (1981). *The nature and measurement of competency in English.* Urbana, IL: National Council of Teachers of English.

Cooper, C., & Odell, L. (Eds.) (1977). *Evaluating writing: Describing, meas ring, judging.* Urbana, IL: National Council of Teachers of English.

Cronbach, L. J. (1988). Five perspectives on validity argument. In H. Wainer & H. I. Braun (Eds.), *Test validity* (pp. 3-17). Hillsdale, NJ: Erlbaum.

Darling-Hammond, L., & Ascher, C. (1991). *Creating accountability in big city school systems.* New York: ERIC Clearinghouse on Urban Education and the National Center for Restructuring Education, Schools, and Teaching, Teachers College, Columbia.

Diederich, P. (1974). *Measuring growth in English.* Urbana, IL: National Council of Teachers of English.

Durst, R. K. (1987). Cognitive and linguistic demands of analytic writing. *Research in the Teaching of English, 21*(4), 347-376.

Eley, E. G. (1955). Should the General Composition Test be continued? The test satisfies an educational need. *College Board Review, 25,* 10-13.

Emig, J. (1982). Inquiry paradigms and writing. *College Composition and Communication, 33,* 64-75.

Faigley, L. (1986). Competing theories of process: A critique and a proposal. *College English, 48,* 527-542.

Faigley, L., Cherry, R., Jolliffe, D., & Skinner, A. (1985). *Assessing writers' knowledge and processes of composing.* Norwood, NJ: Ablex.

Flower, L., & Hayes, J. R. (1980). The dynamics of composing: Making plans and juggling constraints. In L. W. Gregg & E. R. Steinberg (Eds.), *Cognitive process in writing* (pp. 31-50). Hillsdale, NJ: Erlbaum.

Flower, L., & Hayes, J. R. (1981). A cognitive process theory of writing. *College Composition and Communication, 32,* 365-387.

Frederiksen, J. R., & Collins, A. (1989). A systems approach to educational testing. *Educational Researcher, 18,* 27-32.

Frederiksen, N. (1984). The real test bias: Influences of testing on teaching and learning. *American Psychologist, 39,* 193-202.

Frederiksen, N. (1986). Toward a broader conception of human intelligence. *American Psychologist, 41,* 445-452.

Frederiksen, N. (1990). Introduction. In N. Frederiksen, R. Glaser, A. Lesgold, & M. G. Shafto (Eds.), *Diagnostic monitoring of skill and knowledge acquisition* (pp. ix-xvii). Hillsdale, NJ: Erlbaum.

Freedman, A., & Pringle, I. (1981). *Why students can't write arguments.* Unpublished manuscript, Carleton University, Linguistics Department, Ottawa, Canada.

Freedman, S. W. (1981). Influences on evaluators of expository essays: Beyond the text. *Research in the Teaching of English, 15,* 245-255.

Freedman, S. W., Dyson, A. H., Flower, L., & Chafe, W. (1987). *Research in writing: Past, present, and future* (Tech. Rep. No. 1). Berkeley: University of California, Center for the Study of Writing.

Gardner, H. (1988). *Assessment in context: The alternative to standardized testing.* Paper prepared for the National Commission on Testing and Public Policy, Berkeley, CA.

Gere, A. (1980). Written composition: Toward a theory of evaluation. *College English, 42,* 44-58.

Gitomer, D. H. (in press). Performance assessment and educational measurement. In R. Bennett & W. Ward (Eds.), *Construction versus choice in cognitive measurement.* Hillsdale, NJ: Erlbaum.

Glaser, R. (1988). Cognitive and environmental perspectives on assessing achievement. In E. Freeman (Ed.), *Assessment in the service of learning: Proceedings of the ETS Invitational Conference* (pp. 37-43). Princeton, NJ: Educational Testing Service.

Godshalk, F., Swineford, F., & Coffman, W. (1966). *The measurement of writing ability* (Research Monograph No. 6). New York: College Entrance Examination Board.

Greenberg, K. L., Weiner, H. S., & Donovan, R. A. (Eds.), (1986). *Writing assessment: Issues and strategies.* New York: Longman.

Greenberg, K., & Witte, S. (1988). Validity issues in direct writing assessment. *Notes from the National Testing Network in Writing, 8,* 13-14.

Hairston, M. (1982). The winds of change: Thomas Kuhn and the revolution in the teaching of writing. *College Composition and Communication, 33*(1), 76-88.

Haney, W., & Madaus, G. (1989). Standardized testing: Harmful to educational health. *Phi Delta Kappan, 70,* 683-687.

Heath, S. B. (1983). *Ways with words: Language, life, and work in communities and classrooms.* Cambridge, MA: Cambridge University Press.

Hoetker, J. (1982). Essay examination topics and student writing. *College Composition and Communication, 33,* 377-392.

Howard, K. (1990). Making the writing portfolio real. *The Quarterly of the National Writing Project and the Center for the Study of Writing, 12*(2), 4-7, 27.

Johnston, P. (1987). Assessing the process and the process of assessment in the language arts. In J. Squire (Ed.), *The dynamics of language learning: Research in reading and English* (pp. 335-357). Urbana, IL: National Conference on Research in English/ERIC.

Keech-Lucas, C. (1988a). Toward ecological evaluation. *The Quarterly of the*

National Writing Project and the Center for the Study of Writing, 10(1), 1-17.

Keech-Lucas, C. (1988b). Toward ecological evaluation: Part Two. *The Quarterly of the National Writing Project and the Center for the Study of Writing, 10*(2), 4-10.

Langer, J. A., & Applebee, A. N. (1987). *How writing shapes thinking: A study of teaching and learning.* Urbana, IL: National Council of Teachers of English.

Lesh, R., & Lamon, S. J. (Eds.), (1992). *Assessment of authentic performance in school mathematics.* Washington, DC: AAAS Press.

Levine, D. S. (1992). The four P's of context-based assessment: Evaluating literacy across the curriculum. In C. Hedley, P. Antonacci, & D. Feldman (Eds.), *Literacy across the curriculum.* Norwood, NJ: Ablex.

Linn, R. L., Baker, E. L., & Dunbar, S. B. (1991). Complex, performance-based assessment: Expectations and validation criteria. *Educational Researcher, 20,* 5-21.

Lloyd-Jones, R. (1977). Primary trait scoring. In C. Cooper & L. Odell (Eds.), *Evaluating writing: Describing, measuring, judging* (pp. 33–66). Urbana, IL: National Council of Teachers of English.

Lucas, C., & Carlson, S. B. (1989). *Prototype of alternative assessment strategies for new teachers of English.* San Francisco, CA: Report to the California New Teacher Project.

Macrorie, K. (1976). *Telling writing.* Rochelle Park, NJ: Hayden.

Messick, S. (1989a). Meaning and values in test validation: The science and ethics of assessment. *Educational Researcher, 18,* 5-14.

Messick, S. (1989b). Validity. In R. Linn (Ed.), *Educational measurement* (3rd ed., pp. 13-104). New York: Macmillan.

Mislevy, R. J. (in press). Foundations for a new test theory. In N. Fredriksen, R. J. Mislevy, & I. Bejar (Eds.), *Test theory for a new generation of tests.* Hillsdale, NJ: Erlbaum.

Mitchell, R. (1989). *A sampler of authentic assessment: What it is and what it looks like.* Paper prepared for the California Assessment Program Conference, Sacramento, CA.

Mitchell, R. (1992). *Testing for learning.* New York: Free Press.

Moffett, J. (1968). *Teaching the universe of discourse.* Boston: Houghton Mifflin.

Moss, P. A. (in press). Shifting conceptions of validity in educational measurement: Implications for performance assessment. *Review of Educational Research.*

Murphy, S., & Smith, M. A. (1990). Talking about portfolios. *The Quarterly of the National Writing Project and the Center for the Study of Writing, 12*(2), 1-3, 24-27.

Murphy, S., & Smith, M. A. (1991). *Writing portfolios: A bridge from teaching to assessment.* Markam, Ontario, Canada: Pippin.

Newmann, F. (1991). Linking restructuring to authentic student achievement. *Phi Delta Kappan, 72*(6), 458-463.

O'Connor, M. C. (1989). Aspects of differential performance by minorities on standardized tests: Linguistic and sociocultural factors. In B. Gifford (Ed.), *Test policy and test performance: Education, language and culture* (pp. 129-181). Boston: Kluwer.

Odell, L. (1981). Defining and assessing competence in writing. In C. Cooper (Ed.), *The nature and measurement of competency in English* (pp. 95-138). Urbana, IL: National Council of Teachers of English.

Paulson, F. L., Paulson, P. P., & Meyer, C. A. (1991). What makes a portfolio a portfolio? *Educational Leadership, 48*(5), 60-63.

Penrose, A. M. (1989). *Strategic differences in composing: Consequences for learning through writing* (Tech. Rep. No. 31). Berkeley: University of California, Center for the Study of Writing.

Polin, L. (1980). *Specifying the writing domain for assessment: Recommendations to the practitioner* (CSE Rep. No. 135). Los Angeles, CA: Center for the Study of Evaluation.

Pringle, I., & Freedman, A. (1985). *A comparative study of writing abilities in two modes at the grade 5, 8, and 12 levels.* Toronto, Canada: Ontario Ministry of Education.

Rafoth, B. A., & Rubin, D. L. (Eds.). (1988). *The social construction of written communication.* Norwood, NJ: Ablex.

Reif, L. (1990). Finding the value in evaluation: Self-assessment in a middle-school classroom. *Educational Leadership, 47*(6), 24-29.

Resnick, D. P., & Resnick, L. B. (1985). Standards, curriculum, and performance: A historical and comparative perspective. *Educational Researcher, 14*(4), 5-20.

Rose, M. (1989). *Lives on the boundary: The struggles and achievements of America's underprepared.* New York: Free Press.

Ruth, L., & Murphy, S. (1988). *Designing writing tasks for the assessment of writing.* Norwood, NJ: Ablex.

Scardamalia, M., & Bereiter, C. (1985). Research on written composition. In M. Wittrock (Ed.), *Handbook of research on teaching* (3rd ed., pp. 708-803). New York: Macmillan.

Shaughnessy, M. (1977). *Errors and expectations: A guide for the teacher of basic writing.* New York: Oxford University Press.

Shepard, L. A. (1991). Psychometricians' beliefs about learning. *Educational Researcher, 20,* 2-16.

Smith, F. (1982). *Writing and the writer.* New York: Holt, Rinehart & Winston.

Snow, R. E. (1989). Toward assessment of cognitive and conative structures in learning. *Educational Researcher, 18,* 8-14.

Snow, R. E., & Lohman, D. F. (1989). Implications of cognitive psychology for educational measurement. In R. Linn (Ed.), *Educational measurement* (3rd ed., pp. 263-331). Washington, DC: American Council on Education.

Spandel, V., & Stiggins, R. J. (1980). *Direct measures of writing skill: Issues and applications.* Portland: Northwest Regional Educational Laboratory, Clearinghouse for Applied Performance Testing.

Stiggins, R. J. (1988). Revitalizing classroom assessment: The highest instructional priority. *Phi Delta Kappan, 69*(5), 184-193.

Taylor, D. (1989). The many keys to literacy. *Phi Delta Kappan, 70,* 184-193.

Thompson, E. H. (1985). Self-assessment and the mastery of writing. In J. Beard & S. McNaff (Eds.), *Testing in the English language arts: Uses and abuses.* Rochester, MI: Michigan Council of Teachers of English.

Tierney, R. J., Carter, M. A., & Desai, L. E. (1991). *Portfolio assessment in the reading-writing classroom.* Norwood, MA: Christopher Gordon.

Valencia, S., McGinley, W., & Pearson, P. D. (1990). Assessing literacy in the middle school. In G. Duffy (Ed.), *Reading in the middle school* (2nd ed., pp. 124-141). Newark, DE: International Reading Association.

Ward, W. C., Frederiksen, N., & Carlson, S. B. (1980). Construct validity of free-response and machine-scorable forms of a test. *Journal of Educational Measurement, 17,* 11-29.

White, E. (1985). *Teaching and assessing writing.* San Francisco: Jossey-Bass.

White, E. (1986). Pitfalls in the testing of writing. In K. L. Greenberg, H. S. Weiner, & R. A. Donovan (Eds.), *Writing assessment: Issues and strategies* (pp. 53-78). New York: Longman.

Wiggins, G. (1989). A true test: Toward more authentic and equitable assessment. *Phi Delta Kappan, 70,* 703-713.

Witte, S., Trachsel, M., & Walters, K. (1986). Literacy and the direct assessment of writing: A diachronic perspective. In K. Greenberg, H. S. Weiner, & R. A. Donovan (Eds.), *Writing assessment: Issues and strategies* (pp. 109-125). New York: Longman.

Wolf, D. P. (1989). Portfolio assessment: Sampling student work. *Educational Leadership, 46,* 35-39.

Wolf, D., Bixby, J., Glenn, J., & Gardner, H. (1991). To use their minds well: Investigating new forms of student assessment. In G. Grant (Ed.), *Review of Research in Education, 17,* 31-73.

Yancey, K. B. (Ed.). (1992). *Portfolios in the writing classroom: An introduction.* Urbana, IL: National Council of Teachers of English.

3

Holistic Scoring: Past Triumphs, Future Challenges

Edward M. White
California State University, San Bernardino

Those of us who were involved in the missionary activity of promulgating holistic scoring of student essays in the 1970s tended to feel that we had achieved the answer to the testing of writing. By developing careful essay questions, administering and scoring them under controlled conditions, and recording a single accurate score for the quality of writing as a whole (with scoring guides and sample papers defining quality), we had become committed to a flexible, accurate, and responsive measurement method, one that could come under the control of teachers. The rapid and widespread acceptance of such scoring, and the kind of testing that led to it, let us take a relatively uncritical stance. We were promulgating a kind of religious belief in an approach to writing as well as a testing device, and we were more interested in converting nonbelievers than in questioning the faith.

But as we enter the 1990s, with holistic scoring more or less routine, we have a belated scholarly obligation to step back and view it in perspective. Those of us who were personally involved need to convey the flavor and personal touches, as well as the history, of this minor revolution in a profession's approach to writing measurement and writing instruction. But these personal matters are interesting only as they convey underlying truths of a discipline in flux. What, we ought to ask, were the historical forces that allowed a lethargic profession to change the way it evaluated students so radically within a single decade? Further, technology has taught us that every solution brings new problems: What are the new problems that holistic scoring has (inevitably) produced? Finally, we need to consider the challenges to holistic scoring that have recently emerged from the profession. Portfolio assessment, for instance, proposes itself as a new solution to the problems raised by holistic scoring, yet it seems to be repeating many of the same problems and solutions of its predecessor. What have we learned from the profession's experience with holistic scoring that will be useful for new assessment methods?

SOME PERSONAL BACKGROUND

When I published an article entitled "Holisticism" in *College Composition and Communication* in 1984, I summarized, indeed exaggerated, the arguments for holistic scoring of student writing. Though that article has often been cited, and though I still stand behind the essence of what it says, some qualifications are by now in order. Miles Myers has told me that my assertion that I conducted the first holistic scoring on the west coast in 1973 is incorrect; some San Francisco Bay Area teachers had carried the concept and procedure from Advanced Placement readings back home before that time. More significantly, the editor for my 1985 book, to whom I had proudly sent the article (which was being revised into the second chapter), was decidedly unimpressed by the title; every serious writer, the late Ken Eble wrote me, has an obligation to refrain from inventing new and barbarous words. He also suggested that I was making rather too much of a fuss over what any sensible person is likely to use at times in grading or teaching. By turning a simple scoring procedure into an "ism" I was creating ideologies without good reason. Although I felt the deflation of my rhetoric to be healthy, I could not fully agree that things were quite that simple: The remarkable triumph of holistic scoring was bound to be theoretically interesting, and probably ideological as well. Surely it was possible to discuss these matters in clear and direct language, however profound their implications turned out to be. Evaluation in education is never a simple matter, although it is too often simple-minded, since it powerfully embodies the goals of instruction—the real goals, which are often different from the stated ones. I see now that we were part of some major forces acting upon education at the time, of which we were only dimly aware, and I also see that our language, as we began to write about what we were doing, expressed an understandably inflated view of the uniqueness of our enterprise, brought about in part by the polemics of our time and situations.

When those of us who accidentally became the apostles of holistic approaches to writing measurement began our work, we had no such elaborate sense of what we were doing at the time. A few key players were members of the testing community, such as Paul Diederich, Evans Alloway, and Trudy Conlon of Educational Testing Service (ETS), simply going about their jobs as researchers or test administrators. Al Serling of ETS, who was directing the College Level Examination Program (to which I will return shortly), saw essay testing as a way to give substance and academic respectability to a testing program sorely in need of both. Alan Seder of the Berkeley ETS office, a superb administrator, was stimulated by the sheer challenge of managing the complex programs that emerged, and John Bianchinni, also of the Berkeley ETS office, became involved in the statistical challenges that holistic scoring presented. Some of us (Rex Burbank of San Jose State, Richard Lid of California State University-Northridge, Bill Lutz of Rutgers-Camden, and Karen Greenberg and Marie Lederman of the City College of New York) were English teachers, trained as literary scholars, who were unwilling to accept the reductive concepts of reading and writing that were dominant in writing testing at the time, and we found ourselves in administrative positions that allowed us to try to do something to better the situation. We gave ourselves crash courses in testing procedures and statistics, and we tried to handle test administration the way we handled departmental administration: We expected to commit a few years to doing necessary but boring clerical duties that could be handled by anyone with common sense and basic intelligence.

My first clue that I was into something bigger occurred during the summer of 1972, when I undertook to prepare a report for what became the California State University system on what was known about the measurement of writing ability at the college level. Aside from one book published by the College Board (Godshalk, Swineford, & Coffman, 1966) and a series of in-house documents at the Educational Testing Service, I found only material of questionable use and relevance in statistics and education. Various college English faculty on three continents were rumored to be knowledgeable in measurement, and I assiduously gathered their names and requested their help, but each of them hastily denied the allegation, pointing to others as expert. The others repeated the same lateral passing movement. Aside from a few Advanced Placement readers and table leaders with valuable practical experience, no one in college English knew anything about the measurement of writing ability. I nonetheless had committed myself to directing a major statewide testing program using holistic scoring. I received some willing help from ETS, most notably from Paul Diederich and Al Serling, but scholars in my own field were strangely silent, though supportive. For some years I felt myself in an alien world, exposed, ignorant, and almost alone, an odd position for one whose major scholarly energies had been expended on Jane Austen's novels, Thackeray's journalism, and two notably unsuccessful freshman composition textbooks.

COMBAT IN THE 1970S

In the early 1970s, hardly anyone had heard of holistic scoring, and the term had a faddist ring to it, akin to holistic health or holistic physics. Sometimes its Greek roots meaning *unity* disappeared before an awkwardly anglicized "wholistic" spelling. English teachers found it unsettling: Its emphasis on reading and scoring a piece of student writing as a whole flew in the face of an overwhelming professional preference to nit-pick at parts, while its attention to what student writing does well (as opposed to the customary focus on what it does badly, the usual error hunting) seemed weak-willed and slack in the face of the predominant negativism of teacher grading. At the same time, most of those in the testing and assessment communities smiled patronizingly at one more effort by poetic subjectivists to resist the cold numbers of multiple-choice tests, the sure truth givers for hard-headed behaviorists. Even the institutional core of ETS, the originator of holistic scoring, saw it (indeed, still sees it) as a bone to throw to English teachers, while the multiple-choice tests were delivering the data; the essay testing (and, now, portfolio assessment) defenders at ETS have always been a beleaguered crew, with relatively little influence. The few scholars and test administrators who were using holistic scoring were using all their energies to confront the problems of cost and scoring reliability, as practical aspects of the large testing programs they were supervising. Writing researchers were still using error counts, T-units, and other neatly quantifiable measures of doubtful validity for college writers.

So a small group of English faculty apostles set out to promote the word of holistic scoring, quickly developing missionary zeal. While my colleagues in the California State University and I were proselytizing in the west, Karen Greenberg and Marie Lederman (along with Harvey Weiner and Richard Donovan) did the same in the east. Indeed, with characteristic presumption, they established an organization they called the "National Testing Network in Writing" and developed it into a thriving institution whose newsletter, book (Greenberg, Weiner, & Donovan, 1986), and annual conferences have had an important influence on all measurement of writing. We were justifiably self-righteous, on the side of the angels and opposed to a host of devils: the reductionism of multiple-choice usage testing, the hostility to students and pointless negativism of contemporary paper grading, the domination of teachers and curriculum by insensitive tests and testing agencies, and the distortions introduced into teaching by socially biased tests over which nobody seemed to have control. Holistic scoring did not defeat these destructive influences wholly, by any means; they can still be seen everywhere in American education. But college English faculties and many college administrators were fed up with the dominance of multiple-choice testing. To our surprise, the opposition melted before us: Podiums and journal space were made available by every professional organization, government moneys flowed like red ink, and every essay scoring produced new converts to spread the message. By the time my *Teaching and Assessing Writing* appeared in 1985, I could say:

> In the early 1980s, a survey of English departments conducted by a committee of the College Conference on Composition and Communication showed an amazing change: Not only did almost 90 percent of responding English departments state that they used holistic scoring, but nowhere did either the committee chair or the responding parties feel the need to define the term by more than a parenthetical reminder. In one decade, in a notoriously conservative and slow-moving profession, a new concept in testing and (hence) in teaching writing became accepted while no one was watching (p. 19).

The triumph seemed complete. It wasn't actually complete, of course, but it was a sufficiently impressive victory to demand analysis of its causes.

During the 1970s, holistic scoring became a focus for a variety of ideas and conditions that had been impinging upon the traditional teaching of English for some time: awareness of the social and economic bases of privileged language and "correctness," development of poststructural theories of reading and process theories of writing, emergence of writing research as a field of inquiry, and the appearance of a vocal proletariat of regular as well as part-time writing faculty for whom writing was a serious business, not merely a path to literature seminars. (The founders of the Council of Writing Program Administrators in 1980 took some pleasure in the New Deal proletarian ring of the group's initials: WPA.) Some of these developments were related to the virtual disappearance of tenure-track positions in university English departments; others had to do with a new attempt on the part of higher education to enroll student populations traditionally barred from college, as symbolized by the traumatic switch to open enrollment by the City University of New York in 1970. In addition, the force of the student rebellions of the 1960s could still be felt, particularly in their demand for connections and meaning in education, and in their protests against atomization of knowledge, impersonal bureaucracy, subordination of liberal education to economic or government concerns, and rote memorization rather than critical thought.

Multiple-choice testing, particularly in the area of English, became a powerful symbol of what was wrong with education from each of the perspectives I listed above. Part of our zeal, which caused some distortions still evident today, emerged from our opposition to these fill-in-the-bubble tests; like many other reformations, our language and concerns bore a striking resemblance to those of the enemy. (Thus, the overriding concern for scoring reliability on the part of holistic research is a direct result of frustrating combat with the perfect scoring reliability of the machine-scored tests, a combat largely conducted on foreign soil.) While it was clear that multiple-choice testing is merely a human tool (not necessarily the devil's handiwork), and that it could be useful under appropriate circumstances, the uses of those tests to grade, label, place, and screen out students seemed then (as now) to demean education in general and writing in particular.

The two multiple-choice tests that focused the opposition most pointedly at the college level were both produced by ETS: the Test of Standard Written English (TSWE) and the College Level Examination Program (CLEP) General Examination in English. Although the tests had different purposes, they both drew upon the same ETS item bank of dreary usage questions, examining for "correct" editing answers, according to the school dialect. Since these two tests did more to promote holistic scoring than any or all of the missionaries, we should pause to consider why and how they elicited the outrage that they did—and still continue to elicit.

The TSWE was put together by decent and well-meaning ETS people to meet the demand from colleges for a quick and convenient means of placing new and untraditional students in remedial courses, where all right-thinking people in power knew they belonged. Although the TSWE is technically separate from the Scholastic Aptitude Test, it is administered at the same time and place, and TSWE scores are reported along with the SAT. (As this book goes to press, ETS has announced its intention to abandon use of the TSWE.) Since the massive numbers of students taking the SAT made essay testing cumbersome and costly, the TSWE remains even now a fill-in-the-bubble test of "correct" English, which is by association defined as scholastic aptitude. To this day, some of the ETS people involved do not understand why the community of writing teachers and writing researchers were—and are—so opposed to their socially and linguistically naive work. The test serves one buried and inglorious purpose of the institutions that award college degrees in America: It designates as "remedial" most students who grew up in homes where English was spoken in any dialect other than that used by the white upper-middle class. The ETS defense is simple: National tests exist to reflect college needs, not to crusade for change. Since colleges generally demand skill in using the school dialect, and since students must learn that dialect to succeed, ETS tests for editing skills in that dialect (which is defined as "standard") and provides that information as part of what the College Board defines as "scholastic aptitude." This response simply accepts as fact that a major component of such scholastic aptitude involves being born into an upper-middle-class white family; that is the way the world works.

Aside from the test's unquestioning acceptance of one of the most elitist aspects of American society, it also accepts as fact that an ability to identify correctness of dialect is an acceptable definition of writing ability. While the ETS staff is well aware that editing is not the same as writing, those defending the TSWE point to high score correlations (among middle-class white students, of course) between editing and writing tests. Thus, there is no need to spend money to ask students to write, or to pay faculty to read that writing; by giving scores based on the family dialect of students, obtained cheaply, ETS helps colleges identify those who require remedial help in "writing."

I was present at two encounters between English faculty and ETS personnel during the mid-1970s at which these arguments were presented and disputed. The first of these was a special session of the Executive Committee of the Conference on College Composition and Communication (CCCC), to which I had been elected. Incredibly, the ETS developers of the TSWE were seeking approval of the test from the CCCC, as a needed support to college writing programs. Only in retrospect does the lack of communication at that meeting seem comic; powerful emotions and strong language dominated at the time. The CCCC leaders talked of sociolinguistics and the importance of writing as a central form of critical thinking on tests and in the schools; the ETS staff talked of administrative convenience and the practical needs of students. My memory of just how things concluded is a bit dim, clouded not only by time but also by my own remembered fervor and rhetoric. I think the ETS staff finally stormed out of the room, while the Executive Committee unanimously passed a strong resolution condemning the new test. Subsequently, virtually every other professional organization in English endorsed that resolution, or passed one like it. Despite this opposition, the test became, and still remains, a steady thorn in the side of writing faculty, demeaning their work whenever it is used. As a gesture, ETS does include a halfhearted recommendation to institutions to add a writing test to the TSWE usage items, for increased validity, if it is not too terribly inconvenient for the test officer.

The second incident is clearer in my mind, since it was a private conversation I had with an ETS vice president, a statistical specialist who had become administratively responsible for the TSWE in its second year. I had requested the meeting to clear up a statistical problem with an entirely different test, an issue he resolved directly and easily, as befitted the national expert in the area. Now it was time for social talk before leaving. Smiling graciously, he asked, "What do you think of our new Test of Standard Written English?"

"I'm sorry to say this," I replied, trying to smile back, "but I don't know anyone in the field of writing who respects that test."

His smile disappeared abruptly. I watched his neck and jowls turn bright red and when he spoke his voice had turned harsh. "Oh, you mean the student's right to his own language and all that nonsense, don't you?" His reference was to a CCCC document arguing against requiring all students to succeed in the school dialect in order to succeed in college composition. I was a bit uncomfortable with the document, since it did not take sufficient account of social reality, but I was even more uncomfortable with the implicit accusation in his tone. He knew of my Ivy League background, and he was calling me a traitor to my class!

"I think it is wrong to call the dialect you and I grew up speaking 'scholastic aptitude'," I continued. "It's simply unfair to score kids according to social class, and we've been doing that for too long in this country."

Now he was furious. "Don't you think that students should be able to read the literature of the past?" he shouted. I turned to leave, stunned at what I took to be a thundering non sequitur. "I don't see what that has to do with it," I said. He turned away from me and our meeting was at an end.

Remembering that conversation today, after almost a decade of national debate about "cultural literacy" and "reclaiming a legacy" and "the closing of the American mind," I realize that I was wrong to take the vice president's statement as a non sequitur. He saw, as did the authors of the reports and books I have alluded to, the traditions of the West in peril, under attack from barbarian hordes. For him, as for the test he administered, education and educational standards depended on the indoctrination of students into his dialect. Those who were different could be accepted only if they gave up their differences and adopted his traditions and language. This was another version of what a white inner-city high school principal told me once, with self-righteous assurance: "It's impossible to be intelligent in that black dialect; all it is is a bunch of grunts and coughs."

With the TSWE expressing and codifying these attitudes, the forces in education seeking to open the process and offer new opportunities to the excluded rallied around holistic scoring. Here was a procedure that defined writing as producing a text, that could award scores for originality, or creativity, or intelligence, or organization, as well as for mechanical correctness in the school dialect. Most educators in the humanities and many college administrators were, and are, made uncomfortable by the simple class barriers made apparent by the TSWE; they additionally feel a responsibility to help the schools teach writing as well as skills at coping with fill-in-the-bubble tests. The TSWE, then, has spurred the growth of writing tests and holistic scoring, in part because it raises everywhere the banner of low-level class warfare.

The CLEP test is small potatoes compared to the TSWE, since it must be sought out by students who hope that a high score will be accepted in place of freshman English by their college. Nonetheless, that test raised more violent emotions from English faculty in the 1970s than did any other single measurement device. Since it was designed to test for achievement of the goals of freshman English, it presented a definition of the foundation course for most English departments in the country. That definition turned out to be even worse than that given by the TSWE. If the TSWE presumed to place students into freshman English by examining their dialects and editing skills, the CLEP test declared it could recommend the award of college credits by testing the same things. English faculties looking at the test were thunderstruck: Here was freshman English defined without including either reading (aside from the reading of test questions) or writing.

The protests against the CLEP General Examination in English reverberated from coast to coast. When the Chancellor of the California State University sought to award college credits for the test, and for the other CLEP General Examinations, the CSU English faculties revolted and the Los Angeles Times supported the faculties with editorials and front-page stories mocking the "instant sophomores" created by some short fill-in-the-bubble tests. The Florida English Council echoed the California protests (ironically, without acknowledging its source). To complete the geographical coverage, a major conference on "The Politics of CLEP" took place in Peoria, Illinois, sponsored by Bradley University, and the National Council of Teachers of English published the proceedings (Burt & King, 1974). In every case, the opposition to the demeaning multiple-choice test focused on essay testing and holistic scoring as the creative response.

A curious version of the conflict occurred even within the ivied walls of the ETS campus in Princeton. There, the Advanced Placement Program had a considerable stake in the essay portions of AP exams (a stake somewhat diminished these days under financial pressure). The AP exams themselves had become a center for experiment and dissemination of information about holistic scoring. The CLEP exams were seen by the AP bureaucracy at ETS, and even more so at the College Board in New York, as low-level competition for the same market: award of college credit by examination. The CLEP exams, embattled within as well as without, were eventually forced to improve, to add optional essay portions, and even (with the English General Exam) some token holistic essay scoring. But long before that occurred, the rallying cry of CLEP had led to the creation by English departments of competing essay tests with holistic scoring, most notably the Freshman English Equivalency Examination in California (White, 1973-1981).

The triumph of holistic scoring, then, had principally to do with the enemies it faced. To the atomization of education, it brought a sense of connection, unity, wholeness; to the bureaucratic machinery of fill-in-the-bubble testing, it brought human writers and human readers; to a true-false world of memorized answers to simplified questions, it brought the possibility of complexity; to socially biased correctness, it brought critical thinking. On behalf of students, it had the human decency to ask them what they thought as well as what they had memorized; on behalf of teachers, it asked them to make complex community judgments as well as to give grades. Most political of all, despite its ETS parentage, holistic scoring represented a partly successful attempt on the part of teachers to wrest control of the goals of education from the ETS-Industrial Complex; for decades any success at all on this front had been as unlikely as glasnost.

HOLISTIC SCORING: THE TRIUMPH OF THE HUMAN

Moreover, holistic scoring triumphed for personal as well as institutional reasons. In a lonely profession, holistic scoring requires the scarcest of environments: community. I have argued elsewhere that the literary theory developed by Stanley Fish, that an "interpretive community" of readers determines the meaning as well as the value of a text, is embodied by every holistic reading (White, 1984b). But here I am using the term almost in the way Paolo Freire does, as a Community whose work is made meaningful by a joint social purpose. ETS recognized early on that it would have to bring Advanced Placement readers together for some days in order to generate scores; perforce, a community developed, shaped in part by the common grind of scoring during the day and in part by the alcohol that flowed in the evening. ETS has an internal conflict with the requirements of community during holistic readings; with an eye to the bottom line, it tends to see too much debate about scores (or anything else) as time taken away from production of scores. But as campus and other faculty-run holistic scorings became more and more common, the warmth and fellowship they generated became one of their most valuable features. Discussions of scores became discussions of what one valued about writing, and, in turn, became discussions of teaching writing. With its necessary emphasis on agreement, the holistic scoring session provided a wholesome atmosphere for such conversations, as opposed to the contentious jockeying that normally occurs within English departments. Good fellowship, good food and drink, good conversation, constructive community work: This is a rare combination for writing teachers, or for anyone, and if the price is the generation of grades on a test, that is a small price to pay. Even ETS, with its slave wages and empty pretense that an appointment as an ETS reader is a professional plum, has a steady waiting list of eager applicants to read for various tests. I take this as a sign of the hunger for community by isolated writing teachers.

When these same writing teachers returned to their classrooms, they found that their teaching had changed. With newfound confidence in their ability to give consistent and fair grades, they were able to use evaluation as part of teaching, a great change from the customary empty whining about their responsibility for grading and testing. Some teachers brought scoring guides, sample papers, and peer evaluation directly into their teaching of writing. Other teachers were unhappy at the comparison between the stimuli for writing they were giving their students and the questions they had been scoring at holistic readings; the careful questions used in professional essay tests usually put to shame the casual and vague writing assignments they had been accustomed to using. Particularly if they had served on question development committees, they learned to think systematically about what they wanted their students to do, why the tasks were worth doing, and how writing assignments related to each other. Most important of all, they became able to teach revision of writing, since their grading standards could become public, under-standable, accountable, and clear. Most students (as opposed to profes-sional or skilled writers) do not revise their work, and hence do not really write, since they have not learned to see what needs to be changed in their early drafts. With new attention to evaluation, writing classes could attend to the writing process as a way of meeting clearly stated standards. Holistic scoring has become a significant, perhaps the most significant, in-service training project in the profession, its power deriving from its "indirectness."

As the 1980s drew to a close, college-writing testing no longer meant the kind of fill-in-the-bubble test represented by the TSWE or the CLEP. True, it might mean that, and in the public schools it usually still does mean that. But when a university or college opens discussion of the measurement of writing ability these days, the point of departure is usually a holistically scored essay test. The clearest sign of this change emerged, curiously, from medical schools. The Association of American Medical Colleges, which administers the Medical College Admissions Test, funded a 5-year pilot study on ways of testing writing, as part of an overall attempt to enhance the liberal arts preparation of medical students (Koenig & Mitchell, 1988). At the conclusion of the study early in 1989, after exhaustive analysis of results, the AAMC announced that the forthcoming revision of the MCAT would contain two essay tests, which would be scored holistically. When college English departments generally accept holistic scoring for placement, credit, course exit, and university exit exams (as they now do), a major triumph may be declared. When the medical schools look up from their serums and viruses to make the same statement, perhaps we could justly call it an achieved revolution.

PROBLEMS WITH HOLISTIC SCORING

Nonetheless, holistic scoring remains a technique, a means of obtaining information from a test, and only one of many possible scoring mechanisms. Although it embodies a particular humanistic attitude toward teaching, writing, and students, it is not, after all, a religious experience. It may be more or less appropriate to different circumstances; it may be done more or less creatively; it may or may not yield the needed information. Now that we have finished celebrating its successes, it is time to turn to the problems and limitations of holistic scoring.

Validity

Validity has to do with honesty and accuracy, with a demonstrated connection between what a test proclaims it is measuring and what it in fact measures. Although the basic concept is simplicity itself, the ways of determining validity, and the different kinds of validity, can become extremely complex. Holistic scoring has posited its technical claims on its face validity: It is a direct measure of writing, measuring the real thing, and hence, is more valid than indirect measures, such as fill-in-the-bubble tests of correct editing. Indeed this single claim has been persuasive enough to lead to many a decision to use holistic scoring; as a political argument, it has no peer. But when we look at it closely, the validity of holistic scoring poses a series of problems.

In the first place, the claim that the student writing presented for holistic scoring is "real writing" requires a special definition of writing. While it is true that students producing text during a test are doing a kind of writing, its "reality" is of a peculiar kind: first draft (usually), pressured, driven by external motivation rather than an internal need to say something, designed to meet someone else's topic and grading criteria. It is not "unreal" writing; surely pressured first- draft work, for evaluation purposes, has enough reality for most definitions. But many efforts have been made to make the writing on tests more like the kind of writing that takes place in writing courses, or, even, like writing outside writing courses. Some tests have provided ample time for leisurely revision (but since most students don't learn how to revise, they tend merely to recopy a draft in better penmanship), fake supposed audiences for the prose (but students know that the test will be scored by faculty, so the pretend audience only complicates the artificial writing problem) or choices of questions (but students do not know which choice will work best for them), or even opening sentences for students to use (but these demand that the students write to someone else's pattern), and so on. When these efforts lead to more careful and precise question development, as they usually do, they are useful; but they never can turn a test into a picnic, test questions into self-expression, or test scorers into Aunt Sally. We may as well recognize that writing for a test is an artificial situation, as is most writing, and take it for what it is. That lets us recognize that some good writers freeze under pressure, need more time than our test allows, just can't handle the particular question, have a bad hangover, or whatever. Most students will write better when they are not taking a timed test, so we do not need to be overly punitive in our scoring, particularly on minor errors, and we can afford to reward good work despite some glaring errors. In short, we had best moderate our claims that test questions and test conditions produce uniquely valid real writing.

Once we recognize that the "real" writing under test conditions represents a severely limited kind of reality, we can take a more relaxed posture in relation to some of the objections to holistic scoring. We need not feel compromised by combining scores on a responsible multiple-choice test (which represents another kind of limited reality) with our essay scores; a combination of measures is usually more accurate and fair than single measures of any kind. When our colleagues protest that the holistic score does not measure the writing process, we can cheerfully agree; it only measures what it measures and has certain correlations with other kinds of tests. There are many aspects of college writing, such as learning to use the library or to appreciate complexity in reading or to revise repeatedly, that cannot be measured easily and directly on any test.

One aspect of the "reality" of the writing on a writing test is particularly troublesome in these days of dominant process theories of writing instruction. I have already suggested that there is no good way to examine for revision on a holistically scored exam; we are grading a writing product rather than the process by which that writing emerged. If one believes that "writing is a process, not a product," then we are not grading writing at all when we grade a first-draft product. But I think that the slogan is a false simplification: Any sensible person knows that writing is both a process and a product. We must resist narrowing writing to only one kind of activity, just as we must resist imagining that one score reflects all possible writing abilities. Writing as product is a serious and common form, from professional published work to job applications and reports to term papers and essay exams. All of these products count, and we make ourselves foolish if we pretend that they do not exist. Holistically scored essays measure writing products, and they only hint at the writing process. If our colleagues protest that we are not measuring the writing process, and therefore not measuring the only kind of writing that matters, we must answer "of course" to the first and "nonsense" to the second.

It is also foolish to pretend that holistic measurement of writing is a talisman and the only right way to proceed. There will be occasions when specific information about particular traits should be measured, and for such needs primary-trait scoring and other kinds of trait scoring are available. These methods are akin to holistic measurement, since they render a single score, ranking students against each other; but they are focused sharply on particular traits: coherence, logic and organization, sentence sense, or whatever. When special instructional information is required, such as for diagnosis or measurement in relation to a section of a curriculum, a holistic score is too general to be useful. Under such circumstances, trait scoring, focusing entirely on the material taught, will make the best sense. On some occasions, researchers may even want to use analytic scoring, with its improbable assumption that a series of scores on supposed subskills will add up to a total writing measure. Those developing portfolio measurement are coming up with new scoring schemes, responsive to the particular needs of the many kinds of portfolios. Just as there is no firm consensus on the best scale for holistic scorings (though the 4-point and 6- point scales are most common), we cannot expect holistic scoring to be the best kind of measure for all writing.

Sometimes the validity problem with holistic scoring emerges from weak question development. One of the most consistent complaints about holistic approaches is that the writing tasks are both trivial and personal (not the same thing), variations on "what did you do last summer." I have seen such questions on testing programs that have lost energy; the team that originated and developed appropriate and valid questions has gone on to other things and has left the test in the hands of staff. Or sometimes the program began with borrowed questions, which seemed to work pretty well, and never turned its attention to developing questions examining what was central to the instructional need. Since holistic scoring can apply to any kind of writing product, including argument and exposition of all kinds, we ought to be particularly careful about question development; everyone expects a few silly questions on even the best multiple-choice tests, but when the only question on an essay test is an embarrassment, the entire test—and testing method—becomes invalid.

With all of these variations in scoring, and all of these objections to the validity of holistic scoring, what can we say with confidence? In the first place, we need to restrict holistic scoring to overall measures of writing ability, defined as clearly as possible for a particular program and a particular student population. These definitions appear in the written scoring guide and are exemplified in the sample papers used in the reading. Further, these definitions and samples need to represent a clearly developed consensus by the teachers and others using the results of the test. Pretested and revised test questions should be carefully developed, with an eye to the stated test criteria, by a committee constantly refreshed by new members. Then, validity studies relating the scores on the test to other useful measures need to be undertaken. For example, students failing a university upper-division writing test should also be failing courses requiring writing and generally avoiding writing; if students with low test scores are getting high grades in English and philosophy, publishing work in the student paper, and otherwise succeeding with the written word, something is wrong with the test. We cannot assume that an essay test is, by definition, valid. We need to work carefully to ensure its validity, and then, as we would ask of outsiders, we need to produce some evidence to show it is indeed valid.

Finally, we should not overstate the validity of holistic measurement, a severe and common problem. The power and success of holistic scoring normally leads faculty and administrators to imagine that the test results mean more than they do. While we ought to use as much effort as we can afford to make the writing test, or any test, as valid as possible (using multiple measures, conducting validity studies to gather data, and so on), we should know that any test gives only an approximate score and is subject to error. Far too often, a single essay score is used to make important decisions about a student, a procedure that is indefensible. Holistic scoring in no way relieves us of the special obligation to use test results carefully and responsibly.

Reliability

Reliability has been the underlying problem for holistic scoring since its origins in the experiments conducted by Paul Diederich at the Educational Testing Service (1974): Without controls and agreement on standards, a variety of readers will give all possible scores. The reliability issue is a kind of touchstone for seriousness in measurement: Romantic types don't much care about it, thinking that validity (particularly face validity) is all that matters, while hard-headed statistical types take delight in pointing out that no test can be more valid (in a statistical sense) than it is reliable. Reliability is a technical way of talking about simple fairness to test takers, and if we are not interested in fairness, we have no business giving tests or using test results. Writers and writing teachers who get involved in essay testing tend to have conversion experiences in relation to reliability, moving from romantic to statistical views after a moment of blinding insight into this need for fairness; the conversion is partly motivated by guilt over the unreliable tests and essay scorings they have routinely perpetrated in the past. They then focus so fully upon reliability (particularly scoring reliability), trying to emulate the supposed perfection of computer scoring, as to lose sight of the special qualities of essay testing. As I said earlier, the consuming attention to scoring reliability on the part of holistic scoring research has diverted attention from much else, in large part because of the historical combat with multiple-choice tests.

Certain matters relating to reliability are beyond control of those directing holistic scoring: variations in testing conditions, student health on the testing day, or test taker test wiseness, for example. These matters affect the reliability of all tests, which can never be perfect, and while we should do our best to level the playing field, we cannot fret too much about some inevitable tilt. I know I can increase my students' scores on essay tests with some practical tips; the clever writer learns how to write a second draft on a test, despite the lack of time for a first draft. Anyone who leaves the first page blank, to be written after the entire essay has been completed, will gain a point or two on coherence and organization; a writer who saves a few minutes for editing and inserting the (inevitable) missing words will also improve the score. Oddly enough, most students seem not to know, or to use, these techniques, and so score a bit lower than they should. We should have no illusions about achieving perfect reliability in such an imperfect world.

On the other hand, a few matters relating to reliability are entirely in the hands of the director of an essay test program: test development, scoring reliability, and score reporting. I will turn to those issues in a moment, since they offer creative opportunities to increase the reliability and overall fairness of a test, within the conventional contexts of assessment.

Finally, there are those matters which distinguish essay testing and other kinds of performance or subjective measures of ability. These are complex matters that call for some speculation about the meaning of what we are measuring and how: What is the difference between measuring ability in writing or musical performance or artistic production and measuring the weight of a cow or the knowledge of German strong verbs? What, we need to ask, changes about the concept of reliability when we move into these necessarily subjective areas? I will conclude my discussion of reliability with some thoughts on this problematic issue.

Reliability and cost. The thorniest issue in holistic scoring reliability relates the level of reliability to both the cost and purpose. The more money you spend—up to a point—the higher reliability you can achieve; how much reliability do you need? The answer must be local. If all you need is a rough freshman English placement, to be followed by some shuffling about of students after they begin handing in class papers, very high reliability is probably a waste of resources that would be better spent on instruction; but low reliability is also a waste, since instructional time is the most precious commodity in education and any loss of class time caused by inaccurate placement is itself costly. As the uses of the test become more critical, higher reliability becomes increasingly crucial: If you are using a test as a barrier to upper-division standing or to the receipt of a degree, then very high reliability is essential, and reliability data need to be collected and preserved in case of court challenge. There is no longer any excuse, whatever the test, for giving or using the extremely unreliable essay tests that were common in the days before holistic scoring became common. Reasonably high reliability can now be achieved at modest cost.

Question development. While most of those in charge of holistic scoring focus upon reliable scoring, naturally enough, the most important determiner of reliability has been fixed long before the readers convene: question development. A small but useful bibliography on question development reached its climax with the book on that subject by Leo Ruth and Sandra Murphy (1988); Gordon Brossell has also written on his work with the Florida College Level Academic Skills Test essay (1989). The CLAST plan, which restricts questions to a set pattern with replaceable words, is an extreme version of the sensible attempt to reduce the variability introduced into testing by various kinds of essay questions. A California test demonstrated that the correlation between student scores on different kinds of questions was very low: about .35 (White, 1973-1981). But I am not impressed by the restrictions upon writing posed by a predictable and standard question pattern, which defines writing in a particularly artificial way. Question development is a ticklish matter, balancing the needs of the test (reliability in particular) with the definition of writing that the test question defines. At heart, question development is a special, and especially difficult, form of collaborative writing, rather more of an art than a science.

What do we know about question development at this point? We know that a single essay question, however well developed and carefully scored, will not give test reliabilities much above .5 (the Medical College Admissions Test pilot project showed this; Mitchell & Anderson, 1986), probably because of the "question variable" (some students will write better on this question than on another one, because of interest and background, while other students will write worse). To even out this problem, an important test should have two separate essays, which can be expected to achieve reliabilities in the .7 range with careful scoring. We also know that a systematic test development committee will need considerable time and support staff to develop test criteria, develop test questions to these criteria, implement a scheme for winnowing and pretesting questions, and follow through with a means of validating revisions they have made to improve the questions.

It seems odd to say this, at this late date, but very few essay testing programs attend to careful test development; they are more likely to spend quantities of time and money on reliable scoring of an inherently unreliable test. This is one of the legacies of the combat I spoke of earlier between essay and multiple-choice testing. Instead of focusing upon their strong suit—valid, insightful, precise, and reliable questions—essay testing programs have been trying to beat the computer at accurate counting. I don't mean that we should countenance sloppy readings; we should always be as responsible as we can. But we must concede an advantage in mechanical accuracy to machines and turn our particular attention to what machines cannot do, as compensation for our human variability.

If we put some of the money and energy now going into ever more elaborate computer-assisted scoring into essay test development, we would, I am convinced, achieve major gains in both validity and reliability. The great variety of possible writing tasks that might be called for by different testing programs has hardly been looked into, despite some interesting innovations. The Foreign Service examination, for example, used to give a series of facts about a mythical foreign country and ask examinees to produce a report to the state department recommending a level of foreign aid. The new Test of English as a Foreign Language essay portion has experimented with nonverbal prompts, as have a few other tests. Occasionally, one may see charts or graphs, as well as the usual quotations for discussion from Thoreau, Eiseley, or Ann Landers.

The problems that have held back creative question development are not trivial. In addition to the pressure of multiple-choice test scoring, we should note the usual inexperience of most faculty at careful development of, or even attention to, writing assignments, and the overly tight time pressures that hound most test programs. The foolish resistance by many English faculty to systematic thinking about testing or writing is slowly giving way to enhanced professionalism, but there is always someone on hand to waste time by arguing that the enterprise is impossible, or an accessory to racism and imperialism, or a block to passionate inspiration, or an affront to Shakespeare. Nonetheless, a well-formed test development committee, given enough time and support, is crucial to reliable holistic scoring and to reliable testing.

Essay readings.   I have written elsewhere about the machinery of conducting holistic readings (1985), so I will not repeat myself here. But the relationship of a good essay reading to reliable essay scores, obvious though it seems to me, is generally not well understood. No sensible person would run test results through a computer in faulty condition; yet holistic essay readings, the analogous device for producing results for essay tests, are not normally maintained in prime condition. Unreliable scores will surely come from a computer with deteriorating circuits or from an essay reading with low morale. Thus, it is worthwhile to step back and notice what happens at well-conducted readings, and to speculate about why such readings remain rare.

The essential problem of an essay reading is to create a coherent working community of highly educated specialists, with common goals and procedures, to accomplish intense, difficult, boring, and (usually) low-paid labor. Those who are charged with the responsibility for conducting an essay reading need to take time to consider ways to develop a constructive working community, under the conditions at hand. Readers will feel part of the community if they have been included in the discussions that have led to the test; representative readers should have some voice, whenever possible, in deciding upon the kind of test, the test criteria, the meaning of test results, and even the test question. The scoring guide should not be presented as a fixed and revealed truth, but as a guide that can always be improved—until the scoring begins. The sample papers illustrating the score points have not been chosen and scored by divinities, but by selected readers doing their best, subject to overrule by the community of readers. In short, the readers must develop a sense of ownership of the test and the scoring guide if they are to score willingly and reliably. Without this ownership, they are hired hands doing piecework and both community and reliability decline. At its best, a reading embodies and rewards collegiality; readers feel special and will take extra pains to make things work. At its worst, a reading can resemble a sweat shop, with a grumbling and rebellious work force resenting every dreary minute of labor. For the sake of efficiency and reliability, humane working conditions and cordial working relations become necessary. For some readings, this means a bottled vintage rather than a jug wine after the reading is done; at others, it means replacing the rigid chief reader with a colleague blessed with humility and a sense of humor. Some outsiders may wonder at the warm feelings evident at a good essay reading and even complain about the expenses; but without these collegial feelings, the extra effort necessary for reliable reading, hour after hour, day after day, just does not happen.

The "true score." Finally, we return to the statistical issue of reliability at its most profound and most theoretical. I am speaking here of the different definitions of what we are trying to learn about students from a test (or any other measurement device), an important conceptual difference between the measurement community and those in the writing community. At the root of this issue is the concept of a "true score" for a test. In classical test theory, a student taking a test is presumed to have a "true score" which represents the accurate measurement of the construct being evaluated. Since no test is perfect and conditions are never ideal, the observed score a student achieves on a test will normally be at some distance from the true score, a distance whose probability is expressed mathematically by the Standard Error of Measurement for the test. Thus the observed score of a student is made up of the "true score" modified by an error score; the best test will reduce that error score as much as possible.

For many kinds of measurement, such a concept, and such a language, work reasonably well. We need to be aware, however, that to speak of a "true score" suggests a kind of purity and objectivity of measurement, a kind of value-free and meaningful reality associated with other kinds of Truth: true love, perhaps, or true religion. Such language authorizes a profound belief in the value of tests and test scores, and allows even heavily subjective multiple-choice tests to be called "objective," as if they had been created by the same computers that score them. Those who use the language of true scores, objective tests, and the narrowly statistical view of measurement are driven by their language to envision tests as a way of achieving a vision of truth, ideally free from social values or subjective judgment or disagreement; any such matters are called "error," the serpent to be stamped out of the garden. Measurement becomes a reality of numbers and charts, equations and computers, scorecards for the nation's schools, and percentile ratings that rank skills to several decimal places. Most of all, like all truth, it is to be believed.

However, when we evaluate student writing (not to speak of writing programs or high schools), we sometimes find differences of opinion that cannot be resolved and where the concept of the true score makes no sense. Using controlled holistic scoring, we can achieve high interrater reliability, but some papers resist agreement. Despite our scoring guides and sample papers, you grade Sam's paper a 4 while I grade it a 3; there are so many aspects to writing that, despite the scoring guide and sample papers, you are focusing on some while I attend more to others. In practice, we simply add the two adjacent scores, call the paper a 7 and move on, while differences of more than one point are resolved by a third independent score. Is our difference of opinion to be called error? Not at all. In fact, historically, such differences about value in most areas of experience tend to be more valuable than absolute agreement; they combine to bring us nearer to accurate evaluation than would simple agreement (that is, my score is a bit low, probably, and yours a bit high). This is the same principle that allows us to judge work from the past in the light of much critical discussion and disagreement; judgment is a community activity, calling for consensus and compromise. The same is true in measurement of writing ability, where some disagreement (within limits) should not be called error, since, as with the arts, we do not really have a true score, even in theory. Yet, if we imagine that we are seeking to approximate a true score, we exaggerate the negative effects of disagreement and distort the meaning of the scores we do achieve. Sophisticated statisticians have been aware of this issue for some time. A team headed by the distinguished psychometrician L. J. Cronbach developed some decades ago what he called "generalizability theory," based on a "consensus score" rather than a true score (Cronbach, Rajaratnam, & Gleser, 1963). A consensus score can yield very useful measurement, which reflects the social process of judgment and offers sound statistical data. But the usual language of measurement resists so human a matter as consensus, with its acceptance of the value of differing opinions.

The concept and language of the "true score" is so powerful for many statistical test consultants, and the definition of error in measurement so narrow, that generalizability theory seems to rest in an odd byway, reserved for the poets of statistics, who rarely sing. It is rather the harsh language of classical statistics, with its agricultural and phrenological roots, that still governs the world of academic measurement and, hence, that normally determines the analysis of scores produced by essay readings. That is to say, the world of assessment, despite the realities of holistic scoring and essay testing, remains largely a universe of true scores, measurement errors, pretests, posttests, and, in general, numerical positivism. Some leaders of this community, aware, as Cronbach was, of the need to liberate it from its narrowness, have tried to promote larger concepts, such as "performance measures" instead of product measures, or multiple measures instead of single tests (Adelman, 1988); the Assessment Forum of the American Association for Higher Education seeks to bring researchers and practitioners from various academic communities together for discussions on these matters.

So reliability still remains an underlying theoretical and practical problem for essay testing in general, and holistic scoring in particular. We cannot dismiss the issue, as many would prefer to do, because it is a statistical way of talking about simple fairness and accuracy, matters we would be foolish to ignore. Yet, we cannot be bound to a narrow and mechanical version of reliability, designed for simpler measurement, for such limits diminish and trivialize what essay testing can accomplish. Perhaps some card-carrying statistician with an interest in essay testing will emerge before the century is over to produce new theories and practices for the statistical analysis of reliability of holistic scoring.

Meanwhile, we need to be alert to the uncertain reliability of holistic scores in order to defeat their misuse, particularly when they are used alone to damage students. Too many institutions use holistic scores (indeed, all test scores) as if they were infallible measures handed to them by the gods. For example, a number of freshman composition programs require students not only to receive a passing grade from their instructors, but also to pass a writing test, holistically scored. When some students fail the test, despite good or even excellent grades from their instructors, the natural reaction is to deprecate the low standards of the faculty. While it is possible that some instructors will have too low standards and that the test may, over some years, show such a pattern, one test score is simply not reliable enough to warrant such a conclusion. It is far more likely that the instructor's grade, based on multiple measures, will be accurate than that the holistic score will be a reliable single measure. The comedian Richard Pryor once said that cocaine is God's way of telling you that you have too much money; perhaps reliability statistics are a similar message about too much academic arrogance.

THE CHALLENGE OF PORTFOLIO ASSESSMENT

Just as essay testing and holistic scoring developed in the 1970s as a response to the inadequacies of multiple-choice testing of writing, portfolio assessment is developing in the 1990s as a response to the inadequacies of essay testing and holistic scoring. Many of the same issues are reoccurring in this new context, which suggests that history is repeating itself and that we may have something to learn from a review of that history from this new perspective.

Portfolios present possible solutions to the problems of essay testing that have become apparent. Instead of a single, timed test response, or a writing product based on a test maker's question, scored to the criteria of a single test, we now may have for evaluation a folder including a range of writing products, some of them drafts showing the writing process, produced under more natural conditions. Pat Hutchings, of the American Association for Higher Education, one of the most articulate proponents of portfolios, likes to argue that portfolios can replace the usual "snapshot" of measurement with a "motion picture." While there is not much history of successful portfolio assessment outside the fine arts (where it has been standard for generations), the arts do provide a model of performance evaluation that is a more appropriate model for writing than the product models still dominant in writing assessment.

Writing portfolios have been used for many years by individual instructors, who require students to hand in a compilation of all writing for a course at the end of the term. A portfolio grade can then include such matters as improvement, diligence in revision, ability to write in different modes—all matters that will not show up in a single piece of writing, but will become apparent in an entire folder of work. A development of this means of evaluation has been described by Peter Elbow and Pat Belanoff (1986), who used it to certify writing proficiency for all students in a required writing course. Experiments are under way in the 1990s to use portfolio assessment in even larger contexts: for freshman composition placement, for general education outcomes and certification, for entrance into upper-division standing, and the like. In addition, many campuses are experimenting with the use of portfolios for program evaluation, with the principal aim of gathering information about the effects of the major or the general education program, rather than the progress of an individual. A literature describing these experiments, proposing new theories and practices, will surely be available in the near future, though little is in print now (Belanoff & Dickson, 1991; White, 1992).

We need to note, at the outset, that portfolio evaluation is not really parallel to holistic or multiple-choice evaluation; portfolios refer to a method of collecting materials for evaluation, rather than to an evaluation method itself. In fact, many portfolios will be collected for such purposes as record keeping, or mementos of college, or general evidence of progress in learning, and never evaluated at all.

But once a decision is made to collect portfolios for evaluation purposes—for individuals or for programs—the issues of development and scoring interconnect just as they do for holistic assessment of essays. I think that some version of holistic scoring will turn out to be the only manageable way to score portfolios, since the problems of cost and reliability that I discussed earlier in the context of essay testing now become many times more severe. Thus, portfolio assessment is likely to become the next chapter for holistic scoring, with developments that are now hard to foresee.

Just as essay testing has had to adapt to the different purposes and occasions it has served, so portfolios will appear in different forms. Many of the problems such assessment will face as it moves from the classroom to larger contexts have already become apparent. As we have learned from essay testing programs, these kinds of problems need to be dealt with in the context of the institution and the particular assessment; the questions they raise are thorny and complex, and must be thought through before implementation gets under way.

What Is to Be Included in the Portfolio?

In the early days of essay testing, one repeated shock for evaluators was the sheer bulk represented by a large-scale exam. Those responsible for grading the tests discovered an unforeseen need for large boxes, storage rooms, athletic student aides, even trucks for moving the test booklets about. A strong back, we used to say, was as important as a strong mind in preparation for a reading. These discoveries are now being repeated, on a much larger scale, with portfolio assessment. Five thousand essay tests can fit nicely in a storage room; 5,000 portfolios can take up a small building.

The bulk of portfolios represent more than a physical problem; they represent reading time, which in turn costs money. Essay tests can be read holistically, and regularly are so scored, at an average rate of 25 or more an hour (for 45-minute essays). But portfolios can, and often do demand, an hour or more apiece. Holistic scoring made the bulk of large-scale essay testing manageable and affordable, but we are only beginning to experiment with holistic scoring of portfolios. What method of control and management will emerge?

A first step in the management of portfolios is probably a restricted definition of the contents. While different assessment goals will lead to different definitions, a typical portfolio can be limited to three or four documents: an extended term paper, an in-class examination, and a short paper with first and second drafts. A general education portfolio would surely add a laboratory report, while a portfolio in the major would ask for some coverage of the major material. But unless some restrictions and definitions are put in place at the start, the bulk will get beyond management and the measurement will be unreliable, because the folders will not be comparable.

Thus, the definition of the portfolio is parallel to question development for essay testing. They both require careful attention to the goals of the assessment and the uses of the results. They both call for a compromise between requiring all one would like and scoring all that one can afford.

Who is Responsible for the Portfolio?

The first assumption about responsibility for the portfolio is that, quite naturally, the student should be in charge. The history of portfolios in the arts, and in individual classrooms, also argues that the producer of the work should also produce the portfolio. However, enough problems emerge when the student is made responsible that some experiments have decided to require either the faculty or some central office to be responsible for creating and storing the student portfolios.

As soon as a portfolio assessment requires the student to include work from more than one course, the assessment design conflicts with the customary student pattern of deleting previous courses from the mind when the next term begins. Of course, portfolios intend more or less explicitly to fight against such fragmentation of education, and some small campuses (such as Alverno College) have come up with ways to enforce student maintenance of the portfolio from term to term. But some institutions have been forced to abandon that goal in the face of student indifference and carelessness, and have required faculty to send in papers to an office that maintains the portfolios for the student. Under these conditions, the portfolios are maintained and on hand for scoring, but one of the purposes of the entire assessment (students taking responsibility for connecting their various courses) is lost. The maintenance of the portfolio across courses and years becomes even more complicated when we move from the small liberal arts college to large state universities, with their transient student bodies and large number of transfer courses from other institutions. How were students to know that they should have preserved papers written for other institutions, perhaps years ago?

Large-scale essay testing has met similar problems by focusing upon global goals for assessment. Thus, the MCAT essay specifically avoids questions having to do with medicine or other specific information, measuring such traits as ability to develop an idea and to produce reasonably edited prose consistent with first-draft writing. Many essay placement tests in fact measure a student's ability to produce clear sentences and to relate them in some way. The tests deal only with the presumed outcomes of previous education, as demonstrated by writing on the test, not with the products of previous courses. Large-scale portfolio assessment will probably need to make a similar adjustment to the reality of the student body: Only material from courses at the particular institution may be used, perhaps, and only three or so courses may need to be included. In addition, some in-class or test writing may be required, and a student self-assessment of the portfolio is often mandatory.

Writing in the Disciplines?

An additional problem for portfolio assessment emerges from the paucity of writing that faculty in some disciplines require. A student majoring in mathematics or physics will often do little writing beyond freshman composition, despite all the efforts of writing-across-the-curriculum advocates. If one of the goals of the portfolio is to integrate and assess the work of baccalaureate study, such students may be at a serious disadvantage through no fault of their own. On one campus I visited, the psychology department required no writing at all, and some students (in despair? in protest?) submitted a series of multiple-choice answer sheets in their folders. Perhaps a holistically scored essay test needs to be part of such portfolios in order to obtain a sample of writing beyond the freshman year. Or perhaps the very existence of the portfolio system will prevail upon recalcitrant departments to begin requiring student writing as a means of active learning in order to avoid public embarrassment from portfolio assessment of their students.

Authenticity of the Documents

The question of the authenticity of the documents in the portfolio must also be dealt with if the assessment is to be meaningful. If the faculty are responsible for submitting work, and a central office stores the portfolios for the student, the submitting faculty can be asked to guarantee that the student actually did the work. But if the student is made responsible for the contents and storage of the portfolio, and if the evaluation of the portfolio is significant, some other means must be found to ensure the authenticity of the work. Some experiments have required at least one piece of in-class writing, signed off by the instructor as a check against dishonesty. Presumably, a marked difference in quality between the in-class work and the rest of the portfolio raises questions to be pursued elsewhere. In a world filled with readily available fraternal and commercial papers on almost any topic, those evaluating portfolios need to attend to the problem of authenticity, if the assessment is to be reliable and valid.

Essay testing dealt with this problem by adopting the mechanisms of the traditional multiple-choice test. Picture identifications could be used in large-scale testing situations, if authenticity questions were expected, if the testing officer was made responsible for guaranteeing that the student whose name was on the test booklet in fact wrote the test. But such a testing situation is one of the artificial drawbacks that portfolio assessment is designed to overcome. No doubt, experience with portfolios will accumulate methods for assuring authenticity without overly obtrusive policing, but no simple and efficient method has yet emerged for large-scale measurement.

Influence of the Original Assignment

Anyone involved in essay testing has learned about the importance of question development, an issue I have already spoken to at some length. When we read portfolios, this issue returns in an unexpected way. The student writing that appears depends to a large degree upon the quality of the assignment to which it was written. That is, creative and interesting assignments, naturally enough, elicit much better writing from students than do mechanical and boring assignments.

Essay testing takes care of this problem by asking all students to write to the same question, and by attempting to develop the most appropriate question possible. But these options are not available to portfolio assessment. If a wide variety of writing samples, from a wide variety of courses, is included in the portfolio, there is some chance that this disparity of assignments will even out; my personal experience is, however, that it does not. (Such inclusiveness adds to the bulk of all the portfolios, perhaps prohibitively so.) Many college faculty have developed interesting assignments; indeed, some of the best reading in portfolios turns out to be these creative assignments (which must be included so readers can make sense of the writing prepared in response to them). But every college and every department also has faculty who ask for, and hence receive, uncreative and even unedited work.

Reliability

Validity will not be a direct problem for portfolios. Portfolio assessment can argue it is "real writing" even more powerfully than can essay testing, since it collects materials already produced for courses without the artificiality of a test. Yet, as statisticians never tire of reminding us, no assessment can be more valid than it is reliable, and reliability problems have hardly been defined for portfolio assessment. Many of the problems I have been describing turn out to be related to reliability: Regularizing and authenticating the contents of portfolios, for example, are important for reliable measurement.

One important device for developing reliable scoring of portfolios has been developed by the project under way at Miami University of Ohio: the development of a scoring guide. Once again, the experience of holistic scoring of essays becomes a base for the development of portfolio assessment. The written scoring guide for an essay test not only describes the meaning of the points on the scoring scale, but also defines the criteria of the test for both those scoring it and those taking it. In the same way, a portfolio scoring guide will become one of the descriptive documents for the assessment program, as well as a means of achieving some reliability. At a minimum, each portfolio should receive two independent scores, and reliability data should be recorded. While reliability should not become the obsession for portfolio evaluation that it became for essay testing, portfolios cannot become a serious means of measurement without demonstrable reliability.

Role of Instructor Grade and Comments

Should the original instructor's comments and grades be left on the papers in the portfolio, or should they be removed? Further, what role in the portfolio assessment should be played by the original instructor and the context of the assignment?

It seems obvious that the original instructor's comments and grades should be removed from papers so that the portfolio evaluation can be independent. (How this is to be accomplished remains one more tricky administrative problem.) But when that is done, the readers of the papers become relatively uninformed laymen, reading for general literacy, and easily taken in by superficial knowledge. Let me give an example.

At one small liberal arts college I participated in a reading session that evaluated senior portfolios, prepared as a graduation requirement. All instructor comments and grades had been removed from the documents in the portfolios. As with holistic scoring, these readers had developed a scoring guide and the program directors were checking the reliability of independent portfolio ratings. But when the reading was over and we began comparing scores, a serious problem emerged. I had scored one paper, on William Faulkner's novel *The Sound and the Fury*, very low, since it mixed up the characters, misunderstood the story line, and showed only the dimmest understanding of the issues important to the book, which I often teach. All the other readers rated the essay at the highest level, on the grounds of its fluency and clarity. They had not read the novel, so what else could they do? Again, I had rated a brilliantly written paper on the War of the Spanish Succession as superior, while the historian who happened to be a reader scored it very low: The student had such facts as the names and dates completely scrambled, and he had confused that war with another some 200 years later. In almost every case, the reader with specialized knowledge in a field rated the essays in that field much lower than did those outside the field. If the instructor's comments had been left on the papers, we would have had the advantage of an informed response to begin with. But, then, what would we have been grading for?

This issue seems to me far more serious for portfolio assessment than it is for holistic scoring of essay tests. Within the world of a single test question, a team of readers can quickly become informed and can work to consistent standards. It is impossible for any team of portfolio readers to be informed on all topics within a portfolio covering a range of disciplines. Paradoxically, the portfolio assessment can become a rating of more superficial traits than the typical holistic scoring. The problem is not severe when the portfolio consists of papers from a single discipline, read by faculty in that discipline; portfolio assessment in the major is probably the most promising line to follow for that reason. Yet, the promise that portfolio assessment can help unify the fragmentation of general education, or college education, is so great that we must hope that a consistent way to read portfolios can be developed. This is the great challenge that now faces holistic scoring.

CONCLUSIONS

I remember clearly the early days of large-scale essay testing, when we English department types believed we were both exempt from and morally superior to such bureaucratic matters as validity and reliability. Those of us who became responsible for testing programs not only had to learn about such matters in haste, but we had to become aware of many more regulations than we knew existed, including privacy rules, mechanisms to guard against racial, social, and sexual bias, and appeals procedures for students convinced that a score was wrong. Because we were locked in political battle with an entrenched establishment based on multiple-choice testing, we had to proceed with caution despite our belief that our more responsible academic stance gave us the strength of moral superiority. We saw ourselves, properly, standing up for teachers and students, for substantial learning and creativity, for holistic views of writing and people, as opposed to the reductionism of the fill-in-the-bubble tests. But the political situation kept our arrogance in check.

I now see some of this same blissful innocence among those proceeding with portfolio assessment. This retrospective essay will, I hope, help them realize that laws of fairness and responsibility are not repealed, nor held in abeyance for long. Many of the same problems that the essay testing movement met, and solved (more or less), over the last two decades have returned in disguise to confront portfolios as they move from the arts and the classroom into the arena of assessment on a large scale. I hope the national experience of holistic assessment of writing can become a resource for those seeking to identify and cope with these problems as writing measurement moves into its newest phase.

REFERENCES

Adelman, C. (Ed.). (1988). *Performance and judgment: Essays on principles and practice in the assessment of college student learning.* Washington, DC: U.S. Department of Education, Office of Educational Research and Improvement.

Belanoff, P., & Dickson, M. (Eds.). (1991). *Portfolios: Process and product.* Portsmouth, NH: Heineman-Boynton-Cook.

Burt, F., & King, S. (Eds.). (1974). *Equivalency testing.* Urbana, IL: National Council of Teachers of English.

Brossell, G. (1989). *The effects of systematic variations in essay topics on the writing performance of college freshmen.* College Composition and Communication, *40*, 414-421.

Cronbach, L.J., Rajaratnam, M., & Gleser, G. (1963). Theory of generalizability: A liberation of reliability theory. *British Journal of Statistical Psychology, 16,* 137-163.

Diederich, P. (1974). *Measuring growth in English.* Urbana, IL.: National Council of Teachers of English.

Elbow, P., & Belanoff, P. (1986). State University of New York, Stony Brook, Portfolio-based evaluation program. In P. Connolly & T. Vilardi (Eds.), *New methods in college writing programs* (pp. 95-105). New York: Modern Language Association.

Koenig, J., & Mitchell, K. (1988). An interim report on the MCAT essay pilot project. *Journal of Medical Education, 63,* 21-29.

Godshalk, F., Swineford, E., & Coffman, W. (1966). *The measurement of writing ability.* New York: The College Entrance Examination Board.

Greenberg, K., Weiner, H., & Donovan, R. (1986). *Writing assessment: Issues and strategies.* New York: Longman.

Mitchell, K., & Anderson, J. (1986). Reliability of holistic scoring for the MCAT essay. *Educational and Psychological Measurement, 46,* 771-775.

Ruth, L., & Murphy, S. (1988). *Designing writing tasks for the assessment of writing.* Norwood, NJ: Ablex.

White, E. M. (1973-1981). *Comparison and contrast: The California State University Freshman English Equivalency Examination* (Vols. 1-8). Long Beach: California State University. (ERIC Document Reproduction Service No. ED 275 007).

White, E. M. (1984a). Holisticism. *College Composition and Communication, 35,* 400-409.

White, E. M. (1984b). Post-structural literary criticism and responding to student writing. *College Composition and Communication, 34,* 186-195.

White, E. M. (1985). *Teaching and assessing writing: Recent advances in understanding, evaluating, and improving student performance.* San Francisco: Jossey-Bass.

White, E. M. (1992). *Assigning, responding, evaluating: A writing teacher's guide.* New York: St. Martin's.

4

Reliability Issues in Holistic Assessment

Roger D. Cherry
Ohio State University

Paul R. Meyer
New Mexico State University

In the last 15 years, holistic evaluation of written texts has become widely used as a means of assessing writing abilities. In a typical evaluation scheme, writing samples are collected and scored in accordance with a rating scale by two or more trained raters. A substantial—and growing—literature proposes guidelines for constructing and administering writing tasks and for conducting rating sessions (e.g., Davis, Scriven, & Thomas, 1987; Hoetker & Brossell, 1986; Myers, 1980; Ruth & Murphy, 1984, 1988; Spandel & Stiggins, 1981; White, 1985).

Despite the prevalence of direct assessment practices, the reliability of scores obtained through those practices has not been adequately understood. The literature on writing research and assessment reveals a good deal of confusion about the nature of reliability in general and about the relationship between reliability and validity in particular. Moreover, the field has experienced widespread methodological confusion about computing, interpreting, and reporting reliability coefficients that result from direct assessments of writing. This chapter addresses these theoretical and practical issues under the following headings:

- Reliability as a Psychometric Construct
- The Reliability of Holistic Scoring: Instrument Reliability vs. Interrater Reliability

- Problems with Reliability in Writing Research and Evaluation
- Estimating and Reporting Instrument and Interrater Reliability Coefficients
- Needed Research on Reliability

The basic argument of the chapter is that our profession needs to come to a better understanding of reliability, particularly the relationship between reliability and validity. The profession also needs to standardize the statistical methods used for calculating and reporting the reliability of holistic scores. We offer the remarks that follow as a first step toward addressing these needs.

Although we have tried to make the chapter as accessible as possible, it examines the technical aspects of several issues in some detail. The technical discussions are essential because they form the basis for the specific claims and recommendations we make concerning reliability. Understanding why some current holistic assessment practices are problematic or why high interrater reliabilities do not guarantee reliable assessments requires some knowledge of both the theoretical assumptions and the computational formulas on which reliability statistics are based.

RELIABILITY AS A PSYCHOMETRIC CONSTRUCT

Reliability and validity are two of the most basic concepts in measurement theory. *Reliability* refers to how consistently a test measures whatever it measures. *Validity* addresses the question of whether the test measures what it is designed to measure. In order for a test to be a valid measure of a trait such as writing ability, it must be both reliable and valid: It must yield consistent results, and it must actually measure writing ability. A test cannot be valid unless it is reliable, but the opposite is not true; a test can be reliable but still not be valid. *Thus, reliability is a necessary but not a sufficient condition for validity.*

Both reliability and validity are theoretical constructs developed by psychometricians to describe certain properties of test scores and the confidence with which decisions might be based on those scores. Technically speaking, reliability is a property not of particular tests but of the scores derived from those tests. (Although, for economy of expression, we will often speak of "the reliability of a test," it is important to keep in mind that reliability refers to the consistency of information provided by test scores rather than to a property of a given test.) The applicability and proper use of reliability coefficients in various situations is closely tied to the assumptions and limitations of reliability and validity as psychometric constructs.

According to Jackson and Ferguson (1941), "the term reliability was first introduced into mental test theory by Spearman in 1904" (p. 9). Since that time, reliability has been a central problem in measurement and evaluation (Stanley, 1971). Generally speaking, reliability is not as complex and therefore not as problematic as validity. Psychometricians have achieved greater agreement on the nature of reliability and methods of determining whether a test is reliable than on these issues for validity. Three concepts are central to understanding contemporary treatments of reliability: measurement error, analysis of variance, and the contextual nature of reliability.

Like all things human, measurement is not a perfect business. All measurement, whether of physical characteristics or of psychological traits, involves some degree of error. Repeated measurements of even a relatively stable phenomenon will not yield precisely the same results each time. In classical testing and measurement theory, an individual's score on a particular test is considered to be an inexact estimate of his or her "true score." The "true score" is a hypothetical construct that refers to what a given measurement would be if our knowledge were perfect and complete and we could devise perfect tests. In contrast, an individual's *observed score* is considered to be made up of two components: a *true score* and some degree of *error.*

$$\text{observed score} = \text{true score} + \text{error} \tag{1}$$

Modern psychometricians have used a statistical procedure called analysis of variance to analyze measurement error and define reliability. Analysis of variance, as its name suggests, is used to analyze patterns of variation in a set of data. By identifying and measuring independent "sources" of variation, analysis of variance can determine the extent to which particular factors in a testing situation influence the resulting test scores. Analysis of variance defines measurement error as variation that cannot be attributed to a particular source. In the same way that observed scores are conceived in terms of true score and error, variance is broken into true variance and error variance:

$$\text{total variance} = \text{true variance} + \text{error variance} \tag{2}$$

As Sax (1974) pointed out, when we try to measure student knowledge or ability, variance and measurement error have three main sources:

1. Characteristics of the students,
2. Characteristics of the test, and
3. Conditions affecting test administration and scoring. (p. 196)

Students.   We know that students do not perform with perfect consistency from one writing task to another. Even if students were given the same writing task on different occasions, we would expect their performance on a given day to differ at least somewhat from their performance on another day. The necessary implication of this difference is that although a writing sample may reflect a student's writing ability, it cannot do so perfectly. The inherent inconsistency of student performance lessens our ability to rely on a single writing sample to make judgments about a student's writing ability. In statistical terms, variability in student performance contributes to the error in measurements of writing ability.

Tests.   We also know that all essay prompts are not equal. Some writing tasks are easier for students of a certain age or students with particular kinds of knowledge or experience; other writing tasks are more difficult for these same groups. Some tests of writing ability require students to write narratives; others require students to synthesize information. Differences in the way writing tests measure writing ability make it more difficult to assess writing ability consistently. Thus, the writing test itself contributes to the error in measurements of writing ability.

Test Administration and Scoring.   Finally, we know that the rating of writing samples is not perfectly reliable. The way raters are trained influences the way they make judgments about a set of writing samples. Similarly, raters' personal values influence their judgments. Even if a rater were to be given the same writing sample at two different times during the same rating session, he or she might score the text differently. Much of the variability in the scores assigned to writing samples is due to idiosyncratic features of rating sessions and individual raters. Test administration and scoring are major contributors to measurement error in holistic assessments.

Common sense and statistical theory both tell us that when we attempt to measure writing ability holistically, we must consider the three sources of error discussed above. This fact was recognized by Godshalk, Swineford, and Coffman (1966), who used analysis of variance to identify the influence of "students," "topics," and "readings"on holistic judgments.

The reliability of a testing instrument is a function of the magnitude of measurement error associated with that instrument. When analysis of variance is used to quantify measurement error, it provides a way of defining and quantifying reliability. According to Thorndike (1951),

> The numerical value of the reliability coefficient of a test corresponds
> exactly to the proportion of the variance in test scores which is due to

true differences between individuals in the quality being evaluated by the
test. A test is unreliable in proportion as it has error variance. (p. 567)

In other words, reliability is, by definition, the ratio of true variance
to total variance. This ratio can be expressed in two ways:

$$\text{reliability} = \frac{\text{true variance}}{\text{total variance}} = \frac{\text{total variance} - \text{error variance}}{\text{total variance}} \qquad (3)$$

Equation (3) is the basis of all reliability formulas. In general terms, the
higher the proportion of variance due to error, the more likely individual
performance on the measure will vary across repeated testing; low
reliability means that the testing instrument will not provide consistent
information about individual performance. Measurement error and
predictability have an inverse relationship to one another: A greater
degree of error means that individual performance on the test is less
predictable. Quantifying reliability is a matter of determining how true
variance and error variance should be defined and measured in particular
assessment situations.

Because they represent a ratio of true variance to total variance,
reliability coefficients range between 0 and 1. A reliability of 0 would
indicate that a test was entirely unreliable because all of the variance in
scores on the test could be attributed to measurement error. A reliability
of 1 would indicate that the true score and the test score were identical
because there was no measurement error. In practice, reliability
coefficients are greater than 0 and less than 1.

THE RELIABILITY OF HOLISTIC ASSESSMENT: INTERRATER RELIABILITY VS. INSTRUMENT RELIABILITY

Procedures for estimating reliability were developed when "objective"
tests began to gain currency in American education (ca. 1930-1950).
Because classical testing and measurement dealt with "objective" tests
consisting of items with right and wrong answers (e.g., Gulliksen, 1936;
Valentine, 1932; Vernon, 1940), reliability generally has been regarded as
a unitary construct. For "objective" tests, scoring is not problematic, and
reliability is a question of whether the test produces consistent results on
different occasions. For essay testing, reliability is more complicated. In
addition to test consistency, evaluators must also be concerned with the
consistency of student performance and with the scoring of raters who
will never achieve perfect agreement. Thus, the reliability of essay testing
is multidimensional rather than one-dimensional.

Unfortunately, writing researchers and evaluators generally have not
recognized the complexity of reliability. Perhaps following their

predecessors in classical testing and measurement theory, those who discuss the reliability of holistic scoring typically have assumed that reliability is one-dimensional. With few exceptions (e.g., Breland, Camp, Jones, Morris, & Rock, 1987; Godshalk et al., 1966), reliability has been considered synonymous with *interrater reliability*, the reliability with which raters assign scores to written texts. Yet interrater reliability treats only part of one of the three sources of assessment error, that due to scoring. Neglected almost entirely has been instrument reliability, the reliability of the writing assessment as a whole. Instrument reliability is concerned with the consistency of assessments across successive administrations of a test. It necessarily takes into account all three sources of error—students, test, and scoring.

Although the instrument reliability of essay testing corresponds most closely with the notion of reliability assumed in classical testing and measurement theory, this dimension of reliability has been grossly neglected in writing research and evaluation. Despite the fact that instrument reliability rather than interrater reliability provides a basis for making inferences about writing ability, most researchers and evaluators have been more concerned with interrater reliability. To an extent, their concern has been justified because rater judgments can be a major source of error and of low reliability in measurements that involve human judgment. Despite what some advocates of holistic assessment suggest, however, interrater reliability alone cannot establish holistic assessment as a reliable or valid procedure. Focusing only on interrater reliability has resulted in a truncated notion of the reliability of holistic scoring as an assessment procedure.

Interrater reliability tells only part of the story with respect to the reliability of holistic scoring. By describing the consistency with which raters assign scores to written texts, interrater reliability indicates how likely it is that a group of texts would be rated the same way in a second rating. It addresses the question of whether, within the assessment context, raters can reliably judge the quality of writing samples. Interrater reliability, however, says nothing about the reliability of the assessment as a whole.

Instrument reliability, on the other hand, evaluates the consistency of both the writing prompt and the rating of writing samples across successive assessments. Whereas interrater reliability describes how consistently raters judge the *writing quality* of writing samples, instrument reliability addresses the reliability of judgments of *writing ability* made on the basis of those samples. Because most holistic assessments purport to measure writing ability (rather than the quality of a writing sample or the consistency of the raters), instrument reliability should be of greater concern to evaluators than interrater reliability.

The study reported by Godshalk et al. (1966) is one of the few to distinguish between interrater and instrument reliability. Godshalk et al. reported coefficients for both a "reliability of reading" (interrater reliability) and a "reliability of total essay score" (instrument reliability). They explained that their interrater reliability of .921 "means that if a second group of 25 readers as competent as the first group were chosen and the papers were read again, it might be expected that the two sets of total scores would produce a correlation of approximately .921" (p. 12). The "reliability of total essay score" (reported as .841) is an estimate of the reliability of the testing instrument itself, which in this case consisted of a total of five different "essays" produced by each writer. The authors suggested that their overall instrument reliability was "an estimate of the correlation to be expected if the students were to write five more essays on five new topics and if these essays were read by 25 new readers" (pp. 12-13). It is possible to quibble with some of the assumptions underlying this last statement (e.g., Godshalk et al. assume that any writing sample would be an equally good measure of writing ability and that all raters are equally competent), but the examples provide good basic definitions of the concepts of interrater and instrument reliability.

As Godshalk et al. recognized, interrater reliability accounts for only one source of measurement error, that deriving from raters. Regardless of how consistently raters assign scores to written texts, if the writing prompt (the test) is faulty or if examinees do not respond consistently to it, the holistic scores will not reliably reflect writing ability. In order to obtain accurate estimates of the reliability of holistic assessment, all three sources of measurement error—student, test, and scoring procedure—must be taken into account.

Interrater reliability stands in relation to instrument reliability as reliability stands in relation to validity. Just as reliability is a necessary but not sufficient condition for validity, *interrater reliability is a necessary but not sufficient condition for instrument reliability*. As such, interrater reliability provides an upper bound for instrument reliability.

As Stanley and Hopkins (1972) pointed out in a general treatment of essay testing, "agreement in marking the essay test is higher than the reliability of the test itself" (p. 204). This is not a statistical result but a logical consequence of the fact that the total error in a testing situation must be greater than or equal to the error associated with any of its components. Interrater reliability would be equal to instrument reliability only if students responded like automata to writing tasks, performing with identical skill on different occasions without regard to the task. Because students inevitably respond differently on different days and perform differently on different writing tasks, instrument reliability is always lower than interrater reliability, often substantially lower.

PROBLEMS WITH RELIABILITY
IN WRITING RESEARCH AND EVALUATION

Several problems have plagued the treatment of reliability in writing research and evaluation. As we have noted, one problem has been that discussions of "reliability" have typically been limited to interrater reliability. In addition, a number of writing researchers have been confused about the difference between interrater reliability and instrument reliability, about the relationship between the two types of reliability, and about how different types of reliability coefficients can be used in decision making.[1]

A second, but related, problem has been confusion over the notions of reliability and validity in influential studies of writing assessment.

A third problem has been a lack of agreement on appropriate statistics for calculating and reporting interrater reliabilities. A wide variety of coefficients has been reported in the composition research and testing literature, with no discussion of, or apparent consensus on, which statistics are appropriate for which circumstances. In many cases, interrater reliability coefficients have been reported without identification of the particular statistic that has been calculated or of the procedures used to calculate it.

A fourth problem is that a number of procedures typically employed in holistic rating sessions are highly problematic with respect to reliability. For example, the practice of calculating and reporting interrater reliability coefficients based on a "sample rating" involving more ratings per text than are actually obtained during a rating session often results in erroneous reports of interrater reliability. A more serious problem is the common procedure of "resolving" discrepancies between two raters by obtaining a third rating, a practice that results in inflated and misleading interrater reliability coefficients. Each of these problems is considered in some detail below.

Reliability and Validity

The relationship between the reliability and validity of essay tests of writing ability has rarely been discussed explicitly, let alone adequately. In fact, one of the more troublesome tendencies in the assessment literature has been the conflation of the two concepts.

Consider, for example, the study conducted by Godshalk et al. (1966). Several times in this report the authors discussed reliability and

---

[1]Even some who attempt to distinguish between interrater and instrument reliability fail to maintain the distinction or to discuss it clearly. The treatment of this issue by Lauer and Asher (1988, pp. 138-39) is problematic in this respect.

validity as if the two concepts were interchangeable. When discussing objective and essay tests of writing ability, the authors reported that

> In spite of the growing evidence that the objective and semi-objective English composition questions were *valid*, teachers and administrators in schools and colleges kept insisting that candidates for admission to college ought to be required to demonstrate their writing skill directly. In 1953 experimentation was begun on a two-hour General Composition Test, but Pearson (1955) reported that it had proved no more *reliable* than the shorter essay examinations used in earlier years. (p. 3; emphasis added)

Of course, if the General Composition test was not reliable, it could not be valid. Thus, technically speaking, there is nothing wrong with this discussion. But because reliability appears to be the sole criterion for judging validity, the passage can be read as implying that reliability and validity are interchangeable constructs. A clearer statement might have suggested that the General Composition Test had been judged not to be valid *because* it was not sufficiently reliable.

Consider another passage from the report, one in which the authors pose the central question of the study:

> The testing problem . . . may be stated as follows: How *valid* is the English Composition Test as a measure of each student's ability to write? At the time the study was designed, it was known that the *unreliability* of essay tests came from two major sources: the difference in quality of student writing from one topic to another, and the differences among readers in what they consider the characteristics of good writing. (p. 4; emphasis added)

The second source of unreliability mentioned here—"differences among readers in what they consider the characteristics of good writing"—is indeed a problem of interrater reliability. But the first source—"differences in quality of student writing from one topic to another"—is a problem not only of reliability but also of validity. Variation in performance from one topic to another results in part from natural variation in human performance (human beings cannot perfectly replicate any action or performance) and in part from differences in the writing topics. Different writing topics generally make different demands on writers and assume different kinds and degrees of background knowledge. Differences across topics are more a question of construct validity than of reliability.

Consider a final passage from the Godshalk et al. study:

> During the 1940s, when serious efforts were being made to improve the *reliability* of reading of essays, attempts were made to train readers in making a detailed analysis of each essay. . . It looked as if the efforts to

improve reading reliability had been going in the wrong direction. The solution, it seemed, was in subjecting each paper to the judgment of a number of different readers. The consensus would constitute a *valid* measure of writing, assuming, of course, that the readers were competent. (p. 4; emphasis added)

An unjustifiable assumption underlies the reasoning in this passage. The unstated assumption that all writing topics are equally valid tests of writing ability leads the authors to confound validity and scoring reliability and to suggest that the two are interchangeable, if not synonymous. This oversimplification and misrepresentation of the problem of validity in holistic assessment—reducing it to scoring reliability—is a problem not only with Godshalk et al. but with others as well (e.g., Anderson, 1960; White, 1985).

To be fair to Godshalk et al., we would have to acknowledge that their apparent assumption that a reliably scored writing sample would be a valid measure of writing ability is based on an understanding of writing ability that was current in 1966. Godshalk et al. assumed that writing ability is monolithic and manifests itself in some uniform way whenever it is tested. If this were true, their assumption that scoring reliability established validity would have some merit. But if we have learned anything about writing in the 25 years since the Godshalk et al. study, it is that writing is complex and multidimensional. The multidimensionality of writing ability requires us to maintain a distinction between reliability and validity in holistic assessment of writing.

Another source of confusion is that instrument reliability and criterion-related validity are closely related when applied to writing assessment. The only way to determine instrument reliability is to compare student performance on different writing tasks. A common method of determining validity is to correlate student performance on one task with performance on other tasks and with other measures of the same ability. But even though the methods for estimating instrument reliability and criterion-related validity are similar, the two constructs are distinct theoretically.

Instrument reliability makes a claim about what would happen if the same assessment were to be done again in the same way, with the same distribution of students, the same method of assessment, and the same general kinds of topics, but with different topics, students, and raters. Criterion-related validity, on the other hand, makes qualified, contextual claims about the validity of a test by correlating performance on a test with other measures of writing ability: objective tests, performance in a writing course, or other essay scores, for example.

Both instrument reliability and criterion-related validity are context-bound. Instrument reliability cannot be generalized to other assessment situations that do not correspond to the original one in terms of the students, the test itself, and the assessment procedures. Claims of criterion-related validity are similarly limited. The predictive validity of a test, for example, is no better than the validity of the tests with which it correlates. One of the major criticisms of standardized tests such as the SAT, GRE, and LSAT is that they mostly predict performance on one another.

Instrument reliability and criterion-related validity are similar in that they are both concerned with the kinds of generalizations that can be drawn from a given assessment. As Cronbach, Rajaratnam, and Gleser (1963) explained, when assessment is considered from the point of view of generalizability theory,

> the theory of 'reliability' and the theory of 'validity' coalesce; the analysis of generalizability indicates how validly one can interpret a measure as representative of a certain set of possible measures. (p. 157)

What this means in a practical sense is that instrument reliability approaches a common-sense notion of validity. By describing how consistently an assessment instrument measures the performance of a particular group of students on a particular kind of writing task scored in a particular way, instrument reliability comes close to describing how valid the assessment is within the given constraints. In any case, instrument reliability tells us much more about the validity of an assessment procedure than does interrater reliability.

The Reporting of Interrater Reliability Statistics

Two major problems occur with the reporting of interrater reliability statistics in writing research and evaluation: (a) a number of different methods of calculating interrater reliability have been employed, and these different procedures do not yield values that can be compared across studies and (b) reports of interrater reliability coefficients frequently do not indicate which calculations were used to arrive at a given statistic.

Psychometricians have not achieved a great deal of consensus on how to compute and report the reliability of human judgments, in part because their theoretical understanding of reliability has changed over time and in part because of differences of opinion about the most appropriate formulas for computing interrater reliability coefficients. Between 1948 and 1977, for example, at least 15 formulas for inter-observer or interrater *agreement* were proposed. Similarly, between 1950 and 1975, six different coefficients of interobserver or interrater *reliability* were proposed and debated in over 30 scholarly papers (Berk, 1979). The composition literature has reflected the inconsistency of the psychometricians in computing and reporting reliability statistics. At least eight different statistics—and probably more—have been used to compute the interrater reliability (or agreement) of holistic scoring:

- straight percentage of agreement
- Scott's *pi*
- Pearson correlation coefficient
- average intercorrelation
- tetrachoric correlation
- Spearman-Brown formula
- intraclass correlation
- Cronbach's alpha.

This wide array of interrater reliability formulas in the composition literature prompted Coffman (1971a) to lament, "Much of the literature on rating reliability of essay examinations is difficult to assess because of the great variety of procedures that have been used to estimate reliability" (p. 277; see also Coffman, 1971b; Coffman & Kurfman, 1968). Coffman has a gift for litotes. The problem with these various indices is that reliability figures based on different formulas are not comparable. There is simply no way to compare one researcher's findings based on a straight percentage of agreement with another researcher's findings based on Cronbach's alpha.

Worse than the wide variety of statistics that have been employed to calculate and report interrater reliability are the many cases in which reliability statistics are not even identified. It is not uncommon, for example, for a researcher or evaluator to claim simply that "interrater reliability was .90." Unless ".90" is identified as the result of a particular calculation and as the reliability of a single rater judgment or a composite of rater judgments, it is impossible to attach any significance to the figure or to compare it to other interrater reliability coefficients.

Fortunately, in the 1970s psychometricians applying generalizability theory to classical concepts of reliability came close to agreeing on how to think about reliability and reliability formulas. The recommendations we offer later for estimating interrater and instrument reliability derive from that emergent consensus.

Procedures Used During Holistic Scoring Sessions

The procedures used for rating texts holistically can directly affect the reliability of the scores that result. It is well known that careful training of raters can improve interrater reliabilities. In most scoring sessions, raters review and judge a number of sample texts, discuss the criteria that inform their judgments, and gradually move toward greater agreement about how to score the papers. Using two or more raters to score papers and conducting careful training sessions are both sound ways to increase the interrater reliability of holistic assessments.

A problem that occurs with some regularity, however, is that investigators will select a small subsample of texts to be rated by a large number of raters in a "trial" or preliminary rating designed to establish a theoretical interrater reliability. The difficulty is that interrater reliability calculated on the basis of this "trial" session will not reflect the reliability of judgments that are made on the basis of ratings obtained during the actual scoring. Because the more times a text is rated, the more reliable will be its composite score, reliabilities can be artificially inflated by conducting a "trial" rating with more ratings than are obtained during actual scoring. In order for an interrater reliability coefficient to be legitimate, that coefficient must be calculated on the basis of data obtained during the session itself (cf. Tinsley & Weiss, 1975, p. 373).

A much more serious problem in holistic scoring is the practice of "resolving" differences between two raters by seeking a third rating, a procedure we call the *tertium quid method*.[2] The tertium quid procedure is usually invoked when two holistic scores assigned to a given text are more than one point apart on the scale used. Several evaluators (e.g., Myers, 1980; White, 1985) recommend such a procedure, which can take any of several forms. In one version of the procedure, the third party is asked to rate the essay in question and the third score is substituted for one of the original scores. In another version, the third party is asked to choose one of the two previously assigned scores. In the first case, a text assigned scores of 2 and 4, for example, could be assigned a 2 and a 3 or a 3 and a 4. In the second case, the text would be assigned scores of 2 and 2 or 4 and 4. In the system advocated by Myers, the adjudicator "reads the paper a third time and changes one of the original scores, moving the total of the paper up or down" (1980, p. 41). (Note that this advice does not describe what to do when the adjudicator of a 2 and a 4 wants to give the paper a 3. In this case, does the composite score move up or down?)

The motivation behind the tertium quid procedure is admirable when the concern is to make sounder decisions about people's lives. After all, if two doctors disagree about whether a patient needs major surgery, the wise patient goes to a third doctor. However, in such a case, the third doctor doesn't force the odd doctor out to recant his/her opinion. In some cases, the odd doctor out will have made the correct diagnosis.

---

[2]"Tertium quid" is a term derived from medieval dialectic. It refers to a situation in which two disputants have reached a deadlock and a third party is called in to decide on a particular point in favor of one of the disputants so that the debate can proceed.

The tertium quid procedure usually involves three steps.

1. When two ratings of a text disagree by more than one point, a third rating is obtained.
2. The "bad" rating of the three is thrown out.
3. Interrater reliabilities are calculated on the basis of the new set of paired ratings.

The first step is unnecessary. From the point of view of reliability theory, which treats all rater judgments as a combination of true score and error, there is no sound reason to treat a text that receives scores of 2 and 4 differently from one that receives two 3s. Both have an average score of 3 and a summed score of 6. Because there is no a priori reason for thinking that the error in a 2-4 pair of ratings is concentrated in one of the two ratings, rather than residing in both, there is no justification for changing one of the original ratings.

The second step—throwing out a rating—is totally unjustifiable from the point of view of statistics. There is no legitimate way of distinguishing between "good" ratings and "bad" ratings in holistic scoring. In situations in which three ratings are obtained, statistical theory says that the best estimate of the true value (in this case, of writing ability) is the average of the three ratings.

The third step—calculating reliabilities on the basis of the "revised" ratings—is even worse than the second. Adjudication procedures such as the tertium quid method violate the most basic assumptions on which reliability formulas are based: that scoring error is distributed randomly, that each rating is equally likely to be erroneous, and that individual scores are independently determined. When a particular text is singled out for special treatment (for example, when a text is identified as having scores that need to be "resolved" through a third reading), the assumptions on which reliability coefficients are based are seriously compromised. *If pairs of ratings that do not agree are altered through adjudication and if a reliability coefficient is computed with the new numbers as if the numbers had occurred without intervention, the resulting coefficient will be vastly inflated and largely meaningless.*

In fact, calculating interrater reliabilities on the basis of modified ratings constitutes a kind of fraud since such a calculation is guaranteed to result in an inflated and false report of interrater reliabilities. Calculating interrater reliabilities in this way is like a defense contractor calculating the accuracy of its missiles after throwing out data for projectiles that missed their targets by more than 100 feet. It is precisely the big misses that most contribute to low reliability. Because calculating reliabilities using data resulting from the tertium quid procedure is inaccurate and misleading, the practice should be discontinued altogether in writing research and evaluation.

Interrater reliability formulas are quite sensitive to the manipulation of data through tertium quid methods, even in cases in which a relatively low percentage of scores is affected. The example shown in Table 1 demonstrates the results of the worst possible tertium quid procedure—one that forces the adjudicator to choose one of two discrepant scores and repeat it. In this example, less than 10% of the scores have been adjudicated using the tertium quid method (a percentage that may be a little higher than normal according to Myers).

Table 1. Sample Data for Showing the Effect of Tertium Quid Adjudication

Test	Rater 1	Rater 2	Tertium Quid
1	1	2	
2	2	2	
3	2	2	
4	4	3	
5	4	1	4
6	2	2	
7	2	2	
8	2	2	
9	3	2	
10	4	3	
11	4	3	
12	3	2	
13	2	2	
14	2	3	
15	1	3	3
16	3	3	
17	3	3	
18	4	3	
19	4	4	
20	4	4	
21	2	3	
22	3	3	
23	2	1	
24	3	3	
25	4	4	
26	2	1	
27	3	3	
28	2	4	2
29	4	4	
30	2	1	
31	3	3	

If the tertium quid scores are ignored, the interrater reliability coefficient for the summed scores is .63 (using formula 3b, which is discussed in a later section). If the tertium quid score is substituted for the dissimilar score in each of the three cases that have been "adjudicated," the reliability coefficient jumps to .88. Did the reliability of the assessment as a whole actually improve that much? Of course not. Calculating the interrater reliability of the complete set of scores above using a one-way analysis of variance model for situations involving unequal numbers of judgments per subject (Ebel, 1951, p. 412) results in an interrater reliability of .59 for the summed scores.[3]

The important point is that the adjudications do not significantly change the "real" reliability of the scoring session. The gain of .25 (from .63 to .88) resulting from the tertium quid procedure is entirely bogus. Substituting tertium quid scores for even a small fraction of disparate pairs can have a profound (and obviously misleading) effect on interrater reliability coefficients that are calculated for a set of holistic scores. To insure that interrater reliability figures truly reflect the reliability of holistic scoring sessions, researchers and evaluators should choose one of the following options:

- *Option 1.* Do not use the tertium quid adjudication procedure. Use the original scores and report reliabilities based on those scores.
- *Option 2.* If there is a compelling reason to use tertium quid methods to adjudicate disagreements, calculate and report the reliability of the data prior to adjudication, or use a formula such as Ebel's (1951) that takes into account all the ratings.

Each of these options will result in lower reported reliabilities. But those reliabilities will be accurate and meaningful.

ESTIMATING AND REPORTING INSTRUMENT AND INTERRATER RELIABILITY COEFFICIENTS

Estimating Instrument Reliability

Most treatments of reliability focus on "objective" tests rather than on essay testing or direct measurement of writing abilities. These discussions assume that such tests consist of a number of items that collectively cover the domain being tested. It will be helpful to review the methods used to determine the reliability of "objective" tests for two reasons: (a) understanding the procedures used for estimating the reliability of "objective" tests can contribute to a better understanding of the nature of

---

[3]This figure is lower than the original estimation of .63 in part because Ebel uses a more restrictive interrater reliability formula than is possible when all raters rate all texts.

instrument reliability and (b) we must eventually ask whether the methods used for "objective" tests can or should be adapted for tests of writing ability.

Estimating the Reliability of "Objective" Tests

Four methods have been most commonly used for determining the instrument reliability of "objective" tests: (a) comparison of equivalent test forms, (b) division of a test into equivalent halves, (c) repeated administration of a single test form, and (d) analysis of individual items to determine error variance. The first three methods rely on the calculation of correlation coefficients, the fourth on analysis of variance.

Equivalent forms. With this method of establishing instrument reliability, test makers create at least two different forms of a test, administer the test forms to the same group of subjects or to comparable groups, and then compare the scores yielded by the two forms. (See Thorndike [1951] for a discussion of issues involved in determining "equivalence.") Coefficients of correlation are used to compare the scores resulting from the two test forms. The correlation coefficient is interpreted as an indication of the reliability of the test; it represents a measure of the likelihood that the test will produce consistent results across successive administrations. A typical equivalent forms procedure for establishing the reliability of an arithmetic test, for example, would involve constructing two or more exams (or forms) with different problems but ones judged to be testing the same kinds of knowledge and to be of comparable difficulty.

Equivalent halves. This "poor person's alternative" to using equivalent forms is often referred to as the "split-halves" method. When lack of time or resources prohibits development of equivalent forms of a test, an acceptable alternative is to divide the items on the test into equivalent halves. Scores on the two halves are then compared by calculating a coefficient of correlation. As with the equivalent forms method, this correlation coefficient is interpreted as a reliability coefficient.

Repeated administration. Some abilities or traits are defined so narrowly that it does not make sense to develop equivalent tests to measure them. It would not seem useful, for example, to develop different tests in order to measure people's weight. In such cases as these it is more reasonable to administer the same test on two or more occasions. Scores from the different administrations are then correlated and the resulting coefficient interpreted as a reliability coefficient.

Analysis of variance methods. Analysis of variance techniques can also be used to estimate the instrument reliability of a test (Hoyt, 1941). When applied to a group of subjects with scores on individual items in a test, analysis of variance breaks the variance into separate components attributable to subjects, items, and error. True variance is due to real differences across subjects being tested and to differences in items on the test. Error variance is error due to chance and/or poor test questions. The ratio of true variance to error variance is, by definition, the instrument reliability of the test. The reliability coefficients developed by Kuder and Richardson (1937) are based on analysis of variance principles.

Determining the Instrument Reliability of Essay Tests

Correlation and analysis of variance techniques have been widely used for estimating the instrument reliability of "objective" tests, tests that consist of multiple items. But how should we estimate the instrument reliability of essay tests of writing ability, tests that typically consist of a single "item" to which examinees respond—that is, a writing prompt?

Three of the four methods used for establishing the reliability of objective tests are not readily applicable to essay testing. Both the equivalent forms and equivalent halves methods would require writing prompts different enough in content to avoid a practice effect but virtually identical in the demands they place on writers. This kind of equivalence is possible for tests of arithmetic but very difficult to achieve for essay tests of writing abilities.

Some research has examined how students respond to writing topics (e.g., Brossell, 1983, 1986; Brossel & Ash, 1984; Ruth & Murphy, 1984, 1988). Hoetker and Brossell (1986) showed that it was possible to vary the rhetorical specificity of a single topic without affecting student performance. But we have not yet established procedures for creating truly equivalent writing tests—tests that would be different in content but identical in the demands they place on writers. Perhaps future research will allow equivalent halves testing to establish instrument reliability. What is needed are pairs of topics that are so similar that it does not matter which one a student writes about (which was the case in Hoetker and Brossell's study) but different enough so that a student could write about both topics without having the writing of the first paper affect the writing of the second.

Trying to establish instrument reliability by having students write twice in response to the same prompt—the procedure of repeated measures—has similar problems with respect to the practice effect. If the second test is administered soon after the first, student performance on the first test will affect the second. If, on the other hand, the second administration is postponed until subjects have "forgotten" the first test, their writing abilities may well have changed and, in an important sense, they may no longer be the same people.

Largely because of these difficulties, writing researchers and evaluators have turned to analysis of variance as a way of addressing the question of instrument reliability. Thorndike (1951) suggested that "the analysis of variance approach . . . appears useful for obtaining reliability estimates from items or trials which are scored with a range of scores, and not merely as 'passed' or 'failed'" (p. 591). This method, however, requires at least two independent tests of writing. Instead of trying to create "equivalent" writing tasks, examiners sample different dimensions or domains of writing ability and correlate performances on these different domains in order to assess the instrument reliability of particular writing prompts. Scores on different tests can be correlated using one of several forms of the intraclass correlation, which we discuss in greater detail below.

Godshalk et al. (1966) and Breland et al. (1987) estimated the instrument reliability of writing prompts in this manner by correlating students' performance on one writing task with their performance on others. The instrument reliabilities Godshalk et al. reported for five writing prompts (p. 16) ranged from .435 to .592 (based on five readings of each essay). Breland et al. (p. 27) estimated that a single essay exam like those in their study would have an instrument reliability of .42 (if rated once) and .63 (if rated four times).

These two studies provide the best available estimates of the instrument reliability of essay tests of writing ability. Unfortunately, the results of these studies cannot be generalized to other writing topics or other assessment situations. Even if evaluators used one of the Breland topics in an assessment, for example, the same instrument reliability could not be assumed unless two things were true: (a) the assessment procedures (including training and raters) were indistinguishable from Breland's and (b) the examinees were indistinguishable from those in the Breland study by range of writing abilities and average writing ability.

At present, the only way to determine the instrument reliability of a given essay test of writing is for individual researchers or evaluators to obtain multiple writing samples from a representative group of subjects and intercorrelate them. The problem, of course, is the expense and time required to establish the instrument reliability of a writing test using these procedures. Most research or assessment teams are not likely to have the necessary resources at their disposal. Nevertheless, a hard fact remains: If researchers and evaluators continue to use holistic assessment without addressing issues of instrument reliability, they will do so without knowing how reliably they are assessing writing ability.

Estimating Interrater Reliability

For most "objective" tests, interrater reliability is not an issue because true/false or multiple-choice items leave no room for disagreement among scorers or raters (at least in terms of scoring itself). A particular response either agrees with the "right" answer identified by the test maker(s) or it doesn't. With essay tests of writing ability, interrater reliability has been recognized as a critical issue for many years (Coffman 1971b; Coffman & Kurfman 1968; Finlayson, 1951; Follman & Anderson, 1967; Hartog, Ballard, Gurrey, Harnley, & Smith, 1941; Huddelston, 1954; Stalnaker, 1936; Stalnaker & Stalnaker, 1934; Starch & Elliott, 1912; Traxler & Anderson, 1935; Vernon & Millican, 1954). Because there is no single "right" response to the testing instrument and because scoring depends on human judgment, it is inevitable that scorers (or raters) will not agree with one another 100% of the time.

Of the several methods of determining interrater reliability, a particular class of statistical formulas, the intraclass correlation, seems especially appropriate for holistic scoring. Tinsley and Weiss (1975) consider the intraclass correlation "the best measure of interrater reliability available for ordinal and interval level measurement" (p. 373; see also Algina, 1978; Bartko, 1976; Haggard, 1958). The intraclass correlation is based theoretically on analysis of variance, and the rationale for interpreting intraclass correlations as reliability coefficients derives from generalizability theory (Cardinet, Tourneur, & Allal, 1976; Cronbach, Gleser, Nanda, & Rajaratnam, 1972; Cronbach, Ikeda, & Avner, 1964; Cronbach et al., 1963; Gleser, Cronbach, & Rajaratnam, 1965; Rentz, 1980).[4]

According to Berk (1979), "the intraclass correlation expresses the classical theory of measurement error relationship between true and observed variance" (p. 463). The most general form of the intraclass correlation is the simple ratio of true to total variance, which we presented earlier as equation (3) and reproduce here in an equivalent but slightly different form (following Ebel, 1951, p. 409):

$$\text{reliability} = \frac{\text{true variance}}{\text{true variance} + \text{error variance}} \qquad (4)$$

A whole family of intraclass correlations has been developed, but all derive from equation (4).

Shrout and Fleiss (1979) discuss three pairs of the intraclass correlation, each of which is based on a different analysis of variance model. The formulas differ in how they define particular components of

---

[4]Analysis of variance is most commonly used as a statistical test of hypotheses regarding group differences. Generalizability theory applies similar statistical calculations somewhat differently. Instead of analyzing group differences, generalizability theory focuses on the magnitude of variance components in order to determine the ratio of true variance to error variance in a set of measurements or observations.

variance as true variance or error. In some versions of the formula, variance due to differences in mean scores awarded by raters is defined as part of the error term; in others, it is defined as part of the true variance. These differences are important for interrater reliability because definitions of true and error variance depend on how rating sessions are conducted and on the kinds of decisions evaluators intend to make.

The appropriate form of the intraclass correlation depends on a number of contextual factors associated with the assessment: (a) whether individual or composite ratings are the measure of interest, (b) whether all raters rate all texts, and (c) whether ratings are considered relative or absolute.

Below we discuss three typical holistic assessment situations. For each situation, two different forms of the intraclass correlation are introduced. The first formula in each pair (i.e., 1a, 2a, and 3a) is the appropriate equation for determining the reliability of a single rating. The second formula in each pair (i.e., 1b, 2b, and 3b) is appropriate for determining the reliability of a judgment based on summing or averaging scores across two or more raters.[5]

In most situations, researchers and evaluators make decisions based on composite scores and should calculate reliability accordingly. For example, if two ratings have been given to each text and the evaluator is using the summed score for placement purposes, calculating the reliability of the summed scores would be appropriate. In contrast, if a single score of "failing" on an exit exam would prevent a student from passing, then, in terms of reliability, a single score would be serving as the basis for judgment and the reliability of a single score, rather than a composite score, should be calculated and reported.

The three situations described below differ along two lines: (a) whether all raters rate all texts and (b) whether scores will be considered relative or absolute. Situation One describes the very common case in which, instead of scoring all the texts, individual raters score only a fraction of them. In Situations Two and Three, individual raters rate all texts available for scoring. The distinction between Situations Two and Three rests on whether scores are considered relative or absolute. In Situation Two, scores are considered absolute or criterion-referenced; in Situation Three, scores are considered relative.

Assessment Situation One. The evaluators have a large number of texts to rate and a pool of more than two raters. Each rater rates a portion, but not all, of the texts. For example, six raters might each rate one-third of

---

[5]The reliability of composite scores is the same regardless of whether they are formed by summing or averaging.

the texts. The appropriate intraclass formulas in this case are as follows:[6]

Formula 1a (reliability of single rating):

$$r = \frac{MSp - MSwp}{MSp + (k-1)\, MSwp}$$

r = reliability coefficient
MSp = between persons mean square
$MSwp$ = within persons mean square
k = number of raters

Formula 1b (reliability of summed or averaged ratings):

$$\frac{MSp - MSwp}{MSp}$$

Formulas 1a and 1b are based on a one-way, random effects analysis of variance model (see Cho, 1981).[7] When individual raters do not rate all essays, "raters" cannot be treated as an independent variable; thus, the model is "one-way," with "students" as the only independent variable. Because student writing abilities are assumed to be distributed normally, the student effect is considered random. The formulas based on the one-way random effects model take into account the fact that each rater does not rate every essay, a fact that lowers the interrater reliability of the assessment, although often by only a small amount.[8] The example below illustrates the relationships among texts, raters, and ratings in Situation One:

---

[6]The formulas given for these situations are appropriate only if one writing sample per student is elicited. The analysis of variance model gets more complicated if multiple writing samples are considered, although the same general principles discussed here apply.

[7]Glass and Stanley (1970) provide a good explanation of the distinctions among random, fixed, and mixed effects analysis of variance models.

[8]Strictly speaking, the model posited for Situation One assumes that each writing sample is rated by a different set of raters chosen randomly from a larger pool, i.e., no samples share a common set of raters, except by chance. In a typical holistic rating session, raters rate a large number of texts, and many texts are likely to share a common set of raters because texts are grouped into packets that move intact from one rater to another. This circumstance represents a mild violation of the assumptions of the analysis of variance model on which the formula for Situation One is based, but Cronbach et al. (1963) argue that "the absence of true random sampling from a pool of items or judges is unfortunate but no more so than in the ubiquitous studies that make statistical inferences from persons who are not chosen in a strictly random fashion" (p. 160). Thus, because the discrepancy is minor, the model and reliability formulas for Situation One are appropriate for cases in which individual raters do not rate all texts.

Text	Rater	Rating	Rater	Rating
1	R3	1	R5	1
2	R1	2	R4	4
3	R5	3	R1	3
4	R2	3	R6	4

Formula 1a (reliability of a single rating) = .59
Formula 1b (reliability of a composite rating) = .75

Formula 1a or 1b *must* be used when individual raters do not rate all texts in a given scoring session, regardless of whether ratings are considered relative or absolute. In Assessment Situations Two and Three, each rater rates all of the texts available in a given scoring session. The distinction between the two situations rests on whether ratings are absolute or relative. In Situation Two, scores are absolute; in Situation Three, they are relative.

Assessment Situation Two.   Each rater rates every essay. In addition, ratings are considered objective or criterion-referenced rather than relative. The raters are not simply assigning relative ratings on a scale of, for example, 1 to 6. Instead, the rating categories are tied to some outside criterion. An example would be a placement situation in which raters are trained to think of a score of 1 as meaning that a student should be placed in a remedial class, a score of 2 as meaning that a student should be placed in a regular class, and a score of 3 as meaning a student should be exempt from Freshman English.[9] The appropriate intraclass formulas for Situation Two are the following:

Formula 2a (reliability of single rating):

$$r = \frac{MSp - MSe}{MSp + (k-1)\ MSe + k/n\ (MSr - MSe)}$$

r = reliability coefficient
MSp = between persons mean square
MSr = between raters mean square
MSe = error mean square
k = number of raters
n = number of persons

---

[9]Other examples might include some forms of analytic scoring, primary trait scoring, or performative assessment (Faigley, Cherry, Jolliffe, & Skinner, 1985). The formulas presented for Situation Two might also be appropriate for many types of text analysis commonly used in writing research (e.g., asking readers to identify particular text features or to determine when text features should be considered cues to other phenomena).

Formula 2b (reliability of summed or averaged scores):

$$r = \frac{MSp - MSe}{MSp + 1/n \, (MSn - MSe)}$$

Formulas 2a and 2b are based on a two-way random effects analysis of variance model. Because all raters rate all texts, "raters" constitutes an independent variable as well as "students"; thus, the model is "two-way." "Students" is treated as a random effect as in Situation One: "raters" is treated as a random effect as well because scores are criterion-referenced. Because differences between raters' mean scores have an objective meaning, variance due to differences in rater means is included in the error term of intraclass formulas 2a and 2b.[10]

The example below uses the same hypothetical data as used for Situation One. This time, however, the columns in the table for ratings correspond to particular raters, making it possible to account for the systematic effect of raters on the scoring.

Text	Rater A	Rater B
1	1	1
2	2	4
3	3	3
4	3	4

Intraclass formula 2a (reliability of a single rating) = .65
Intraclass formula 2b (reliability of a composite rating = .76

Because scores are considered objective in Situation Two, differences in raters' mean scores must be taken into account. Between-rater variance has been factored into the error term of the intraclass formulas, resulting in lower estimates of interrater reliability than will result using the same data in Situation Three. In fact, formula 2 treats rater disagreement more strictly than does formula 3, and because it considers any differences between raters' scores as error, formula 2 can be thought of as an agreement formula (Shrout & Fleiss, 1979, p. 425).[11]

---

[10]A number of statisticians have discussed the circumstances in which it is appropriate to treat between-rater variance as true variance (Cronbach, 1951; Cronbach et al., 1963; Ebel, 1951; Shrout & Fleiss, 1979; Tinsley & Weiss, 1975). Ebel's (1951, 411ff.) discussion is accurate and detailed but somewhat confusing. Berk's (1979, p. 466) treatment of the issue is clearer and easier to follow.

[11]The terms *reliability* and *agreement* are often used interchangeably in treatments of holistic scoring and other types of judgments that raters are called upon to make about written texts. Although the two notions are related, they should be distinguished both conceptually and computationally. Space does not permit a full treatment of this issue here. Lawlis and Lu (1972), Tinsley and Weiss (1975), and Berk (1979) provide helpful discussions of this issue.

Assessment Situation Three. Each rater rates every text. In addition, ratings are considered relative rather than objective. Each rater simply evaluates the relative quality of the writing samples. An example would be a case in which a researcher wanted to identify groups with different levels of writing ability. The ratings are not tied to an outside criterion but are considered relative within the group of texts to be assessed. The appropriate forms of the intraclass formula in this situation would be the following:

Formula 3a (reliability of single rating):

$$r = \frac{MSp - MSe}{MSp + (k-1)MSe}$$

r = reliability coefficient
MSp = between persons mean square
MSe = error mean square
k = number of raters

Formula 3b (reliability of summed or averaged scores):

$$r = \frac{MSp - MSe}{MSp}$$

Formulas 3a and 3b are based on a two-way mixed effects analysis of variance model. As does the model for Situation Two, this model includes both "students" and "raters" as independent variables. "Students" is again considered a random effect, but because scores are relative rather than objective, "raters" is treated as a fixed effect. This means that the difference in average scores between two raters (or among three or more raters) is attributed to raters consistently applying slightly different standards of judgment rather than to error, and the difference in average scores is therefore considered true variance. Because the student effect is random and the rater effect is fixed, this model is described as "mixed."

The example below uses the same hypothetical data as used for Situations One and Two:

Text	Rater A	Rater B
1	1	1
2	2	4
3	3	3
4	3	4

Intraclass formula 3l (reliability of a single rating) = .69
Intraclass formula 3b (reliability of a composite rating) = .81

Because they consider raters' scores to be relative, Formulas 3a and 3b treat between-rater variance as true variance, which results in higher interrater reliability estimates than the inclusion of between-rater variance in the error term (as in Situation Two). When all raters rate all texts and scores are relative, differences among raters' mean scores are of no consequence because the differences cancel out when scores are added or averaged. It makes no difference, for example, if one rater's scores average 3 and another rater's scores average 4 as long as their judgments are consistent relative to one another.

Versions 1 to 3 of the intraclass formula are progressively less "restrictive," and coefficients will generally be higher for Situation Three than for Situation Two and in turn higher for Situation Two than for Situation One.[12] With the exception of formula 3b, which is equivalent to Cronbach's alpha, the different versions of the intraclass correlation are not easily obtained through standard statistical packages such as SAS and SPSS, but the formulas can be calculated from an analysis of variance table. An extensive knowledge of ANOVA theory and procedures is not necessary for computing the formulas; Cho (1981) provides a clear description of the necessary procedures.[13]

Needed Research on Reliability

Further research will be needed to answer a number of questions concerning the reliability of holistic assessment. Among the questions we consider most important are these: What standards should be expected for the reliability of holistic ratings? Specifically, how high should interrater reliability figures be? Should different standards apply for different assessment purposes? For example, should one standard be employed for research and another for educational decision making? For educational decision making, should different standards apply, for example, for placement testing as opposed to proficiency testing?

---

[12]It is important to note, however, that when assessments are conducted with writing topics that have been thoroughly tested and with raters who have been carefully trained, the differences among various forms of the intraclass correlation may be much less pronounced than in the examples above. In some cases, even though it would not be appropriate to calculate all versions of the formula, the different intraclass coefficients might yield very similar results. Careful testing of topics and training of raters helps to reduce random variation between ratings and between-rater variance, the most important potential sources of lower interrater reliabilities when formulas 1 and 2 of the intraclass correlation are appropriate.

[13]It is not difficult to write a computer program using Cho (1981) as a guide. A source listing of such a program in C and in BASIC is available free of charge by sending a stamped, self-addressed envelope to Paul Meyer, Department of English, Box 3E, New Mexico State University, Las Cruces, NM 88003.

How High Should Interrater and Instrument Reliability Coefficients Be?

As we suggested above, it is difficult to provide definitive expectations for interrater reliability coefficients, in part because the wide range of statistics used to calculate them reduces our ability to compare the interrater reliability figures reported in various studies.

Berk (1979) suggested that "coefficients in the .80s are indicative of a high level of agreement" (p. 467), and it does seem clear from a number of studies that interrater reliability coefficients in the .80s or .90s can be reached with careful training and monitoring of raters. In our view, however, about the best that can be said about high interrater reliabilities is that they are better than low ones. It is essential to keep in mind that high interrater reliabilities do not insure that the testing procedure as a whole is reliable. The more important concept to consider is instrument reliability.

Godshalk et al. (1966) reported an instrument reliability of .841. This figure represented the reliability of composite scores formed by summing five scores for each of five essays by each student in the study (i.e., 25 pieces of information for each subject). The instrument reliability of a single writing task in the Godshalk study was about .5.

Psychometricians generally strive for instrument reliabilities of over .8 for tests that are used to make important judgments about individuals. When a test with a reliability of .5 is used to discriminate between students at the 50th and 75th percentiles of a group, over one-third (36.8%) of those at the 50th percentile would seem to be better than those at the 75th percentile on a second testing (Sax, 1974, p. 194). What this means, of course, is that those who rely on holistic assessments of writing ability should be concerned about whether a single writing sample provides enough information to make reasonable and fair judgments about individual students.

If most holistic assessment tasks have an instrument reliability comparable to that of the tasks in the Godshalk and Breland studies (i.e., in the range of .5 to .6 for a single writing sample scored twice), then the true instrument reliability of such tests may be too low for making important decisions about individuals. There is reason to believe that the Godshalk et al. and Breland et al. studies were conducted under very favorable conditions and that studies conducted in more typical circumstances would likely result in testing instruments with even lower reliabilities.

Kelly (1927) suggested that instrument reliabilities of .5 were fine for making decisions about the behavior of groups, but he recommended instrument reliabilities of at least .94 for making decisions about individuals. Breland et al. projected achieving such a level of reliability would have required nine writing samples and somewhere between four and an infinite number of ratings of each one (p. 27). Kelly's standards would probably be considered a bit strict today, and indications are that .94 is not a realistic number for writing assessment. But most psychometricians would be very uncomfortable about using a test with an instrument reliability of only. 5 for making decisions about individuals.

Should Different Standards Apply for Different Assessment Purposes?

Reliabilities should be high enough to justify whatever decisions are being made on the basis of the scores. This is not a simple numerical answer, but it is the only good answer. Evaluators need to be concerned about the reliability of their decisions in proportion to the impact their decisions will have on individuals. Common sense and good judgment must come into play in su h situations. The more significantly a decision will affect an individual's life, the more the evaluator needs to be concerned with instrument reliability.

For research decisions for which the goal is to differentiate between or among groups, instrument reliabilities of .5 are generally considered high enough. In addition, placement decisions, although they affect people's lives, are probably not as critical as other types of educational decisions. In contrast, exit exams that determine whether a student graduates from high school or college, writing exams that determine whether a student can take advanced coursework or whether someone with a teacher's certificate will be allowed to teach—these are serious assessment decisions for which instrument reliability is critical. Anyone making such decisions based on a single writing sample for which the reliability is probably no more than .5 is on shaky ground at best.

How high should instrument reliabilities be, then? In our view, a definitive answer to this question is not possible at this time. We need additional research on instrument reliability in different assessment situations before we begin to answer the question with any confidence. Our hope is that researchers and evaluators will begin to recognize the importance of instrument reliability and that such research will be forthcoming.

What Can Be Done To Achieve Higher Instrument Reliabilities?

As we mentioned above, the procedures for determining the instrument reliability of direct writing assessments are time-consuming and costly. Although it may not be feasible for individual researchers and evaluators to undertake the necessary testing, they must still be concerned about instrument reliability and do everything in their power to achieve instrument reliabilities that are as high as possible.

A number of procedures will contribute to a higher instrument reliability. First, important decisions should be based on more than one piece of information. The more independent pieces of information used in making a decision, the more reliable the decision will be. A writing sample and an objective test can be used, as Breland et al. suggested. Or two or more writing samples can be elicited. Or a writing sample and a course grade can be used.

Second, great care should be taken in the development of writing topics and in the training of raters. The three main sources of error in the assessment of writing are the student, the test, and the assessment situation. Thorough development and testing of writing topics will help to improve instrument reliability. Careful rater training will result in higher interrater reliability and reduce error from this component. Evaluators may not have much control over student performance, but they should attempt to make the testing situation as favorable for students as possible by providing manageable topics and well-trained raters.

Finally, evaluators should develop procedures for appeal and review so that incorrect placements or assessments can be identified and corrected.

CONCLUSION

Reliability should not be regarded as a fixed, monolithic attribute of a particular testing instrument. Strictly speaking, "reliability" refers not to a characteristic (or set of characteristics) of a particular test but to the confidence that test users can place in scores yielded by the test as a basis for making certain kinds of decisions. For essay tests of writing ability, reliability is multidimensional, consisting of components associated with the test, the student, and the assessment situation. An essay test of writing ability can be said to be reliable only for a certain population for a certain purpose.

Reliability is a necessary but not sufficient condition for validity. Holistic scoring must be reliable, but reliable testing is not necessarily valid testing. For a complete understanding of the reliability of holistic assessment, we must distinguish between scoring reliability and instrument reliability. We must employ rating methods that ensure high agreement among raters, but we must also gauge the extent to which our assessment instruments yield comparable results across successive testing occasions. We must keep in mind that reliable scoring is not necessarily reliable testing.

As research on holistic scoring progresses and as writing assessments become more refined, our profession must begin to use common formulas for computing and reporting interrater and instrument reliability. In our view, much research remains to be done to provide answers to the questions still surrounding the reliability of essay tests of writing ability. We consider it imperative, however, that this research be conducted and reported using common procedures and statistics. Researchers and evaluators must begin to provide explicit, detailed descriptions of the methods and computational formulas used to arrive at estimates of interrater and instrument reliability. Only then can results be compared across studies and only then can the research community move toward informed, intelligent answers to important questions that still remain about the direct measurement of writing skills.

REFERENCES

Algina, J. (1978). Comment on Bartko's "On various intraclass correlation reliability coefficients." *Psychological Bulletin, 85*, 135-38.

Anderson, C. C. (1960). The new STEP essay test as a measure of composition ability. *Educational and Psychological Measurement, 20*, 95-102.

Bartko, J. J. (1976). On various intraclass correlation reliability coefficients. *Psychological Bulletin, 83*, 762-765.

Berk, R. A. (1979). Generalizability of behavioral observations: A clarification of interobserver agreement and interobserver reliability. *American Journal of Mental Deficiency, 83*, 460-472.

Breland, H. M., Camp, R., Jones, R. J., Morris, M. M., & Rock, D. A. (1987). *Assessing writing skill.* New York: College Entrance Examination Board.

Brossell, G. (1983). Rhetorical specification in essay examination topics. *College English, 45*, 165-173.

Brossell, G. (1986). Current research and unanswered questions in writing assessment. In K. Greenberg, H. Weiner, & R. Donovan (Eds.), *Writing assessment: Issues and strategies* (pp. 168-82). New York: Longman.

Brossell, G., & Ash, B. H. (1984). An experiment with the wording of essay topics. *College Composition and Communication, 35*, 423-425.

Cardinet, J., Tourneur, Y., & Allal, L. (1976). The symmetry of generalizability theory: Applications to educational measurement. *Journal of Educational Measurement, 13*, 119-35.

Cho, D. W. (1981). Inter-rater reliability: Intraclass correlation coefficients. *Educational and Psychological Measurement, 41*, 223-26.

Coffman, W. E. (1971a). Essay examinations. In R. L. Thorndike (Ed.), *Educational measurement.* Washington, DC: American Council on Education.

Coffman, W. E. (1971b). On the reliability of ratings of essay examinations in English. *Research in the Teaching of English, 5*, 24-36.

Coffman, W. E., & Kurfman, D. (1968). A comparison of two methods of reading essay examinations. *American Educational Research Journal,* 5, 99-107.

Cronbach, L. J. (1951). Coefficient alpha and the internal structure of tests. *Psychometrika, 16,* 297-334.

Cronbach, L. J., Gleser, G. C., Nanda, H., & Rajaratnam, N. (1972). *The dependability of behavioral measurements.* New York: John Wiley.

Cronbach, L. J., Ikeda, M., & Avner, R. A. (1964). Intraclass correlation as an approximation to the coefficient of generalizability. *Psychological Reports, 15,* 727-736.

Cronbach, L. J., Rajaratnam, N., & Gleser, G. C. (1963). Theory of generalizability: A liberalization of reliability theory. *The British Journal of Statistical Psychology, 16,* 137-163.

Davis, B. G., Scriven, M., & Thomas, S. (1987). *The evaluation of composition instruction* (2nd ed). New York: Teachers College Press.

Ebel, R.L. (1951). Estimation of the reliability of ratings. *Psychometrika, 16,* 407-424.

Faigley, L., Cherry, R. D., Jolliffe, D. A., & Skinner, A. M. (1985). *Assessing writers' knowledge and processes of composing.* Norwood, NJ: Ablex.

Finlayson, D. S. (1951). The reliability of the marking of essays. *The British Journal of Educational Psychology, 21,* 126-134.

Follman, J. C., & Anderson, J. A. (1967). An investigation of the reliability of five procedures for grading English themes. *Research in the Teaching of English, 1,* 190-200.

Glass, G. V., & Stanley, J. C. (1970). *Statistical methods in education and psychology.* Englewood Cliffs, NJ: Prentice-Hall.

Gleser, G. C., Cronbach, L. J., & Rajaratnam, N. (1965). Generalizability of scores influenced by multiple sources of variance. *Psychometrika, 30,* 395-418.

Godshalk, F. I., Swineford, F., & Coffman, W. E. (1966). *The measurement of writing ability* (Research Monograph No. 6). New York: College Entrance Examination Board.

Gulliksen, H. (1936). The content reliability of a test. *Psychometrika, 1,* 189-194.

Haggard, E. A. (1958). *Intraclass correlation and the analysis of variance.* New York: Dryden Press.

Hartog, P., Ballard, P. B., Gurrey, P., Harnley, H. R., & Smith, C. E. (1941). *The marking of English essays.* London: Macmillan. (International Institute Examinations Enquiry, Britain).

Hoetker, J., & Brossell, G. (1986). A procedure for writing content-fair essay examination topics for large-scale writing assessments. *College Composition and Communication, 37,* 328-335.

Hoyt, C. (1941). Test reliability estimated by analysis of variance. *Psychometrika, 6,* 153-160.

Huddelston, E. M. (1954). Measurement of writing ability at the college-entrance level: Objective vs. subjective testing techniques. *Journal of Experimental Education, 22*, 165-213.

Jackson, R. W. B., & Ferguson, G. A. (1941). *Studies on the reliability of tests.* Toronto: University of Toronto Press. (Department of Educational Research, Bulletin 12).

Kelly, T. L. (1927). *Interpretation of educational measurements.* Yonkers-on-Hudson, NY: World Book Co.

Kuder, G. F., & Richardson, M. W. (1937). The theory of the estimation of test reliability. *Psychometrika, 2,* 151-160.

Lauer, J., & Asher, J. W. (1988). *Composition research: Empirical designs.* New York: Oxford.

Lawlis, G. F., & Lu, E. (1972). Judgment of counseling process: Reliability, agreement, and error. *Psychological Bulletin, 78,* 17-20.

Myers, M. (1980). *Procedures for writing assessment and holistic scoring.* Urbana, IL: National Council of Teachers of English.

Rentz, R. R. (1980). Rules of thumb for estimating reliability coefficients using generalizability theory. *Educational and Psychological Measurement, 40,* 575-592.

Ruth, L., & Murphy, S. (1984). Designing topics for writing assessment: Problems of meaning. *College Composition and Communication, 35,* 410-422.

Ruth, L., & Murphy, S. 1988). *Designing writing tasks for the assessment of writing.* Norwood, NJ: Ablex.

Sax, G. (1974). *Principles of educational measurement and evaluation.* Belmont, CA: Wadsworth.

Shrout, P. E., & Fleiss, J. L. (1979). Intraclass correlations: Uses in assessing rater reliability. *Psychological Bulletin, 86,* 420-428

Spandel, V., & Stiggins, R. J. (1981). *Direct measures of writing skill: Issues and applications* (Revised ed.). Portland, OR: Northwest Regional Educational Laboratory.

Stalnaker, J. M. (1936). The measurement of the ability to write. In W.S. Gray (Ed.), *Tests and measurements in higher education.* Chicago: University of Chicago Press.

Stalnaker, J. M., & Stalnaker, R. C. (1934). Reliable reading of essay tests. *School Review, 42,* 599-605.

Stanley, J. C. (1971). Reliability. In R. L. Thorndike (Ed.), *Educational measurement.* Washington, DC: American Council on Education.

Stanley, J. C., & Hopkins, K. D. (1972). *Educational and psychological measurement and evaluation.* Englewood Cliffs, NJ: Prentice-Hall.

Starch, D., & Elliott, E. C. (1912). Reliability of the grading of high-school work in English. *School Review, 20,* 442-457.

Thorndike, R. L. (1951). Reliability. In E. F. Lundquist (Ed.), *Educational measurement* (pp. 560-620). Washington: American Council on Education.

Tinsley, E. A., & Weiss, D. J. (1975). Interrater reliability and agreement of subjective judgments. *Journal of Counseling Psychology, 22,* 358-76.

Traxler, A. E., & Anderson, H. A. (1935). The reliability of an essay test in English. *School Review, 43,* 534-539.

Valentine, C. W. (1932). *The reliability of examinations.* London: University of London Press.

Vernon, P. E. (1940). *The measurement of abilities.* London: University of London Press.

Vernon, P. E., & Millican, G. D. (1954). A further study of the reliability of English essays. *The British Journal of Statistical Psychology, 7,* 65-74.

White, E. M. (1985). *Teaching and assessing writing: Recent advances in understanding, evaluating, and improving student performance.* San Francisco, CA: Jossey-Bass.

5

Assessing the Reliability and Adequacy of Using Holistic Scoring of Essays as a College Composition Placement Technique

William L. Smith
University of Pittsburgh

INTRODUCTION

For the past 8 years, we have been conducting research at the University of Pittsburgh on our placement testing. During those years, we have examined a wide range of topics: the effects of different kinds of probe structures (cf. Smith et al., 1985), direct versus indirect measurement (cf. Garrow, 1989), the conditions under which students write their essay, the "lasting power" of placement decisions for students who defer enrolling in their first composition course, and—the four topics to be addressed in this chapter—the reliability of raters, the decisions made by split-resolvers, the adequacy of the raters' judgments, and the training of raters.

In this chapter, I first provide some necessary background on the University of Pittsburgh composition and testing program, on types of direct assessment, and on problems specific to placement testing. Then I present and discuss our research on the four topics. Finally, I present my tentative conclusions and discuss the implications of what we have learned.

During the past two decades, many colleges and universities have changed their composition courses from one or two courses required of all students to a set of "differentiated" courses where each course is designed to meet the specific needs of students with specific writing problems and abilities. In such a curriculum, the students are required to take a specific course or a sequence of courses tailored to their individual needs.

Two interrelated reasons have motivated this change. First, there has been an increase in the amount of research on composition; thus, we know more about the composing processes of writers and more about the characteristics and problems of student writers. Second, because of this research, we are better able to distinguish the needs of each student, and we have found that requiring the same courses of all students does not adequately serve the needs of individual students.

In some cases, this change was accomplished by adding a "remedial" course for those students considered to be less able writers. In other cases, the entire curriculum was altered to provide several courses appropriate for the needs of every student, from those students with significant problems to those with superior abilities. Regardless of the kind or amount of change, the new system requires a method for determining which students should take which courses. The efficacy of the system depends upon the adequacy of the placement test.

Two types of placement tests have emerged in the literature. The first uses indirect measures of writing. That is, writing ability is measured by performance on standardized, "objective" tests which test "about writing." The most commonly used are the SAT, the Test of Standard Written English (TSWE), and locally created tests. The second type of placement test was developed in reaction to the first, for it had become apparent that there were flaws in indirect measurement. This second type, direct measurement, requires students to write an essay which is then read and rated using a method generically called holistic rating (Cooper, 1977; Williamson, this volume).

Although the value of the two types continues to be debated at meetings and in journals, it has become increasingly evident that composition specialists favor direct measurement for both measurement and political reasons. Even staunch supporters of objective tests have been persuaded that holistic ratings are valid, useful, and sufficiently reliable (e.g., Rentz, 1984).

A considerable amount of research has been conducted on the methods for conducting holistic ratings, on the training of raters, and even on the cost of holistic ratings (Veal & Hudson, 1983). However, little research has been conducted on holistic rating for placement testing, and the question of validity has not been sufficiently addressed. Because validity carries a considerable amount of baggage (see chapters by Camp, this volume, and Williamson, this volume, for more discussion), I, instead, address the question of "adequacy of placement" into writing courses. This avoids controversy about the kinds of validity and allows me to focus more precisely on what I consider to be the real validity issue for placement testing in writing. The question of adequacy has not been addressed, I believe, because we have seen no need to do so.

In conversations with colleagues from other universities using holistic ratings of essays (direct measurement) as their placement method (i.e., universities which have differentiated composition courses), I have found a general consensus: only about 5% of the students are misplaced and, thus, must be moved (usually early in the term) to a different course. Five percent is certainly a most tolerable error rate; human judgment cannot be expected to be much more precise. Thus, anecdotal evidence would indicate that placement based on holistic rating of essays is adequate. However, if one probes a bit deeper, cracks appear in this facade. In most cases, the determination that a student has been misplaced is made by the classroom teacher. I interviewed my fellow composition teachers at the University of Pittsburgh about their reasons and procedures for suggesting that a student should be placed into a different course. Their responses indicate that they do not want to make many changes on their class roster; in particular, they don't want new students coming into their courses after the first or second week of class. Thus, they do not move as many students as an external reader might, yet external readers are seldom used because the expense is too great. Therefore, our sense that our method is adequate is based on only a belief, a belief which, not surprisingly, keeps us from questioning the placements and the method.

PITT'S COMPOSITION AND PLACEMENT PROGRAMS

Pitt's composition program is based on four concepts (or dimensions):

1. That writing is an effort to make meaning;
2. That writing is closely related to reading;
3. That to make meaning a writer must develop a sense of authority; and
4. That students gradually come to that sense of authority.

Consequently, in all of our courses, the students respond to a sequence of assignments on a central topic (see Coles, 1981, Bartholomae, 1983, and Bartholomae & Petrosky, 1987, for more detailed expositions of the basis of the program). It is also important to note that we do not consider composition courses to be "service" courses. That is, they are not intended, specifically, to train students to write for other courses in the university. Consequently, we, for example, do not have students write research papers, nor are they required to write papers in the various modes (narrative, exposition, etc.).

Because our students have varied abilities along these dimensions, the composition program consists of three courses, each addressing different writing problems and different writing abilities. Course A is designed for students who have serious writing problems which indicate problems with reading and appropriating a text they have read. These students' essays lack development of ideas, lack coherence, are not well organized, and do not address the issue. Commonly, these students either inadequately summarize what they are asked to read or make general statements about the issue or topic. But they do not interrelate what they read with their own ideas. These students also typically have patterns of surface-level errors caused by their inability to read and proofread.

Course B is designed for students who have significant writing problems (e.g., coherence, development of ideas, and organization), but these problems are not related to their ability to read a given passage. Instead, they indicate a lack of a sense of text and a lack of authority. Surface error is common in their texts, typically caused by their lack of a sense of text. If asked whether they read their own texts as they read other texts, they will say they do not, and if pressed for reasons, they will say that their own writing does not merit such reading.

Course C is designed for students who have the ability to read and make meaning but need more experience in developing their abilities, particularly in dealing with problematic texts and in using writing as a means for working their way through complex problems.

Some students are exempted from these courses because the writing ability they demonstrate on the placement test suggests that these courses would not be of significant value to them. Thus, when we conduct our placement ratings, we use a 4-point nominal scale: Course A, Course B, Course C, and Exempt. I will also use "D" or "Course D" to refer to Exempt.

The Testing Program

Nearly all of the students at Pitt write their placement essay during the summer months prior to enrolling. A few, primarily those who are transferring to Pitt, write their essays at other times. Those who come during the summer write their essays in large groups during five or six sessions spread across the summer. They come to campus to take a battery of placement tests (math, foreign language, etc.), for orientation to college, and to register for courses. The session to which each is assigned is based on the student's preference. Because our composition program is based on the interrelation of reading and writing, the students are given a passage to read and a series of questions designed to focus their response. These prompts, therefore, closely resemble the assignments given students in the courses. They are allowed 2 hours to finish the task. Our research on time allowed and time taken indicates that less than 5% of the students use the full 2 hours, so the time allowed seems ample.

The essays are rated immediately after the students finish writing them. Our standard procedure has been to use the composition faculty to read and rate the essays. Each essay is read by two primary raters who provide independent placement decisions. If they are in agreement (the no-split condition), the student is placed into that course. If there is disagreement (the split condition), a third reader, a split-resolver, reads and rates the essay, determining final placement.

The raters are paid for their services. Reading placement essays is not required; it is not part of anyone's contract. Reading is not expected of junior faculty or graduate students. The teachers who volunteer to read do so by choice. Consequently, the pool of readers is composed primarily of graduate students and part-time instructors.

As Director of Testing, I select all readers. Typically, all who apply participate in at least one session. Some are selected for all sessions. The readers know that I conduct research on placement testing, and several have worked with me on various studies. Many are conducting their own research (including dissertations) in the area of composition. All teachers have access to all of the data from the studies.

A TYPOLOGY OF DIRECT ASSESSMENT

All direct assessments are not the same; there are several different types which can be put into two groups according to the purpose/effect of the testing. The first, the one almost exclusively reported in the literature, is to assess writers' abilities by assessing the quality of written compositions—but with no direct impact on the writer. That is, regardless of the results, the writers are not affected by their grade in course, progress in curriculum, or placement into or out of a course. Quite commonly, the results of such assessment are used to draw conclusions about writing ability (e.g., research on instructional methods or large-scale descriptive studies such as the National Assessment of Educational Progress studies), but these conclusions apply only to groups of writers, not individuals. Such assessment would more precisely be called "assessment of writer-groups through direct assessment of text."

When this is the purpose, the researcher/tester has great freedom in the ways the assessment can be designed and in the ways the data can be analyzed. For example, the scale can have any number of points and the final rating can be derived in at least three ways:

1. The raters' ratings on each essay can be summed. This technique creates greater variance and gives the appearance of spreading out the scale.

2. The final rating for each essay can be the average of the raters' ratings. This technique produces lower variance than summing, but it too spreads the scale by creating "between-scale-point" scores (e.g., 2.5 or 2.33).

3. The final rating for each essay can be the modal rating for that essay. This results when either several raters are used or split decisions between the two primary raters are resolved by a third rater. When the primary raters agree, then that rating is the modal rating, but when they disagree, the split-resolver's rating creates the modal rating. When the primary raters disagree by more than one scale point, it may be necessary to use more than one split-resolver. This technique provides a single score and has lower variance. Its advantage is that it may provide the best (i.e., most agreed upon) score; its disadvantage is that a text may require several readings, and that is why it is seldom used.

The scale may be whatever is desired, and the technique used to derive the final score depends on what the user desires to learn. But there is a tradeoff: as one increases the number of scale points, the readers must make finer distinctions, and this decreases the probability of agreement between readers.

The second type is to assess the writers' abilities by assessing the essays—but with a direct impact on the writer. That is, the real purpose is not to assess the text but to assess the writer in order to make a decision about that writer. This purpose underlies all placement testing, either into courses (e.g., preenrollment placement into diversified college composition courses) or out of courses (commonly called "exit exams" or "competency exams"). This purpose would more precisely be called "assessment of individual writers through direct assessment."

When a decision about an individual is the purpose of assessment, the scale and technique used to derive the final score will depend on the constituency being served. If that constituency is broad, for example, several schools or colleges, each with different curricula and/or pedagogy, the scale and the techniques used can be the same as described above for the first purpose. Each school or college would then establish local cut-off points for each course placement.

However, when the constituency is one school or college, the scale and the techniques are limited. The scale must be curriculum derived; that is, each scale point (or set of scale points) must represent a specific course, and thus, the real purpose of the assessment is to use the student's text as a window into that student so as to place the student into the course which best matches his/her needs and abilities. The technique used must produce a final score which refers to a course. Thus, the raters' ratings cannot be summed, for that would produce "below/above course" scores. It would be necessary to determine, through rather extensive research, how to place students with those scores. The scores cannot be averaged, for that too would produce "between course" scores (e.g., 2.5) which do not correspond to any course. Thus, modal ratings are most commonly used. When the primary raters (usually two) agree, that is the modal score. If these raters disagree, the split-resolver creates the modal score, or sometimes creates the final score when the primary raters disagree by more than one scale point. (From discussions with colleagues at other universities, I have found none which use multiple split-resolution to determine a modal final score.) Cherry and Meyer (this volume) present an extended discussion of the issues involved with split-resolution.

Although there is a considerable body of literature on direct assessment, little is devoted to placement testing (e.g., Alexander & Swartz, 1982; Smith, Winters, Quellmalz, & Baker, 1980; Smith et al., 1985). Even the best works on testing in composition (e.g., White, 1985) devote little space to this type of testing. Furthermore, no research has been done on the relationships between the two purposes of direct assessment. No one has examined how a difference in purpose might affect the motivation of the writers and, thus, the quality of their texts. No one has compared, using the same texts, how the two purposes affect final ratings or the distribution of ratings or the way raters read and rate the essays. Therefore, I will limit my interpretations only to placement testing within a local constituency.

Although we publicly call our method for assessing incoming freshmen and transfers holistic rating, it should really be called placement rating because it is significantly different from prototypic holistic rating. Placement rating is like holistic rating in that the readers use the basic holistic method: a single, quick reading leading to a single, overall judgment. Placement rating is also somewhat like analytic rating because the raters are looking for specific features in the text. However, placement rating is unlike either holistic or analytic rating in three very important ways.

First is the basis on which the judgment is made. In holistic rating, the rating scale (for example, 1 to 6 with 6 being the best score) is preset, but the top and bottom points on the scale are determined by the quality of the essays within the set of essays to be rated, and at least one essay from the set must receive top and bottom scores. There can be no empty cells because the set determined the range. Typically, the leader (or some group) selects, from within the set, some essays which represent the points on the scale. The readers then use these "range finders" or "calibrators" to target their reading. This method prevents readers from rating too idiosyncratically. The method also creates higher agreement among the raters. The important point here is that the meaning of the points on the scale is internally derived; it depends on both the range finders and the range of the essays in the set to be rated. Consequently, the results from one holistic rating cannot be compared with another rating—even if they have the same number of scale points—because the range of the essays might differ. If an essay were placed in two sets of essays, it could receive quite different ratings.

In placement rating, the points on the scale are externally derived. They do not refer to the range of the essays in the set but instead to the specific courses (the differentiated composition courses). The scale is, therefore, based on the curriculum, the assumptions about composition, and the purposes of each course. But not on the set of essays. Range finders, therefore, exemplify the kind of writing indicative of each course.

This first difference is crucial because, to claim that placement testing is adequate and fair, we must be able to demonstrate that students entering in one year would be given the same placement if they entered in another year. It even must be possible that, given an abnormal distribution of incoming students, no one would receive one of the ratings, for example, noone would receive a placement in Course A, because no student wrote an essay which evidenced those characteristics. Furthermore, since it is not likely that the distribution of students will remain exactly the same across years, it must also be the case that the distributions from the placement ratings will vary. Thus, one test of the validity of placement rating is that the distribution across years is not constant. If it does remain constant, then it is highly likely that students are being placed in order to fill seats in classes, not to put them in the most appropriate class. This changing distribution, of course, creates a problem for administrators, for they must change, often at the last minute, the number of sections of each course.

The second difference is in the final decision derived from the scale. In typical holistic ratings, the ratings are numbers (e.g., 1 to 6, with 6 being the highest score) and the final score can be either the average of the primary raters' scores (e.g., 1 and 2 becomes a 1.5) or the sum of those raters' ratings (e.g., 1 and 2 becomes 3). If a split-resolver is used when the two primary raters disagree, one can either use the modal score (Rater 1 gives a 2, Rater 2 gives a 3, Split-resolver gives a 3; final score becomes 3), or one can average all three ratings (2 and 3 and 3 become 2.7). None of these are possible in placement testing because that would produce between-course scores. That's one of the reasons why I use letters rather than numbers in our placement rating. Letters cannot be summed or averaged. (I will present an argument later that numerical scales cannot be used in any holistic rating.) In placement testing, each scale point refers to a course. Since there is no 2.5 course (or B-C course), there can be no 2.5 final score. Furthermore, the problem of numerical scales is exacerbated when the primary raters disagree by more than one scale point or when the split-resolver does not agree with either primary rater. In a typical holistic rating where numerical ratings are used, if Rater 1 gives a 1, Rater 2 gives a 2, and the Split-resolver gives a 3, the final score is usually a 2. However, in placement testing, there is no final decision. There is no agreement, so there is no resolution. The student apparently exhibits characteristics of all three courses. Thus, the essay must be read by additional raters until some resolution is reached. Fortunately, we have found that such splits do not occur often. Nevertheless, they do occur, and they cannot be resolved through simple arithmetic.

The third difference is in the impact of the assessment. In typical holistic ratings, the focus is on the text, on placing the texts on a scale. But there is no immediate, direct impact on the student who wrote the text. In placement testing, there is a very direct impact. Some students will be required to take more courses (in some universities, these courses do not carry credit toward graduation), and any error in placement will mean that the students are not being well served, and their needs are not being addressed. This has to put an additional burden on the raters, especially since the raters used for placement testing are almost always teachers of the composition courses.

PROBLEMS SPECIFIC TO PLACEMENT TESTING

All direct assessment of writing has inherent problems. For example, the amount of time the writers are allowed, the physical context within which they write, and the topic on which they write all may affect the results. Placement testing has these additional problems as well as others. In the sections below, I discuss some of these.

The Pragmatics of Testing

The pragmatics of the rating are not the same as the pragmatics of other types of direct assessment. In many cases, and certainly in Pitt's case, the raters are drawn from a limited pool—those who teach the composition courses and wish to serve as raters. Since almost all of our placement rating is done during the summer, the pool is further limited to those who are available then. A second pragmatic difference is the time allowed for the rating. In other types of direct assessment, there is no crushing deadline for finishing the job. At Pitt, the students come to campus for three days, during which they take all placement tests (composition, math, foreign languages, etc.) and are registered for courses. The composition placement rating team is given the essays immediately after the students finish writing them, and they must finish the rating immediately so that the students' academic advisors can register them for the appropriate courses during the following day. Thus, speed— efficiency—is important in placement rating. Until a few years ago, the students wrote their essay in the afternoon, and, thus, we had to rate them in the evening, often finishing near midnight. This took its toll on the raters in two ways. First, the pool of raters was reduced because fewer were willing to work in the evening, and, second, raters became less efficient and probably less effective. Now the students write in the morning, and we rate during the afternoon. Although there is no conclusive data on the effects of when one writes—and we may put some students at a disadvantage—the raters tell me that they now feel better about their ratings.

Size of the Set of Essays to be Rated

Although there is no conclusive evidence, the general belief is that the size of the set may affect the results. Larger sets produce better (more generalizable, more reliable, more valid, etc.) results. In other types of direct assessment the scale itself affects the size of the set, for there must be at least one essay in each point. If the scale is 1 to 8, the set must be larger than if the scale is 1 to 4. There must also be enough essays so that range finders can be found within the set for each scale point. Since these other types of testing concern groups of writers, not individual writers, the size of the set also affects statistical analyses. Although placement testing is not concerned with groups and statistical analyses are of secondary importance, it still may be the case that the size of the set is important. This situation, then, creates a problem for placement testing because, although most of our students (about 90%) are tested in large groups during the summer, the remainder dribble in during the year. They are tested in small groups, or even may be the only person being tested that day. Yet, they need placement results in order to register, so their essays cannot be shelved until some critical mass is reached. These essays must be rated in smaller sets.

In placement testing, all students must be afforded the same potential for an adequate, fair decision. Thus, the size of the set question is not just "Does the size of the set affect the raters and their ratings?" but also "Is there a difference between writing in a small group and in a large group?" "Do students perform the same in both conditions?" "What is the minimum size of the necessary critical mass?" The last question is especially important for us.

The Rating Scale and the Raters' Construal of It

The rating scales for placement and other types of testing differ on how they are determined. Placement testing must have at least one scale point for each possible placement, a constraint not affecting other types of testing. But there may be another, more important, difference. In other types of testing, the scale is assumed to be linear and the "distance" between scale points is the same. This condition is necessary if parametric statistics are used. Furthermore, it is assumed that the scale points abut each other, and that the raters have similar ranges for each point. Noone, of course, assumes that the scale points are really points on a scale. They are ranges. During the calibration training, each rater infers from the range-finding essays and the group discussion the range for each point.

Schematically, these assumptions look like Figure 1 (my reason for using letters rather than numbers will become apparent shortly).

Rater 1	Scale-point A	Scale-point B	Scale-point C	Scale-point D
Rater 2	Scale-point A	Scale-point B	Scale-point C	Scale-point D

Figure 1. The Assumed Scale with Equal Scale-point Ranges.

However, any deviation from this assumption creates serious problems. Assume, for example, that the scale-point ranges are not identical. Then the diagram might look like Figure 2.

Scale-point A	Scale-point B	Scale-point C	Scale-point D

Figure 2. An Alternative Scale with Non-equal Scale-point Ranges.

If the scale points are not the same size, then the distance between the mid-points of any two adjacent scale points is not the same, and in this particular case, most of the essays would fit into "B" and "C". I derived this scale by examining the percentage of essays receiving each of the 1 to 4 scores in several pieces of published research. None of the studies I have read have had equal numbers of essays in each scale point. This finding is predictable since one would expect more essays in the middle. Nevertheless, this also means that one could declare the values of the mid-points of the four scale points to be 7, 28, 66, and 93 (a simple conversion of the percentage of essays in each scale point) instead of 1, 2, 3, and 4. The new numbers would alter the statistical results, especially if one averages split decisions. All A/B splits would be 17.5, yet this point actually falls within the range of scale point B.

But there is a more troubling possibility. One could assume that the higher frequency of essays in the middle scale points is caused by normal distributive effects, that is, most students fall into the middle ranges. Yet, it is also possible that the raters infer or possess different sized scale point ranges, and thus more essays would fit into their larger ranges. No research has been conducted to determine whether a change in the calibration would alter the resulting distribution. (For example, would making the range of scale point A larger alter the final distribution?) Our assumption of linearity and equal intervals remains an assumption, and probably not a valid one. The implications of these scaling assump-tions for placement testing is profound. If one changes the range of a scale point, the number of students placed into that course should change proportionally, and if the size of the range varies from year to year (or within a year from rating session to rating session), we cannot claim that all students are being treated fairly.

In all the studies I have read, there has been less than perfect interrater agreement. Disagreement can be caused by rater error (the common assumption), but it might also be caused by raters having different sized scale-point ranges. For example, consider the two raters diagrammed in Figure 3.

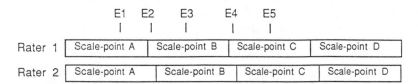

Figure 3. The Effect on Raters' Decisions When a Scale Has Non-equal Scale-point Ranges.

If both raters were given the five essays labeled E1 through E5, they would agree on only three—E1 (both would say "A"), E3 (both would say "B"), and E5 (both would say "C"). However, on E2, Rater 1 would say "B" whereas Rater 2 would say "A", and on E4, Rater 1 would say "C" whereas Rater 2 would say "B". The percentage of disagreement would indicate low interrater reliability, but each rater might have perfect intrarater reliability.

There is also one other reason why there is such great consistency in the distributions cited in the literature. It is possible that the raters have a sense of how many students should be placed into each scale point; they may have a "distribution mind-set." Raters do not expect to find 10 "1's" in a stack of 20 essays. This "distribution assumption" has profound implications for placement testing. Since placement raters are almost always teachers of the composition courses into which the students are placed, they know roughly how many students should be placed into each course. Consequently, they may force the students into the expected distribution.

Because this possibility of a distribution mind-set is so important, I conducted a study of our raters to determine whether they would force an abnormal distribution into the expected distribution. From a batch of previously rated essays, I selected an abnormal distribution. For our four placements, the typical distribution (plus or minus 3 or 4%) is Course A, 5%; Course B, 35%; Course D, 59%; and Exempt, 1%. The distribution I gave the raters was Course A, 6%, Course B, 56%, Course C, 38% and Exempt, 0%. The distribution they returned was not remarkably (or statistically) different from the one I gave them. Consequently, I concluded that our raters do not have a distribution mind-set. This study involved a relatively simple procedure and required less than 1 hour of each rater. If similar studies were conducted in nonplacement testing, we would have greater confidence in the distributions.

The assumption that the scale point ranges abut each other is also tenuous, given the fact that disagreements among raters are normal. During range finding, the raters determine their ranges for each scale point, but that doesn't mean that the scale points abut. Instead, there may be gaps, grey areas, and between-scale points. Schematically, a rater's ranges might look like Figure 4:

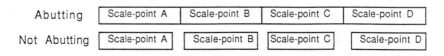

Figure 4. A Comparison of Abutting and Non-abutting Scale-points.

This diagram can be altered further if the rater has scale point ranges and grey areas of different sizes. For example, Figure 5 shows two raters with different sized scale point ranges and different sized grey areas:

If these two hypothetical raters were given the nine essays (labeled E1 through E9), they would agree on four (E1=A, E3=B, E6=C, and E9=D). For the remaining five essays, there is potential for disagreement. E2 is a coin flip for Rater 1; it is exactly in the middle of the grey area between scale points A and B. For Rater 2, the probable rating would be A, but at least some of the time, the rating could be B. E4 would be a consistent B for Rater 1, but not consistently for Rater 2. Similarly, E5 would be

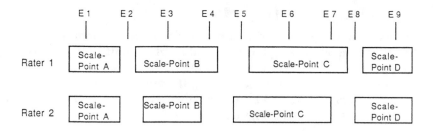

Figure 5. The Effect on Raters' Decisions When a Scale Has Non-equal, Non-abutting Scale-point Ranges.

consistently a C for Rater 2, but not for Rater 1. E7 and E8 would also follow this pattern. Thus, interrater reliability could range from 44% to 100%. However, intrarater reliability would be quite different. Assuming that any essay within a scale-point range will consistently be given that rating and those in the grey areas would not, Rater 1's intrarater reliability would be higher than Rater 2's.

In theory, both the grey area and the different sized scale-point problems could be resolved with sufficient calibration training with an adequate number of essays representing the range of each scale point. However, the number of essays needed would be large because there would have to be, at the very least, essays representing the lowest and highest end for each scale point (the middle could then be inferred). Thus, for a 4-point scale, assuming four essays are sufficient to allow raters to infer each "end," 32 well-chosen essays would be required. If the scale has more than four points, the number of essays needed increases at least proportionally.

The "Fit" of the Students to the Scale

While the grey area hypothesis is only a hypothesis for anything other than placement testing, it is almost a certainty for placement testing. If we assume that the writing abilities (or whatever is being measured) of the students are distributed on a continuum, the probability of having courses which adequately overlay this continuum is small. The more likely case is that at least some of the students do not fit neatly into the courses. Some are between courses, and these are the students who pose the most difficult placement problems for raters .

It is also highly probable that students do not fit one continuum; their abilities may instead be arrayed on several continua, but the courses may not match those continua. In the research I have conducted, I have found that those grey areas are very real, and that different raters have different sized grey areas.

Determining Adequacy of Placement

The issue of adequacy of the raters' decisions is of importance to all direct assessment testing, but it crucial in placement testing. In other types of testing, there is no external metric to allow one to determine adequacy directly. In placement testing, the assessment of adequacy can be more carefully measured by triangulating several data sources, none of which is adequate by itself. There are at least five data sources:

1. The number of students who are moved to a new course at the beginning of the term because they were misplaced;
2. The final course grades of the students in each course;
3. The students' impressions (during and after the course) of the degree to which the course met their needs;
4. The teachers' impressions of how well the students fit into their courses; and
5. Exit exams (or other "posttests").

Keeping records of the number of students moved to different courses at the beginning of the term provides some information, but that information contains some serious flaws. In most colleges, the classroom teacher (perhaps with the help of senior faculty or some other panel) makes the decision to move the student. This method is practical, for to retest all students during the first week of the term would be impossible. But, there are factors other than writing ability (or "fit to course") which affect the teachers' decisions. In interviews with our teachers, I have found that they do not want to move many students because that would create openings and, thus, other students could transfer into their courses. In effect, this means that the first week must be repeated for those new students. The teachers, especially those teaching the courses for "lower ability" students, have also told me that they don't want to move a "high" student, not because that student will write better, more enjoyable essays, but because they can use that student as a leader, a type of teacher, in the class. Several have said that they believe in their abilities, so they don't move a low student because they feel certain they can bring that student up to an acceptable level. (Our data on exit exams indicates that their belief is not bravado. I am convinced that writing teachers can bring any willing student, or any number of willing students, up to an acceptable level of writing, but not for several terms in a row. The toll on their morale would be too great.)

Final course grades are also useful, but they too are problematic. In theory, the distribution of grades in each course should be the same. If it is not, then there is either a problem in placement (a skew toward higher grades in a course would indicate that the students may have been misplaced low) or a problem in the way the teachers are grading (e.g., if a lower course has a distribution skewed toward higher grades, the teachers may be assuming too little of their students). The final grade distributions, by themselves, cannot determine which of these possibilities is most likely. But in concert with other data, the grades become important. Determining how to calculate final grades is also a problem. Different teachers may have different standards for the grade "B". For some, it can mean "acceptable performance," for others, "noteworthy performance." To control for this teacher difference, one can use a median grade analysis. Instead of using the actual grades, the median grade for each class or each teacher is determined, and then the students are sorted in three groups: above the median, on the median, and below the median. The number of students on the median will be very small if one includes, as we do, the "plus" and "minus" grades. This method also helps to control for nonwriting reasons for grades. Students can fail because their writing performance was inadequate, because they quit coming to class, or because they did not hand in enough assignments. The latter two are not related to writing performance but to "studenting" performance. Studenting performance is not a minor factor in final grades. A strong case can be made that teachers cannot grade just writing performance because they know too much about the students and because they, being human, are affected by the way students act in class.

Although I would not trust students' impressions if they were gathered during the course (students placed into lower courses commonly do not believe they belong there), impressions gathered after the course can be quite useful. For example, my interviews with our Course C students who had previously been in Course A or Course B indicates that they feel more ready to tackle the kinds of assignments given in Course C and have a better understanding of what the teachers (and the program) are looking for. That is, they have a better understanding of the rhetorical context for instruction in Course C. This perception, however, must be weighed in relation to final grades and teachers' perceptions, for our data indicate that many of these "move from A or B into C" students do not perform as well as the students who were placed directly into Course C. Furthermore, many of the "move from A or B into C" students realize that they would be in serious trouble if they had been placed directly into Course C.

Teacher perception of how well the students fit into their courses may be the best single measure, but it too has problems. It is important to restate here that placement testing places students, not essays, but it does so on the basis of one essay. Teacher perception, however, is based on several essays from each student (and even multiple drafts of each essay), and is also based on knowledge of the student as a student and as a person. In our research we have found that teacher perception of the adequacy of placement changes considerably across the term. During the first two weeks, the teachers have too little evidence, so their perception wavers considerably. After mid-term, in our 15-week term, their perceptions correlate very highly with final grades. Thus, I have concluded that teacher perception data must be collected somewhere near the end of the first third of the course, between week 3 and week 5. I will discuss teacher perception data more thoroughly later.

Exit exams (or other posttests) are becoming more common, especially for students placed into lower or remedial courses. These exams are similar to final grades, but the data, even if it is just pass/fail, can provide useful evidence about placement adequacy because, unlike final grades, only the students' writing is being considered (I assume that a student's teacher is not one of the judges). As any teacher of composition knows, occasionally a student whom we award a "B" or even an "A" will fail the exit exam, and it is even more common for a student whom we consider weak (a "D" or "F" student) to pass. The discrepancy may be attributed to making the decision based on one essay versus the teachers' many essays, but it is also probable that the teachers' grades are based on much more than just writing performance.

As a package, these five measures can provide direct evidence about the adequacy of placement. One would conclude that the placement testing was adequate if the following conditions were met:

1. The number of students moved is near the norm;
2. Final grade and exit exam distributions are as expected;
3. The students believe the course met their needs; and
4. The teachers are pleased with the students put in their courses.

Any deviation from this pattern should trigger research into the reasons for the possible problems.

A side note: These five measures are useful in other contexts as well. For example, each year Pitt admits a small population of "at-risk" students. These five measures provided the following information which our administrators found very useful:

1. Although the students are considered at risk in general, they are not all at risk in writing. Their placement distribution is skewed low, yet many are placed into our Course C, and they cannot be distinguished from the general population on the other measures.
2. We have found a difference between the at-risk students placed into Course A and those placed into the other courses. Those who take Course A during their first term (our Fall term) do not perform as well as those who wait a term before taking the course. This pattern does not exist for the regular admits, and there is no similar pattern among the at-risk students who are

placed into Course B or Course C. Thus, at least as far as writing is concerned, the at-risk population cannot be considered one population. We hypothesize that "socialization to college" may be a stronger factor for some than for others. The logical conclusion should be to have the at-risk students take Course A during their second term. However, this might put them at risk in other courses where writing is important. We have not yet resolved this Catch 22.

Public Accountability

What makes placement testing so different from other types of testing is the direct impact on each student. Any mistakes have a personal effect on the number of courses the student must take (and possibly on the tuition bill) and even on the student's sense of self-worth. A student who believes she is a competent writer but who is required to take a "remedial" course (in some colleges, such courses carry no credit) is likely to feel both frustration and self-doubt, and the parents who are paying for the courses are distressed. My experience with such students and parents has taught me that public accountability is a necessity. If I can provide data on our placement testing, data to which appropriate administrators are privy, students and parents are much more likely to accept the placement decision. Moreover, students who accept the decision are less likely to resist the teachers' efforts.

If the student is misplaced, the classroom teacher will also feel resentment. By its very design, placement testing is supposed to presort students so that teachers can be assured that their students match what they plan to teach. Thus, for the sake of the composition program, the teacher, the students, and their parents, research on placement testing makes sense.

THE RESEARCH STUDIES

As I stated previously, we have been conducting research on placement testing for several years. In the sections below, I will focus on two of our topics: rater reliability and the adequacy of placement decisions. Entailed within these topics are the two other topics promised in the intro-duction—split-resolvers and training of raters.

Rater Reliability

It is generally agreed that in all direct assessment, including placement testing, raters must be highly reliable, that is, give the same ratings to the same essays. There are two common methods for increasing reliability.

The first, and most common, is to train or "calibrate" the raters in practice sessions so that they come to agreement prior to rating the essays (see Myers, 1980, and White, 1985, for methods). It is generally agreed that the minimum acceptable level of agreement is .70 (Cooper, 1977). The other method, one particular to placement testing, is to use raters who have taught the range of courses and thus are perceptive to the kinds of students typical of each course. This creates what might be called a local discourse community calibration (cf. Follman & Anderson, 1967, concerning homogeneity versus heterogeneity of raters [academic experiential backgrounds] as sources of reliability and unreliability). To increase that reliability, the raters participate in practice sessions, typically before each rating session.

Practical knowledge tells us that even two highly trained readers commonly disagree about the relative quality of a text. This potential for disagreement is especially true if we believe that students' texts are a form of literature—that is, if the purpose of writing is to make meaning (cf. Bartholomae, 1983, and many others). This is a crucial point in the research presented below, for the curriculum and the pedagogy driving each of our composition courses are built on this belief. However, disagreements about quality do not necessarily mean disagreements about placement because the raters focus on the writer, not the quality per se of the text. Disagreements about placement, then, may be quite different than disagreements about quality. But this does not mean that disagreements will not occur in placement testing, or that they should not occur. The commonly stated reasons for disagreement typically focus on the raters, for example, insufficient training or fatigue. However, there is one other possible reason: the scale. In placement testing, that scale is externally derived—it is based on the curriculum—not on the set of essays. Thus, it is entirely possible that raters might disagree because the student either shows evidence of belonging in two courses or is between two courses. If this is the case, then disagreement would reflect reality and should not be considered a failing on the part of the raters.

Since disagreements inevitably occur, the common practice is to have third raters resolve split decisions. However, using split-resolvers creates problems. The pragmatics of our placement testing dictate that splits must be read after the primary raters have finished reading, and thus the split-resolvers usually know they are resolving disagreements. Well-trained split-resolvers may know the potential range of the split and, thus, they cannot be truly independent raters. Furthermore, different split-resolvers might give different ratings, thus resolving the split in a different direction, especially if their scale-point ranges or grey areas are different.

I examined this knowledge-of-range effect because it seemed important to the research on reliability. In our rating sessions, the essays are first placed into a "primary rater" stack from which the first and second raters draw. When there are split decisions, those essays go into the "splits" stack which are read by the third rater. In one rating session, instead of the usual procedure, all essays which received split ratings were put back into the primary rating stack. Thus, the third raters thought they were primary raters. This process was continued until two raters agreed. The essays were then put into the split resolving stack. On 84% of the essays, the first third rater agreed with one of the primary raters. However, 3% of the essays received all possible ratings (on our 4-point scale) before an agreement was reached. (This 3% is not a unique phenomenon. It is consistent across all of our research, cf. Smith et al., 1985.) The final agreement, regardless of the number of third raters needed, was the same as the decision made by the raters who thought they were split-resolvers in 69% of the cases. These results indicate that when raters know they are split-resolvers, they do not consistently rate the same as when they think they are primary raters. In the research presented below, more evidence about this difference will be shown.

Intrarater Reliability

The data we have gathered over years on placement testing shows that our raters have what must be considered low interrater reliability. The percentage of agreement among the primary raters has ranged from as low as 45% to as high as 70%, with a median of 62%. While this might indicate a cause for concern about our placement system (e.g., that the conditions under which the essays are read is a problem, that the training of the raters is insufficient), it could also be a product of natural disagreement about students who do not not fit neatly into courses. Therefore, I turned my attention to intrarater reliability.

In theory, when raters agree with each other, they should agree with themselves, but this is not necessarily the case. Raters may disagree with each other but be consistent in their own ratings. This is an important distinction because, in placement testing, it must the case that student placement is consistent across all rating sessions during a year as well as across years. If raters do not agree with themselves, if they vary from essay to essay, then there can be of claim to fairness to the students.

To examine this form of reliability, I established a schedule of raters such that seven raters (from the pool of 41 raters) read the placement essays in three of the placement testing sessions. Since there were five sessions, these raters worked the first, third, and fifth sessions. This allowed me to do intrarater comparisons across that time. Approximately one month separated these sessions, and I reasoned that that should be sufficient time for the raters to forget the essays and their ratings of them, especially since they, with one exception, read many other essays in sessions 2 and 4. During the first reading session in mid-June, I randomly selected 10 essays read by each of the seven raters. Ten was the greatest number I could select without making those repeat essays too obvious and without overloading the readers in the subsequent sessions. These essays were merged into the stacks of essays these raters read in the third (late July) and fifth (late August) sessions.

In the placement reading sessions, each essay is read by two primary readers, then, as necessary, by split-resolvers. Since it is possible that readers do not read their first stack of essays (when they are the first primary reader) the same way they read the second (when they are the second primary reader), in the third rating session, five of the essays from the first session were placed in the raters' first stack and five in the second. For the fifth session, the order of the essays was switched. The students write their essays in a standard "blue book" which we provide, and the raters mark their decisions on a roster I prepare. Thus, there would be no physical evidence that the essays had been previously rated, and it was possible to unobtrusively merge the old essays into the new.

Raters commonly state, or complain, that some of the essays they are reading seem like essays they have read before (in the same session or in previous sessions), so it is not surprising that these raters told me that they thought they had read the essays already. However, because this statement is so common, they accepted my response that they were just recalling prototypes, not specific instances. Whether they believed me or not is a separate question for which I have no answer.

The normal record keeping for each placement session allowed me to determine the percentage of essays which received the same "vote" from the two primary readers. Thus, I could determine the interrater reliability for each session and for the entire placement for the year.

As can be seen in Table 1, the distribution, by final placement, of the essays selected from the first rating session did not match the distribution for that session, for that year, or for the ranges across years. By chance, 8.6% of the essays were written by students placed into Course A, 55.7% by students placed into Course B, 35.7% by students placed into Course C, and none by students who were exempted from composition courses. This abnormal distribution could cause two problems. First, one of the tenets of sampling is that samples should resemble the population in order to allow generalizability. Second, the abnormal distribution might affect ratings if raters have a preset notion of the expected normal distribution. That is, they might try to force the essays into the normal distribution. The results (cf. Tables 2 and 4) show that the raters' ratings are significantly different from the normal distribution, thus indicating that the raters did not have a sense of the normal distribution, or if they did, they did not use that knowledge when making their decisions.

I had anticipated that there might be differences in the raters' agreement when acting as the first and second reader, but no such

Table 1. Comparison of Distributions of Sample Essays, Year-Population Essays, and Across-Years Range (in Percentage)

Course Range	Sample	All in the First Session	Year	Across-Year
A	8.6	3.0	6.4	2.7– 6.8
B	55.7	38.2	40.2	35.9–43.0
C	35.7	57.8	52.4	52.8–58.1
Exempt	0.0	1.1	1.0	.2– 1.4

differences were found. Apparently, being a first or second reader, unlike being a split-resolver, does not affect raters. Therefore, all data were merged into one pool.

Overall, the results (Table 2) indicate that intrarater reliability was fairly high and quite consistent. The comparison of the first and second readings of essays showed that the raters gave the same ratings to 75.7% of the essays. As might be expected, the agreement declined somewhat (to 64.3%) when the raters read the essays for the third time (Session 5). Nevertheless, the intrarater reliability was higher than interrater reliability for the rating sessions or the year (see Table 3 for those data). These raters agreed with themselves much more than they agreed with the people who were the other primary raters when the essays were first rated.

Table 2. Intrarater Reliability by Rater (Number of Essays on Which Raters Gave the Same Rating as in Session 1)

	Second Rating (Session 3)	Third Rating (Session 5)	Session 5 Rating Compared with Second Rating (Session 3)
Rater 1	8	8	9
Rater 2	8	6	7
Rater 3	7	5	7
Rater 4	6	5	7
Rater 5	6	7	5
Rater 6	9	7	9
Rater 7	9	7	9
Total	53	45	53
% Agreement	75.7	64.3	75.7

The results of the second rating (Session 3) afforded another base for determining intrarater reliability. It might be the case that the second rating was the "better" one, and if this were the case, when rating in Session 5, the raters should agree more with their Session 3 ratings than

Table 3. Interrater Agreement of all Raters, by Final Placement Decision, by Rating Session (in Percentage)

Final Placement Decision	Session			
	First	Third	Fifth	Combined
A	38.5	33.3	62.2	51.3
B	37.0	54.1	56.7	43.8
C	68.9	71.9	33.7	62.7
Exempt	33.3	50.0	60.0	46.7
ALL	55.7	64.2	40.3	54.7

their Session 1 ratings. As Table 2 shows, the raters' Session 5 did agree more with their Session 3 ratings than with their Session 1 ratings (75.7% vs. 64.3%).

But these data mask potentially important information. First, it might be the case that the raters would be more reliable on decisions about some courses and less reliable on other courses. For example, raters might be more consistent on Course C decisions. Therefore, the data were reanalyzed by the decision. The results (Table 4) show that agreement increases with each course level, and this is consistent across ratings. Thus, it would appear that consistency

1. Depends on the level of the essay (higher rated essays being read more consistently);
2. Is affected by the width of a rater's scale points (for example, the width of the Course C scale point might be much greater than the Course A scale point); or
3. Is a product of a student not fitting neatly into a course.

Table 4. Intrarater Reliability by Rating Given

Rating Given	N (Session 1)	Compared with First Rating (Session 1)				Session 5 Rating Compared with Second Rating (Session 3)		
		Second Rating (Session 3)		Third Rating (Session 5)		Session 3	Session 5	
		N	%	N	%	N	N	%
A	6	4	66.7	3	50.0	7	4	57.1
B	39	29	74.4	24	61.5	35	26	74.3
C	25	20	80.0	18	72.0	27	23	85.2
D	0	0		0		1	0	0.0

The third reason is of considerable importance to intrarater reliability, for variability in raters' successive ratings of an essay would not indicate true low reliability, but rather a variability which reflects the fact that the student doesn't fit neatly into a course. One would expect, therefore, that the raters in this study would be more consistent (have higher intrarater reliability) on essays which were nonsplits in the original (Session 1) rating.

To test the third possibility, that consistency is a product of a student not fitting neatly into a course, the data were again analyzed by sorting the 70 essays according to the ratings given by the original sets of raters (the two primary raters and any split-resolvers). Of course, one of the primary raters for each essay was one of the subjects in this study. The results (Table 5) indicate that the raters' disagreements on their second and third decisions may be explained by the original raters' decisions. Recall that placement raters must put each student into some course, but since some students don't fit neatly into our courses, split decisions are natural. Therefore, it would also seem natural for raters to disagree with themselves when given an essay on which the original raters disagreed. That seems to be what happened here. The original sets of raters produced splits on 26 of the essays. Thus, one might expect the raters in this study to split also. That is what happened. The raters in this study agreed with the split 20 times (76.9%). For example, on the 18 essays where the original three raters' ratings were some combination of B and C (i.e., B-C-B or B-C-C), the raters in this study produced some combination of B and C 16 times. This level of agreement is nearly as high as the percentage of agreement on the nonsplits produced by the original sets of raters (88.6%). Thus, overall agreement (i.e., the subjects' nonsplits and splits matching the original raters' nonsplits and splits) was 84.3%. Therefore, the lack of intrarater reliability among the raters in this study could be attributed to the raters' recognizing, as did the original sets of raters, that some students do not fit neatly into courses.

The small Ns, of course, prevent any firm conclusions. However, increasing the sample may not be worth the effort, for the number of essays each reader would have to reread would constitute too large a percentage of that reader's stack of essays. There would be little room for the new essays the reader is to rate, unless of course these raters' stacks are made noticeably larger than the other raters. This procedure might affect intrarater reliability through a fatigue or motivation factor. Furthermore, it would be nearly impossible to find sufficient Course A or Exempt essays because, in any session, there are not many students placed into these categories. Therefore, for practical reasons, this procedure would be nearly impossible.

The data showing the close matches between the original raters' ratings and the subjects' repeated ratings provided the first clue that

Table 5. Comparison of Raters' First, Second, and Third Decisions with Original Sets of Raters' Decisions (Primary Raters and Split-Resolver)

	Decisions by Original Set of Raters	Decisions by Raters in this Study (Sessions 1, 3, 5)	
		All Three Ratings the Same	All Three Ratings Not the Same
No-Split			
A-A	3	3	0
B-B	24	21	3
C-C	17	15	2
ALL No-Split	44	39	5
%		88.6	11.4
Split			
A-B-A	4	0	4
A-B-B	3	3	0
B-C-B	10	2	8
B-C-C	8	0	8
C-D-C	1	1	0
ALL Split	26	6	20
%		23.1	76.9

raters may not have high intra- or interrater reliability, but still could have high reliability of a different sort, which I call "rater-set" reliability. While the raters who rate any given essay may disagree (presumably because the student does not fit neatly into a course), they may agree with another rater-set, just as the raters in the above study did.

Rater-Set Reliability

A rater-set is the two primary raters' decisions taken as a whole. The split-resolver is excluded because other data showed that split-resolvers rate differently than primary raters. Since disagreements between two raters are natural (i.e., caused by students who do not fit perfectly within a scale point), I hypothesized that essays which are given split and nonsplit ratings by one set of raters would also be given those ratings by a new set of raters from within the same local discourse community. That is, students who belong in a course and even those who are "between courses" (I call them "tweeners") would be spotted by both sets of raters. The tweeners pose the real test. If those splits are reliable, then the placement ratings would be reliable even though the individual raters' ratings were different. However, if that were not the case, then there would be grounds to claim that the raters and the rating system are fundamentally flawed, even if the system produced adequate placement.

The ratings given by the primary raters who actually did the placement rating (I will refer to them as Rater-Set 1 [RS1]) were compared with the ratings given by a new set of raters, Rater-Set 2 (RS2). The new raters were led to believe that they were the real placement raters because the essays were embedded into the placement rating session. This is important because I have found that raters respond quite differently when they suspect that they are being tested.

The scale used for the rating had four points (A, B, C, D). Each letter refers to a composition course, except D, which refers to "exemption from all composition courses." Thus, there are 10 possible combinations of ratings (AA, BB, CC, DD, AB, etc.). The essays were specifically selected from a large pool so that they represented 9 of the possible 10 degrees of agreement and disagreement. However, within each set of "possible degrees," the essays were randomly selected. Only nine combinations were tested because AD ratings are so rare that they could not be meaningfully included.

It is important to note that these essays do not represent a typical distribution. A disproportionate number of essays that had received split ratings were selected. In the real distribution (from over 2,500 placement essays), the primary raters agreed on 62% of the essays (see Table 6 for the sample and population distributions).

The raters used in the second rating (Rater-Set 2) were drawn from the same pool as the original raters. Thus, prior training and experience were identical. All raters in RS1 and in RS2 (like all raters in the pool) had taken the same teaching seminars. They also had taught at least two of composition courses and, thus, were familiar with those courses and the students in each course. All raters in RS1 and in RS2 had previously done placement rating and knew the procedures and methods.

The decisions of the split-resolvers from the real placement rating session were also analyzed in order to determine how such ratings related to the ratings given by the second set of raters (See Table 6 for the distribution of split-resolver decisions).

Because the raters in both rater-sets were drawn from the same pool and thus had the same experience and training, it is possible that they might be calibrated by their shared experience in teaching, in teaching seminars, and in placement rating. Thus, I could be biasing the research by selecting "clones" who might not be the same as raters drawn from a different year or the same as raters who have less experience in our program. Furthermore, it seemed reasonable to determine the degree to which locally drawn raters would agree with raters who had similar backgrounds but who were not from the local rater pool and who were not privy to first-hand knowledge about our students. Therefore, in the second part of this study, the essays were rated by rater-sets from another university which also has diversified composition courses for students of

Table 6. Distribution of Sample and Population by Rater-Set 1 and Split-Resolver Ratings (Split-Resolver's Decision in Parentheses)

| | SAMPLE | | POPULATION |
	N	%	%
NO-SPLIT			
A-A	14	12.96	2.11
B-B	14	12.96	19.28
C-C	14	12.96	40.41
D-D	4	3.70	.56
SUM NO-SPLIT	46	42.59	62.36
MICROSPLIT			
A-B (A)	6	5.56	2.07
A-B (B)	8	7.41	4.12
SUM A-B	14	12.96	6.19
B-C (B)	7	6.48	12.11
B-C (C)	7	6.48	14.22
SUM B-C	14	12.96	26.33
C-D (C)	10	9.26	2.36
C-D (D)	4	3.70	.58
SUM C-D	14	12.96	2.94
SUM MICROSPLIT	42	38.89	35.46
MACROSPLIT			
A-C (B)	14	12.96	1.29
B-D (C)	6	5.56	.89
SUM MACROSPLIT	20	18.52	2.18
SUM ALL SPLIT	62	57.41	37.64

varied abilities. These raters had taught composition courses and had taken a course or courses in composition theory and practice. They were given a description of the course represented by each point on the scale and a description of a typical student's writing. They did not participate in formal calibration training. These raters will be referred to as Rater-Set 3 (RS3).

For both RS2 and RS3, the essays were randomly distributed and all sets of raters were randomly composed.

Split-Resolving. Before discussing the rater-set results, some comments about the split-resolvers are in order. In the previously cited research on split-resolvers, two split-resolvers agreed in 69% of the cases. That percentage was higher than the agreement between primary raters. For the essays selected for this study, the split-resolvers, when given essays with the AB or BC microsplits (one scale-point different), were equally divided between the two original ratings. This is reasonable because they were making a decision on an essay which, theoretically, did not fit cleanly into either rating slot but was somewhere in between. When given essays with the CD microsplit, 71% decided on C. This is also as expected because D means that the student is exempt from all composition courses. Thus, the split-resolvers, who know this fact, would be more likely to lean toward the more conservative side, preferring to err on the side of requiring one course. This is quite similar to the general pattern for the whole year (see Table 6).

When the split-resolvers were given essays with macrosplits (AC, BD), they always gave the rating in the middle. Not once did they give a rating which agreed with one of the primary raters. Because this finding has powerful implications, I examined all placement scores for the year. In only one case did the split-resolver on a macrosplit agree with one of the primary raters. This implies that the split-resolvers are inferring the degree of split and thus give the rating in the middle, further evidence that raters do not rate the same when they know they are split-resolvers.

Rater-Set 2 (Within Same Local Discourse Community). Overall, the second set of raters gave exactly the same ratings as RS1 for 80% of the essays (see Table 7). This shows higher reliability than the actual percentage of agreement for all placement ratings for the year (62%) and, obviously, for the within-set ratings.

No split. When there was no split within RS1, RS2 produced those same ratings in 93% of the cases. This degree of agreement is important, for if our sample had been based on the normal distribution of splits and nonsplits (38% and 62% rather than the 57% and 43% in this study), the overall agreement would have been even higher than the 80% agreement. In the three cases in which RS2 disagreed with RS1, that disagreement was always by only one rater, and the divergent rating always differed by one scale point (e.g., RS1:BB; RS2:BC). Furthermore, these disagreements only occurred on BB and CC ratings. This may indicate that students who "fit" into the extreme points on the scale are more easily and more reliably discerned. (See Alexander & Swartz ,1982, and Cohen ,1973, for evidence of rater discrepancy in the middle range of scores, and Hughes, Kelling, & Tuck ,1980, for evidence concerning how the average is more affected by context effects.) The data from the year's set of ratings partially confirm this. There was far higher agreement between raters on A than on B or C. However, agreement was lower on D. But this may be "funny" data because D means "exempt from all composition courses." One of the two primary raters might have been leery of allowing students to exempt.

Table 7. Ratings Given by Rater-Set 1 and Rater-Set 2 (Split-Resolver Decision for Rater-Set 1 in Parentheses)

	RATER SET 1		RATER SET 2					
			AGREE WITH RS1		DISAGREE WITH RS 1			
NO SPLIT	AA	14	AA	14				
	BB	14	BB	13	BC	1		
	CC	14	CC	12	BC	2		
	DD	4	DD	4				
SUM NO-SPLIT		46		43 (93.48%)				
MICROSPLIT	AB(A)	6	AB	6				
	AB(B)	8	AB	6	BB	2		
SUM AB		14		12 (85.71%)				
	BC(B)	7	BC	5	BB	2		
	BC(C)	7	BC	5	CC	2		
SUM BC		14		10 (71.43%)				
	CD(C)	10	CD	6	CC	4		
	CD(D)	4	CD	2	CC	1	DD	1
SUM CD		14		8 (57.41%)				
SUM MICROSPLIT		42		30 (71.43%)				
MACROSPLIT	AC(B)	14	AC	9 (64.29%)	AB	2	BC	3
	BD(C)	6	BD	4 (66.67%)	BC	2		
SUM MACROSPLIT		20		13 (65.00%)				
SUM ALL SPLIT		62		43 (69.35%)				
ALL		108		86 (79.63%)				

Microsplit (One Scale-Point Different). When RS1 produced a microsplit, RS2 produced that same split in 71% of the cases. This would indicate that the writers of these essays do not fit neatly into the established courses. Instead, they are reliably between two courses. This "no neat fit" reliability may provide a very useful method for determining the degree to which the courses meet the needs of the population.

In all cases in which RS2 differed from RS1, RS2 raters both gave the same rating (i.e., produced a No Split) and that rating was always the same as one of the RS1 ratings (e.g., RS1:BC; RS2:BB). Furthermore, in all but one of the cases, the RS2's nonsplit rating agreed with the split-resolver. These results indicate that the split-resolvers' decisions were appropriate. This may also indicate that we erred in using only the primary raters as RS1. That rater set may, in reality, be comprised of all three raters. The results also indicate that it is possible that some students whom we now consider "between courses" (because they received split ratings) are actually "almost in one course" (if numbers were used instead of letters, these students might be 2.8 or 2.2, not 2.5). By using three (or perhaps even more) raters, it might be possible to locate such students and then track them through the curriculum in order to determine how they perform, and more important, to determine whether we put them at risk by our placement.

Macrosplit (Two Scale Points Different). When RS1 disagreed by two scale points (AC or BD), RS2 produced those same ratings in 65% of the cases, slightly below what is considered to be the minimum acceptable interrater reliability and about the same as the 62% interrater agreement for the year. Thus, what appears to be a lack of reliability seems to be high reliability for problematic students. When RS2 differed from RS1, only one rater was different and that rating was always one point less in spread (e.g., RS1: AC; RS2: AB or BC). RS2 raters never produced a nonsplit. These results seem to confirm that some students in the population do not fit neatly into the present courses. Here again, the rater-set method may be useful in locating such problematic students so that they can be tracked through the curriculum, and useful in determining when a new course should be created (e.g., when a sufficient number of such students appear in the population).

Rater-Set 3 (Raters from Another University). Overall, RS3 raters agreed with the placement raters (RS1) in 72% of the cases, somewhat lower than RS2 (80%), but this still meets the minimum acceptable level of agreement. Thus, overall, it appears that readers who are from different local discourse communities provide very similar placement ratings. One interpretation of this finding is that raters who are teachers of composition, regardless of their local discourse community, can agree on placement if given the criteria for each placement point. Thus, there is a larger discourse community, a "college composition teacher" community. (See Pula & Huot, this volume, for another view of this phenomenon.)

No Split. When given essays on which RS1 had produced no split, the raters in RS3 agreed nearly as often as RS2 raters did (see Table 8). In

Table 8. Ratings Given by Rater-Set 1 and Rater-Set 3 (Split-Resolver Decision for Rater-Set 1 in Parentheses)

	RATER SET 1		RATER SET 3					
			AGREE WITH RS1		DISAGREE WITH RS 1			
NO SPLIT	AA	14	AA	13	AB	1		
	BB	14	BB	13	BC	1		
	CC	14	CC	12	BC	2		
	DD	4	DD	3	CD	1		
SUM NO-SPLIT		46		41 (89.13%)				
MICROSPLIT	AB(A)	6	AB	2	AA	3	BB	1
	AB(B)	8	AB	7	BB	2		
SUM AB		14		9 (85.71%)				
	BC(B)	7	BC	4	BB	2	CC	1
	BC(C)	7	BC	6	CC	1		
SUM BC		14		10 (71.43%)				
	CD(C)	10	CD	7	CC	3		
	CD(D)	4	CD	1	DD	3		
SUM CD		14		8 (57.41%)				
SUM MICROSPLIT		42		27 (64.29%)				
MACROSPLIT	AC(B)	14	AC	6 (64.29%)	AB	3	BC	5
	BD(C)	6	BD	4 (66.67%)	BC	2	CD	1
SUM MACROSPLIT		20		10 (50.00%)				
SUM ALL SPLIT		62		37 (59.68%)				
ALL		108		78 (72.22%)				

89% of the cases, they produced the same placement rating. It would appear, then, that some essays are prototypic of the criteria for the scale points. Raters who are not from within the same local discourse community can spot these quite reliably. A comparison of the RS2 and RS3 ratings which disagreed with the RS1 ratings showed that there was only one essay on which RS2 and RS3 agreed. On all the rest, either RS2 or RS3 produced a no-split rating. Thus, there is no evidence in this sample that the RS1 no-split ratings were unreliable.

Microsplit.   When given essays which had received a microsplit from RS1, RS3 raters agreed on 64%. This is only 7% lower than RS2, and it is only slightly lower than what is considered the minimum acceptable level. In all cases in which they disagreed with RS1, RS3 raters consistently agreed with each other; that is, they produced a nonsplit rating. This is consistent with the performance of RS2 raters. Given a BC essay, RS3 raters would give it a BB or a CC, and on all but two cases, RS3 raters agreed with the split-resolver. Since RS2 raters agreed with the split-resolver every time, there may be an indication here of discourse community differences. However, it is also possible that if an essay is read by enough rater-sets, disagreement will eventually occur.

Macrosplit.   When rating the essays which were macrosplits (AC, BD), RS3 raters agreed with RS1 on only 50% of the cases. This is considerably lower than the 65% agreement produced by RS2. But, like RS2 raters, when RS3 raters did disagree, they always returned a split vote (e.g., given an AC, they would give either AB or BC). In no case did they ever give an AA or a BB or a CC. The fact that both the raters from the same pool (the within-university raters) and those from another university never produced a nonsplit decision is much stronger evidence that RS1 raters reliably sensed that the writers of these essays did not fit neatly into the current curriculum.

Conclusions.   These results indicate that the placement ratings given by these trained, qualified raters are reliable even when the raters disagree and, thus, appear to be unreliable. This contradicts the claim by Smith et al. (1980) that low interrater reliability challenges the validity of placement decisions. Consequently, using traditional methods for determining rater reliability may not accurately portray what the raters are actually doing nor how reliable their judgments are. This conclusion may apply only to local placement rating, where the scale points refer to specific courses. However, the results indicate that similar research on other types of holistic ratings might be profitable.

Furthermore, it appears that raters from another university—raters who have experience in teaching composition and who are given some guidelines—can replicate the placement ratings quite closely when the essays are prototypic of a placement, but they are not nearly as close with problematic essays. (Figure 6 depicts the decreasing percentages of agreement produced by Rater-Sets 2 and 3.) This conclusion may indicate that training raters using practice sessions (reading a set of essays and coming to agreement) is not sufficient. At least for placement testing, it may be necessary to have taught the courses and thus have a "teacherly"

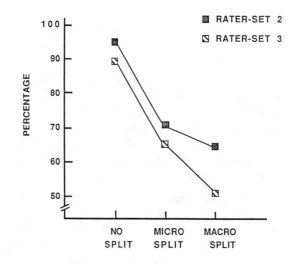

Figure 6. Percentage Agreement with RS1 by Degree of
RS1 Split

sense of best placement. If so, then raters should not be drawn from a
larger population. The raters must have the privileged knowledge of
students that can only come from teaching the courses.

The results also indicate that the use of split-resolvers does not always
produce more "truthful" ratings in a real placement setting. In placement
testing, there are a finite number of possible placements, and not all
students seem to fit neatly into those courses. Some students are not
within a scale point. Some, the macrosplits, may not even be between two
points; they may be within both scale points but not the one in the
middle. In the case of students who are between two scale points (the
microsplits), the split-resolver may be making the appropriate decision.
But when a student is both points, the split-resolver's tendency to place
the student into the middle course seems arbitrary. An alternate
conclusion is that the split-resolvers are not arbitrary; at least some of
them are enacting the philosophy that, when in doubt, it is better to
require an additional composition course.

Revising the Conclusions

While these conclusions seemed warranted from the data, something
about the data troubled me, especially the data on students who received
the macrosplits. I had thought it reasonable that some students could

show characteristics of two distinct courses, but that might not be the real reason for the macrosplit. Therefore, I reanalyzed the data, looking at the raters' backgrounds. I discovered that one other possible reason might be the course that the rater had most recently taught. It is important to remember here that all of the raters in the pool are teachers of composition courses and that they are placing students, not just rating essays. Furthermore, in order to teach course B, one must have successfully taught Course C, and to teach Course A, one must have successfully taught Course B. Thus, the Course B raters would have knowledge of courses B and C, and the Course A teacher would have knowledge of all three courses. However, that knowledge may not be recent. My reanalysis of the data showed that when the two raters in each of the two rater-sets were matched—for example, when the Most Recent Course Taught by the raters in RS1 were B and C and the same was true of RS2, then agreement was extremely high. In fact, almost all of the disagreements between the two within-university rater-sets (RS1 and RS2) happened when the raters had most recently taught different courses.

During the normal summer placement rating sessions, I had been collecting some Think-Aloud Protocols (TAPs) on raters while they were rating, and those data led me to a new perspective. The TAP data showed that when raters were reading an essay which they would place into the course they had most recently taught, their comments were not just about the essay. They also made specific comments about the writer as a student. They would say such things as "This student is one of those who never talks in class" or "This student will make significant progress in the first few weeks." When reading an essay they would place into some other course, there were no statements about the writer as student, only comments about the text or the writer as writer.

Thus, it seemed that I might have missed the real point. The raters' expertise—the expertise which comes from working with their students— might be more powerful than any training session in which they are told about the various courses and read essays prototypic of those courses. I call this "Most Recent Course Taught" expertise (hereafter CT). In effect, a rater's expertise may be linked to the course that rater has most recently taught because those are the students most recently encountered. If, for example, fourth-grade teachers are asked to grade-rate essays written by students from a wide range of grades, they would make the most errors on the grades furthest from their own grade. Their expert vision would be greatest when the students were near the fourth grade. Thus, it might be the case that raters are less able to make expert judgments when reading essays written by students who don't belong in their course. Therefore, I reanalyzed data from a previous year to determine whether this course-taught effect had some impact on reliability.

For that year, 2,704 students were tested during the summer, thus giving me a large pool to draw from. The interrater reliability for the year was a bit on the low side, 57.2%, but not radically different from the across-year median, 61%. The distribution of ratings given by the primary raters (Table 9) was consistent with other years so it presented enough diversity to allow testing of the Course-Taught hypothesis.

Table 9. Distribution of Ratings Given by Primary Raters

Non-Splits		Splits	
A-A	42	A-B	164
B-B	524	B-C	856
C-C	973	C-D	78
D-D	8	A-C	49
Total	1547	B-D	9
		A-C	1
		Total	1157

One ramification of the Course-Taught hypothesis might be that when the two primary raters have taught the same course, they would agree more than if they had taught different courses. The data did not support this conclusion. When two raters had the same CT, they agreed 54.6% of the time and when they had different CTs, they agreed 59.1% of the time, a nonsignificant difference. This result, however, is somewhat muddied because there were no cases in which two raters from Course A were paired. In fact, there is some evidence that Course A raters might be different. A comparison of the distributions of the ratings given by various pairs of raters indicates that when Course A raters are paired with other raters, they produce a different distribution (see Table 10). When the rater-set CT is AC, they give proportionally more AA ratings and fewer CC ratings, and when the rater-set CT is AB, they given proportionally more AB ratings and fewer CC ratings.

There was one other anomaly. The rater-sets composed of BB, CC, and BC raters all produced a different proportion of ratings identical to their CT than did the other rater-sets. The BB raters gave a BB rating 17.1% of the time, whereas the other rater-sets gave a BB rating on 30.4% of the essays they rated. Similarly, the CC rater-set produced a CC rating on 31.9% of their essays, whereas the other rater-sets gave the CC rating on 49.8%. Thus, these raters, who should have special knowledge of whom to place into their courses, were less likely to agree to place a student in their course. The BC rater-set, however, produced a BC split on 28.6% of their essays, whereas the other rater-sets produced this split on 51.1% of their essays.

Table 10. Distribution of Ratings Given by each Primary Rater-Set, By Rater Course Taught (CT)

Primary Rater-Set (by CT)	Ratings Given										
	AA	BB	CC	DD	AB	BC	CD	AC	BD	AD	SUM
AA	0	0	0	0	0	0	0	0	0	0	0
BB	8	136	301	4	47	255	31	10	4	0	796
CC	2	57	107	2	25	120	7	12	2	1	335
AB	8	102	102	0	30	142	6	11	1	0	402
AC	13	46	82	2	16	77	9	9	0	0	254
BC	11	183	381	0	46	262	25	7	2	0	917
ALL	42	524	973	8	164	856	78	49	9	1	2074

The fact that the AB, BC, and AC rater-sets produced odd ratings led me to analyze them further, looking inside the pairs at each rater's rating. The results of this analysis are presented in Table 11. What is most apparent in this table is that the ratings given by the AB, BC, and AC rater-sets depend on which rater is giving what. The AB rater-set produced 30 AB ratings, but 27 of these were the result of the rater not giving the rating corresponding to his/her course. In effect, the raters were "rejecting" the student from their course. The same is true to a lesser degree for the BC rater-set. On two-thirds of the BC splits they produced, both raters rejected the student, fairly clear evidence that these students do not fit neatly into either course.

Table 11. Distribution of Split Ratings Given by the Rater-Sets, By Rater-Set (CT)

Rater 1 CT	Rater 2 CT	AB	AC	AD	BC	BD	CD
A	B	3	1	0	80	1	3
B	A	27	10	0	62	0	3
A	C	7	0	0	57	0	3
C	A	9	9	0	20	0	6
B	C	28	5	0	89	1	16
C	B	18	2	0	173	1	9
B	B	47	10	0	255	4	31
C	C	25	12	1	120	2	7

The AC rater-set is also similar, but the implications may be different. Of the nine AC splits they produced, not once did either rater "accept" the student. They always rejected, and rejected by a considerable degree. These nine cases account for only 8% of the total number of disagreements by AC rater-sets, so no firm conclusions can be drawn. Nevertheless, one hypothesis is that when a student is a "definite reject" (i.e., certainly does not belong in one's course), the rater's rating may be of a noncontiguous course, a possible explanation for the BB rater-set's giving more BD and CD ratings than any other rater-set. One of the raters may have decided that the student definitely did not belong in his/her course.

I will return to this study in the next section, when the research on adequacy is presented.

The results from these studies seemed to confirm the "course-taught" hypothesis, but one more study was needed to make sure I was not just finding serendipitous occurrences.

A Third Rater-Set Study

For this final study, I selected essays from a previous placement rating session (a month previous) which had been rated by rater-sets with specific CTs (see Figure 7). I could not use all possible combinations of rater–sets and their decisions because that would have overloaded the placement session and, thus, might adversely affect placement decisions. I excluded all "D" ratings because there were too few and because D is not a course, hence there could be no "course-taught expertise." I randomly selected eight essays from within six high-frequency combinations, including when a rater-set with the same CTs agreed that the student belonged in their course (i.e, they "accepted" the student into their course), and when a rater-set with different CTs disagreed, both rejecting the student from their course. This method of sampling provided nonsplits and both micro and macrosplits. Consequently, the data could be compared with the data from the first rater-set experiment.

Rating	RS1 Raters, by Course Taught
AA	Both ratings given by Course A rater (i.e., "accept into course")
AB	"A" rating given by Course B rater. "B" rating given by Course A rater. (i.e, both "reject from course")
BB	Both ratings given by Course B rater (i.e., "accept into course")
BC	"B" rating given by Course C rater. "C" rating given by Course B rater. (i.e, both "reject from course")
CC	Both ratings given by Course C rater (i.e., "accept into course")
AC	"A" rating given by Course C rater. "C" rating given by Course A rater. (i.e, both "reject from course")

Figure 7. Essays Selected for the Second Study
(8 essays per)

The raters were randomly selected from the raters working in the placement session. They were put into rater-sets such that the sets matched the sets which had produced the ratings. In all, 6 rater-sets were created, each of which read a total of 48 essays, 8 from each of the 6 categories.

As in the first study, the target essays were randomly placed into the stacks of essays the raters were to read. Original versions were used so that the raters would not know that these essays had been previously rated. The design allowed me to divide the data into a two by two matrix: when RS1 and RS2 were matched/not matched for RCT, and when the essays were no splits and splits (see Table 12 for the matrix).

Results. Overall, the results (see Table 12) show that when Rater-Set 1 and Rater-Set 2 are composed of raters with the same CT, and when RS2 is reading nonsplit essays, the agreement is 100%. When reading splits, the agreement is 83%. Out of 48 opportunities, the matched RS2 agreed with its RS1 counterpart 45 times (93.75%). Conversely, the nonmatched RS2s (e.g., RS1's CT was AA, RS2's CT was BB) agreed only 48.75% (117 matches out of 240 possible), but this low agreement is almost entirely due to the very low (17%) agreement on splits. Thus, the data indicate that reliability, regardless of the raters' CTs, is high on nonsplits, but varies considerably on splits.

Table 12. Percentage of Agreement on No-Splits and Splits When RS1 and RS2 are Matched and Not Matched

	RS1 Produced a No-Split Decision (e.g., AA)	RS1 Produced a Split Decision (e.g., AB)
RS1 matched with RS2	100.00	83.33
RS1 not matched with RS2	81.67	16.67

A closer examination of the rating patterns (see Table 13) provides a better picture of the effects of rater course-taught expertise.

NonSplits Produced by RS1. When two raters agree that a student belongs in their course (which is what the RS1 raters were doing when they produced a nonsplit), that student should be fairly prototypic for the course and thus well within that scale-point range for all raters, even if their ranges differ somewhat. Thus, it should be the case that other raters, regardless of their CT, would agree often. The results from the nonsplits produced by RS1 (i.e., AA, BB, and CC) show that when RS2 was matched with RS1 (e.g., both RS1 and RS2 were composed of two Course A raters), there was total agreement, but when RS2 was composed of raters with

Table 13. Ratings Given by Raters in Rater-Sets (CT: Course Most Recently Taught) (When RS2 is matched with RS1, Results are in Boldface)

Given Essay	R1:CT-A R2:CT-A			R1:CT-A R2:CT-B			R1:CT-A R2:CT-C			R1:CT-B R2:CT-B			R1:CT-B R2:CT-C			R1:RT-C R2:RT-C			Total Agree.
	R1	R2	N	R1	R2	N	R1	R2	N	R1	R2	N	R1	R2	N	R1	R2	N	
A-A	**A**	**A**	**8**	A	A	8	A	A	6	A	A	8	A	A	6	A	A	5	41
							A	B	2				A	B	2	A	B	3	
A	B			B	A	7	B	A	2	A	B	1	A	B	2	A	B	3	15
										A	A	7	A	A	6	A	A	4	
	B	B	8	B	B	1	B	B	6							B	B	1	
B-B	B	B	5	B	B	6	B	B	7	**B**	**B**	**8**	B	B	8	B	B	6	40
																A	B	2	
	B	C	2	C	B	2	C	B	1										
	C	C	1																
B-C	B	C	2	B	C	4	C	B	4				**C**	**B**	**8**	A	B	1	18
	B	B	1				B	B	4							B	B	7	
	C	C	5	C	C	4				C	C	8							
C-C	C	C	5	C	C	6	C	C	6	C	C	8	C	C	8	**C**	**C**	**8**	41
	B	C	1	B	C	1	B	C	1										
	C	D	1	D	C	1	D	C	1										
	D	D	1																
A-C				C	A	1	**C**	**A**	**5**				C	A	1				7
													A	A	1	A	A	2	
										A	B	3	B	A	2	A	B	4	
	B	B	4	B	B	1	B	B	3	B	B	3	B	B	2	B	B	2	
	B	C	3	C	B	5				B	C	2	C	B	2				
	C	C	1	C	C	1													

different CTs, the agreement dropped to 84.7%, a quite adequate agreement if one accepts .7 as criterion for acceptability. The high overall agreement on nonsplits may indicate that all raters, regardless of course-taught expertise, are able to reliably discern students who are prototypic of a course. The decisions by individual RS2 raters, however, provide some indications that course-taught expertise is important.

When given essays which the two Course A raters in RS1 had rated AA (i.e., accepted), only the Course C RS2 raters disagreed. In seven cases, a

Course C rater produced a B rating. When given essays which the two Course B raters in RS1 had rated BB (i.e., both accepted), only the Course A and the Course C RS2 raters disagreed. Course A raters produced seven C decisions, and Course C raters produced two A ratings. When given essays which the two Course C raters in RS1 had rated CC (i.e., both accepted), only the Course A RS2 raters disagreed, producing three B ratings and five D ratings. What these data indicate is that the Course B raters never disagreed with RS1 on any nonsplit, and that when Course A and Course C raters disagreed with RS1, they never placed the student into their own course. Since Course B is between Course A and Course C, when Course B raters reject students, they must either place them above or below, and this creates agreement with RS1 raters. Thus, it would be expected that they would disagree less on prototypic essays (although they might give a Course C student a D rating).

When Course A or Course C raters reject students, there is more "room" for placement. Course A raters select from three ratings above their course. When Course A raters disagreed on a student rated B by RS1, they couldn't select A because they had already rejected the student from their course. Thus, they had to select C. (Selecting D would be unlikely because the essay would not have the right characteristics for exemption.) When they disagreed on a student rated C by RS1, they could, and did, produce B, C, and D ratings. The pattern here is that a disagreement will be "one course off," that is, a course contiguous to the course determined by RS1. This replicates the findings from the first study. Similarly, when Course C raters reject, they have two courses below theirs, and all of their disagreements were also one course off. It should be noted, however, that disagreements were far less common than agreements. Twelve raters read each of the 24 nonsplit essays, yet there were only 24 disagreements. Thus, they agreed on 91.6% of the cases.

Splits Produced by RS1. Split decisions offer a more taxing condition for the course-taught expertise theory. If the theory is right, when two RS1 raters disagree (i.e., produce a split vote), then the matched RS2 raters should agree with that decision. As Figure 7 shows, all split-vote essays selected for this study share one commonality: the raters never accepted the students into their own courses. Thus, for the RS1 AB split, the A was given by a Course B rater and the B by a Course A rater. The theory would predict that RS2 Course A raters would not accept regardless of whom they are paired with in the rater-set.

The data confirm the theory partially. For the microsplits (AB and BC), the matched-pair raters agreed 15 out of 16 times (93.75%), whereas the nonmatched pairs agreed only 18 out of 120 times (22.50%). Closer examination of the decisions produced by the nonmatched pairs, however, confirms the prediction that raters would reject rather than accept. When given an AB split, the RS2 Course A raters always rejected as did the Course C raters. The Course B raters rejected in 93.75% of the cases. When the Course A raters rejected a student, they always placed the student in B, presumably because the essays did not contain the characteristics of a C or D placement. Thus, since A is not possible, B is the only remaining possibility. The Course C raters had more room for a decision. A rejected student could be either an A or a B, and these raters were clearly not in accord with each other on which placement to select. Nineteen of the 32 decisions (59.38%) were for A, 13 (40.62%) for B. Thus, it seems that the Course C raters, when given an essay which has characteristics of both Course A and Course B, very nearly flip a coin. This confirms the course-taught-expertise theory, for since Course C raters had not taught Course A or Course B, they did not have expert vision when making their decisions and, thus, their scale-point ranges may have been quite different.

When given a BC split, the same phenomenon occurs. The raters from all three courses always reject the students. Course B raters always give a C because that is the only alternative for a student who isn't a B but is higher. (They could have given a D, but the students apparently didn't have the right characteristics for exemption, or the raters were being conservative. Whatever the reason, none of the raters gave these students a D rating.) The Course C raters always rejected, and since the students were not at the C level, they would have to be either A or B. B is the more probable choice (RS1 had already determined that), and thus the Course C raters produced a B rating in all but one case. The Course A raters rejected the students, and thus had to select between B and C as ratings. They favored the C rating, giving this rating in 20 of the 32 cases (62.50%). Thus, the data from the BC split are almost exactly the same as the data from the AB split. This confirms that the original split decision was probably well deserved.

The one macrosplit tested in this study, the AC split that provoked this experiment, provides a somewhat different picture. The most notable difference is that it elicited every possible combination of votes (assuming D was not a possibility). When the matched RS2 raters (i.e., from Course C and Course A) rated these essays, they produced five agreements out of the eight opportunities (62.5%). However, the nonmatched pairs produced only 2 agreements out of 40 opportunities (5.0%). Thus, although the matched-pairs agreed only slightly better than chance, that rate of agreement was 12 times higher than the nonmatched pairs.

The AC split data, like the AB and BC split data, reveal that Course A and Course C raters never accepted a student. However, these raters had equal dispersion in their decisions. The Course A raters gave 15 Bs and 17 Cs; the Course C raters gave 17 As and 15 Bs. Thus, it seems pretty much chance that the essays were true macrosplits. Given different raters from within the same Course-Taught pool, the splits could just as easily have been microsplits.

The Course B raters produced more problematic results. If these eight students really belonged in Course A and/or C but not B, then the Course B raters should have rejected them. That was not the case. Of their 32 individual decisions, 5 were A, 21 B, and 6 C. Thus, in nearly two-thirds of the cases, the Course B raters accepted the students. Further-more, when RS2 was composed of two Course B raters, they agreed on B three times. Thus, it would appear that what I had considered an AC split might have really been something else. In fact, it could be the case that the three essays to which the two Course B raters paired up in RS2 both gave B ratings might really be true B students.

However, analysis of the rating patterns on the three essays indicates that this does not seem to be the case. When the other RS2s' decisions on these three essays are compared with their decisions on the nonsplit BB essays (see above), the pattern is quite different. When given essays rated by RS1 as BB, 32 of the 40 individual decisions (80%) made by the raters in the other (non-BB) rater-sets were also BB. However, these same rater-sets, when reading the three essays, produced only 5 BB ratings out of 15 opportunities (33.3%). Thus, it appears that these three essays are just problematic, and raters must make some decision.

Contrary to my earlier conclusions, it seems clear that the AC splits are neither A nor C. Not once did a Course A or Course C rater accept a student. Thus, since these students are neither A nor C (and not likely to be D), they must by default be B. This is what the split-resolvers decided in the first experiment and in nearly all instances in placement sessions.

The data also show that only the Course A raters gave D ratings, and these were given only on essays rated CC. Only the Course C raters gave A ratings to essays previously rated as either BB or BC. These data, therefore, indicate that when the student, according to RS1, is far from the course the rater has most recently taught, there is the greatest chance of disagreement and potential error. I will return to this possibility of error in the "adequacy" section below.

Because the AC macrosplit was the only one of its kind, and because it was consistently resolved to a B by split-resolvers, I had one additional rater-set, composed of two Course B raters, rate those essays. They agreed with the Course B rater-set, with only one exception. Clearly, these eight students showed evidence of not fitting neatly into our courses. They were always rejected by the A and C course raters, and were rejected by one-third of the Course B raters.

To further test the assumption that some students do not fit neatly into our courses, and thus would be rejected by the raters, I selected essays which had been accepted by raters in Courses A, B, and C, and had those essays rerated by raters from the other courses. Not one of the 36 essays was accepted. Thus, I could conclude that the raters were highly reliable. They knew whether an essay fit into their course, and, as these data show, they knew when it didn't.

I also selected 63 essays which had been rejected by raters of contiguous courses and had them rerated by two other raters of those courses. Of these, only one was accepted by another rater. Thus, out of 126 ratings, there was a 99.2% agreement rate. One essay, an essay which a Course B rater had rejected high and a Course C rater had rejected low (thus, by inference, that student could not belong in A or D), was put through 13 iterations, that is, it was read by 13 Course B raters and by 13 Course C raters. That essay was never accepted. Although they never agreed on the final placement (and thus would seem unreliable using standard reliability measures), in fact, they were perfectly reliable.

Thus, it appears to me that our standard methods of examining reliability—of determining reliability by asking how often raters agree on a scale point—misses the point. The scales we use are made up by us. In the case of placement, the scale is determined by the number of course placements. In other types of testing, that scale—whether it has 4 or 12 points—is still concocted by us. To assume that that there are only 4 or 12 categories of students or texts seems untenable. Some students (or essays), regardless of the number of points on the scale, will not fit neatly into that scale, and thus disagreements must be expected. The truer test of reliability seems to be the rater-set method.

ADEQUACY

Although the studies on reliability indicate that raters, especially when considered as rater-sets, are reliable, that still does not mean that their decisions are correct or that they make the best decisions for the students. If their reliable decisions are not appropriate, then the testing is flawed in some important way. Thus, tests of adequacy are extremely important in two ways:

1. To determine whether the placement testing is doing what it should (placing students into the appropriate courses); and
2. To allow more precise interpretation of the reliability research.

Assessing adequacy, however, is not an easy task. The most powerful direct tests cannot be used. Students cannot, ethically or morally, be purposefully misplaced; nor can they be randomly assigned to courses. And even pretest and posttest measures will not suffice, for good teachers will do whatever is necessary to help misplaced students. Thus, any tests of adequacy must be indirect, and they must be post hoc. That is, adequacy cannot be judged until the students have been placed, and that is too late to put the students where they really belong. Thus, any placement system must include double checks, such as first-week testing.

In our research, we have focused primarily on two measures of adequacy: the classroom teachers' perception of the correctness of placement of their students, and, to a lesser extent, the final grades received by students. Other possible measures, such as student's perceptions, subsequent performance in courses requiring writing, and exit exam scores, are either too difficult to gather and too unreliable to use (as in the case of student perception and subsequent courses) or not available for all students (at Pitt, only the students in Courses A and B must take the exit exam, thus producing no information about the adequacy of placement in Course C).

Although the teacher perception and final grade measures are useful, both have flaws and drawbacks, and these need to be mentioned before discussing the research using them. Teacher perception is just that, a perception, and as I discussed earlier, it depends on how much the teachers knows about their students. Too little knowledge (e.g., gathering the data very early in the term) produces useless results. Too much knowledge (e.g., gathering the data late in the term) produces confounded results, so the teachers may not be assessing placement. Although I assume that teachers take the task seriously when I ask them to provide perception data, I cannot be certain, nor can I be certain that they all equally know their students or have sufficient knowledge of our composition program to make adequate assessments. For example, when we first used the teacher perception measure, I was concerned that new teachers, those teaching their first course in our program, would provide different responses than the veteran teachers. A comparison of these two groups' responses showed no distributional differences, and thus they could be considered equivalent groups. This provided support for using the teacher perception measure, even though the distributional equivalence does not necessarily mean that the new teachers were as capable of making distinctions as the veterans, especially the veterans who had taught more than one of our courses and who had participated in placement rating sessions.

The final grades are even more problematic because they are affected by many variables. Students who do not turn in assignments or meet other conditions (e.g, miss classes, do not participate in class discussions) may receive lower grades. Conversely, students who are active in class and evidence interest may be rewarded with grades higher than their development as writers might warrant. The most nettlesome problem, however, is the "F" grade. It might indicate unsatisfactory progress, but it too can be the result of several nonwriting variables (e.g., quitting) and may be awarded for different reasons by different teachers (e.g., different teachers have different standards concerning the number of classes a student may miss). Determining what final grade to use also poses a problem. Because different grades have different meanings for different teachers, we use the median analysis, determining the median grade for each course and then dividing the students into "above median," "on median," and "below median." But this analysis is extremely tedious and expensive. Consequently, we have not used it extensively.

The first use of these two measures was in a study we conducted on students whose first-week essay (the essay students write during the first week of class to determine who might be misplaced) did not match their placement essay. A sample of those first-week essays had been placement-rated, that is, read and rated using our placement method. The results showed that the teacher's perception of the students whose first-week essay was given a different rating differed from those whose first-week essay was the same as the placement essay. For example, the distribution of those students who had been placed into Course B but whose first-week essay was given a "Course C" rating (thus indicating that these students may have either been misplaced or were tweeners) was skewed toward the high side of the scale (see the "CODES" in Table 14 for the scale), whereas there was a normal distribution of the students whose first-week essay confirmed the placement results. The pattern in the final grades was quite similar. Since this confirmed intuition, I concluded that both measures could provide useful information about the adequacy of placement.

The First Study of Adequacy

The two adequacy measures were used as one part of a reliability study. That sample consisted of students placed into Courses A, B, and C. The teacher perception (hereafter TP) data on these classes (see Table 14) showed that the teachers considered slightly more than half of the students to be "prototypic." The remaining students were distributed differently for each course. Since there is no placement lower than Course A, Table 14 shows empty cells for "could have been placed lower" and for "slightly below". This may have created a skew in the distribution. The distribution for Course B is skewed slightly toward the high side, whereas the distribution for Course C is skewed slightly toward the low side. If one assumes (an assumption supported by the placement raters) that the Course C teachers are wary of exempting students, one would expect a low percentage in the "could have been placed higher" category for Course C.

These data tell us only that the distributions are not the same for each course and that less than 8% of the students are considered to be misplaced. Thus, the conclusion must be that, overall, the placement testing produced adequate results. However, 14% of the Course A

Table 14. Distribution of Teacher Perception Responses for Students (in Percentage)

PLACEMENT	TEACHER PERCEPTION				
	A	B	C	D	E
COURSE A	0.0[a]	0.0[a]	51.3	34.2	14.5
COURSE B	1.2	12.0	56.1	28.1	2.6
COURSE C	8.1	16.7	62.1	11.7	1.4
ALL	4.3	13.1	58.5	21.0	3.1

[a] A and B were not used for COURSE A

CODES (The prompts on the scale given to the teachers)
A= COULD HAVE BEEN PLACED IN LOWER COURSE
B= IS SLIGHTLY BELOW THE PROTOTYPIC STUDENT FOR THIS COURSE
C= IS PROTOTYPIC OF THIS COURSE
D= IS SLIGHTLY ABOVE THE PROTOTYPIC STUDENT FOR THIS COURSE
E= COULD HAVE BEEN PLACED IN HIGHER COURSE

students were considered to have been placed too low and 8% of the Course C students placed too high. Thus, it would seem that too few students were placed into course B. Further analysis of these data provide some information concerning why this might have happened.

The data were sorted to determine what happened when at least one of the raters who placed the student into a course had course-taught expertise in that course. That is, when a rater accepted the student. The remaining students were placed into a course by a rater-set which did not include a rater with course-taught expertise for that course. This could be called the "no accept" condition or perhaps the "reject" condition, for the raters were rejecting the student from their courses. These data are presented in Table 15. The differences in the two distributions for each course (the "accept" distribution and the "no accept" distribution) are striking. There is a clear central tendency in the accept condition. The logical conclusion is that when one of the raters is making an expert decision, the probability that the student is misplaced drops to near zero.

If this is the case when one rater has expertise, the central tendency should be even greater when two raters with course-taught expertise agree. That is exactly what happened. These data are presented in Table 16. (Data on Course A are not presented because there were no instances in which two Course A raters were paired.) The data for the "Two Accept" distributions are problematic because the numbers are so small (38 for Course B and 19 for Course C), but the differences are so great that at least one can hypothesize that when two raters with the same course-

Table 15a. Distribution of Teacher Perception Responses for Students. When At Least One Rater's Course-Taught Expertise Corresponded to That Rater's Decision—"Accept" Condition (in Percentage)

	TEACHER PERCEPTION				
PLACEMENT	A	B	C	D	E
COURSE A	0.0[a]	0.0[a]	83.3	16.7	0.0
COURSE B	0.0	7.5	68.3	24.2	0.0
COURSE C	2.1	15.3	72.5	9.5	.5
ALL	.8	9.9	70.7	18.5	.2

[a] A and B were not used for COURSE A

CODES (The prompts on the scale given to the teachers)
A= COULD HAVE BEEN PLACED IN LOWER COURSE
B= IS SLIGHTLY BELOW THE PROTOTYPIC STUDENT FOR THIS COURSE
C= IS PROTOTYPIC OF THIS COURSE
D= IS SLIGHTLY ABOVE THE PROTOTYPIC STUDENT FOR THIS COURSE
E= COULD HAVE BEEN PLACED IN HIGHER COURSE

Table 15b. Distribution of Teacher Perception Responses for Students. When At Least No Rater had Course-Taught Expertise Corresponding to Final Placement—"No Accept" Condition (in Percentage)

	TEACHER PERCEPTION				
PLACEMENT	A	B	C	D	E
COURSE A	0.0[a]	0.0[a]	30.4	45.7	23.9
COURSE B	4.5	24.3	22.5	37.8	9.9
COURSE C	13.0	17.7	53.7	13.4	2.2
ALL	9.0	17.5	42.0	24.5	7.0

[a] A and B were not used for COURSE A

taught expertise agree to accept a student, the classroom teacher will consider the student appropriately placed.

If this hypothesis is correct, then it also stands to reason that students who receive split votes may receive them because the rater is "rejecting" but is uncertain as to where to place the student. This problem is greatest for the Course A rater. If the student doesn't belong in A, then B, C, and D are the options. For a Course C rater, students who don't belong in C but are "higher" must go into D, but those who are "lower" could go into either A or B.

Table 16. Teacher Perception Distributions under Three Conditions: "No Accept," "One Accept," and "Two Accept" (in Percentage)

			TEACHER PERCEPTION				
COURSE	CONDITION	N	A	B	C	D	E
B	No Accept	111	4.5	24.3	22.5	38.7	9.9
	One Accept	268	0.0	8.6	64.6	26.9	0.0
	Two Accept	38	0.0	0.0	94.7	5.3	0.0
C	No Accept	231	13.0	17.7	53.7	13.4	2.2
	One Accept	170	2.4	46.5	70.6	10.0	.6
	Two Accept	19	1.1	5.3	89.5	5.3	0.0

To examine what happens when students receive split votes from the primary raters, illustrative cases where the N would be sufficient were selected. To simplify the presentation, I use the following notation: RCT is the Rater's Course-taught expertise. Thus, RCT-A:B would indicate a rater with Course A expertise who gave a B rating, and RCT-A:B/RCT-B:A would be a pair of raters and their decisions. The following patterns were selected: (a) RCT-B:C/RCT-C:B where final placement was B or C; (b) RCT-B:B/RCT-C:C where final placement was B or C; (c) RCT-B:B/RCT-B:B where final placement was B; (d) RCT-C:B/RCT-C:B where final placement was B; (e) RCT-B:C/RCT-B:C where final placement was C; and (f) RCT-C:C/RCT-C:C where final placement was C. These patterns allowed comparisons, using teacher perception data, among and between course-taught expertise on both accept and reject decisions. The data are presented in Table 17.

The first pattern, RCT-B:C/RCT-C:B, was of the greatest interest, for it specifies that both raters reject the student, and thus the student should be between the two courses. If that were the case, the students placed into Course B should receive high TP ratings and the students placed into Course C should receive low ratings. The data support this. About half of those placed in Course B were considered "slightly above" and about half of those placed into Course C were considered "slightly below." One could conclude, then, that both raters' ratings were correct—the student didn't fit neatly into either course.

The median analysis of these students' final grades provides confirming evidence. The grades of those placed into Course B were skewed toward the "above median" side, whereas the grades of those placed into Course C were skewed toward the "below median" side. However, below median does not mean failing grade. In fact, none of the 28 students placed into Course C failed the course. Thus, one must assume that they performed adequately.

In the second pattern of interest, RCT-B:B/RCT-C:C, both raters

Table 17. Teacher Perception Distributions for Selected Patterns of Raters and Ratings (in Percentage)

PATTERN	PLACE-MENT	N	TEACHER PERCEPTION				
			A	B	C	D	E
RCT-B:C/RCT-C:B	B	51	0.0	5.9	41.1	51.0	2.0
	C	28	3.6	50.0	39.3	7.1	0.0
RCT-B:B/RCT-C:C	B	27	0.0	3.7	59.3	33.3	3.7
	C	21	9.5	33.3	57.1	0.0	0.0
RCT-B:B/RCT-B:B	B	26	0.0	3.8	88.5	7.7	0.0
RCT-C:B/RCT-C:B	B	38	0.0	0.0	78.9	18.4	2.6
RCT-B:C/RCT-B:C	C	180	2.2	11.1	70.0	15.0	1.7
RCT-C:C/RCT-C:C	C	15	0.0	6.7	93.3	0.0	0.0

CODES (The prompts on the scale given to the teachers)
A= COULD HAVE BEEN PLACED IN LOWER COURSE
B= IS SLIGHTLY BELOW THE PROTOTYPIC STUDENT FOR THIS COURSE
C= IS PROTOTYPIC OF THIS COURSE
D= IS SLIGHTLY ABOVE THE PROTOTYPIC STUDENT FOR THIS COURSE
E= COULD HAVE BEEN PLACED IN HIGHER COURSE

accepted the student. Thus, assuming that the raters did not simply err, the student must be within the scale-point ranges of both raters. Here again, the teachers' perceptions confirm the raters' decisions. Regardless of where the students were placed, the teachers considered over half of them to be correctly placed. There is, however, an off-angle skew in the data. One-third of the students placed into Course B were considered "slightly above," whereas one-third of those placed into Course C were considered "slightly below." However, the final grades for these students exhibited no skew.

In the third and fourth patterns, the student was placed into Course B and the two raters both agreed. However, the Course C raters rejected while the Course B raters accepted. This provides another test of the theory. For the two Course B raters to accept, the student must be within both of their scale-point ranges. However, for a Course C rater to reject, the student must be somewhere below the low end of the Course C scale point. The theory would predict that the students placed in Course B by the Course C raters would have a wider or flatter distribution than those placed by Course B raters. The data confirm this. Although the teachers considered most of the students correctly placed, the distribution of those placed by Course B raters shows more of a central tendency. The distribution of the students placed by the Course C raters indicates that these raters' scale-point range for Course B is either larger or is elastic. This is confirmed by other evidence which shows that most of the students considered misplaced by Course A teachers were placed in Course A by Course C raters.

In the final pair of patterns, the students were placed into Course C by either two Course B or two Course C raters. Here again, the theory would predict that the TP distribution for the students placed by Course B raters would be flatter, that there would be fewer students considered to be prototypic. Unfortunately, there is a problem with these data: The sizes of the two groups is radically different. Thus, even though the distributions are as predicted, there can be less confidence in the results.

The data from this study of adequacy allow two conclusions. First, there does not seem to be a serious problem of misplacement. Very few students are considered to be misplaced. But for the students and for the teachers, "very few" is too many. Second, the misplacements seem to be predicted by the theory of course-taught expertise. The misplacements were consistently a product of the wrong raters making the judgments.

A REVISED RATING METHOD: NEW RELIABILITY AND ADEQUACY EVIDENCE

The fact that the reliability and adequacy data consistently showed the power of course-taught expertise led me to reconsider our standard method for rating. That method specified that the essays be randomly assigned to raters, regardless of the course they have most recently taught and that those raters place students into the appropriate course (i.e., make full-scale decisions). The new method I devised specified that raters determine only whether a student should be accepted into or rejected from the course they have most recently taught. This method relies, therefore, on the "expert" opinion of each rater, that is, that rater's expertise gained by teaching the students. This expert method does not require raters to make judgments based on the full scale, a scale which includes courses they have not taught or have not taught recently. They are only concerned with accepting into their course or rejecting from it.

Therefore, during the subsequent year, I altered the rating so that each rater's decisions were limited to "accept" or "reject-high" or "reject-low." Of course, the Course A raters could only accept or reject-high. The essays of those students who were rejected-high by Course C raters were then read by a panel who determined who deserved Exemption. Every essay was read by at least two raters until it was "located" on the following distribution:

In Course A
Between Course A and Course B
In Course B
Between Course B and Course C
In Course C
Between Course C and Exemption
Exempt

A student who was never accepted (a tweener) was placed into the higher course, except for those between Course C and Exemption—they were placed into Course C. Although this decision might put some students at risk, the data from the previously described studies indicated that there was a low chance of failure. Of course, the teachers might have to work harder.

The raters were told that they should accept students who resembled students in their course during the first half of the term. This cut-point was arbitrary but reasonable. Interviews with teachers and some small-scale studies of student progress across-term had indicated that the "progress curve" is not a straight 45-degree slope. Instead, the line is relatively flat for the first few weeks and then curves upward. In effect, the curve is closer to logarithmic. If a student can perform as well as students during the last half of the term, there should be no reason for requiring that student to take the whole course.

There should be four immediate consequences of this new rating method. The first is that the troublesome macrosplits disappear. The new method precludes them. The second is that the problem of split-resolvers in general is resolved, because there are no split-resolvers. The third is that the placement distribution should be different from previous years' distributions. The data on split-resolvers show that their decision is affected by their course-taught expertise. Thus, some tweeners are placed into the higher course, and some into the lower course, depending on who resolved the split. With the new method, all students between Course A and Course B would go into Course B. This would decrease the number of students in Course A and increase the number in B. Those between Course B and Course C would go into Course C. This would decrease the number in B and increase the number in C. Finally, those between Course C and Exemption would go into Course C. This would increase the number in Course C. The net effect, given the number of students typically placed into each course and the calculated percentage of students who were tweeners, would be a decrease in Course A and Course B and an increase in Course C. As Table 18 shows, the percentages did change as predicted.

The fourth consequence should be a different distribution in the teacher perception data. Because the tweeners are moved up, the

Table 18. Distribution of Students Under the Nonexpert (the Old) Rating Method and the Expert (the New) Rating Method

Placement	Nonexpert Method		Expert Method	
	N	%	N	%
Course A	161	6.0	68	2.7
Course B	1089	40.3	755	29.9
Course C	1430	52.9	1671	66.2
Exempt	24	.9	29	1.2
Total	2704		2523	

teachers' TP distribution should show an increase in Course B and Course C in the proportion of students considered "slightly below" and a decrease in the proportion of Course A students considered to be "slightly above." The data in Table 19 show that this did happen. But there is also a considerable increase in the proportion of students considered to be prototypic and a notable decrease in the proportion considered to be in the wrong course. Thus, it seems that this new rating method produces more adequate results. Less than 3% of students were considered misplaced.

There are two other possible consequences that are of pragmatic concern. The first is the raters' "comfort" with the system and with their decisions. In my interviews and conversations with the raters, all of the raters who had worked with both the old and new methods said they greatly preferred the new. They said they believed in their decisions more because they didn't have to worry about deciding exact placement for rejected students. Several first-time raters stated that they liked being considered experts, that this made them feel more important. Conversely, some veteran raters said they missed being able to place students in all courses, and especially missed determining who deserved exemption. One possible interpretation is that they felt they had less control over the composition program; another is that they felt their knowledge of the whole program and its courses was not being fully used.

The other consequence concerns the time required to do the rating, an important consideration because time is directly related to cost and to rater fatigue. Under the old method, in which the average agreement between primary raters was about 60%, the average number of readings per essay was about 2.4. Every essay was read twice and about 40% of the essays were read three times. The experimental design for the expert rating specified that every student's essay be read either until it was accepted by two raters from the same course or rejected by two raters from contiguous courses. The basic design was as follows:

Table 19. Distribution of Teacher Perception Responses for Students Placed Using the Nonexpert and Those Placed Using the Expert Rating Models (in Percentage)

| PLACEMENT | METHOD | TEACHER PERCEPTION | | | | |
		A	B	C	D	E
COURSE A	N-E	0.0[a]	0.0[a]	49.4	34.8	15.7
COURSE A	E	0.0[b]	3.0	68.2	25.2	3.6
COURSE B	N-E	1.2	12.0	56.1	28.1	2.6
COURSE B	E	0.2	20.0	68.2	9.7	1.9
COURSE C	N-E	8.1	16.7	62.0	11.6	1.5
COURSE C	E	1.1	21.1	71.2	5.1	1.4
ALL	N-E	5.0	13.1	57.7	21.2	2.9
ALL	E	0.9	20.1	70.4	5.7	1.9

[a] A and B were not used for COURSE A; A was not used for Course A

[b] A not used for Course A

CODES (The prompts on the scale given to the teachers)
A= SHOULD HAVE BEEN PLACED IN LOWER COURSE
B= IS SLIGHTLY BELOW THE PROTOTYPIC STUDENT FOR THIS COURSE
C= IS PROTOTYPIC OF THIS COURSE
D= IS SLIGHTLY ABOVE THE PROTOTYPIC STUDENT FOR THIS COURSE
E= SHOULD HAVE BEEN PLACED IN HIGHER COURSE

- If the first reader accepts, the next reader has the same CT.
- If CT-A rejects high, the next reader is CT-C (because most of our students end up in Course C).
- If CT-B rejects low, the next reader is CT-A.
- If CT-B rejects high, the next reader is CT-C.
- If CT-C rejects low, the next reader is CT-B.
- If CT-C rejects high, the next reader is CT-D.

In theory, given at least two disagreements by raters from the same CT, an essay would be read by six readers. In fact, no essay required more than four. Forty-seven percent were read by two, 46% by three, and only 6% by four. The average number of times an essay was read was 2.6. This is an 8% increase over the 2.4 readings per essay under the nonexpert rating model. Thus, the rating should have taken longer. In fact, the raters finished the job much faster. The reason, as best I can determine from observing them and from what they said, is that they read more efficiently because they didn't have to make as many decisions. If they rejected a student, they didn't have to decide on the course. They also know how their students write, thus, they could make faster decisions, for any student who didn't write that way would be a reject. Furthermore, the agreement among raters with the same CT was very high. Course A raters agreed on 96% of the essays they read together, Course B raters agreed on 93%, and Course C raters agreed on 86%. The Course C raters' agreement may have been lower because they were involved in the reading of nearly 90% of the essays.

It appears, then, that the expert rating method produces better results for a cheaper price. However, I have conducted far too little research on it to conclude that it is better for placement testing. Since it has never, to my knowledge, been used in other types of testing, no conclusions can be drawn. However, I would speculate that this method could be profitably used in a wide variety of testing conditions and with any type of scale.

CONCLUSIONS AND IMPLICATIONS

The research I have presented permits some tentative conclusions, and, if these conclusions are correct, it some powerful implications for placement testing and even for other types of direct assessment.

Rater Reliability

Two conclusions about rater reliability seem warranted by the research. First, the standard methods for assessing reliability assume too much of both the rater and the rating scale. They assume that raters have the same ranges for each scale point, that they are no grey areas between scale points, that the scale adequately covers the range of the essays, and that a rater should be equally able to distinguish essays within each of the scale points. They also assume that disagreements indicate a lack of reliability. My research provides some indications that each of these assumptions may not be valid. I found great reliability in disagreements, considerable evidence of varied scale-point ranges, and differing "rater power" for each scale point.

Second, if essays (or students) do not fit neatly into our scales, qualified raters will sense this. It is not uncommon for raters to put little pluses or minuses next to their ratings, presumably because they are uncomfortable with the scale. Since there seems to be no easy solution to this problem, alternative methods for determining reliability are needed. The rater-set method may be one such alternative. Since I have used it only within one limited context—placement rating at Pitt—I cannot make generalizations about the results of using it in other types of direct assessment, but it does make sense to test it.

Adequacy

Although reliability is important, in placement testing adequacy is what counts. The students must be correctly placed. Determining adequacy and determining an acceptable level of adequacy, however, are significant problems. Unquestionably, errors in placement will occur. Some students will not exhibit their true abilities because of the testing conditions (time of day, what they did the night before, the topic they must write on, the number of students in the room, etc.), and raters will make mistakes. Nevertheless, we must seek methods for assessing the adequacy of placement (and of other types of assessment).

Our research provides some clues to ways one can determine whether the placement decisions are appropriate. Final grades can provide some evidence about the adequacy. If there is a serious problem with students being misplaced, there should be some indication in the distributions of grades. Final grades were very useful in our efforts to examine the tweeners (the students who were between our courses). Consistently, they performed differently than the students who were prototypic for the course. If the tweeners' pattern of grades changes in the future, that will provide a signal that a problem may exist in our placement testing. However, there are too many reasons for assigning any grade—especially a failing grade—to depend on grades alone as a measure.

Although I did not present our research on exit exams, these data are also useful. The students in Course A and Course B must pass this exam in order to take Course C. For the exit exam, they write an impromptu essay (the topic is parallel to the placement topic) and submit a portfolio of revised essays. Thus, we can compare the essays which are judged to be "passing" with placement essays written by students placed into Course C. We have found that the Course A and B students' exit exam essays are slightly lower than the prototypic Course C placement essays. Thus, when these students enter Course C, they resemble tweeners, and the teacher perception data on these students shows that they are somewhat lower than the prototypic Course C student. However, their grades are not different from the tweeners (those between B and C) whom we placed into C, and their failure rate is no higher than the students placed directly into Course C.

The most powerful method for assessing adequacy seems to be the teachers' perceptions of where their students should have been placed. This instrument seems to provide reliable evidence. We found that it was sensitive enough to distinguish tweeners, to indicate differences between the various rater-sets, and to distinguish expert and nonexpert raters. In effect, the evidence probably is no different from that which any program director would obtain by informal, personal inquiry or by normal feedback. Certainly, the teachers would complain if too many students were misplaced. But the instrument allows the collection of larger databases and, thus, should provide more comprehensive information about adequacy of placement within a year and across years. It also can be used to track students as they move across courses.

Training Raters

One of the critical issues in placement rating and in all holistic rating is the training of the raters. Every authority discusses this issue because it is believed that this training (whether it is called range finding or calibration) is essential for achieving reliability, and reliability is considered necessary for validity. My research calls our standard reliability methods into question at two levels. First, the idea that all essays will fit into arbitrary points—points created by someone—on a scale is unrealistic. It is even more unrealistic to assume that readers, no matter how well trained, will agree consistently. After all, trained literature specialists disagree about novels, and trained critics disagree about plays and movies. Disagreement, therefore, is to be expected. What this research has shown is that the disagreements are reliable. When rater-sets, not individual raters, are tested, they produce the same agreements and the same disagreements.

Second, when the readers have what I call course-taught expertise, efforts to calibrate may not be necessary if the raters' expertise is used profitably. All of my evidence suggests that building the rating system around this expertise is crucial to increased reliability and adequacy. Furthermore, I suspect that calibration may not be able to overcome the effect of expertise. I suspect that if I used range finders which were not consistent with the raters' knowledge of their own students, those raters would reject the training.

The concept of expertise-from-experience has not been tested in the other forms of evaluation of writing, but some implications seem clear. First, the time needed to train the raters is decreased if they are pretrained by experience. Second, if discourse communities do exist (and I think they do), then those within a community share a form of expertise. For example, reviewers for journals are selected because they are within the community. They are not trained by calibration or range finders; they are trained by experience. Their holistic judgments (accept, reject, or revise and resubmit) determine the fate of manuscripts. When I review an article, I do not know who else will review it; yet in all the years I have been reviewing, I have disagreed with my fellow reviewers less than 2% of the time. If teaching a particular composition course creates that same expertise and community, the raters from within that community should agree with each other. Conversely, if I were asked to review an article for a journal in some other discipline, the chances of disagreement with fellow reviewers would increase. The fact that the raters with different course-taught expertise were more likely to disagree indicate that teaching a course (including working on colleagues' assignments and sharing essays and all the other things that teachers of a course do) can create a discourse community.

Cost of Rating

Placement and other types of holistic ratings can be quite expensive. Although there is research which indicates that holistic rating is cheaper than atomistic or analytic ratings (e.g., Veal & Hudson, 1983), cost is still a factor. But total cost alone is not the issue. If it were, then indirect measures which are faster and more efficient would be the best. In all types of writing assessment, the key issue is not efficiency, but relevance. What we are measuring must be worth measuring, and the current belief is that direct measures give us the information we seek. In placement testing, and in some other types of testing, individual students are directly affected. Therefore, in such testing, one must consider the ratio of efficiency to effectiveness, where effectiveness is determined by adequacy. In holistic ratings, the time factor includes the training of the raters as well as the actual rating of the essays. In placement testing, the time factor also includes any double checks, such as the essay written during the first week of class.

My research indicates that reliability among judges does not lead to higher adequacy, as judged by teacher perception, when the raters were making judgments outside their areas of course-taught expertise. But I also found strong indications that, when judgments are within that area of expertise, the reliability and adequacy are so high that if one rater accepts a student, a second rater from that course is largely redundant. In fact, the expert placement rating method decreased the cost of the rating sessions and adequacy was increased. However, the expert model is expensive for very small groups, those who dribble in throughout the year, because there should be two raters from each course. Consider the extreme case: If one essay was to be rated for placement in our system, I would hire six raters. If the student was a pure Course B, and if a Course B rater read the essay first, the decision would be made after two readings. The other raters would have done no work, but they would be paid for making their expertise available. Although expensive, the process doesn't seem unfair, especially when my evidence indicates that the final judgment is more apt to be correct.

We have only scratched the surface of the various cost, efficiency, and effectiveness issues. Much more work needs to be done to determine, for each type of rating, the various efficiency/effectiveness ratios. This is of considerable importance, for the consensus opinion is that direct measurement of writing ability is better than indirect measurement. However, indirect measurement seems to be cheaper. If we can show that the cost of direct measurement can be reduced without loss of validity, more administrators will be willing to accept this argument.

Reconceptualizing Rating Scales

The rating scales typically used are numerical, with equal intervals between the numbers (e.g, a 1 to 6 scale). These scales are used because they are amenable to parametric statistical operations (means and standard deviations, ANOVAs, *t*-tests, etc.). For each scale point, there is either a set of criteria ₁r a set of model essays which serve to target the reader. Yet, the intervals (and the scale) are arbitrary. We don't have any real knowledge that students' writing ability is normally distributed or that the intervals represent the real differences between students. Certainly, in all of the literature I have read, there have been no claims that a student who received a "4" wrote a text which is twice as good as the student who received a "2." Nor is it claimed that the student who received a split rating of "2" and "4" is the same as a student who received two "3" ratings. Yet, the numbers proclaim this, and the statistical operations assume it.

It is, therefore, much more reasonable and prudent to use categorical or nominal scales. There are appropriate and powerful statistical operations for such data (cf. Hollander & Wolfe, 1973; Reynolds, 1982). Such scales do not force us into assumptions for which we have no firm evidence, and do not force us to buy into a paradigm which is not relevant to our research. I have found that using nominal scales and nonparametric statistics is quite liberating and much easier to explain, especially to colleagues and administrators, who do not have strong backgrounds in design and statistical analysis. In short, the data make more sense to them.

In a placement context, nominal scales are more reasonable because they prevent such methods as averaging or summing in order to derive a final placement score. If a student receives a split vote, for example, A and C, the essay must be read until there is some agreement. Even if the split-resolver gives a B (which I have found to be the ⋅isual case), the student does not belong in the course which B represents. Another reader must confirm the placement.

However, the potential for numerical scales should not be slighted just because our current scales are inadequate. With some serious investigation, we might discover ways to determine the distance between the points on a numerical scale. The advantage of this method is that data from different sources and contexts could be compared. For example, data from our (Pittsburgh's) scale cannot currently be compared with data from another university's placement because the scales are not the same. If we were to find a method which placed our scale, and the other university's, on a numerical continuum, comparisons could be made. Because placement testing occurs yearly and in many universities, a large database exists. Thus, placement testing seems the logical "test bed" for research on scaling. The implications of such research spread far beyond placement testing. One of the nettlesome problems with all holistic rating is that the results are not comparable to other ratings (across year or between sets of essays). Any method which allows us to determine the distance between scale points would, therefore, allow us to do metaanalyses.

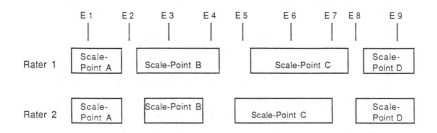

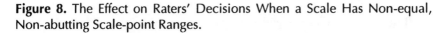

Figure 8. The Effect on Raters' Decisions When a Scale Has Non-equal, Non-abutting Scale-point Ranges.

In an earlier section, I described some alternative conceptualizations of the normal linear scale. The problem with all scales is that raters have to use them; that is, the raters, not the scale maker, have to create a usable concept of the range of each scale point. As the number of scale points increases, the task of conceiving the ranges increases. In theory, a scale which has only two points would be the easiest for the raters and would decrease disagreements. Disagreements would not cease to exist because each rater would have a slightly different range for each scale point, and all might have the grey areas between the ranges. Therein lies the power of the expert rating model. Because it combines course-taught expertise with a binary decision-making model, more precision results.

In an earlier section I presented a hypothetical case of two raters, each with different scale-point ranges and different sized grey areas, rating nine essays. This is reproduced in Figure 8.

These raters would agree on four essays and might disagree on the rest. The other raters, with their slightly different ranges and grey areas, would have similar disagreements. However, the potential for agreement among raters in the expert method is much higher. Figure 9 depicts these same nine essays as rated by eight raters, two expert raters from each scale point.

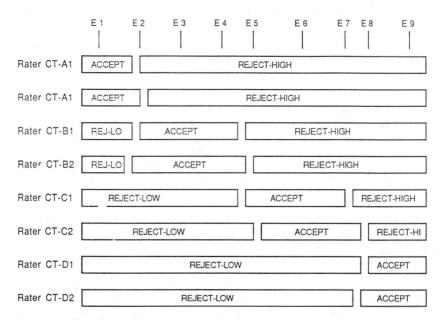

Figure 9. The Effect of the Expert Method on Raters' Decisions.

The two CT-A raters will certainly agree on eight (E2 could be a disagreement), the two CT-B raters on seven (E2 and E5 could be disagreements), the two CT-C raters on six (E5, E7, and E8 could be disagreements), and the two CT-D raters on seven (E7 and E8 could be disagreements). If the raters with different CTs are paired, they too will agree far more often then not. Of course, agreement for such pairs does not mean "same response;" it mean "same direction." Thus, if CT-A says "Reject-Low" and CT-B says "Reject-High," that would indicate an essay which is between the B and C scale-point ranges. E5 would be such an essay. However, if E5 was read by CT-C1, that rater would accept it, because it would then be read by CT-C2 who would "reject-low" and, thus, send if off for a reading by a CT-B rater. Both of these raters would be most likely to "reject-high," although there is a chance that CT-B2 might accept because the essay is in his grey area. The final resolution, then, must depend on rational decision-making protocols for tweeners.

The expert model assumes tweeners exist and creates a structure within which they are most likely to be placed in an appropriate course. It does so by taking away the possibility that the wrong reader makes the final resolution, as in the case of the Course A reader giving a C rating and a Course C rater giving an A rating. If split-resolvers were truly independent, then a Course A rater would most likely resolve the split by agreeing with the C rating. That cannot happen with the expert model.

The Course A rater would "reject-high," the Course C rater would "reject low," and the Course B rater's decision (interpreted through the protocol) would determine where the student should be placed. In placement testing, the student would, most likely, be placed into Course B. But if that student is at the high end of B (exemplified by CT-B's rating of "reject-high"), we would place the student into Course C.

In other types of testing, this essay would simply be given some code which would indicate its position on the scale continuum being used. If that continuum has only, for example, four points and no between-point possibilities, the essay would receive a B because we know that it isn't an A or a C (and therefore cannot be a D). However, if one wishes to expand the scale, the expert model allows that. For example, consider five essays given the following ratings:

E1: CT-B: accept/CT-B: accept
E2: CT-B: accept/CT-B: reject-high/CT-C: reject-low
E3: CT-B: reject-high/CT-C: reject-low
E4: CT-B: reject-high/CT-C: accept/CT-C: reject-low
E5: CT-C: accept/CT-C: accept

If we construct the space for scale-points B and C, it would look like Figure 10, within which I have placed the five essays.

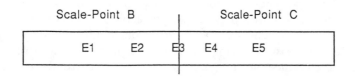

Figure 10. The Distribution of Five Essays Across the Conceptual Space of Scale-points B and C.

E1 occupies the center space in scale-point B because two CT-B raters accepted it. Similarly, E5 occupies the center space in scale-point C because two CT-C raters accepted it. E3 is between because it was rejected by both CT-B and CT-C. E2 and E4 are within their respective scale points because one expert accepted them, but they are out of the central space because another expert rejected them. Therefore, instead of two scale points, there are five. However, the difference between this 5-point scale and the usual 5-point scale is that no additional demands were made on the raters. Their decision making was kept at the binary level. Consequently, if my data on rater efficiency are generalizable, the time necessary for the rating would be considerably less than if the raters had to make a five-way decision. I also suspect that reliability would be much higher.

A Final Note

There are two potential problems with the expert model. The first is a product of the implication that training raters, for example, with range-finding exercises, is not necessary because the raters are pretrained by their teaching experience. Selecting raters, therefore, is more difficult because one must have raters who have recently taught each course. In my case, this means that I no longer hire anyone who wishes to read. I must have a certain number of readers for each course. I also don't hire as many because using the expert model increases efficiency. Consequently, some readers get to work more than others, and this preferential treatment might cause some discord, especially since reading placement tests is one of the few ways our graduate students can earn money during the summer. Furthermore, colleagues at other universities have told me that placement rating sessions are a vehicle for the staff coming together. The calibration training, it seems, is an important part of staff development, of creating unity, and of allowing teachers to view their efforts in relation to other teachers' efforts. If this is the case, then using the expert model might create more problems than it would solve.

The second problem is one that will occupy my time for the next few years. Since my experience with raters shows that "having taught" training is more powerful than calibration training (the TAP data most clearly showed this), the potential problem is that there could be a shift in the "having taught" training because we place the tweeners in the higher course. Thus, the teachers of each higher course might develop a "lower threshold" for decision making. In effect, the method would have created a shift in their scale-point range. Students who are currently rejected-low would be accepted into the higher course, and a new set of tweeners would evolve. It will take several years of research to determine whether this problem exists, but it can be done.

REFERENCES

Alexander, J., & Swartz, F. (1982, October 29-31). *The dynamics of computer assisted writing sample measurements at Ferris State College.* Paper presented at the annual meeting of the Michigan Council of Teachers of English, East Lansing, MI. (ERIC Document Reproduction Services No. ED 233 344).

Bartholomae, D. (1983). Writing assignments: Where writing begins. In P.L. Stock (Ed), *Fforum: Essays on theory and practice in the teaching of writing* (pp. 300-312). Upper Montclair, NJ: Boynton/Cook.

Bartholomae, D., & Petrosky, A. (1987). *Ways of reading: An anthology for writers.* New York: Bedford/St. Martin's Press.

Cohen, A. M. (1973). Assessing college students' ability to write compositions. *Research in the Teaching of English, 7,* 356-371.

Coles, W. E., Jr. (1981). *Composing II: Writing as a self-creating process.* Rochelle Park, NJ: Hayden Book Company.

Cooper, C. R. (1977). Holistic evaluation in writing. In C. R. Cooper & L. Odell (Eds), *Evaluating writing: Describing, measuring, judging.* Urbana, IL: National Council of Teachers of English.

Follman, J. C., & Anderson, J. A. (1967). An investigation of the reliability of five procedures for grading english themes. *Research in the Teaching of English, 1,* 190-200.

Garrow, J. R. (1989). *Assessing and improving the adequacy of college composition placement.* Unpublished doctoral dissertation, University of Pittsburgh.

Hollander, M., & Wolfe, D. A. (1973). *Nonparametric statistical methods.* New York: John Wiley and Sons.

Hughes, D. C., Kelling, B., & Tuck, B. F. (1980). Essay marking and the context problems. *Educational Research, 22,* 147-148.

Myers, M. (1980) A procedure for writing assessment and holistic scoring. Urbana, IL: National Council of Teachers of English.

Rentz, R. R. (1984). Testing writing by writing. *Educational Measurement: Issues and Practices, 3,* 4.

Reynolds, H. T. (1982). *Analysis of nominal data.* Berkeley, CA: Sage.

Smith, L. S., Winters, L., Quellmalz, E. S., & Baker, E. L. (1980). *Characteristics of student writing competence: An investigation of alternative scoring systems* (Res. Rep. No. 134). Los Angeles: Center for the Study of Evaluation. (ERIC Document Reproduction Services No. ED 217 074).

Smith W. L., Hull, G. A., Land, R. E., Moore, M. T., Ball, C., Dunham, D. E., Hickey, L. S., & Ruzich, C. W. (1985). Some effects of varying the structure of the topic on college students' writing. *Written Communication, 2,* 73-89.

Veal, L. R., & Hudson, S. A. (1983). Direct and indirect measures for large scale evaluation of writing. *Research in the Teaching of English, 17,* 290-296.

White, E. M. (1985). *Teaching and Assessing writing.* San Francisco: Jossey Bass.

White, E. M. (1975-81). *Comparison and contrast: The California State University and College Freshman English Equivalency Examination.* Long Beach: English Council of the California State Universities & Colleges. (ERIC Document Reproduction Services No. ED 227 510).

6

The Influence of Holistic Scoring Procedures on Reading and Rating Student Essays

Brian A. Huot
University of Louisville

INTRODUCTION

Four main objections have been raised about holistic scoring procedures:

1. Ratings have been shown to correlate with handwriting and text length (Bertrand, 1985; Chou, Kirkland, & Smith, 1982; Markham, 1976; Nold & Freedman, 1977; Remondino, 1959; Sloan & McGinnis,1978; Stewart & Grobe, 1979; Thomas & Donlon);
2. Ratings are product-driven and not suitable for informed decisions about composition instruction or students' composing processes (Faigley, Cherry, Jolliffe, & Skinner, 1985; Gere, 1980; Odell & Cooper, 1980);
3. Ratings cannot be generalized beyond the scoring sessions in which they are produced; and
4. Ratings are generated by scoring procedures which alter fluent reading processes and impede the ability of raters to make sound judgments about writing quality (Charney, 1984; Gere, 1980; Huot, 1990b).

The first three criticisms point to limitations that are properly the subject of continuing validation work on holistic scoring. Some of these limitations have been addressed in previous research and in other chapters in this volume. The fourth criticism, however, seems the most damaging, since it is a direct challenge to holistic scoring validity, asserting that the very procedures used to read and rate student writing may distort the ability of raters to render valid scoring decisions.

Unfortunately, the theoretical basis for holistic scoring has never been explicitly articulated (Gere, 1980; Huot, 1990b), and its validity, though asserted, has never been demonstrated (Charney, 1984; Huot, 1990b). The study reported in this chapter focuses on this primary concern for validation research on holistic scoring and the effects of the procedures themselves on reading and rating student texts in holistic scoring sessions.

Holistic scoring procedures require adherence to a scoring rubric by raters who read text rapidly and independently. These characteristics seem incongruous to normal reading processes. Charney (1984), Gere (1980), Hake (1986), and Nold (1978) object to the use of uniform scoring criteria and the emphasis on rater agreement. Smith (this volume) suggests that readers' criteria never uniformly overlap, and perfect agreement will always be impossible.

Fluent reading normally involves two important aspects—the readers' purpose for reading and their prior experience (Anderson & Pearson, 1984; Fish, 1980; Holland, 1968, 1975; Iser, 1978; Smith, 1972, 1983; Stock & Robinson, 1987; Tierney & Pearson, 1983). More importantly, raters' judgments about texts emerge from their responses to these texts. Holistic scoring procedures would impede the fluent reading process if these procedures altered the way raters respond to texts. For instance, reading a text quickly for a limited set of criteria instantiated within a scoring rubric would seem to disconnect the holistic rater from the whole or gestalt of that text. The rubric, reading rate, and need for agreement would seem, therefore, to impede a rich, personal response in the interest of producing reliable scores. Thus, holistic scoring procedures provide a purpose for reading which may disconnect raters from their personal responses.

Bleich (1975) asserts that all critical judgment begins with the subjective reaction of a reader. Thus, personal response is a vital feature of readers' experiences with making meaning from a text, much in the same way that differences in prior experience account for independent response from different readers to the same texts (Stock & Robinson, 1987, p. 105). The relationship between judgment and response in reading is crucial: "an interpreting entity endowed with purposes and concerns, is, by virtue of its very operation, determining what counts as the facts to be observed" (Fish, 1980, p. 8). The effects of a reader's purposes and prior experience raise serious questions about the influences of training on the nature of the reading process. Similarly, the speed of reading in holistic scoring sessions could restrict the individual nature of the reading process. Both the speed and the rubric could cause raters to limit their focus, so they can agree with their fellow raters. But, this agreement would come at a price.

What happens to the personal reaction of a holistic rater? Is it subsumed by the training with the rubric? If so, how does this training affect the judgment made by individual raters? Gere (1980) contends that holistic scoring procedures inhibit a rater's ability to interact with a text.

> The interaction between reader and text, the context in which the writing is produced, and the textual representation created by the reader are subsumed by pervasive attention which focuses on the written text and emphasizes reader consensus in response to this text. (p. 47)

An important misgiving about holistic scoring is the possibility that a personal stake in reading might be reduced to a set of negotiated principles, and then a true rating of writing quality could be sacrificed for a reliable one. Baritt, Stock, and Clark describe the conflict between personal response and group rubrics: "We discovered in our enquiry that the engagement of mind by text has the power to disengage even the tightest of pre-ordained schemes" (1986, p. 322). What we have is a "tension between a reader as reader and a reader as rater" (Huot, 1990a, p. 255). It is conceivable that raters who have been trained according to a common rubric would base their judgments upon that set of criteria, and therefore their personal engagement with the writing would be considerably diminished.

Summary of the Research Problem

In understanding the purpose of this study it is important to remember how holistic scoring developed and where it is in terms of becoming the standard measurement of writing quality. To gain any kind of acceptance, direct writing evaluation had to establish some record of consistency. The price of this consistency has been the preoccupation of writing assessment literature with reliability and the procedures used to obtain it. The validity of holistic scoring has largely gone unexplored. There have been few attempts to analyze the reading and rating activities of holistic scorers. Any attempt to understand holistic scoring as a true measure of writing quality requires a focus on the processes of reading and rating student writing within a holistic scoring session.

This study attempts to answer the general question of whether or not holistic scoring procedures modify the way raters read and judge student writing. To find out if holistic methods of scoring writing are an obtrusive force on the process of reading and rating student writing, this research is organized around the following questions:

1. Are holistic raters limited by their training to a selective reading, and would an untrained rater comment more often on the same papers?
2. Do holistic raters base their judgments of writing quality on the same criteria as raters without holistic scoring experience or training?
3. Do holistic raters respond less personally to student writing than those without training or experience?
4. Are the reading and rating processes of trained and untrained raters essentially different?

METHOD

To answer questions about the possibility of holistic scoring procedures impeding the process of reading and rating student writing, this study sought to compare the rating process of two sets of essay readers, one with holistic scoring experience and training and one without. There were four raters in each group. I employed protocol analysis to access the process of reading and rating student writing and to compare and analyze the process of each group. Protocol analysis has become a familiar method in composition research; it has been used in several studies of students' writing processes (Flower & Hayes, 1981; Hayes & Flower 1983; Perl, 1979; Pianko, 1979; Swarts, Flower & Hayes, 1984; Witte, 1987; and others), in a study involving student reaction to teacher commentary (Hayes & Daiker, 1984), and in a previous study on the rating processes of holistic scorers (Vaughan, 1987).

Sample Description

The essays scored in the study were drawn from those written as part of the English Department's Task Force for the Evaluation of the Teaching of Writing conducted from 1984 through 1986 at Indiana University of Pennsylvania (IUP) (McAndrew, Swigart, & Williamson, 1986). IUP's enrollment during the fall semester of 1984, when the essays used in the study were written, was about 10,500 students on the main campus. All essays used in this study were written by native speakers of English.

Data Selection and Preparation

Over 30,000 essays were written by students in all sections of three different writing courses as part of the task force study on writing (McAndrew et al., 1986). The essays used in the study had been previously scored as part of the IUP task force project for which the data was originally collected. I drew 24 essays from each of the seven possible scale points, the sum-scores of 2 to 8 given on a 4-point scale by the two task force raters, thus insuring a full, stratified sample representative of the wide range of writing quality within the original population. To protect any of the results obtained from this study from being labeled task-specific, I drew the essays from two different topics, creating a pool of 84 essays for each of the two tasks.

Writing Tasks

The compositions used in the study were written in response to two tasks (Appendix A) developed during the summer of 1984. These tasks were among eight created by a panel of 15 experienced teachers who all had graduate-level course work in composition theory. The panel began with 20 possible topics which would require no special knowledge, and the panel members individually rated each topic for its interest to first-year college students (McAndrew et al., 1984). Panel members individually constructed 45 tasks that were reviewed, discussed, and narrowed down to a consensus of eight which were piloted, and six that were eventually used in the task force's study (McAndrew et al., 1984). All six tasks proved to be relevant to student writers and successful in the task force's collection of student writing. For the present study involving the process of reading and rating student writing, I chose one task each from the persuasive and expository categories.

Protocol Analysis

Protocol analysis, a research method developed in cognitive psychology for accessing the mental activity of research subjects as they perform a specific task (Ericsson & Simon, 1984), was chosen because this study attempted to define the nature of the influence of holistic scoring procedures upon a rater's process of reading and scoring student writing. One study (Vaughan, 1987) reported on the use of the talk-aloud responses of raters as they read and scored student writing. Vaughan's study provided a field test for the application of protocol analysis to the rating process. However, the design of her study, in which 15 raters read the same six essays, did not duplicate the inquiry of the present study into the effects of scoring procedures on judging student writing quality.

Protocol analysis can be used concurrently, while a task is being performed, or retrospectively, immediately after a task is completed. Both types of protocol procedures were used in an attempt to secure different kinds of information. Concurrent protocols revealed what raters were concerned about as they read and rated, and retrospective probing was employed to determine what raters thought they were concerned about.

The reflective nature of retrospective probing allowed a rater to think about the rating process without the pressures of the task at hand. In this way, the two protocol procedures were used to test each other and to provide a broader picture of rater behavior and the rating process.

Training Raters for Protocol Analysis

General instructions to protocol subjects have been found to be superior to particular directives because they yield a richer database and are less disruptive to the normal processing which goes on during the performance of a task (Ericsson & Simon, 1980, 1984; Nisbett & Wilson, 1977; Tversky & Kahneman, 1973). For this reason, raters were only told to talk aloud as they read, making sure that they kept up a steady stream of speech as they read and rated the essays. Raters were not directed to comment on any specific textual criteria, but rather were asked to verbalize any thoughts they had while reading and rating. Each rater was instructed and warmed up individually according to a uniform set of instructions (see Appendices B & C). These instructions and training procedures were based on a general set of guidelines developed by Ericsson and Simon (1984, pp. 375-377). The training period included the comparison of two passages. Raters were asked to read both passages and judge which they preferred. All the recordings of the concurrent protocols provided continuous spoken discourse. All raters were offered but refused additional training for the second protocol session.

Raters took part in the study by groups of two on four consecutive days. Novice raters scored the first two days, and expert raters scored the second two days. This scheduling reflected the individual preferences of the raters and the scoring leader who was needed for the sessions involving the expert raters. Every rater read four packets of 21 papers each; two packets were read while raters talked aloud (42 papers), and two were read silently. Raters read silently and protocolled in an alternating scheme with Raters 1 and 3 protocolling first and Raters 2 and 4 reading the first group of essays silently.

Raters worked in two separate office-size rooms which were far away from each other so that neither rater could hear the other while protocolling. Raters had a choice of chairs and worked with adequate lighting and a temperature which they could control. A microphone was positioned on the table in front of the rater, but away from the folder of papers so that it did not interfere with the turning of pages or the reading of the essays. Raters were allowed breaks as needed, and the sessions were regulated so that the raters read two packets of papers (one silently and one aloud) in the morning, went to lunch, and returned to read the remaining essays in the afternoon.

Holistic Rater Training

Expert raters were trained according to standard procedures outlined in the literature (Myers, 1980; White, 1985). Appendix D provides copies of the rubrics used by the raters in the present study. In both training sessions, the raters reached agreement on a full set of training papers after discussion and some adjustment to the rubric. In the training session involving Expert Raters 3 and 4, the two raters agreed on every one of the anchor papers used in training. In the morning the raters each read two folders containing 21 papers each . The raters were retrained on two sets of anchor papers in the afternoon, and both groups of raters reached full agreement on all papers in the afternoon training sessions. The scoring leader was also a veteran of several holistic scoring sessions and two composition research studies.

The Raters

The raters who participated in the study were all practicing English teachers who represented a wide range of experience. Six possessed high-school-level teaching experience, and six had taught at the college level. The least-experienced rater had 6 years teaching experience. Five of the raters had between 12 and 17 years experience, while two of the raters had taught for over 20 years. Seven of the raters held Masters of Arts degrees, and one had a Bachelor's. All of the raters had completed graduate-level course work in composition theory and practice. The raters' fairly impressive backgrounds ascertained that they were qualified to act as judges of student writing quality.

While the raters in the novice group had all heard of holistic scoring practices through their familiarity with the composition literature, none of them had ever participated as a holistic rater or considered themselves familiar with holistic scoring procedures. It was important to the design of the study that the novice group rated without the benefit of present or past training, so that any differences between groups could be attributed to the training and holistic rating experience of the expert rater group.

All members of the expert group had served as holistic scorers on at least two other occasions. Two of the four raters had performed as trainers and scoring leaders in the past, and one of the raters had participated in eight separate holistic scoring sessions. The scorers in the expert group were also familiar with the holistic scoring literature and with all phases of holistic scoring procedures.

Transcribing the Tapes

All protocol sessions were recorded on cassette tape. I verified the accurate identification of the raters by listening to a small portion of each tape. These tapes were given to two typists who transcribed the tapes for the present study. Both typists were experienced in transcribing from their work in law offices, which make extensive use of transcribed verbal material. All transcribing was done on a word processor and printed double spaced to make reading and coding easier.

The Development of the Code

The initial step in attempting to provide a coding system with which to quantify salient characteristics of the raters' reading during the concurrent protocols was to read the transcripts of all raters' protocols and make a list of their responses. The coding system had to account not only for what the raters saw as they read, but also what the raters did, how they read, and when they performed certain rater functions.

The coding system, then, was generated from the reading of the raters' transcripts. Using the notes written while trying to code the transcripts, I created a grid which matched the data. To test the suitability of the grid, the transcripts were coded once again. I kept notes on responses which would not fit into the grid. During this second reading of the transcripts I made many revisions and reread two of the raters' transcripts to make sure that they would fit the many modifications to the coding system.

The Coding System

The type of response.   No matter what response a rater made during a talk-aloud rating session, the response contained three distinct characteristics: it was made either after or while the rater read the essay; it was either a positive, negative, or neutral comment; and the comment was either directed at the paper or the writer. Using these three characteristics, I derived 12 different possible types of response.

1. Neutral Comments Made to the Paper While Reading
2. Neutral Comments Made to the Paper After Reading
3. Neutral Comments Made to the Writer While Reading
4. Neutral Comments Made to the Writer After Reading
5. Negative Comments Made to the Paper While Reading
6. Negative Comments Made to the Paper After Reading
7. Negative Comments Made to the Writer While Reading
8. Negative Comments Made to the Writer After Reading
9. Positive Comments Made to the Paper While Reading
10. Positive Comments Made to the Paper After Reading
11. Positive Comments Made to the Writer While Reading
12. Positive Comments Made to the Writer After Reading

Rating criteria.   Along with the 12 types of responses, the coding system had to account for the various criteria on which raters based their judgments and the behavior raters exhibited while rating. Ten areas covering 62 separate categories were extracted from the transcripts of the concurrent protocols. Seven of the rating criteria categories pertain to the features on which raters base their judgments of writing quality: Content, Organization, Tone, Style, Print Code, Appearance, and Instructional. The other three categories—Reading Process, Personal Comments, and Series of Actions—pertain to what raters did while rating a student's essay. (See Appendix E for a copy of the grid.)

Coding the data.   All essays read and rated while talking aloud were coded on a separate grid. Each rater's comments were coded from the transcripts directly to the grid. The design of the grid allowed me to code not only to what kind of rating or behavior criteria a rater's remark pertained, but also to record when the comment was made, to whom or what it was directed, and whether it was positive, negative, or neutral.

Data Analysis

The data collection for the present study yields three different kinds of information about the process of reading and rating student writing. The first type of data were the transcripts of the raters' concurrent protocols. While the transcripts themselves are a rich source of information, their length (over 800 pages) makes them unruly to use except in smaller segments. For reasons of manageability and to provide a quantifiable form of data to compare the rater groups, the transcripts of the concurrent protocols were coded according to the procedures described earlier. The coded data provided a more manageable form for the information in the concurrent protocols and also gave an overall picture of trends and patterns. In addition to the information available from the raw and coded versions of the concurrent protocols, the verbal data from 16 retrospective probing sessions were collected and transcribed, one after each of the concurrent protocol sessions. This retrospective data were the answers to eight identical questions given by each rater twice during the rating session (see Appendix F). The retrospective protocols allowed each of the raters to give additional insight about their method of rating and any other pertinent information not mentioned during their talk-aloud protocols.

The design of the data analysis utilizes three separate data sources in attempting to examine and interpret the results of the study. The intent in designing the data analysis was to provide a sense of the individual nature of the protocol data, while at the same time preserving the trends and patterns available in quantifying rater response. The use of three different indices to explore the data collected in the present study employs the method of triangulation articulated in Miles and Huberman (1984) and others as a means to verify qualitative data analysis. In a strict sense, the use of transcripts and the data coded from these transcripts did not qualify as separate data sources (Miles & Huberman, 1984, p. 235). However, the data did come from two instruments: the transcripts from the raters and the code from my analysis of the verbal reports. An important aspect in employing these two means of examining the data was that the quantifiable, coded results needed to be compatible with the tone of each rater's verbal report. In other words, the transcripts of the verbal reports verified the code.

The purpose of this study was to discover how raters read and scored student writing, as the process of rating would not be present merely in the verbal reports themselves, in the number and type of response, or in raters' reflections about their scoring experience. The fullest possible picture of the rating process required that each rater be viewed from at least three different perspectives. With this three-tiered analysis I built a comprehensive rater profile for each of the raters in the study. Ultimately, the three forms of data allow for the fullest model of rating behavior for the two rater groups. This method of analyzing the data from three distinct perspectives enriches the findings and the interpretations available from these findings. Most importantly, the examination of the verbal reports of the raters in the study provides the best possible insight into the process of reading and rating student writing.

RESULTS AND DISCUSSION

This study was conducted to question whether or not holistic scoring procedures are obtrusive on the process of reading and rating student writing, and whether this obtrusiveness could challenge the validity of holistic scoring. I will examine and discuss the results of the data analysis that pertain to an understanding of each of the four specific questions (see p. 209) addressed in the study. The answers to the four specific questions are used to answer the larger question of whether or not the findings of the study can be interpreted to suggest that holistic scoring interferes with the ability of raters to effectively assess writing quality.

Rater Response Rate

As predicted, novice raters responded many more times—over 1,400 more—than did their expert counterparts (see Table 1).

Table 1. Rate of Response by Group

Total Responses	Novice	Expert	Difference
6307	3873	2434	Novice 1439+

This discrepancy between the total number of responses for each of the rater groups averages out to over 350 more responses per rater for the novice group. The reasoning behind the prediction of more responses for the novice rater group was due to the speed at which holistic raters are encouraged to read (McColly, 1970; Myers, 1980), and the fact that the rubric focuses the raters' attention on specific textual features. This focus, I theorized, would work in much the same way as a reader's alignment does (Tierney & Pearson, 1983), and as such, reading specifically from a rater's point of view would blot out that part of the text not relevant to a determination of writing quality. The reasoning was that expert raters would comment less because they would see less due to their tighter, constrained reading. At first glance, the research findings of the present study would support this theory. However, under closer scrutiny the difference in response rate between the two rater groups cannot be attributed to the constraining influence of holistic scoring procedures (see Table 2).

Table 2. Number of Responses for Each Rater

Novice 1	Novice 2	Novice 3	Novice 4
1506	706	1244	417

Expert 1	Expert 2	Expert 3	Expert 4
773	551	416	694

First of all, the majority of the difference in response rate was not attributed to all of the novice raters. Novice Rater 4 was only one response away from producing the least number of responses for any rater in the study. As it is, Novice 4 tallied over 550 less responses than the average for the novice group and almost 400 responses below the mean rate for all raters in the study. In addition, Novice Rater 2 tallied over 250 less responses than the mean for the novice rater group. Novice 2's response rate was closer to three of the expert raters than to any of the raters in the novice group. The inflated response rate for the novice group is due to three of the protocol sessions for two of the novice raters. Novice Rater 1 amassed over 500 more responses than the mean rate for the novice group. In fact, Novice 1 made more responses in one concurrent protocol session than 5 out of the 8 raters made in two talk-aloud sessions. The most responses made in any protocol session was made by Novice Rater 3 who made over 500 less comments during the second talk-aloud session. Given the great discrepancy between raters in the novice group—almost 900 responses between the high and low raters—it is impossible to attribute the difference in mean response rate between the novice and expert raters to holistic scoring procedures.

Rating Criteria

Table 3. Percentage of Response for Rating Criteria

	Novice (%)	Expert (%)
Content	29.34	29.01
Organization	12.00	11.58
Tone	5.35	7.54
Style	10.54	7.29
Print Code /M x	12.08	8.90
Appearance	6.03	5.40
Instructional	1.43	1.40

Clearly, the two rater groups based their judgments of writing quality upon the same criteria (see Table 3). Of the seven rating criteria categories—content organization, tone, style, print code, appearance, and instructional—the two rater groups are within one percentage point for four of the criteria and within three points for the other areas. The most popular area of comment was for content, around 30% for each of the two rater groups. Organization was the second most common response. These findings indicate the preoccupation of the raters in the present study with content and organization and reflect the findings of other studies which attempted to discern what raters were interested in when they scored student writing (Breland & Jones, 1984; Freedman, 1979a, 1979b; Pula & Huot, this volume; Vaughan; 1987). The results for content and organization verify the data collection methods and coding system with studies which achieved the same results with other research methodologies.

While the information about rater preference for content and organization matches other studies, the data in this study were obtained with a methodology that more closely duplicated the rating situation than any research I can cite. This study is the only one, besides its replication which appears in this volume (Pula & Huot), designed to replicate the context of a holistic scoring session. Freedman's work (1977, 1979a, 1979b), which has been the benchmark for research in holistic scoring, really measures how rewritten student writing, strong or weak in particular areas, can influence scores given by raters. The Breland and

Jones study (1984) correlated raters' annotations with later judgments of holistic quality. Even Vaughan (1987), who used verbal data from raters, had a handful of papers scored by 10 raters, hardly the context of a holistic scoring session. The importance of this study in providing data gathered from raters working within a holistic scoring situation is important not only in verifying earlier studies, but in providing strong opposition to those studies which found raters more influenced by mechanics (Harris, 1977; Rafoth & Rubin, 1984), since neither of those studies gathered data from raters working within a scoring session. Harris's work centered on raters' inability to respond to syntactic variables, and Rafoth and Rubin used propositional analysis to manipulate student texts. Clearly, the present study and its replication (Pula & Huot, this volume) command some authority concerning the question of what most influences holistic raters' scoring decisions.

Personal Engagement

The third research question this study addressed was the degree of personal response to student writing. While the influence of holistic training procedures upon the degree of personal response was a logical question for this study to answer, the notion that raters in the novice group would respond more personally to student writing was not proven by the research results. In fact, just the opposite was true. Instead of holistic training procedures impeding the level of response, expert raters commented 10 percentage points more often (17%) than did their novice counterparts (7%), the largest discrepancy in any of the coded areas between the two rater groups.

Some insight into why the expert rater group made more personal comments than the novice raters in the present study might come from examining the 10 categories which made up the Personal Response Area (see Table 4).

Table 4. Percentage of Responses From the Personal Comment Area

	Novice (%)	Expert (%)
Indecision	.65	4.23
Opinion	2.35	2.26
Expectations	2.17	.94
Laugh	.9	2.71
Justification	.18	.08
Nonevaluative Comments	.57	3.9
Sarcasm	.21	.94
Questions Own Judgment	.18	1.6
Time Management	0	.16
Explains Decisions	.26	.04

In the Opinion category, the two rater groups were less than a tenth of a percentage point away from each other, and in the category of Expectations, novice raters amassed twice the percentage of responses. However, in proportion, expert raters expressed indecision 6 times more often, questioned their own judgments 9 times more often, laughed 3 times more often, and gave nonevaluative remarks 7 times more often than did the raters in the novice group. From the greater number of comments for the expert raters in the Indecision and Questions Own Judgment categories, it might be assumed that novice raters were more sure of their decisions. However, expert raters made over 7 times more comments which weren't concerned with assessment. The novice raters, on the other hand, made many more comments of an evaluative nature. Therefore, it might be said that since the expert raters made fewer evaluative comments, they might have been more sure of the ones they did make. As well, expert raters commented more often on the process of arriving at a decision about writing quality, a notion supported from the comparison of the retrospective probes.

One interesting trend available from the patterns of responses for the two rater groups is that the expert group seemed to make a greater variety of comments than did the novice rater group. The novice group basically expressed their expectations and then assessed the writing. On the other hand, expert raters expressed expectations much less, perhaps because of the scoring rubric which served as a declaration of group expectation. Expert raters read from a greater variety of stances, taking the time to interact with student writing without having to evaluate what they were reading. Expert raters even indulged in fits of sarcasm and word play, and they laughed much more often. Expert raters appeared to have read more freely and from a greater number of viewpoints than did the novice raters who were constrained by a need to evaluate. The expert raters' reading represents a fuller range of response than the limited, expectative, judgmental reading given by the novice raters. Not only did the expert rater group interact more personally with student texts, but the expert raters were also able to create meaning beyond their roles as evaluators, constructing a reading that reflected a wider sense of student writing. On the other hand, the novice rater group commented many more times as a group, but their remarks were limited to expressing their expectations, opinions, and judgments of the student essays; without holistic training, raters seemed unable to read beyond their role as evaluators.

In further interpreting the difference in personal comments between the two rater groups, it is important to consider the essential differences between the conditions experienced by the two sets of raters. The biggest difference between the two groups of raters was the use of a scoring rubric. Of course, the scoring rubric and training also brought about the burden of wanting to agree with a scoring partner. During the retrospective protocols, all expert raters mentioned their concern about agreeing with their partners, while none of the novice raters expressed any concern about agreement.

Initially, the difference involving the scoring guide would seem to favor the novice group's ability to provide a more flexible and comprehensive reading, since the expert group was contracted, so to speak, to score by a set guideline and to agree with a partner. However, the members of the novice group had no real preparation or expectations as raters, while the expert group had a clearer idea of what was expected of them. The scoring guide could be conceived to function not only as a mechanism which helps a rater agree with his/her rating partner, but which also provides a clear set of rater expectations. The results of this study may indicate that the rubric or scoring guideline frees the holistic rater from having to be a full-time evaluator, allowing him/her to read outside his/her role as examiner. Members of the novice group struggled in their roles as evaluators and were unable to assume any other reading stance because they lacked the clear set of expectations provided to the expert raters.

The Process of Reading and Rating

The last of the four research questions around which this study was organized has to with the process of reading and rating student writing in a holistic scoring session. There are three places in the results where I find pertinent information about the rating process: in the rating behavior Area of the Reading Process; in the rating behavior Area of Series of Actions; and in the types of comments readers made.

The reading process.   The two rater groups showed little difference in the total percentage of comments they made concerning the process of reading. In fact, the percentage figures were about one half of one point higher for the novice rater group. There were only three categories where a real difference existed between the two groups. Expert raters recorded no comments which rephrased an essay; while novice raters did rephrase student work, the frequency of rephrasing was so slight, .25%, that this difference cannot be used to promote a difference in the reading process for the two rater groups. Proportionately, novice raters repeated words (4%) twice as often as did members of the expert rater group (2%). As well, novice raters broke down when reading (1%) at about twice the percentage rate than did expert raters (.5%). The difference between the two groups in the Reading Process Area occurred in the Rereads for Evaluation Category where novice raters reread to evaluate essays only .36% of the time, and the expert group reread to evaluate 2% of the time.

All of the numbers from this area are too slight to make any strong assertions about what the differences may mean. However, if there are any trends available in the findings, they would point to a more fluent reading for the expert group and a greater tendency on the part of the expert raters in the study to evaluate after, rather than while, reading an essay.

Series of actions. It is safe to say that the novice raters in the study monopolized the Series of Actions Area (see Table 5).

Table 5. Number and Percentage of Series of Action Comments

Novice	*Expert*
131 or 3.42%	4 or .16%

While Novice Rater 1 made almost half of all comments directed at the area, each of the novice raters accumulated more series of actions comments than all expert raters combined. This area, by definition, differs from all the others coded in this study because it involves more than one action. The first category of Expectations/Follow/Judge (EFJ) received about half of the responses. It's not too surprising that the novice rater group would use this comment often since they were much more prone in the Personal Comment Area to express their expectations.

It seems probable that the EFJ category is a logical extension of the need of the novice rater group to use their expectations, since they didn't have a scoring guideline upon which to base their judgments of writing quality. Instead, the novice rater set up his/her expectations and followed through on them to assess the quality of the writing. Expert raters did not have to employ a similar strategy because they were able to fall back on the rubric.

The Alternative/Justification (AJ) and the Corrects/Explains (CE) categories work in much the same way as the EFJ does. Without a rubric with which to gauge an assessment of a piece of writing, the members of the novice rater group were forced to develop ad hoc measures to express their decisions and reasons about their decisions. Novice raters felt more compelled to explain and justify because they did not have the added dimension of a rubric to validate and verify their judgments.

An interesting way to view the whole Series of Actions Area and the novice preoccupation with such comments is that the rubric could be seen as working much the same way as the two or three parts of a Series of Actions remark works for a novice rater. The expert rater does not have to express his/her expectations for a piece of writing, because the scoring guide does it for him/her. Consequently, the expert rater is able to comment on a specific aspect of an essay without a series of actions because the rubric acts as his/her expectations, justifications or explanations. It's important to reiterate that the rubric actually seems to make it easier for the rater to read and judge writing quality. The use of a scoring guide cuts down on the amount of commentary or mental activity necessary to make judgments about writing quality. The expert raters, then, did not need a two- or three-part comment because all of their comments were connected to the guidelines sketched out in the scoring rubric.

The types of comments.   Comment type refers to whether a rater's remark was directed to the paper or the writer, whether or not the remark was positive, negative, or neutral, and whether the remark was made during or after the rater had read the composition he/she was rating. There were only slight differences between the two groups of raters for whether the comment was directed at the writer or paper and whether the comment was positive, negative, or neutral. The only marked difference in comment type had to do with when a rater made his/her remarks. All expert raters accumulated a greater percentage of comments after a paper was read than did the members of the novice rater group. Proportionately, expert raters amassed 25% more responses after reading than did their novice counterparts.

The expert raters' tendency to reserve response to student writing until after reading a text can also be related to the use of the scoring guideline or rubric. Because of the scoring guideline, expert raters knew exactly what features they would use to judge a composition's quality. Expert raters could read the essay with less disruptions and then comment after reading, while they used the rubric to judge the quality of the paper. Novice raters tended to comment on a piece of writing as they read because they did not have the luxury of a scoring guide. Commenting after reading would seem to make a rater's task a little easier. Instead, novice raters attempted to judge and read at the same time and were unable, as their expert counterparts were, to reserve judgment until after reading a student's essay.

MODELS OF THE RATING PROCESS

In the Method section I outlined a three-tiered data analysis that allowed for the triangulation of findings to sketch a profile for each rater in the study. While space here does not allow a full presentation of rater profiles (Huot, 1988, pp. 149-200), this section will use those profiles as the basic structure in building a model of the rating process. Furthermore, a review of profiles by group separates the processes of the novice and expert raters and focuses on the difference between the two groups in determining the effect of holistic scoring procedures on the way raters read and assess student writing.

Model of the Novice Rating Process

Novice Rater 1 made almost a quarter of all the comments (1,506) which comprise the verbal report data of this study (6,307). She directed the greatest percentage of her comments (30%) to the Content Area. Novice 1 depended on correct writing and was easily distracted by errors in grammar, mechanics, and usage. She seemed uncomfortable with the demands of scoring a large number of papers and remarked that she would prefer two separate rating sessions where she could annotate the papers during the first reading. Also, she said she relied on correctness as a rating criteria because it was the easiest feature for her to recognize.

Novice Rater 2 used the Organization Area more than any other rater in the study (21%). Also, Novice 2 chose to compare student's papers, but this strategy proved ineffective for her: ". . . but it's hard to remember if another student really did better." Overall, Novice 2 appeared to be searching for a rating method, and when asked what could have improved her rating performance, she outlined a typical holistic training procedure: "Look for this, look and as soon as you get to a paper that does this, put it in this category."

Novice 3 totaled the second highest number of responses (1,244) of any rater in the study. She seemed preoccupied with the format of the papers she read, mostly whether or not they contained a letter-type salutation. Overall, she commented more often (54) to the format area than all the other raters combined (22). However, three quarters of the format comments were made in the first protocol session, and Novice 3 commented 500 fewer times during the second session, remarking during the retrospective probe that she rated differently the second time around.

Novice Rater 4 recorded the fewest number of remarks for any rater during her second protocol, and she reported that fatigue was a major factor in her performance. Her strategy as a rater revolved around trying to make sense of the essay from the viewpoint of the audience in the writing task. Novice 4's transcripts portray her as a sympathetic reader, and she accumulated a high percentage of positive remarks (35%), at least 10 percentage points higher than any other rater.

One thing seems to stand out from this summary of the four novice raters; they appear to have chosen four distinctive and unrelated rating strategies: correctness, organization and essay comparison, format , and audience awareness. However, three out of the four raters reported that their rating technique broke down some time during the scoring session, and Novice 1, the only constant novice rater, acknowledged that she chose to rate so strongly on correctness because it was easy for her. The novice rater appears to be in search of a rating system, a set of criteria which she can apply and on which she can rely. This search for an effective rating process appears to have caused novice raters to try too many things at once. For one thing, novice raters commented much more often while reading (79%) than after (21%). This technique of commenting while reading appears to have been inefficient as novice raters broke down and repeated words more often (195) than their expert counterparts (67). Novices attempted to carry on many functions at once, and this was also reflected in their greater amount of Series of Actions remarks (139 for novices and 4 for experts). An interesting note about the Series of Actions Area is that almost half the comments (62) involved the expression of expectations, and the other half (77) involved the justification of alternative language forms or the explanation of corrections. In this light, the novice raters seemed to not only be searching for a rating strategy, they appear to be insecure about the strategies they used.

Beyond the novice rater's attempt to comment, read, and express herself in multiple-step remarks, there are some other similarities within the apparent disparate criteria used by the novice raters. Some of the novice strategies appeared to have come from the essays themselves. Novice 3 commented heavily on whether students included a salutation or not. She would not have been able to use such a criterion if the task had not asked for students to write a letter. Similarly, Novice 4 relied on students' use of the fictional audience contained in the writing prompt. My point is that these two novice raters extracted their criteria for judgment from the task itself and would have had to use other bases for their decision making had the prompt not asked for a letter or contained a fictional audience. Their rating strategies were a reaction to the demands of rating student writing much in the same way Novice 1 reacted by choosing that aspect of student writing which was easiest for her to recognize. Similarly, Novice 2 chose organization just as arbitrarily, remarking that she wished she had been trained to look for certain features and to know which rating to assign those features.

The novice rating process, then, appears to be formulated from the demands of rating a specific set of papers. The novice rater group lacks any cohesive rating technique and instead attempts to institute ad hoc measures adapted from the essays themselves. What's important to remember in all of this is that the novice rater group did succeed, since novice raters used pretty much the same rating criteria as did their expert counterparts. The difference is that the novice effort to provide a good evaluation cost them any personal interaction with the student texts; all of their effort was diverted in assessing writing quality.

Model of the Expert Rating Process

The model of the expert rating process begins with a brief synopsis of the profiles for each of the expert raters. Expert Rater 1 appeared to carry on a monologue with the student paper as her audience. She remarked in the retrospective probe that she liked talking to the papers as she would talk with one of her students in a writing conference. Expert 1's personal, conversational style is reflected in the large number of remarks she made to the Personal Comment Area (143), more than any other rater in the study.

In her rater profile, Expert Rater 2 could be dubbed the reflective rater. She was the only rater to respond about the process of rating papers in the retrospective probe, as well as commenting on the particular papers she had just finished reading. Expert 2 seemed concerned about any aspect of the scoring session which could bias her assessment of student writing. Expert 2 made 43% of her comments (240) after reading student papers, and this percentage is over 20 points higher than any novice rater in the study. Also, she compiled 16% of her remarks (87) to the Personal Comment Area, 9 points higher that the mean rate (7%) for the novice rater group.

Expert Rater 3 made the fewest comments (416) of any rater in the study. In her retrospective, she mentioned that assigning scores gets harder the longer she takes to do it. Expert 3 employed a very rapid rating style. However, excerpts of her transcripts and the coded responses indicated that she spent a good amount of her time interacting with student writing on a personal level, since 19% of all her commentary was directed to the Personal comment Area. Expert 3 is proof that a holistic rater can read rapidly without sacrificing personal engagement. Expert 3 was one of the most consistent raters in the study, making only 28 fewer comments during the second protocol session. She expressed confidence in her rating style and emphasized the need for flexibility and adjustment in scoring holistically.

Expert Rater 4 was the only rater in the study who commented more often after reading essays (63%). Her percentage rate of after-commentary was 33% higher than the closest novice rater (30%). As well, Expert 4 tallied the highest percentage of responses to the Content Area (37%) and the lowest percentage rate to the Print Code Area (1%). In the retrospective probe, Expert 4 showed her concern with being a good rater. She was the only rater in the study to respond that her greatest concern while rating was to give a fair reading to the essays. Her rating style can be categorized as focused on understanding the meaning of a student's writing while she reserved comment until after she had an opportunity to read the entire essay.

While none of the expert raters really resemble each other that much in terms of the particulars of their rating strategies, there are some similarities which characterize expert raters as a group. For one thing, all of the expert raters appear to have been satisfied with a particular rating style. Also, this style revolves more around a method of rating than it does any criteria for judging writing quality. This apparent lack of concern for rating criteria among the expert raters in the study probably comes from the fact that expert raters have a definite guideline on which to base their scoring decisions. In addition, expert raters appear to bring fairly well-formulated strategies not only about what criteria with which to judge writing quality, but how to conduct themselves during the session itself. This preformed rating schema is in contrast to the novice rater group's scoring style which appears to evolve from the essays themselves.

Any model of the expert rating process would have to contain a fair amount of preordained procedure about the process of rating the essays. Expert 1 converses with her papers as if she is speaking with her students in person about their writing. Expert 2 is on guard for any biases or flaws which might influence her judgment, while at the same time being interested in the writing content. Expert 3 reads very rapidly, believing that her first impression is her best decision. Expert 4 is concerned with being a fair reader, and she tends to focus on content and minimize mechanical correctness. In addition to a personal style, all the raters share the propensity to reserve commentary until after reading the entire composition while at the same time providing a fair amount of personal interaction. The technique of reserving judgment and relying on a tried and true rating procedure helps to facilitate the more personal reading by the expert rater group.

Comparison of the Novice and Expert Models of Rating

Overall, expert raters made a greater percentage of personal comments (17%) than their novice counterparts (7%). Also, the expert rater group tallied over 20% more comments after reading (46%) than did the novice raters (20%). It appears that the expert rater's stronger sense of method allowed him/her to reserve comments and to interact more personally with a student's writing than did the rating style of the novice rater group. An important difference in the models of rating for these two groups comes from the fact that for the most part the novice group had to improvise a strategy or rely on what it could do best. The expert group not only had the assistance that a scoring guideline provided, it also appears to have organized its past experience into a coherent set of rating strategies which helped to facilitate the personal involvement lost to those novice raters who had to improvise a rating strategy.

THE OBTRUSIVE NATURE OF HOLISTIC
SCORING PROCEDURES

At this point in the discussion of the results of this study, it goes almost without saying that there is no evidence to conclude that holistic scoring practices impede the ability of raters to read and assess the quality of student writing. Attacks against holistic scoring validity on the grounds that it prevents raters from fully interacting with student writing (Charney, 1984; Gere, 1980; Nold, 1978) are not supported by the results of this study. The first question about the influence of holistic scoring to limit a rater's ability to see the whole text could not really be answered from the findings of the present study. Even though the novice rater group made a more substantial number of remarks than did the expert rater group, the difference in response rate could be attributed to individuals within the group rather than to the group as a whole.

The second question concerning the rating criteria for the two rater groups yielded some interesting information in terms of the ability of the methodology to match findings with other studies utilizing different data collection techniques. However, raters in both groups essentially based their rating decisions on similar rationale.

The third question about the personal engagement of raters with the student writing they were reading and rating was answered contrary to expectations when the findings showed that expert rather than novice raters amassed a more considerable number of personal comments. Not only did the expert rater group respond more often in the Personal Comment Area, it also contributed a wide variety of responses which were unavailable from the comments made by the novice rater group.

The fourth question about the types of comments made by the two rater groups showed a slightly more fluent reading for expert raters, the use of a series-of-comments strategy for the novice rater group, and most important, the finding that expert raters made many more responses after reading a student text than did members of the novice rater group.

Given the summary of the discussion to the four particular research questions, I cannot help but speculate that not only do the findings of the present study squelch any ideas about holistic rating practices being an impediment to a true and accurate reading, but it may be that holistic scoring procedures actually promote the kind of rating process that insures a valid reading and rating of student writing.

There are two main reasons that lead me to speculate that holistic scoring techniques might actually promote a receptive reading for a rater. One, holistically trained raters contributed substantially more personal responses, representing many viewpoints besides just evaluative ones than raters who read the same papers and were not trained. Two, holistic training appeared to have influenced raters to comment more after reading a paper. While both of these findings are important, I think they can be best explained together. I believe that the use of a scoring rubric made it easier not only to agree with each other, but to actually score the papers.

The two findings of the present study which showed that expert raters responded more after reading and that they made more personal comments make a fairly good case for reviewing the notion that holistic scoring procedures and the use of a scoring rubric only accomplish the task of rater consistency. I think that the findings of this study, which can be used to advocate the idea that holistic scoring procedures can promote a systematic and personal reading of student writing, must be seen within the context of reading for evaluation. While the findings of this study cannot be used to infer content or construct validity for holistic scoring, they do raise the possibility that holistic scoring practices may be a sound and valid measure of directly assessing student writing.

FUTURE RESEARCH

The most important information to come from the present study as it relates to future research is the use of verbal data collection for more insight into the rating process. Protocol analysis could be used to explore many of the facets of holistic training including, but not limited to, the influences of trainers, differences in the scoring rubric, or other variables in the rating process. Studies into factors which affect rater judgment, such as that done by Freedman (1981) on the variable of training, environment, and text might be replicated using protocol analysis. There is little doubt that the successful use of protocol analysis in the present study should provide an opportunity for future research studies into the process of rating student writing and the factors which most affect this process.

Protocols can be used with other methodology-like interviews or examinations of assessment teams (see Pula & Huot, this volume) to create a larger picture of how and why raters arrive at judgments about student writing quality. Between this present study and the Pula and Huot chapter later in this volume, there are appropriate methods to begin tackling many research questions concerning how teachers and raters make evaluative decisions about student writing. Some of the more interesting questions still to be answered concern how purpose and context affect the criteria teachers use to assess student writing. It is safe to say that research about how and why teachers assess student writing should be an active area of inquiry in the near future.

REFERENCES

Anderson, R. C., & Pearson, P. P. (1984). A schema-theoretic view of basic processes in reading. In P. D. Pearson (Ed.), *Handbook of reading research* (pp. 255-292). New York: Longman.

Barritt, L., Stock, P. L., & Clark, F. (1986). Researching practice: Evaluating assessment essays. *College Composition and Communication,* 37, 315-327.

Bertrand, C. V. (1985). Factors in holistic rating of children's writing. *Dissertation Abstract International,* 46, 09A. (University Microfilms No. DA 8524206).

Bleich, D. (1975). *Readings & feelings: An introduction to subjective criticism.* Urbana, IL: National Council of Teachers of English.

Breland, H. M., & Jones, R. J. (1984). Perceptions of writing skills. *Written Communication,* 1, 101-109.

Charney, D. (1984). The validity of using holistic scoring to evaluate writing: A critical overview. *Research in the Teaching of English,* 18, 65-81.

Chou, F., Kirkland, J. S., & Smith, L. R. (1982). *Variables in college composition.* (ERIC Document Reproduction Service No. 224 017).

Ericsson, K. A., & Simon, H. A. (1980). Verbal reports as data. *Psychological Review,* 87 215-51.

Ericsson, K. A., & Simon, H. A. (1984). *Protocol analysis: Verbal reports as data.* Cambridge, MA: MIT Press.

Faigley, L., Cherry, R. D., Jolliffe, D. A., & Skinner, A. M. (1985). *Assessing writers' knowledge and processes of composing.* Norwood, NJ: Ablex Publishing.

Fish, S. (1980). *Is there a text in this class? The authority of interpretive communities.* Cambridge MA: Harvard University Press.

Flower, L., & Hayes, J. R. (1981). A cognitive process theory of writing. *College Composition and Communication,* 32, 365-387.

Freedman, S. W. (1977). Influences on the evaluators of student writing. *Dissertation Abstracts International,* 37, 5306A.

Freedman, S. W. (1979a). How characteristics of student essays influence teachers' evaluations. *Journal of Educational Psychology,* 71, 328-338.

Freedman, S. W. (1979b). Why do teachers give the grades they do? *College Composition and Communication,* 30, 161-164.

Freedman, S. W. (1981). Influences of evaluations of expository essays: Beyond the test. *Research in the Teaching of English,* 15, 245-255.

Gere, A. R. (1980). Written composition: Toward a theory of evaluation. *College English,* 42, 44-48.

Hake, R. (1986). How do we judge what they write. In K. L. Greenberg, H. S. Wiener, & R. A. Donovan (Eds.), *Writing assessment: Issues and strategies* (153-167). New York: Longman.

Harris, W.H. (1977). Teacher response to student writing: A study of the response patterns of high school English teachers to determine the basis for teacher judgment of student writing. *Research in the Teaching of English, 11,* 175-185.

Hayes, J. R., & Flower, L. (1983). Uncovering cognitive processes in writing: An introduction to protocol analysis. In P. Mosenthal, L. Tamor, & S. Walmsley (Eds.), *Research in writing: Principles and methods* (pp. 206-229). New York: Longman.

Hayes, M. F., & Daiker, D. A. (1984). Using protocol analysis in evaluating responses to student writing. *Freshman English News, 13,* 1-10.

Holland, N. N. (1968). *The dynamics of literary response.* New York: Oxford University Press.

Holland, N. N. (1975). *5 readers reading.* New Haven: Yale University Press.

Huot, B. (1988). *The validity of holistic scoring: A comparison of the talk-aloud protocols of expert and novice raters.* Unpublished dissertation, Indiana University of Pennsylvania, Indiana, PA.

Huot, B. (1990a). The literature of direct writing assessment: Major concerns and prevailing trends. *Review of Educational Research, 60,* 237-263.

Huot, B. (1990b). Reliability, validity and holistic scoring: What we know and what we need to know. *College Composition and Communication, 41,* 201-213.

Iser, W. (1978). *The act of reading: A theory of aesthetic response.* Baltimore, MD: The John Hopkins University Press.

Markham, L. (1976). Influences of handwriting quality on teacher evaluation of written work. *American Educational Research Journal, 13,* 277-83.

McAndrew, D. A., Anderson, M., Baumgartner, V., Condravy, J. C., Davis, W., Dreyer, D., Gaunder, E., Huot, B., Pence, P., Puma, V., Xu, Q., Risk, S., Shi, S., & Wieland, S. (1984). *Report of the pilot study: Teaching of writing in the English department's education program.* Indiana, PA: Indiana University of Pennsylvania, Department of English.

McAndrew, D. A., Swigart, F. H., & Williamson, M. M. (1986). *Final report and recommendations: English department's task force for the teaching of writing.* Indiana, PA: Indiana University of Pennsylvania.

McColly, W. (1970). What does educational research say about the judging of writing ability? *The Journal of Educational Research, 64,* 148-56.

Miles, M. B., & Huberman, A. M. (1984). *Qualitative data analysis.* Beverly Hills, CA: Sage.

Myers, M. (1980). *A procedure for writing assessment and holistic scoring.* Urbana, IL: National Council of Teachers of English.

Nisbett, R. E., & Wilson, T. D. (1977). Telling more than we know: Verbal reports on mental processes. *Psychological Review, 84,* 231-259.

Nold, E. W. (1978, December). *The basics of research: The evaluation of writing.* Paper presented at the Meeting of the Modern Language Association of America, New York. (ERIC ED 166 713)

Nold, E. W., & Freedman, S. W. (1977). An analysis of reader's responses to essays. *Research in the Teaching of English, 11,* 164-174.

Odell, L. (1981). Defining and assessing competence in writing. In C. R. Cooper (Ed.), *The nature and measurement of competency in English* (pp. 95-134). Urbana, IL: National Council of teachers of English.

Odell, L., & Cooper, C. R. (1980). Procedures for evaluating writing: Assumptions and needed research. *College English, 42,* 35-43.

Perl, S. (1979). The composing processes of unskilled college writers. *Research in the Teaching of English, 13,* 317-36.

Pianko, S. W. (1979). A description of the composing processes of freshmen college writers. *Research in the Teaching of English, 13,* 5-22.

Rafoth, B. A. & Rubin, D. L. (1984). The impact of content and mechanics on judgments of writing quality. *Written Communication, 1,* 446-458.

Remondino, C. (1959). A factorial analysis of the evaluation of scholastic composition in the mother tongue. *British Journal of Educational Psychology, 30,* 242-51.

Sloan, C. A., & McGinnis I. (1978). *The effect of handwriting on teachers' grading of high school essays.* (ERIC Document Reproduction Service No. 220 836).

Smith, F. (1972). *Understanding reading.* New York: Holt, Rinehart and Winston.

Smith, F. (1983). The writer as reader. *Language Arts, 60,* 558-567.

Stewart, M. R., & Grobe, C. H. (1979). Syntactic maturity, mechanics, vocabulary and teacher's quality ratings. *Research in the Teaching of English, 13,* 207-215.

Stock, P. L., & Robinson, J. L. (1987). Taking on testing: Teachers as testers researchers. *English Education, 19,* 93-121.

Swarts, H., Flower, L., & Hayes, J. R. (1984). Designing protocol studies of the writing process. In R. Beach & L. Bridwell (Eds.), *New directions in composition research* (pp. 53-71). New York: Guilford.

Thomas, D., & Donlan, D. (1980). *Correlations between holistic and quantitative methods of evaluating student writing.* Paper presented at the combined Annual Meeting of the Conference on English Education and the Secondary School English Conference, Omaha, ME. (ERIC Document Reproduction Service No. 211 976).

Tierney, R. J., & Pearson, P. D. (1983). Toward a composing model of reading. *Language Arts, 60,* 568-580.

Tvesky, A., & Kahneman, D. (1973). Availability: A heuristic for judging frequency and probability. *Cognitive Psychology, 5,* 207-32.

Vaughan, C. (1987, March). *What affects raters' judgements?* Paper presented at the Conference on College Composition and Communication, Atlanta, GA.

White, E. M. (1985). Teaching and assessing writing. San Francisco: Jossey Bass.

Witte, S. P. (1987). Pretext and composing. College *Composition and Communication, 38*, 397-425.

APPENDIX A

High School Principal Task

As a recent graduate from high school, you have had some time to reflect on your education during those years. Prepare the body of a letter to your high school principal in which you tell him/her what you think the strengths and/or weaknesses of the program are. Explain them completely so the principal will really understand what you thought were the highs and lows of your high school career.

Radio Manager Task

Your favorite radio station has just switched its format to a type of music that you do not like listening to. Prepare the body of a letter to the radio station manager in which you tell him/her that you are not pleased with the recent changes in programming. Your letter should attempt to convince the manager that the station should return to its original format.

APPENDIX B

Instructions for Talk-Alouds

During the rating session I am interested in what you are saying to yourself while you read and rate these essays. To accomplish this, I will ask you to talk aloud as you read and decide what score to give each essay. What I mean by talk aloud is that I want you to say out loud everything that you say to yourself silently. Just act as if you are talking to yourself. I will stay long enough to make sure you can keep up a steady stream of speech. As you move from one essay to another please call out the number of the essay you are reading. Do you understand what I want you to do?

Good. Before you begin to read and rate these compositions, I want you to answer a few questions while you talk aloud. How many words can you think of that rhyme with meet? How many things do Hemingway, Fitzgerald, and Thomas Wolfe have in common?

APPENDIX C

Read the following two passages and decide which version you like best.
(Given to the subject)

Passage 1

While he lay sleeping, Don was bitten on the nose by a large, black and yellow striped bee. The bed was pushed against the wall as Don fell to the floor and grabbed his pulsating proboscis. "Ouch," he screamed as the bee flew in concentric circles trying to escape the magazine being waved in its direction. Finally the life of the bee was ended as Don crushed it with a mad swing of the magazine he held in his hand. Somehow the death of the bee seemed to make his nose hurt less.

Passage 2

A large, black and yellow striped bee bit Don on the nose as he was sleeping. Don pushed the bed up against the wall, fell to the floor and grabbed his pulsating proboscis. He screamed, "ouch" and waved a magazine at the bee which flew in concentric circles trying to escape. Finally Don madly swung the magazine and crushed the bee against the wall. Somehow his nose hurt less now that the bee was dead.

APPENDIX D

Rubric for Radio Manager Task

4. Illustrations and specifics for persuasion.
   Tone is formal but personal.
   Logic intended for audience. The writer buffers the complaint.
3. More abstract. Conclusions but fewer illustrations, specifics and examples.
   Less persuasive and audience aware.
   Expressive, blunt, and complaining
2. Effort to address audience, but audience not satisfied.
   Solution by advice.
   Problems in logic.
1. Begging and pleading.
   No audience consideration, egocentric.
   Complaints and threats.
   Little logical argument.

Rubric for High School Principal Task

4. On task, addressing strengths, weaknesses.
   Well developed, using specifics.
   Appropriate tone.
   Well organized.
   Clear purpose.
   Effective use of transitions.
3. Shifting focus.
   Shifting tone.
   Less clear development.
   Minor surface problems.
2. A sense of audience.
   Consistency of tone.
   Inappropriate word choice.
   Less effective use of transitions.
   LOC's somewhat distracting.
1. No sense of audience.
   Inappropriate tone.
   Focused on less important issues.
   Not effectively organized.
   Unsupported claims, lack of specifics.
   LOC's distracting.

APPENDIX E
Coding Grid

Paper No. _____ Score _____ Rater: _____

CONTENT		Unity	
Sophistication		Introduction	
Logic		Conclusion	
Originality			
Development		TONE	
Redundancy		Audience	
Judgmental		Point of View	
Convincing		Personal	
Challenges		Attitude	
Agrees			
Shows Interest		STYLE	
Ideas		Word Choice	
Asks for Info		Clarity	
Whole Paper		Awkward	
		Fluency	
ORGANIZATION		Diction	
Focus		Wordy	
Transitions			

PRINT CODE			PERSONAL COMMENTS	
Punctuation			Indecision	
Sentence			Opinion	
Meaning Impeding			Expectations	
Spelling			Laughs	
Grammar			Justification	
Corrects			Non Ev. Comments	
Explains Rule			Sarcasm	
			Questions Judgment	
APPEARANCE			Time Management	
Comparing Essays			Explains Decisions	
Length				
Handwriting			INSTRUCTIONAL	
Paragraphing			Student Training	
Format			Rewriting Strategy	
			Papers Needs	
READING PROCESS				
Repeats Sentences			SERIES OF ACTIONS	
Rephrases			Exp/Fol Judge	
Break Down			Alt/Justifications	
Restates Ideas			Corrects/Explains	
Repeats Words				
Rereads for Eval.				
Supplies Meaning				

APPENDIX F

Instructions for Retrospective Probe

1) What kinds of concerns seemed most important as you read the students' essays?
2) What was the hardest thing about assigning scores?
3) What was the easiest?
4) Do you remember anything important or unusual about the essays?
5) Is there anything you would want to change about the way you read or scored the essays?
6) What was the best thing about your training (expert raters)
7) What was the worst thing about your training (expert raters)
8) What could have been done to make your reading and rating better? (novice raters)

7

A Model of Background Influences on Holistic Raters*

Judith J. Pula
Frostburg State University

Brian A. Huot
University of Louisville

INTRODUCTION

As a replication and extension of Huot (this volume), the validation study of holistic scoring reported in this chapter employs much of the same methodology. We hope to verify Huot's earlier results with a different sample of raters and to elaborate those findings through the use of extended interviews with those raters. The most interesting finding from the earlier study is that holistic training procedures do not appear to dictate rater responses, since both trained, experienced raters and English teachers without prior training or experience in holistic scoring procedures based their rating decisions on very similar criteria.

Although no explanations for these similarities were readily apparent, Huot (1990b) suggests a possible explanation in his review of the literature on expectation in reading and rating student writing:

> What seems to emerge here is a sort of tension between the reader as reader and the reader as rater. Reader expectation shaped by *personal and professional experience* will always be a strong yet hard-to-define influence on holistic raters. (p. 255; emphasis added)

*The authors thank The Delta Kappa Gamma Society International for partial funding of this research, and Karen M. Bambacus and Michael S. Pula for help developing the visuals which appear here.

Following Huot (1988; this volume) and others (Barritt, Stock, & Clark, 1986; Breland & Jones, 1984; Freedman & Calfee, 1983; Rafoth & Rubin, 1984; Vaughan, 1987) who have investigated how raters read and judge student writing during holistic scoring sessions, this study examined the influence of background, training, and experience on reading and rating in holistic scoring sessions.

An exploration of the influence of personal background, professional training, and work experience on rater performance, as an element of the validity of holistic scoring, is consistent with recent advances in the study of writing which emphasize the contexts and interrelationships among psychological processes and social systems in understanding writing (Anson, 1988; Berkenkotter, Huckin, & Ackerman, 1988; Bishop, 1990; Cooper, 1986; Diesing, 1971; Doheny-Farina & Odell, 1985; Faigley, 1985, 1986; LeFevre, 1987; Mishler, 1979; Phelps, 1985; Pula, 1990; Shuy, 1981; Williamson, 1984, 1988). Such broad-based framing of validation research on holistic scoring connects writing assessment to its function as a network of teachers who make individual judgments based on a group consensus which defines and regulates decisions about student writing quality. This study falls into the realm of what Williamson (1988) calls "functional research" (p. 90), based on the work of Diesing (1971) and Garvin (1977). Functional research can be more fully understood as

> an explanation of human behavior against the background of a social system or culture as a whole . . . term[ed] . . . *holistic*, because it preserves the unity of personal, psychological events and their public, social functions. . . . [I]t is the meaning that humans themselves impute to their behavior. (pp. 90-96)

Functional research in rhetoric and composition is subsumed under what Faigley (1985) calls a social perspective on writing. One way to examine the importance of context is to consider how raters' training, experience, and personal background help them to create a context for their reading of student texts in holistic scoring sessions. This notion of context is based on the importance of reader purpose as detailed within the psycholinguistic version of the fluent reading process (Anderson & Pearson, 1984; Goodman, 1982; Smith, 1986; Tierney & Pearson, 1983). This reading theory emphasizes the influence of readers' background and experience as they attempt to make sense or meaning of a text. Psycholinguistic theories of reading hold that as raters attempt to make meaning of texts they will be influenced by their previous experience stored within their memories as schemata. Experience plays a dual role, since often it is also a major social influence on the enculturation of individuals within a community of readers and writers (Jolliffe, 1984; Jolliffe & Brier, 1988; Toulmin, 1972; Williamson, 1988).

One theoretical and methodological model for understanding the context of rating student writing within a holistic scoring session comes from Williamson (1988) who defined "two powerful contexts" (p. 91) which illustrate the social setting for members of an academic community. The first context is the disciplinary community itself, and the second context is the colleagues with whom individuals interact daily. This definition seems to suit holistic raters, since they belong to two distinct groups, one of which is the English teaching profession at large, and the other the individual set of raters who meet to decide on the quality of student writing for a specific purpose. This dual membership is important for an understanding of holistic scoring, since so little is known about the way raters arrive at decisions about writing quality.

Other than results which measure the importance of content and organization in rater judgment of writing quality, little is known about the way raters arrive at these decisions. "It seems that if assessment literature is to progress, more inquiries are needed about how raters arrive at judgments about writing quality and what part rating procedures have in this process" (Huot, 1990b, p. 258).

The notion of dual discourse communities provides a working model of how raters bring with them individual ideas concerning writing quality and how they interact, are influenced by each others' opinions, and otherwise produce the consensus in judgment that is so important to holistic scoring effectiveness. This notion of holistic scoring as a discourse community building activity is common in the literature in which various methods are advocated to advance the feeling of community. For example, White (1985) and Myers (1980) advocate having the raters draw up the rubric's final form since this participation fosters a sense of community among the raters, a "community of assent" (White, 1985, p. 164), which in turn contributes to a successful reading. The fact that all the raters have common working hours (including breaks) in the same facility further contributes to what White (1985) terms a controlled essay reading, an extension of the training procedures. Each of these activities, used to promote community among raters and uniformity among rating decisions, can be understood as part of the enculturation process, whereby raters learn to incorporate past experiences and training into acceptable rating behavior.

METHOD

This study employs some of the methods (concurrent protocols were coded with the same system) and data (raters read the same essays and were warmed up for protocol analysis with the same prompts) used by

Huot (1988; this volume), who sought to examine whether or not holistic scoring procedures were an obtrusive force on the reading and rating of student writing. This follow-up research seeks to discover whether Huot's results were specific to his sample of raters, to explain why raters without holistic training used the same rating criteria as those who were trained as holistic scorers, and to develop a model of the rating process. To build such a model, we asked raters to relate how background variables of personal and professional experience and training influenced their rating experiences.

The data collection consisted of concurrent protocols for each rater and a series of long interviews. Raters were interviewed after all protocol data had been collected, coded, and summarized, and initial charts of the process had been sketched out to share with them.

Data Gathering Procedures

The sequence of the data collection sessions follows:

- think-aloud instruction and warm-up activity
- concurrent protocols of one folder of 21 essays
- a retrospective probe/focused interview
- concurrent protocols of a second folder of 21 essays
- a second retrospective probe/focused interview
- a confirmatory interview.

Interview Research

Yin (1984) describes interviews, which he says may be open-ended, focused, or highly structured, as "an essential source . . . of evidence . . . about human affairs" (p. 84). We used a focused interview technique which allowed us to concentrate on a set of questions, while still remaining open-ended and conversational. We conducted these exploratory inter-views from a series of questions, following Williamson's (1988) guidelines for functional research; confirmatory interviews allowed us to share with the informants our conceptualizations of their rating process taken from their protocols and earlier interviews. We solicited raters' feedback and amended our models.

The Retrospective Probe/Focused Interview Sessions

Following each essay rating and concurrent protocol session, we conducted a focused interview session. The set of questions that each rater was given in common for this exploratory interview was adapted from the list Huot (1988; this volume) composed for his retrospective probes.

The intent was to encourage raters to tell their own stories and to listen carefully in order "to take full advantage of exploratory investigation when the opportunity presents itself" (McCracken, 1988, p. 25). To get the raters to continue talking, the interviewer would, for example, ask them to tell more about aspects of their experiences as they mentioned them, or repeat part of their previous statement in a questioning manner (Egan, 1975; McCracken, 1988). The open-endedness of the questions facilitated conversational requests for elaboration of points that the interviewees offered in response to initial queries.

Also, the open-ended focused interview format may have encouraged raters to volunteer more information. Miles and Huberman (1984) indicate that data volunteered by informants may be more valid than data generated by a specific, and perhaps closed-ended, prompt; so, ample opportunity was built into the interview to permit voluntary amplification.

Model Building

Successful model building requires appropriate measures of reducing raw data, limiting the model to the purposes and questions of the study, and confirming the accuracy of the reduced data with participants. The next sections explain the methods we used to build the model detailed in this study.

Data reduction. To begin to identify themes for model building, we took notes while the raters were completing their concurrent protocols and just after their exploratory or confirmatory interviews. Shortly after each contact with a rater we completed a Rater Contact Summary Sheet. On the Rater Contact Summary Sheets we incorporated reflections from field notes, insights that came during the sitting devoted to filling out the sheet, others that came unbidden after the sheet was filled out, and still others that came from reading the transcripts of concurrent protocol and interview sessions. The summaries enabled us to see convergent and divergent aspects of each rater's background experiences.

Model-building charts. With the concurrent protocol data thus reduced, we began building the model, using the coded protocol data and interview transcripts. Charting out influences for each rater provided us with a visual element which further reduced the complexity of the data. The charts reflected the scope of the study and focused on rater scoring, personal background, professional training, and work experience.

The confirmatory interview sessions. After developing initial rating influence models, we then held confirmatory interviews with each rater.

We began the confirmatory interview session by discussing the percentage tables and graphs which represented the final reduction of data from each rater's concurrent protocols, and which reflected individual scoring priorities. Then we looked at the charted rating influence models, based on our previous interviews, for rater confirmation and elaboration of those models. The confirmatory interviews clarified and often elaborated themes explored in the initial interview sessions. Each confirmatory interview session was also taped and transcribed. The feedback from the interviews helped to refine the model.

Additional confirmatory procedures. We confirmed our information during the drafting of the chapter by reviewing all data (concurrent protocol and interview transcripts) to check for additional elements that may have influenced raters' scoring processes and for additional examples of elements or themes we had already identified. After that, we further refined rater descriptions.

We then sent each rater a synthesis of the personal background, professional training, and work experience influences on his/her scoring process drawn from the transcripts of our work together. In addition, we sent each rater the part of this work which detailed the results, and overviewed the holistic scoring context, so each would have a fuller picture of the whole. Shortly after that, we spoke with each rater on the telephone to gather additional confirmatory feedback. Expert 4's feedback typified that of his colleague raters. He said he found the passages about himself "revealing and sensible" and indicated that our label chosen to characterize him, "the rhetorician," was "an accurate metaphor for the way I was doing it [holistic scoring] and do it." He offered "personal responses rather than corrective or evaluative annotations" to the writing.

RESULTS

Summary of the Coded Responses

Raters' verbal responses from the concurrent protocols were coded according to Huot's system (1988; this volume). The five most frequent categories of response were Content, Organization, Reading Process, Appearance, and Personal Comment (see Table 1 for percentages and the complete listing of response frequencies and categories). These findings are consistent with earlier studies (Breland & Jones, 1984; Freedman, 1979a, 1979b; Jones, 1978; Vaughan, 1987), which indicate that ho-

Table 1. Raw Scores and Percentage Scores for Expert Total, Novice Total, and Group Total by Category

	Raw Scores			Percentage Scores		
	Exp	Nov	Grp	Exp	Nov	Grp
CONTENT	624	1431	2055	25.8	35.7	31.9
Sophistication	5	24	29	0.2	0.6	0.5
Logic	84	85	169	3.5	2.1	2.6
Originality	22	92	114	0.9	2.3	1.8
Development	316	757	1073	13.1	18.9	16.7
Redundancy	11	35	46	0.5	0.9	0.7
Judgmental	4	8	12	0.2	0.2	0.2
Convincing	50	78	128	2.1	1.9	2.0
Challenges	35	25	60	1.4	0.6	0.9
Agrees	18	70	88	0.7	1.7	1.4
Shows Interest	16	41	57	0.7	1.0	0.9
Ideas	6	65	71	0.2	1.6	1.1
Asks for Info	16	50	66	0.7	1.2	1.0
Whole Paper	41	101	142	1.7	2.5	2.2
ORGANIZATION	243	663	906	10.0	16.5	14.1
Organization	43	97	140	1.8	2.4	2.2
Focus	38	145	183	1.6	3.6	2.8
Transitions	68	101	169	2.8	2.5	2.6
Unity	20	66	86	0.8	1.6	1.3
Introduction	49	126	175	2.0	3.1	2.7
Conclusion	24	110	134	1.0	2.7	2.1
Body	1	18	19	0.0	0.4	0.3
TONE	278	373	651	11.5	9.3	10.1
Tone	51	32	83	2.1	0.8	1.3
Audience	88	125	213	3.6	3.1	3.3
Point of View	136	205	341	5.6	5.1	5.3
Personal	3	11	14	0.1	0.3	0.2
STYLE	112	178	290	4.6	4.4	4.5
Word Choice	21	47	68	0.9	1.2	1.1
Clarity	19	47	66	0.8	1.2	1.0
Awkward	5	9	14	0.2	0.2	0.2
Fluency	56	66	122	2.3	1.6	1.9
Diction	6	5	11	0.2	0.1	0.2
Wordy	5	4	9	0.2	0.1	0.1
PRINT CODE	113	194	307	4.7	4.8	4.8
Punctuation	20	23	43	0.8	0.6	0.7
Sentence	3	15	18	0.1	0.4	0.3
Meaning Impeding	0	16	16	0.0	0.4	0.2
Spelling	39	38	77	1.6	0.9	1.2
Grammar	50	95	145	2.1	2.4	2.3
Corrects	1	7	8	0.0	0.2	0.1
Explains Rule	0	0	0	0.0	0.0	0.0

Table 1. Raw Scores and Percentage Scores for Expert Total, Novice Total, and Group Total by Category (continued)

	Raw Scores			Percentage Scores		
	Exp	Nov	Grp	Exp	Nov	Grp
APPEARANCE	245	483	728	10.1	12.0	11.3
Comparing Essays	34	78	112	1.4	1.9	1.7
Length	34	90	124	1.4	2.2	1.9
Handwriting	37	76	113	1.5	1.9	1.8
Paragraphing	115	171	286	4.8	4.3	4.4
Format	25	68	93	1.0	1.7	1.4
READING PROCESS	467	287	754	19.3	7.1	11.7
Repeats Sentence	220	65	285	9.1	1.6	4.4
Rephrases	47	79	126	1.9	2.0	2.0
Break Down	12	11	23	0.5	0.3	0.4
Restate Ideas	58	49	107	2.4	1.2	1.7
Repeats Words	81	57	138	3.3	1.4	2.1
Reread for Eval	27	16	43	1.1	0.4	0.7
Supplies Meaning	22	10	32	0.9	0.2	0.5
PERSONAL COMMENT	321	241	562	13.3	6.0	8.7
Indecision	52	34	86	2.1	0.8	1.3
Opinion	16	41	57	0.7	1.0	0.9
Expectations	22	84	106	0.9	2.1	1.6
Laughs	56	8	64	2.3	0.2	1.0
Justification	43	20	63	1.8	0.5	1.0
Non Eval Comment	65	67	132	2.7	1.7	2.1
Sarcasm	61	7	68	2.5	0.2	1.1
Questions Judgment	3	3	6	0.1	0.1	0.1
Explains Decisions	3	22	25	0.1	0.5	0.4
INSTRUCTIONAL	9	91	100	0.4	2.3	1.6
Student Training	7	29	36	0.3	0.7	0.6
Rewriting Strategy	2	62	64	0.1	1.5	1.0
SERIES OF ACTIONS	8	73	81	0.3	1.8	1.3
Exp/Fol Judgment	8	22	30	0.3	0.5	0.5
Alt/Justification	0	6	6	0.0	0.1	0.1
Correct/Explain	0	0	0	0.0	0.0	0.0
TOTAL	2420	4014	6434			

listic raters are most concerned with content and organization, but more important, they verify Huot's (1988; this volume) results with a different sample of raters, using the same essays and coding system. Even with different raters, the coded responses from this study replicate his findings that holistic scoring does not impede raters' ability to read and score student writing. In fact, the increased rate of personal response for holistically trained raters indicates that holistic reading procedures may allow raters the ability to respond more personally, since the procedures free raters from having to set their own criteria for judging writing quality. The background data we collected permit us to go beyond the scope of the Huot study and to examine why raters make the scoring decisions they do, and to explain how raters arrive at similar decisions about student writing, whether or not they are trained and experienced as holistic raters.

Overview of Influences On Scoring: The Extended Discourse Community Model of English Teacher Disciplinary Enculturation

The data from this study confirm Williamson's (1988) notion of "two powerful contexts" (p. 91) as a description of disciplinary socialization within an academic discourse community. The effects of personal background, professional training, and work experience for each rater are components of an extended interpretive or discourse community at large, analogous to Williamson's first powerful context of the disciplinary community, for each of the eight raters in the study. Within the scope of this study, only the four experts, however, enjoy the benefit of Williamson's second powerful context, in this case an immediate discourse community of colleagues with whom they interacted almost daily in the holistic scoring sessions (see Figure 1).

Raters underwent the socialization process that Williamson explains as part of the disciplinary enculturation which takes place in these two contexts. As English teachers, raters appeared to undergo long-term socialization or disciplinary enculturation which began with their earliest literacy encounters in their extended discourse community, the community of writers, or what Bazerman (1979) labels the "community of literacy" (p. 6).

Along with illustrating and expanding Williamson's notion of discourse communities within discourse communities, this study also answers Rafoth's (1990) call for research to advance "critical inquiry into the reasons why sameness and difference co-exist" (p. 145) in a given discourse community. Both novice and expert raters share many common influences within the extended discourse community (see Figure 2). Where they differ is demonstrated most clearly in the influence of the holistic scoring experience. Experts had it. Novices did not. Examining criteria used by each rater during scoring coupled with examining interview texts reveals that holistic scoring experience separated the experts from the novices, but the common influences of the larger discourse community enabled all raters to rate essays similarly. Thus, we can redefine Rafoth's call for inquiry into sameness and differences within a discourse community as a call for explorations of how com-

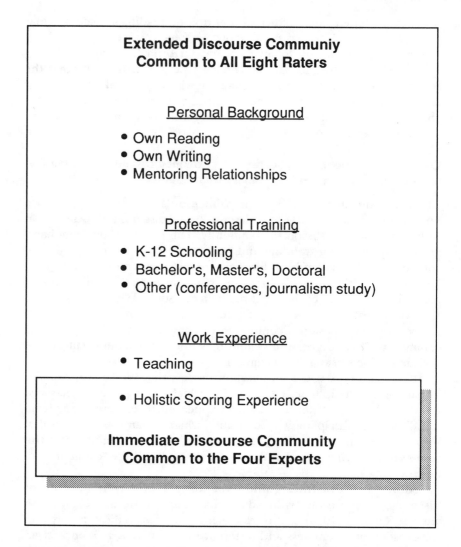

Figure 1. Holistic Scoring Influences in Raters' Extended and Immediate Discourse Communities.

munities overlap and intersect, creating individual memberships which hold various differences and similarities.

Drawing upon the constructs of extended and immediate discourse communities, we present a model of the holistic scoring process based upon interview data from the eight informants. The model represents eight independent sources and allows for "corroborative and replicative testing" (Miles & Huberman, 1984, p. 240) of the findings. In this model

	E1	E2	E3	E4	N1	N2	N3	N4
Personal Background								
* Own Reading	•	•	•	•	•	•	•	•
* Own Writing	•	•	•	•	•	•	•	•
Mentoring Relationships		•	•	•	•			•
Professional Training								
K-12 Schooling		•	•	•				
Bachelor's	•		•		•		•	•
* Master's	•	•	•		•	•		•
* Doctoral	•	•		•	•	•	•	•
Other								
- Professional Conferences				•				
- Journalism Study	•				•			
Work Experience								
* Teaching	•	•	•	•	•	•	•	•
- Teachability of Material	•	•	•	•	•	•	•	•
- Mentoring Students			•	•		•	•	
- Coaching						•		
- Textbooks							•	
- Writing Exam			•					
* Holistic Scoring Experience	•	•	•	•				

* Most frequently mentioned influences

Figure 2. Summary of Influences on Each Rater.

of influences on the holistic scoring process, raters' own reading and writing experiences, their most recent coursework, their teaching experience, and—for the experts—their holistic scoring experience exerted the most influence on holistic scoring behaviors.

Influences in the Extended Discourse Community

Personal Background.

Own reading. Each rater's own reading experiences, repeated in many contexts for multiple purposes, seemed to have the most influence on their rating practices. Reading gave each one internal models for good writing. These models, internalized over years of reading (Chomsky, 1979; Krashen, 1984; Smith, 1983, 1986), emphasized content development and organization as paramount. For each rater, accumulated reading experience constitutes what Expert 4 called the "real rubric," an internal sense of the features of quality writing.

Raters recalled reading to discover explicitly how a particular text "worked," and why that writing was successful. In turn, the raters applied what they learned to their own writing, what Smith (1983) calls "reading like a writer" (p. 558). Raters enjoyed thinking about how writing worked. They viewed it as a game, not a chore. The language play these raters engaged in during their early literacy experiences was a factor in their ultimate entry into the English teaching profession. Bloom (cited in Hillocks, 1986) notes that achievers across a variety of professions have in common early playful experiences with the activities or content of their ultimate chosen professions. Reading and introspection may have established content and organization as primary criteria for each rater; however, the actual texts, and therefore the introspection they triggered, were different for each individual. These differences help account for some of the variation in rating styles from rater to rater, but the commonalities in the texts and introspection help to explain the similarities. These early experiences with reading mark their entry into what would eventually become the larger of the two discourse communities which help to shape their decisions as raters.

Own writing. Since individuals already had notions about writing quality based on their wide reading, apparently common experiences in writing refined their ideas about what constitutes good writing. The fine-tuning process helped raters make certain elements of their conceptions about writing conscious and explicit.

For example, while each rater described life-long writing activities, five looked back to their writing prowess at earlier stages and recalled deficits that bothered them even now. These same five isolated feedback from certain individuals or from particular writing instruction (e.g., journalism training) that triggered improvement in their writing and helped them see more exactly what good writing was.

Raters often noticed that sample essays showed students wrestling with the same problems the raters had struggled with in their own writing. Raters reacted in two different ways to that observation. Some indicated that they downgraded essays for insufficiency in these areas. Others in effect said, "I learned, so the student can. It's just a temporary stage." Experiences with their own writing helped to develop and refine the "real rubric" they used to score student essays.

Mentors. Mentoring relationships also influenced raters' holistic scoring practices, although fewer raters mentioned them than mentioned reading and writing. Raters most often credited parents for fostering early literacy experiences, the bedrock of a rater's internal rubric. Raters mentioned that a grandmother, a spouse, and children had provided critical feedback or insights which led to raters' modification of their writing or scoring. Five of the subjects mentioned a mentor who helped them look at their writing from a reader's viewpoint.

Professional training: Bachelor's, master's, and doctoral study. Professional training was the second major category of experience that influenced raters' scoring. The components of professional training reveal more common ground in addition to the shared importance of the joy of reading and the impulse to tinker with text. A pattern of school-related influences was evident. Every rater cited their most recent academic training as influential. Novice 1, as well Expert 1, said that journalistic study strongly influenced their rating habits. Expert 4 felt his standards had been influenced by a pivotal professional conference. Most recent schooling nevertheless was overwhelmingly the strongest professional training influence on all the raters.

Some novice and expert raters mentioned specific instructors, courses, and course-related readings and writing projects that influenced their perceptions of good writing. However, all seven who held or were working toward a Ph.D. cited the influence of their doctoral work as important, perhaps because those experiences were the most recent.

Raters mentioned being influenced by first or primacy exposures to important concepts, by novel concepts encountered in recent course-work, and by repeated exposures to a concept (see Freedman, 1982, for an analysis of how these four factors affect memory). In short, primacy, recency, novelty, and repetition in their professional training seemed to have an important impact on raters' scoring practices and priorities.

Primacy. Initial insight into the metacognition of how writing works seemed to be primal. Expert 1 recalled that his first exposure to the importance of transitions in his bachelor's program had never left him. Three of the four expert raters, Experts 1, 2, and 3, specifically mentioned Reigstad and McAndrew's (1984) *Training Tutors for Writing Conferences* as a central influence on their personal holistic scoring criteria and on the criteria for the rating group's external rubric. Each of them first encountered the monograph in master's coursework in rhetoric and composition. It had a strong impact on Expert 1 and Expert 3. They encountered it in their training as writing center tutors. Expert 3 said she had "practically memorized" the document. It would seem, therefore, that the initial impact of Reigstad and McAndrew (1984), plus subsequent frequent use, shone through even recent coursework.

Recency. Most recent coursework also had a strong effect on how raters scored student placement essays. Expert 1 indicated that the recency of his doctoral work gave it more importance as influences of M.A. courses receded with time and experience. For two years after his M.A. program, he called himself "the fresh disciple," strongly under the influence of the program's philosophy, which seemed to minimize lower order or mechanical concerns to better support student growth in literacy. However, a different Ph.D. environment and recent teaching experience with better writers—English majors as opposed to first-year college students—led him to say that print-code facility was now third in importance to him (after content and organization) as an indicator of writing ability. He found himself less willing to overlook surface errors and based some rating decisions on how well a writer could produce correct prose, a stance he would not have advocated a few years before. The standards learned in the M.A. program had not disappeared, but recent learning had more impact on his rating than past experiences. Most recent schooling was overwhelmingly the strongest professional training influence on all the raters. The impact of the recency of an influence on raters is also evident in W. Smith's work (this volume) with raters who place students in courses based on their experience and expertise as instructors of the course. Raters appear to be more capable of identifying writing which fits the course they most recently taught.

Novelty. If recent education and primary contact with literacy motivate rating practices, so do unusual and vivid revelations. Novice 4 expressed difficulty remembering specific educational experiences from her master's and doctoral program which influenced her scoring. What she remembered were unusual experiences. She recalled most vividly learning about right-branching modification. It struck her as an innovative way to judge writing quality. She also put great emphasis on well-organized papers when scoring; however, she could recall no graduate studies which reinforced her high estimation of organization. Perhaps, she concluded, graduate-level experiences related to text organization did not make much impression on her because they were not new or novel. Organization was already a major part of her norm of what constituted good writing; but right-branching was new. The new stuck out in her memory.

Repetition. As easy to recall as novel concepts were, most of the raters attributed part of their rating values to concepts repeatedly emphasized during their recent education. Some raters noted that they may have tended to remember those specific doctoral program influences on their scoring—instructors, courses, or readings—that affirmed directions in which they already felt inclined by repeating concepts which they already considered important. Expert 4 mentioned that he thought that he looked for evidence of the rhetorical logos, ethos, and pathos in papers because he had heard those concepts stressed so often in so many contexts. Novice 3 affirmed that he appreciated essays that took risks because the doctoral program gave weight to collaboration and risk taking in writing, concepts that he already appreciated from coaching. Repetition cemented values in the raters' minds.

To summarize, while each rater was affected by a different complex of professional training, primacy, recency, novelty, and repetition played a discernible role in creating an individual rating style.

Work experience. Work experience also revealed extensive common ground among the raters. All eight taught English. All were concerned with the teachability of material in scoring. Differences also existed. Some raters saw themselves as mentors. Others saw their scoring colored by textbooks, a writing exam, and coaching.

Teaching. Raters' teaching experience was second only to reading and writing experience in its impact on scoring criteria and practices. Raters did not always volunteer information that teaching slanted their rating styles. Sometimes prompting was necessary to uncover this area; so evidently such influence was not as central to scoring styles as were reading and writing biases. Miles and Huberman (1984) say that less weight may be given to information that is elicited rather than volunteered. However, every rater reported being influenced by teaching experience, so it would seem that teaching experience does influence rating style.

As teachers, raters realized that some aspects of writing are more easily learned than others and they began to use that information in making scoring decisions. Teaching experience, along with writing and reading experience, formed a basis for assessments of which features of writing might be most easily taught (e.g., details, organization, transition, paragraphing, voice). Raters looked for particular key features, and from their presence or absence, made predictions about how well the writer would meet expectations in a given course.

The practice of using teaching experiences in making scoring decisions relates to the placement context of the scoring situation. Raters know that their decisions are being used to place students in appropriate classes (see W. Smith, this volume).

Scoring by key features is W. Smith's "symptomatic scoring" (Huot, 1990a). The key features, and resulting symptomatic scoring, are somewhat different for each rater. Members of both the novice and expert rater groups reported penalizing students less for problems in areas that teaching experience had shown them were easy to teach. Expert 1 refused to downgrade papers for paragraphing problems, since he found it easy to teach paragraphing and did not consider it much of a problem. Novice 3 felt much the same way about faulty closings.

Other raters, however, downgraded college students more for not having learned something the raters felt younger students already controlled easily. Even though Expert 3 believed that writers had to have room to develop rather than to continually be summarily judged, she had seen her seventh graders the previous year learn to control voice with relative ease using creative drama techniques. She felt first-year college students should have voice under control and revealed that she lowered scores when they did not control voice well. It seemed that her most recent teaching experience outweighed her developmentalist philosophy of making allowances for writer inexperience. Even if varied teaching contexts produced different key features, the experience of teaching informed each rater's assessment.

In other words, teaching influenced each one; but each person's teaching experience varied. These types of variations within raters, based upon their perceived teachability of certain skills, furnishes a basis for the validity of W. Smith's (this volume) placement scoring scheme which uses teacher judgments about their specific course experience as the criteria for placement decisions.

Previous holistic scoring experience—the experts' discourse community context. Personal background, professional training, and work experience defined the larger discourse community and influenced all raters to choose content and organization as their primary criteria in scoring. What separated expert from novice was not background or training, but the influence of the particular work experience of holistic scoring. Actual experience with thousands of essays in fact has become a part of the expert raters' own reading experience and their internal rubrics, what Expert 4 called the "real rubric." Expert 3 specifically noted that reading thousands of essays has given her confidence in her ability to make fair and accurate placement decisions quickly.

The need to decide between placing students in regular versus basic first-year English guides the expert raters' practices during actual holistic scoring sessions. The placement is, of course, also why they rate. The purpose clearly overrides the letter of their task of assigning scores of 1 to

4. As Huot (1990a) notes, in placement scoring "raters are aware that their decisions have a direct impact on a student's life" (p. 208). As Expert 2 observed, the repercussions of placing a student in basic writing might include student disappointment and discouragement, the cost involved in taking not one course but two, and the inconvenience of the delay caused by the need for a second course.

All the expert raters felt the weight of making placement decisions, although the more experienced ones were better able to ignore the burden in making the decisions. Expert 3, the least-experienced expert rater, said she was glad that she had never heard of a student committing suicide over having to take basic writing. She said she had learned to let worries about how a low-scoring student would react trouble her less the second summer she scored than it had the first summer. Part of being an expert rater, in short, seemed to be the ability to separate the student from the student essay.

Each expert rater conveyed a sense of urgency while rating, a realization of the effects of time pressures in the evaluation task. Expert 1 said, "[Rating] really is depersonalized, but you are playing off efficiency versus being the humanist." Expert 4 noted that he always had in mind "that sense that there are more papers to come." The sense of urgency helped the experts in this study score nearly twice as fast as the novices.

The expert group's actual experience with scoring essays holistically, of having made the decision before, seemed to outweigh the influence and importance of any rubric per se. For example, once Expert 2 made the gut-level determination that an essay was not a 4, she said she used the group's rubric as a guide to explain why it was not a 4. For the expert, then, the intuition guided by the internal rubric determined the score. Justification came later.

The ongoing training sessions in which the veterans participated for actual placement purposes point resoundingly to the memory effect of recency, since each of the veteran raters saw training as a time of warm-up to refocus on the task at hand after intervening experiences. The intervening experiences included reading student writing in other situations and for other purposes. Expert 4 said training served as a reminder of what they had agreed was important. In their distinction between their individual internal rubric, based on their own literacy experiences, and the actual rubric that the group negotiated, we sensed the swapping of individual for group expectations. Huot (1990b) hypothesizes that such negotiation between individual expectation and group consensus is one stage en route to the group's becoming enculturated into what White (1985) calls a "community of assent" (p. 164).

The swapping seems to be done in a deliberate and conscious manner. Being willing to negotiate is part of what constitutes being a good member of the group. Group cohesiveness promoted group stability over time and may, therefore, have increased interrater consistency. Expert 2 reported that, when the group stabilized, the rubric stabilized. In this way the rubric takes on a larger role than merely being a written-down scoring criteria which raters agree to and are trained by. The rubric becomes the reported consensus of agreement eked out through the tension between individual values and group concerns.

Expert 1 remarked that one of the low points in his holistic scoring experience had occurred when two newcomers actively resisted the compromise necessary to agree on a rubric. Drawing up the public rubric became an uncomfortable experience that took too long and wasted the valuable energy and goodwill needed to do the task at hand. He implied that enculturating individuals with philosophically disparate views into the scoring group was one of the least comfortable facets of the experience.

His implication fits a description by Expert 2. She felt that a group had to "read" new and substitute scorers until group members could determine whether the newcomers would fit in. She recalled with some discomfort that for the first two of her six years with the group she felt like an "outlier" who "couldn't get calibrated" to the other raters' "freshman prose" frame of reference. But the group members "liked" her, because she made other contributions to the scoring community by helping to keep the group together with her sense of humor, a maintenance function (Benne & Sheats, 1948). Her humor contributed to group cohesiveness, and kept her in the group until she did in fact calibrate her expectations to the group's standards. She felt trusted, liked, and validated.

According to Hare (1976), group validation of member judgments enhances cohesiveness. The members of the expert group studied validated each other's judgments when they negotiated a mutually agreeable scoring guide or rubric. The consensus required by the formal rubric contributed to the acceptance a new rater felt after the successful training session and scoring experience. In addition, at each training session, scorers recalibrated themselves using training papers, participating in the communication that Bormann (1975) maintained is the most important determinant of group cohesiveness. Agreement on the scores to be assigned to training papers validated members' judgments about themselves and each other, as did achieving high interrater reliability in agreeing on the scores assigned to actual or "live" student papers.

Yet, the expert group rubric did not come easily or without friction. Expert 1 described occasional "fights" over scores assigned to training papers or live papers. The discussions often became heated, but did not divide the group, because the group members respected each others' opinions and capabilities. They had, in fact, a high level of group cohesiveness.

Bormann (1975), Hare (1976), and Beebe and Masterson (1986) say the high trust level in truly cohesive groups encourages constructive conflict. Although groups which communicate freely may take longer to reach decisions, Hare (1976) says these more considered judgments are usually more accurate. The kind of critical thinking and idea testing reported by the experts during our interviews prevents premature or unreasoned conformity—or groupthink (Janis, 1971, 1982)—from occurring. Cohesive groups see the need to achieve consensus, but can avoid a rush to premature closure. This is an important distinction because several composition scholars have warned against the loss of valuable rating judgments due to the need for rater agreement (Charney, 1984; Gere, 1980; Hake, 1986; Huot, 1990a; Odell & Cooper, 1980).

Then, too, the expert group felt that they had been very effective in their work. A history of task effectiveness added to the group's cohesiveness level. As Beebe and Masterson (1986) observe, "The mutuality of concern for the group's task, which provides the focal point for group process along the task dimension, becomes socially rewarding when the task is completed successfully" (p. 96). The success group members experienced as each day's scoring tasks drew to a close amplified the positive feelings or affection Schutz's (1958) theory predicted would accompany task closure. In fact, Expert 2 noted that group members often went to dinner together after completing the scoring day, perhaps in part a reflection of those positive feelings. The after-session socials certainly helped to build even more cohesive ties within the immediate expert scorer community.

One final subtheme of the experts' professional holistic scoring experience was the dynamic of being involved in the group. That dynamic extended beyond the current day-to-day workings of the scoring proceedings to include their ongoing contacts and friendship apart from the sessions. As Figure 3 shows, they had prior opportunities to get to know each other well. They tutored together, took the same classes, and worked together through two or more years of holistic placement sessions. In addition, when members of the experts' discourse community met socially (including lunch on scoring days), they always talked shop. They discussed and debated their scoring values until each came to understand how the others read as they scored. They made predictions about what scores other members of the group would give certain essays and checked the accuracy of their predictions as a calibration exercise evolving from their natural curiosity at knowing each other as raters. Expert 3 said she was usually accurate at predicting the scores Expert 2 would give, since the latter had supervised her teaching internship. When she needed to decide between assigning a score of 2 or 3, Expert 3 said

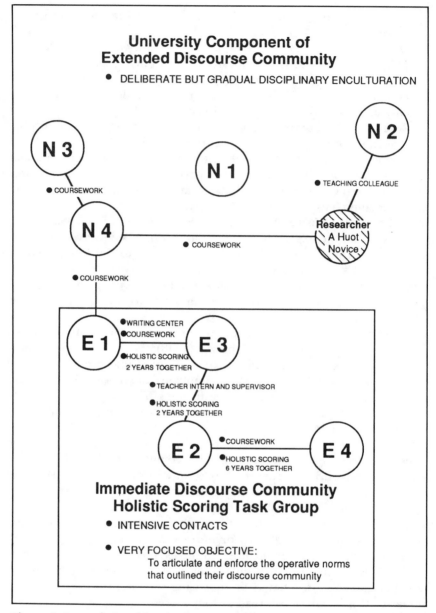

Figure 3. Interrelationships Among Raters Across Discourse Communities.

she would often ask herself, "What would Expert 1 give it?" She thought his current university teaching put him "closer to the reality of what college would be" than did her own seventh-grade teaching experience.

Then, too, the experts liked each other. Thibaut and Kelley (1959) say one of the strongest components of cohesive groups is interpersonal attraction. The immediate expert rater discourse community had that component.

DISCUSSION

Overview of Influences on Scoring: The Extended Discourse Community Model of English Teacher Disciplinary Enculturation

The common influences of the larger or extended discourse community, commonalities in personal background, professional training, and work experience, enabled all raters to give similar scores based on similar criteria. Our model of influences on the holistic scoring process includes raters' own reading and writing experiences, their most recent coursework, their teaching experience and, for the experts, their holistic scoring experience (see Figure 4). These influences were further affected by recency, primacy, novelty, and repetition which create a separate set of expectations and biases for each rater. These influences are also affected by raters' individual sense of context and purpose within a scoring session.

In order to work as efficiently as possible, Experts 1, 2, and 4 distanced themselves from the essays and their writers by focusing on the immediate short-term objective, deciding whether the student should be placed in regular or basic first-year composition. Their evaluations were summative, checking for certain prerequisite skills which they thought the student should have already mastered. For Experts 1 and 2, grammar and spelling were clear indicators of student placement. Student difficulty in those areas, especially for borderline papers, usually prompted the raters to decide in favor of basic rather than regular English. Expert 2 learned "freshman prose" several years before as a researcher studying videotapes of first-year student writing because her teaching experience was at the middle-school level. Choosing grammar and spelling as key features seemed to come most directly from her recent interactions with the others in her scoring community, several of whom had taught first-year composition during the preceding semester. Expert 4 looked for logos, ethos, and pathos as his key textual features, earning him the nickname "the rhetorician" in the study.

All three of these expert raters felt the press for task completion. Expert 4 saw "consciousness of time" as an important part of the holistic scoring process because he thought "every rater's goal is to dust off this folder and get to the next one." Clearly, the expert raters' sense of context and purpose is related to a task awareness of just what is required as a member of a holistic scoring team.

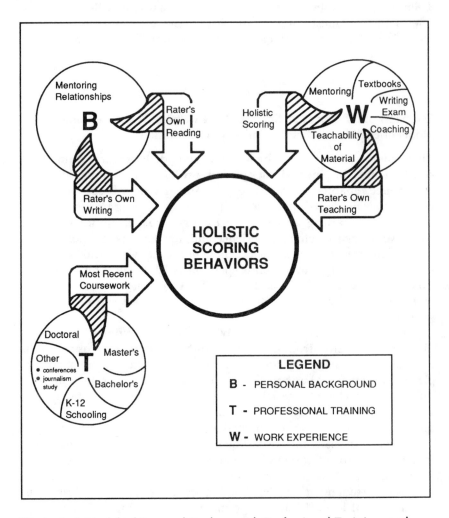

Figure 4. A Model of Personal Background, Professional Training, and Work Experience Influences on Rater Performance in Holistic Scoring Sessions.

The novices and Expert 3 (the least experienced teacher in the study, and the least experienced scorer in the expert group), exhibited more developmental orientations. They seemed generally less focused on actual student achievement at a discrete point in time, the time of assigning scores to the essays they read. Rather, they tolerated a wider margin of what they considered normal limits in writing and were interested in deciding whether (or how) students would achieve an ultimate, instead of an immediate, standard of good writing. Their formative judgments lack the strong focus on immediate teachability or other factors so important to more experienced raters' determinations for placement. For these raters, there seems to be a less conscious awareness of context and purpose. They tended to view student writing without the overriding sense that their reading was for the express purpose of placing students in particular courses.

The task awareness and clear sense of the placement context in experts' ratings should not be taken to mean that experts only read student writing according to narrowly defined criteria. In fact, as with Huot's study (1988; this volume), experts exhibited more personal engagement in their verbal responses as they rated. More than twice as often as their novice counterparts, they laughed, made nonevaluative comments, and indulged in sarcasm. Training and experience also helped them rate more efficiently, as they made about half the comments in approximately half the time of the novices.

Validity and Our Model of the Rating Process

Huot (1990a) notes that the three most widespread uses of holistic scoring are probably program placement, large-scale writing assessment, and research. In alignment with the position of the *Standards for Educational and Psychological Testing* (American Psychological Association, 1985), which states that the concept of validity "refers to the appropriateness, meaningfulness, and usefulness of the specific inferences made from the test scores" (p. 9), he argues that judgments about the validity of holistic scoring should be made in light of the purpose for which the scoring is being used. Anastasi (1988) and Popham (1988) reinforce the importance of the score-based inference, rather than the test or score itself, as the object of concern in matters of validity.

Thus, for the purpose of our study, any statements about validity should be viewed within a test's use as a college placement procedure, which has as its focus the "narrow aim of fitting students into a known curriculum" (White, 1985, p. 62). The validity of placement decisions is tied to the accuracy with which they predict student success in the course into which the student has been placed. This is predictive validity, a criterion-related means of confirming validity (Popham, 1988).

One factor impacting upon the predictive validity of placement decisions is raters' "sense of the classes they teach, and their decisions are influenced by whether or not they feel the writing represents a student who is ready for their courses" (Huot, 1990a, p. 208). In fact, citing a personal communication from W. Smith, Huot reports that Smith challenges placement assessment as true holistic scoring. Instead, Smith conceives of the process as "symptomatic scoring," during which raters look for certain "symptoms of text" (p. 208) as indicators of student readiness, or absence of readiness, for a given course. W. Smith's research (this volume) suggests that the most important influence on a teacher placing incoming students into a known curriculum may be that teacher's sense of the most recent course she taught.

This course and its influence extend beyond the principle of recency and trigger a rater's awareness of student ability and pedagogical context. Not unlike the immediate discourse community which provided reliability training for the experts in this study, the immediate discourse community of the classroom provides recent and repeated interaction with student texts which calibrates the teacher-rater for accurate scoring of placement essays.

More important than mere predictive validity, our model for holistic scoring displays how English teachers bring their personal and professional pasts into a holistic scoring session. Our model confirms Huot's findings that holistic scoring does not impede the rich and personal reading necessary for an appreciation of student texts. In fact, the holistic scoring training, rating sessions, and other attendant socialization actually work as a type of enculturation where raters create an immediate discourse community within the larger community to which they already belong. This smaller community permits raters to work as a group, achieving rating consensus, but at the same time retaining the individual and personal nature of their reading, which is so important to any description of the fluent reading process.

IMPLICATIONS FOR HOLISTIC SCORING AND FURTHER RESEARCH

Holistic Scoring

This study supports the importance of fostering a sense of community in holistic scoring sessions (White, 1984, 1985, 1986), since those experts who discussed their transition to veteran status suggested that their sense of belonging fostered their enculturation into the holistic scoring group.

Findings also suggest characteristics of people who might make good holistic scorers. Such individuals would have done the extensive reading necessary to give them an internal sense of the qualities of good writing, a real rubric. This study also suggests that teaching experience helps raters make an assessment of teachability, and that placement rating is best carried out by those who teach the courses into which they are placing students. Also important for individuals attempting to achieve scoring reliability with a group might be previous experience with holistic scoring or a commitment to the scoring task, with a concomitant willingness to agree with other members of the group on a negotiated external rubric. As Cooper (1977) and Expert 1 state, individuals with similar backgrounds seem likely to reach this agreement most readily. Thus, in addition to using individuals from similar backgrounds for scoring tasks, training should encourage raters to respond to the essays using their similar backgrounds as they score.

Further Research

It seems that the next step in the research process started by Huot (1988; this volume) would be to replicate his study, and this one, with a different group of English teachers not of the same immediate discourse community, to see if similar patterns of rating criteria exist elsewhere.

Another important context to study would be scorers working in actual placement or exit sessions, with live essays, to gain more insights into the realities of these contexts. Such a study could include, for example, observing and analyzing the dynamics of holistic scoring training sessions evolving the rubric. This research could be part of an on-site, longitudinal, ethnographic study of a holistic scoring community as it develops over a period of time.

We have just begun to explore how teachers and raters arrive at decisions about student writing quality. One interesting but untapped set of influences comes from the context and purpose of the rating itself. So far, this study and the Huot (1988; this volume) and W. Smith (this volume) studies have focused on placement scoring. It is time to take some of the methodology, especially the combination of protocols and interviews developed for the current study, and apply them to other rating and evaluation situations, including how teachers arrive at grades for students' writing in their classes. It is also appropriate to begin to look at how our teachers evaluate portfolios. As well, it is important to view large-scale rating sessions done by state agencies or educational corporations such as the Educational Testing Service (ETS), since much of the community-building we found in this study where raters had worked together over years would be absent. Clearly, questions surrounding raters' decisions about writing quality are many, and the answers are few. We hope to see much research in this area in the future.

REFERENCES

American Psychological Association. (1985). *Standards for educational and psychological testing.* Washington, DC: Author.

Anastasi, A. (1988). *Psychological testing* (6th ed.). New York: Collier Macmillan.

Anderson, R. C., & Pearson, P. D. (1984). A schema-theoretic view of basic processes in reading comprehension. In P. D. Pearson (Ed.), *Handbook of reading research* (pp. 255-292). New York: Longman.

Anson, C. (1988). Toward a multidimensional model of writing in the academic disciplines. In D. A. Jolliffe (Ed.), *Advances in writing research, volume two: Writing in the academic disciplines* (pp. 1-33). Norwood, NJ: Ablex.

Barritt, L., Stock, P. L., & Clark, F. (1986). Researching practice: Evaluating assessment essays. *College Composition and Communication, 37,* 315-327.

Bazerman, C. (1979). *Written language communities: Writing in the context of reading.* (ERIC Document Reproduction Service No. ED 232 159).

Beebe, S. A., & Masterson, J. T. (1986). *Communicating in small groups: Principles and practices* (2nd ed.). Glenview, IL: Scott, Foresman.

Benne, K. D., & Sheats, P. (1948). Functional roles of group members. *Journal of Social Issues, 4,* 41-49.

Berkenkotter, C., Huckin, T., & Ackerman, J. (1988).Conventions, conversations, and the writer: Case study of a student in a rhetoric Ph.D. program. *Research in the Teaching of English, 22,* 9-44.

Bishop, W. (1990). *Something old, something new. College writing teachers and classroom change.* Carbondale, IL: Southern Illinois University Press.

Bormann, E. G. (1975). *Discussion and group methods:Theory and practice* (2nd ed.). New York: Harper & Row.

Breland, H. M., & Jones, R. J. (1984). Perceptions of writing skills. *Written Communication, 1,* 101-109.

Charney, D. (1984). The validity of using holistic scoring to evaluate writing: A critical overview. *Research in the Teaching of English, 18,* 65-81.

Chomsky, C. (1979). Language and reading. In R. E. Shafer (Ed.), *Applied linguistics and reading* (pp. 112-128). Newark, DE: International Reading Association.

Cooper, C. R. (1977). Holistic evaluation of writing. In C. R. Cooper & L. Odell (Eds.), *Evaluating writing: Describing, measuring, judging* (pp. 3-31). Urbana, IL: National Council of Teachers of English.

Cooper, M. M. (1986). The ecology of writing. *College English, 48,* 364-375.

Diesing, P. (1971). *Patterns of discovery in the social sciences.* New York: Aldine.

Doheny-Farina, S., & Odell, L. (1985). Ethnographic research on writing: Assumptions and methodology. In L. Odell & D. Goswami (Eds.), *Writing in nonacademic settings* (pp. 503-535). New York: Guilford.

Egan, G. (1975). *The skilled helper: A model for systematic helping and interpersonal relating.* Monterey, CA: Brooks/Cole.

Faigley, L. (1985). Nonacademic writing: The social perspective. In L. Odell & D. Goswami (Eds.), *Writing in nonacademic settings* (pp. 231-248). New York: Guilford.

Faigley, L. (1986). Competing theories of process: A critique and a proposal. *College English, 48,* 527-542.

Freedman, J. L. (1982). *Introductory psychology* (2nd. ed.). Reading, MA: Addison-Wesley.

Freedman, S. W. (1979a). How characteristics of student essays influence teachers' evaluations. *Journal of Educational Psychology, 71,* 328-338.

Freedman, S. W. (1979b). Why do teachers give the grades they do? *College Composition and Communication, 30,* 161-164.

Freedman, S. W., & Calfee, R. C. (1983). Holistic assessment of writing: Experimental design and cognitive theory. In P. Mosenthal, L. Tamor, & S. Walmsley (Eds.), *Research in writing: Principles and methods* (pp. 75-98). New York: Longman.

Garvin, P. L. (1977, March). *An empiricist epistemology for linguistics.* Inaugural Lecture at The Fourth Annual LACUS Forum, Montreal.

Gere, A. R. (1980). Written composition: Toward a theory of evaluation. *College English, 42,* 44-48.

Goodman, K. (1982). *Language and literacy: The selected writings of Kenneth S. Goodman.* London: Routledge & Kegan Paul.

Hake, R. (1986). How do we judge what they write? In K. L. Greenberg, H. S. Wiener, & R. A. Donovan (Eds.), *Writing assessment: Issues and strategies* (pp. 153-167). New York: Longman.

Hare, A. P. (1976). *Handbook of small group research* (2nd ed.). New York: Free Press.

Hillocks, G. (1986). *Research on written composition.*Urbana, IL: National Conference on Research in English.

Huot, B. (1988). The validity of holistic scoring: A comparison of the talk-aloud protocols of expert and novice raters. (Doctoral dissertation, Indiana University of Pennsylvania). *Dissertation Abstracts International, 49,* 2188-A.

Huot, B. (1990a). Reliability, validity, and holistic scoring: What we know and what we need to know.*College Composition and Communication, 41,* 201-213.

Huot, B. (1990b). The literature of direct writing assessment: Major concerns and prevailing trends. *Review of Educational Research, 60*(2), 237-263.

Janis, I. L. (1971). Groupthink. *Psychology Today, 5,* 43-46; 74-76.

Janis, I. L. (1982). *Victims of groupthink: Psychological studies of policy decisions and fiascoes* (2nd ed.). Boston: Houghton Mifflin.

Jolliffe, D. A. (1984). Audience, subject, form and ways of speaking: Writers' knowledge in the discipline. *Dissertation Abstracts International, 46,* 367A.

Jolliffe, D. A., & Brier, E. M. (1988). Studying writers' knowledge in academic disciplines. In D. A. Jolliffe (Ed.), *Advances in writing research, volume two: Writing in academic disciplines* (pp. 35-77). Norwood, NJ: Ablex.

Jones, B. E. W. (1978). Marking of student writing by high school English teachers in Virginia during 1976. *Dissertation Abstracts International, 38*, 3911-A.

Krashen, S. D. (1984). *Writing: Research, theory, and applications.* Oxford: Pergamon Institute of English.

LeFevre, K. B. (1987` *Invention as a social act.* Carbondale: Southern Illinois University Press.

McCracken, G. (1988). *The long interview.* Newbury Park, CA: Sage.

Miles, M. B., & Huberman, A. M. (1984). *Qualitative data analysis: A sourcebook of new methods.* Beverly Hills, CA: Sage.

Mishler, E. (1979). Meaning in context: Is there any other kind? *Harvard Educational Review, 49*, 1-19.

Myers, M. (1980). *A procedure for writing assessment and holistic scoring.* Urbana, IL: National Council of Teachers of English.

Odell, L., & Cooper, C. (1980). Procedures for evaluating writing: Assumptions and needed research. *College English, 42*, 35-43.

Phelps, L. W. (1985). Dialectics of coherence: Toward an integrative theory. *College English, 47*, 12-29.

Popham, W. J. (1988). *Educational evaluation* (2nd ed.). Englewood Cliffs, NJ: Prentice-Hall.

Pula, J. J. (1990). The function of personal background, professional training, and work experience on rater performance in holistic scoring sessions: A study of disciplinary enculturation and placement context. (Doctoral dissertation, Indiana University of Pennsylvania). *Dissertation Abstracts International, 51*, 3714-A.

Rafoth, B. A. (1990). The concept of discourse community: Descriptive *and explanatory adequacy.* In G. Kirsch & D. Rosen (Eds.), *A sense of audience in written communication* (pp. 140-152). Newbury Park, CA: Sage.

Rafoth, B. A., & Rubin, D. L. (1984). The impact of content and mechanics on judgments of writing quality. *Written Communication, 1*, 446-458.

Reigstad, T. J., & McAndrew, D. A. (1984). *Training tutors for writing conferences.* Urbana, IL: National Council of Teachers of English.

Schutz, W. (1958). *The interpersonal underworld.* Palo Alto, CA: Science & Behavior Books.

Shuy, R. (1981). A holistic view of language. *Research in the Teaching of English, 15*, 101-111.

Smith, F. (1983). Reading like a writer. *Language Arts, 60*, 558-567.

Smith, F. (1986). *Understanding reading* (3rd ed.). Hillsdale, NJ: Lawrence Erlbaum Associates.

Thibaut, J., & Kelley, H. (1959). *The social psychology of groups.* New York: Wiley.

Tierney, R. J., & Pearson, P. D. (1983). Toward a composing model of reading. *Language Arts, 60,* 568-580.

Toulmin, S. (1972). *Human understanding.* London: Oxford University Press.

Vaughan, C. (1987, March). *What affects raters' judgments?* Paper presented at the Annual Meeting of the Conference in College Composition and Communication, Atlanta.

White, E. M. (1984). Post-structural literary criticism and the response to student writing. *College Composition and Communication, 35,* 186-195.

White, E. M. (1985). *Teaching and assessing writing.* San Francisco: Jossey Bass.

White, E. M. (1986). Pitfalls in the testing of writing. In K. L. Greenberg, H. S. Wiener, & R. A. Donovan (Eds.), *Writing assessment: Issues and strategies* (pp. 53-78). New York: Longman.

Williamson, M. M. (1984). The functions of writing in three college undergraduate curricula. (Doctoral dissertation, State University of New York at Buffalo). *Dissertation Abstracts International, 45,* 775-A.

Williamson, M. M. (1988). A model for investigating the functions of written language in different disciplines. In D. A. Jolliffe (Ed.), *Advances in writing research, volume two: Writing in the academic disciplines* (pp. 89-132). Norwood, NJ: Ablex.

Yin, R. K. (1984). *Case study research: Design and methods.* Beverly Hills, CA: Sage.

8

The Field Testing of Writing Prompts Reconsidered

Sandra Murphy
University of California, Davis

Leo Ruth
University of California, Berkeley

INTRODUCTION

The importance now placed on accountability at all levels of schooling has intensified the pressures to produce large-scale writing tests on demand. As a result, local test developers are sometimes tempted to "borrow" topics from a state or national assessment to save the time and effort of developing and field testing original topics. This practice sometimes rests on the assumption that writing produced in response to a single topic can serve as a general, all purpose measure of "writing achievement." In 1982, Emig challenged this assumption and in the last decade, research has validated her argument, demonstrating that different modes or purposes for writing draw on different strategies and cognitive operations (see Camp, this volume).

But even when a topic has been designed to sample a particular type of discourse in a state or national assessment, it may not necessarily align with the local writing curriculum, the purpose of the local assessment, or the nature and experience of the target population. Moreover, topics that have worked well in one setting may not work well in another, even when these three factors happen to coincide. The practice of borrowing and using topics without local tryouts is always questionable because writing behavior varies as a function of particular communicative contexts. For example, the "school" topic below is modeled after a writing exercise judged to be successful by the National Assessment of Educational Progress (NAEP).

> There is probably one thing about your school that you would like to see changed. Write a letter to your principal and tell him about the problem. Be sure to describe the situation as it is now and tell why it bothers you, as well as how you would like to change it.

In several district-wide assessments, this topic has evoked varying results. Keech (1982) describes a situation where it had to be abandoned in two schools in California after a field tryout. In one school, teachers monitoring the trial administration reported that students responded to the topic with derisive laughter, complaints, and even refusals to write. These students saw their principal as close-minded and unwilling to listen to any ideas they might have. At another school, where the principal was especially effective in developing a unified, contented student body, the students complained that they couldn't think of a problem worth writing about. The trivial nature of their letters validated their contention.

Test makers need to be sensitive not only to the impact of what sociolinguists such as Cook-Gumperz and Gumperz (1982) call "situated meanings," that is, context-specific interpretations, but also to other reasons why borrowing poses a threat to the validity of the assessment. Validity is not a property inherent in a test item per se; it is bound up with the inferences made from it in relation to local testing purposes, writing curricula, and instructional practices. Because validity does not transfer as a property of the borrowed topic, it has to be established *and maintained* through rigorous field-testing procedures in local contexts, whether or not a topic is homemade or imported. This is a dilemma facing designers of all types of psychometric measurement instruments, not just those intended to assess writing. Thus, measurement theorists have begun to call for contextualized validation. "What is to be validated is not the test or observation device as such but the inferences derived from test scores or other indicators . . . Inevitably, then, validity is an evolving property and validation is a continuing process" (Messick, 1989, p. 13).

Having made the point that a local trial is an essential part of an ongoing situated process of writing test validation, we need to consider the adequacy of traditional psychometric field-testing procedures for auditing and appraising the interactions of examinees with topics in writing assessments. In this chapter we do not suggest that psychometric procedures should be discarded, but we do argue that the community of assessors needs to move beyond them as much as is necessary to accomplish more authentic, more meaningful, and more useful evaluations of student accomplishment in writing. We will consider how well the basic quality control procedures in psychometrics, field testing, and item analysis align with advances in literary theories of interpretation and cognitive theories of language comprehension. Specifically, we will consider the implications of changing theoretical conceptions of the act of reading for conducting a writing assessment.

Issues of reader response and interpretation have been largely ignored in writing assessment. When such issues have been raised—for example, the legitimacy of alternative readings of a text—concern has focused on the "reading" of the student writing sample. Relatively little attention has been paid to the "reading" of the topic for writing. In fact, test makers often assume that each writer gets the same message to direct the writing performance. But contemporary reader response theory and psychological theories of reading comprehension cast doubt on this assumption.

While these theories differ in many respects, they share certain important assumptions, namely, that meaning is not simply retrieved from texts; it is constructed by readers, or, in Rosenblatt's terms, created in the transaction between reader and text (Rosenblatt, 1938, 1978). As Squire (1990) points out, many of the reading research studies on comprehension have supplied empirical data which support insights into reader response long since advanced by theorists such as Rosenblatt. Thus, both reader response theory and psychological theories of text comprehension emphasize the impact of prior knowledge and prior experience on comprehension (Squire, 1990). What these theories tell us, then, is that interpretation of any given text will vary from individual to individual and in relation to a number of variables.

Our own studies of approaches to the assessment of writing, conducted in collaboration with the Bay Area Writing Project, support constructionist views of text comprehension. During the 1980s, we reported results of investigations which suggest that readers of the topic (both the student writers and the teacher raters) choose among cues embedded in the text of the task, both honoring and ignoring elements which may enable them, with varying degrees of success, to match the test maker's intentions and expectations (Ruth & Murphy, 1988). This prior work leads us to pose further questions about the validity and efficacy of traditional types of field testing as quality control procedures in psychometrics. Drawing upon this earlier work, as well as work conducted in collaboration with the Bay Area Writing Project and the California Academic Partnership Program, we argue in this chapter that we need a model of writing assessment that respects the legitimacy of alternate interpretations of the writing task.

STATUS OF TRADITIONAL PSYCHOMETRIC PRACTICE IN THE DIRECT ASSESSMENT OF WRITING

Dominance of the Psychometric Model

Psychometric discourse now provides the dominant vocabulary and formulations for designing and evaluating all types of school achievement tests. To be deemed psychometrically sound, the writing test is expected to be constructed, administered, and interpreted within the restraining boundaries of reliability, validity, utility, appropriateness, and cost (Coffman, 1971; Stalnaker, 1951). Well-ensconced general methods for constructing psychometrically stable measures of achievement appear in any of the standard works on "measurement" and "evaluation" in education and psychology (Anastasi, 1988; Gronlund, 1985; Hopkins & Stanley, 1981; Kubiszyn & Borich, 1987; Millman & Green, 1989; Osterlind, 1989; Popham, 1981). A preponderance of content in these works is devoted to issuing procedural rules and to resolving issues relating to reliability, validity, objectivity, and standardization in the development, administration, scoring, and interpretation of multiple-choice-type tests (indirect assessment techniques) rather than essay tests. Nevertheless, we need to examine carefully the major tenets of psychometrics—actually a form of applied statistics—because they provide the framework for what often counts with test makers as the appropriate methodology for direct assessments of writing.

Psychometric Definition of a Test Item

Tests are constructed out of items or essay topics, so it seems fitting to begin with a psychometric definition of a test item. Osterlind (1989), who has prepared a new comprehensive manual describing methods of constructing and evaluating the quality of test items, illuminates how current theory, practice, and assumptions in measurement guide much of the prevailing practice in designing test items, including essay topics. Osterlind considers his definition of a test item to have general application to any type of achievement test:

> A test item in an examination of mental attributes is a unit of measurement with a stimulus and a prescriptive form for answering; and it is intended to yield a response from an examinee from which performance in some psychological construct (such as an ability, predisposition, or trait) may be inferred. (p. 20)

From the perspective of behavioral psychology, Osterlind explains how a test item functions as a "stimulus" and "directs response":

> A test item is a stimulus that causes a response. The response given by an examinee to a test item is prescribed in the sense that the item guides a particular form that the answer should take. Even in "open-ended" test-item formats, the examinee is guided to make a specific response.It would violate the definition of a test item if the test taker were not directed to make a particular kind of response. (p. 21)

Osterlind claims that writing exercises or essay-type questions also meet the conditions of his definition: "They are a stimulus situation, they have a prescriptive form of response, and they are intended to yield scores that allow for inferences to be made about examinee performance in a psychological construct" (p. 29).

PSYCHOMETRIC PROCEDURES FOR EVALUATING TESTS

To evaluate the quality of a test, the psychometrician looks at a restricted range of phenomena through strict methods of item analysis to determine how well a test and its components are performing their functions. The psychometrician's concern about the quality of the whole test leads him to ask a number of questions related to issues of validity and reliability: Is the test covering the content it is supposed to? Is the test being used in relation to its intended purpose? Is the test producing consistent results on different occasions of administration? To what extent are scores likely to be affected by irrelevant or chance factors? Does the test measure the examinee's "true" level of ability? The concepts of *validity* and *reliability* which deal with these kinds of questions are central to the psychometric theory now governing either multiple-item tests or direct assessments of writing ability.

Psychometricians are interested not only in the validity and reliability of the test as a whole entity, but they are also concerned about particular characteristics of individual items: How difficult are the items of the test? Do they discriminate adequately among test takers, that is, are they sensitive to differences in knowledge among the test takers? Do any of the items introduce error or bias into the test? To answer these questions, psychometrists use two basic approaches to investigate the quality of test items: the judgment of experts about content and form, and empirical studies of response data from field trials (Millman & Greene, 1989). Both procedures aim to detect and reduce sources of error and to improve the items for their intended purposes.

Judgmental Approaches

Judgmental approaches involve asking panels of reviewers to comment on particular items according to some criteria in a systematic process. Panels of expert judges may rate the content of items to provide evidence of validity. The procedure seeks the consensus of informed opinion about the fit between particular test items and specific descriptions of the content domain to be assessed by those items. Judges may also be asked to review the wording of items. These judges may meet face to face or function as a "blind" panel. In the latter case their opinions or ratings are gathered by mail or telephone and then quantified to produce the item scores and the criterion levels used to establish passing or failing items.

Statistical Item Response Methods

To answer other questions, psychometricians have refined complex statistical procedures to estimate various kinds of validity and reliability and to prepare item analyses for the purpose of establishing indexes of difficulty and indexes of discrimination for individual items. The empirical procedures lead to the gathering of data about the statistical properties of particular test items. These data collected in field trials are examined to determine the response distributions for the various items constituting the test. Desirable and undesirable items are sorted out through procedures of *item analysis.* For example, the difficulty level of an item is calculated on the basis of the proportion of students who score at different levels on the scale in use to produce an *index of difficulty.*

An *index of discrimination* is also calculated to show how "good" and "weak" students score on particular items during the field trial. These indices enable test makers to predict how populations comparable to the ones participating in the field test are likely to do on particular questions. When topics don't "work," that is, when they are too easy or too hard, when they fail to "discriminate" between strong and weak students, they can be eliminated. Items with good psychometric values need to discriminate between the examinees who exhibit high mastery of a subject and those who exhibit low mastery. Items that all examinees answer correctly or that all examinees miss do not serve this purpose; hence, they do not discriminate. Items that do not discriminate yield no information about differences between individuals (Osterlind, 1989, p. 283). The first study presented below explores the sensitivity of these statistical procedures to various features of the "response" data within the essays themselves and in the negotiations of meaning occurring during the research process.

BEYOND NUMBERS: ANALYZING STUDENT RESPONSE

One problem with the statistical model is the basis on which items are eliminated. As Wesman (1971) points out, traditional statistical procedures in item analysis identify "clearly bad items" (p. 81). But what is a "bad item?" In this kind of model, a bad item is one which fails to discriminate. For example, if our purpose is to sort students in some way, we need a test which will discriminate. On the other hand, when we test students, it is only fair to give them every opportunity to do their best, the weak students as well as the strong. Thus we need to be careful lest we discriminate blindly, focusing only on the ends and not the means.

When we focus on the means, we are dealing with a question of validity. One traditional notion of validity is concerned with whether we are in fact testing what we intend to test. Statistical field-testing procedures are limited in this respect because, as Wesman (1971) points out, such procedures do "not assure the goodness of an item" (p.81). Although a psychometric approach may provide an evaluative procedure for eliminating bad essay questions or other test items, this perspective does not provide empirically derived analytic methods for determining what has gone wrong in the first place (Payne & McMorris, 1967). Statistical procedures can only signal that something has gone wrong, that something unanticipated has occurred in the process of selecting the correct answer or in the process of composing the expected essay. Some of the limits of these statistical procedures are evident in the following study.

Limits of Traditional Tryout Procedures

Eight topics on trial.   Early in our research on essay examination topics, we encountered a field-testing procedure which employed a mathematical model analogous to the one described above. The field test was part of an effort to develop a bank of topics that could be used for assessing writing in local county schools. In this field trial, eight topics were randomly assigned to students in ninth- and tenth-grade classes in schools identified as high, average, or low according to their students' performance on other measures of their writing ability, including the students' percentile ranking on the *California Test of Basic Skills*. Students were given 30 minutes to write a paper in response to the topic they received. Their responses were scored holistically by two raters who used a 9-point scale. The assessors then gathered data on the scores generated by each topic to determine which topics produced an adequate distribution of scores. This procedure provided information to the school agencies about how well each topic "worked" with the three different school populations. It identified which topics should be saved to form a bank of topics from which to draw for annual assessments in the participating districts. Following the tryout, the assessors used typical statistical procedures to gather response data. However, they failed to obtain an important piece of information. They did not compare the mean scores generated by each topic; they simply assumed that the different topics were "equivalent."

The subsample for analysis.   The data from the original field test of the eight topics were subsequently made available to a research team of our Writing Assessment Project. When we compared the mean scores generated by the topics in three mid-range schools, we found that the mean scores of the two topics presented below were significantly different in the mid-range sample (Kinzer, 1987; Kinzer & Murphy, 1982). Topic B had received significantly higher scores.

Topic A

Think of a friend, real or imaginary, that you had when you were younger. Describe something you and this friend did together; try to show your reader the kind of person this friend was and why you chose this person as a friend.

Topic B

The school newspaper has asked students to submit suggestions about how to improve the school. Think of ONE and only one problem which you would like to see solved to make life at school better for you and others. In a letter to the school newspaper, describe the problem and tell how you would like to see it solved.

These topics may seem to make similar demands on the prior knowledge of the writer, because they allow students to draw on their own experiences to find content for their compositions. "Personal experience" topics such as these are often employed in tests of *general writing competency*, because it is assumed that they do not require the "special knowledge" that might be the focus of a written examination ending a course of instruction. However, the differences in mean scores suggest that topic A may have been more difficult than topic B.

Papers written in response to these two topics in the three mid-range schools formed the source of data for a more detailed analysis (Kinzer & Murphy, 1982). The researchers selected a subsample of 40 papers, 20 written in response to each topic. To ensure that the subsample was representative, Kinzer and Murphy determined the percentages of papers at each score point in the original pool of papers from the mid-range schools. They then randomly selected an equivalent percentage of papers at each score point for their analysis. Thus, the percentages of papers within each score point selected for analysis reflected the percentages of the original response pool.

Analysis of "topic-related" variables. Kinzer and Murphy's analysis examined two quite different kinds of student response variables which may influence quality ratings: "text-based variables" and "topic-related" variables. Text-based variables included features of the students' writing which could be analyzed without reference to the topic for writing— legibility, amount of writing, cohesion, and errors. They defined topic-related variables, on the other hand, in relation to the topics that were employed to prompt the writing. Of particular interest here is their analysis of topic-related variables(Kinzer, 1987; Kinzer & Murphy, 1982). They identified three categories of topic-related features after repeated readings of the students' essays with the holistic score removed:

Category A. Responses *directly related* to explicitly stated task demands in the topics;

Category B. Responses that were *elaborations* which could be judged to be related to either explicitly stated or implicit (inferred) task demands in the topics;

Category C. Responses that were *divergent*, that is,responses which contained issues or themes not called for in the topic or which contradicted explicitly stated task demands.

Kinzer and Murphy then identified the specific topic-related features in samples of student writing for each topic. Their disagreements about the categories and the specific topic-related features were examined with a third party serving as arbiter. The topics, categories, and specific features were also given to three experienced English teachers with holistic scoring experience who judged the categories and specific features to be appropriate. Kinzer and Murphy then coded individual papers on a "yes/no" basis in relation to the identified task demands of each topic.

For example, Topic B explicitly asks students to describe a problem at their school: "In a letter to the school newspaper describe the problem. . ." If the student described a problem, the paper was coded "yes" for that particular topic-related feature (Category A). Conversely, if the student failed to describe a problem, the paper was coded "no" for that feature. Some students went beyond simple description to explain why the issue they chose to discuss was problematic or to explain why the problem was significant in comparison to other problems. These students' papers were coded "yes" for these topic-based features (Category B). Other students, often the weakest writers, simply listed separate problems or issues and failed to describe any one of them in any detail. These papers were coded as "yes" for this particular feature (Category C).

There was 89% agreement between coders on features within papers for topic A and 91% agreement between coders on features within papers for topic B. When the two coders disagreed, the features and papers were discussed with a third party and a consensus was reached. In one case in which there was disagreement on three features within one paper, the paper was eliminated from the analysis, reducing the subsample for topic B to an N of 19.

Results of the analysis of "topic-related" variables. Table 1 shows the results of the analysis used to investigate possible relationships between score and the three topic-based categories of responses[1] (calculated in proportion to total words) as they were coded in the student papers:

---

[1]In this analysis, Kendall's Tau was used to measure the correlation between a dichotomous variable (characteristics of responses coded within categories on a yes/no basis) and a quantitative variable (score) (Marascuilo & McSweeney, 1977).

explicit, elaborative, and divergent. There were no statistically significant relationships between score and any of the three categories of response to topic A. However, results for topic B indicated that as scores increased, instances of elaborated responses also increased. The reverse was true for divergent responses. As scores in topic B increased, inappropriate responses decreased.

Table 1. Scores Related to Explicit, Elaborated and Divergent Responses by Topic (Kendall's Tau)

	Explicit	Elaborated	Divergent
Topic A (N = 20)	–0.47	–0.50	–0.18
Topic B	0.11	0.31*	–0.34*

*$p < 0.05$

Table 2 presents the results of *t*-tests on the means for the three categories of topic-based variables between topics. The results indicate (a) that significantly more students addressed explicitly stated task demands when responding to topic B, (b) that there was no significant difference between responses to the two topics in the number of elaborations, and (c) that topic A papers contained significantly more divergent responses than topic B papers.

Table 2. Means, Standard Deviations and t-Test Results for Explicit, Elaborated, and Divergent Responses Between Topics

	Explicit			Elaborated			Divergent		
	X	SD	t	X	SD	t	X	SD	t
Topic A (N = 20)	0.01	0.13		0.01	0.01		0.01	0.01	
			–6.82*			0.17			4.23*
Topic B (N = 19)	0.04	0.01		0.01	0.01		0.00	0.01	

*$p < 0.05$

Discussion of results. As Kinzer (1987) notes, the data from this study "support the viewpoint that topic effects are reflected in student responses and influence holistic scores" (p. 119). The results of Kinzer and Murphy's study indicate that topics do effect scores. Topic B had the higher group mean score. In addition, the post hoc analysis showed that student responses to topic B contained more responses to explicitly stated task demands than did responses to topic A. The results of this pilot study suggest that it is very important to compare the scores generated by different topics during field testing if there is any possibility that more than one topic will be used either within a single population or to compare samples of writing collected at different times. If multiple topics are to be used, all the topics must make comparable demands; otherwise, the students within the same administrative unit are, in effect, taking different tests. It would be unfortunate, for example, if some students failed a minimum competency test simply because they were unlucky enough to draw the more difficult form of a test.

The Need to Gather Qualitative Data

Beyond comparing mean scores, the results of this study also suggest that an effective field test requires the gathering of pertinent qualitative as well as quantitative information. It would be useful, for example, to go beyond relying on numbers to analyze the compositions produced in a field test, if only to see whether topics do, in fact, elicit the kind of writing we expect them to elicit. For example, topic B asks students to write in the form of a letter, yet many of the students did not honor this topic demand. However, looking only at scores and compositions still may not provide sufficient information in a field test. The limitations of this study and problems encountered during its execution may serve to illustrate this point.

A problem of topic interpretation.   Even though Kinzer and Murphy were experienced teachers, they still encountered difficulty in agreeing on their interpretations of the topics and what these topics were asking the students to do. Their initial interpretations differed, and, although they found it easy to agree on explicitly stated task demands, it was not always easy for them to reach agreement on implicit demands and on what could be counted as an elaboration in a student's essay. Although they ultimately were able to reliably identify features in the students' writing and agree upon categories for coding the features, the initial process of developing the categories revealed perhaps as much disagreement as agreement. During this phase, they often found themselves disagreeing, both on the nature and importance of particular demands, as well as on the question of whether or not particular students had met those demands. However, once Kinzer and Murphy specified the categories and task demands, that is, negotiated an agreement as to exactly how each category or demand was to be interpreted, they were able to score the papers with a relatively high degree of interrater reliability.

In some ways, the process that Kinzer and Murphy undertook was similar to what takes place in preparing for analytic scoring when readers are trained to recognize particular features described in a rubric and to code the student papers accordingly. Definitions of features are agreed on in the process, although they might not be the definitions that readers would offer spontaneously before training. After all, the goal is *agreement* not diversity.

However, it was the disagreement Kinzer and Murphy initially encountered, not the agreement they ultimately achieved, as well as the diversity they observed in students' responses to the two topics, which eventually led them to begin to rethink their methods and consider new questions. They realized that they were analyzing the students' responses in relation to their own negotiated interpretation of the topic, not the students'. But if they disagreed initially, might not the students also disagree? Did the students interpret the task in some unanticipated way? For example, did students who produced lists of events in response to topic A misunderstand the intention of the topic author? Were the varied responses in the students' essays really attributable to features of the topics or to some other factor? Did some of the students interpret the topic as Kinzer and Murphy had interpreted it, but fail in the execution of a written response? Given the post hoc nature of this pilot study, these questions could not be answered. Kinzer and Murphy had only the student compositions and scores as data to examine. They had no way to document a link between the student interpretations of the topics and the written compositions; in fact, they had no way to know what the students' interpretations of the topic really were. Like many others, researchers and field testers alike, Kinzer and Murphy fell prey to the erroneous assumption that everyone was getting the same message, that the meaning was in the text. As Emig (1982) might say, they were trapped in a positivist point of view.

A lack of sensitivity in statistical data.   A second problem that Kinzer and Murphy encountered in the study stems from the assumption of the statistical analysis that all identified features carried equal weight. Topic B, for example, explicitly asks students to "describe the problem," "in a letter to the school newspaper." But is it equally as important to observe the form of a letter as it is to describe the problem? Which aspects of the task might carry more weight with raters? Which would they judge to be more crucial to the production of an adequate response to the task? Again, given the design of this study, the researchers couldn't know.

Many current field-test procedures operate under these same assumptions and within these same limitations. Analyses are done post hoc and combine statistical procedures with judges' ratings. This is not to say that these kinds of activities aren't useful. They are. Yet, when assessors rely solely on such methods, they are ignoring the connections between the powerful forces of language, cognition, and context. They are behaving as if the language of the topic merely acts as a convenient filter between the intent of the test maker and the expressive outcome of the examinees. Too often test makers (and researchers) tend to conceive of the topic for writing as a uniform stimulus. They sometimes forget that the same topic can set off very different reverberations of meaning within individual writers, and they tend to forget that "words do not function in isolation, but always in particular verbal, personal, and social contexts" (Rosenblatt, 1989, p. 156).

STUDYING THE CONSTRUCTIVE ACTIVITIES OF PARTICIPANTS IN A WRITING ASSESSMENT EPISODE

Overview of the Study

In a later study (Murphy, Carroll, Kinzer, & Robyns, 1982; Ruth & Murphy, 1984), the research team collected data at various points during an entire writing assessment episode. Given the questions emerging from the study described above, the research team decided to focus on points within the assessment episode which emphasized the sense-making activity that participants, including both students and raters, must undertake in relation to the two focal texts in any writing assessment: (a) the text of the writing topic and (b) the text of the paper generated in response to it. The composing of the text of a writing test, the construction of a reading of the topic and the writing of a response by the student, and the constructing of an evaluative reading of the student's paper by the test rater—all of these sense-making activities—involve reciprocal processes of constructing meanings between texts and participants.

The research team selected a subsample of 12 students to interview about their interpretation of the topic before they wrote their essays and again afterwards. The researchers collected the students' papers. They also tape-recorded the topic development session so that they would know what expectations the authors of the topic had in mind, and they interviewed the teachers who scored the essays to discover their own expectations. In addition, the researchers collected data from a questionnaire given to all of the tenth-grade students who had completed the test and from another questionnaire given to the raters who had scored the papers.

The researchers interviewed the subsample of students to discover whether or not there would be substantial variation in the ways students interpreted the topic given to them. The interview procedure involved a minimum of prompting. In effect, students were asked to "think aloud" about what came to mind as they read the topic used in the assessment. Its text follows:

Many different suggestions for improvement of Central High School have recently been made. Describe one problem or situation at Central which you feel needs correction or improvement, giving reasons for your choice and selecting one or more solutions.

Possible Paths of Interpretation in Reading the Topic

By now the substance of this topic should seem quite familiar. It is yet another version of the NAEP school topic mentioned at the beginning of this chapter and it is similar in many ways to Topic B in the Kinzer and Murphy study. It's emergence in this latter study was entirely seren-dipitous. A committee of teachers at a local high school where the assessment was to be conducted met with one person from another high school to design a topic. The substance of the topic—a school problem—was suggested by the chair of the English department as a member of the design committee. A careful reading of this particular version should reveal that it supports a number of plausible interpretations.

Several paths of interpretation are possible. To begin, there are at least two ways in which the first sentence could be read. If a reader knows, for example, about suggestions "recently made," the first sentence could function as a reference to the context of a familiar discussion. On the other hand, if a reader understands the first sentence as new information being introduced for the first time, it will inform the reader of an existing state of affairs of which he/she is yet unaware. However, the second sentence does not provide additional information about either what the suggestions are or who made them. Whether or not the reader has knowledge of suggestions recently made, he/she might still wonder about what purpose the first sentence serves. A student-reader might ask, for example, "Is this the subject of the composition I am about to write, or is it intended to be merely an introduction to what follows."

A reader could also interpret other segments of this topic in a variety of ways. The phrase "giving reasons for your choice," for example, could be interpreted variously as meaning "giving reasons why the problem could be considered a problem," as "giving reasons why the problem was chosen above others," or as "giving reasons why the problem was personally relevant." The choice of describing either a "problem" or a "situation" can also lead to divergent task interpretations. Some readers might decide to describe a "situation" and give suggestions for "improve-ment," while others might decide to describe a "problem" and propose a "solution," a process that is quite different from making "improvements."

Evidence in Student Interviews of a Range of Topic Interpretations

That the tenth-grade students did, in fact, interpret the topic in a variety of ways is shown in the following excerpts from the interview data. To collect data about topic interpretations before students wrote their essays, the researchers asked them to use a "think-aloud" procedure which the students had practiced with another topic. This method invited the students to tell what came to their minds as they read the topic. The researchers also interviewed students after they had written their essays. The first four segments are from the prewriting interviews, and the last example is from a postwriting interview.

Data from Prewriting Interviews

Alice   Um . . . that comes to mind how everybody's always talking about: "All we need is grass." You know, "There should be a swimming pool!" Cause we were supposed to have a like uh a football stadium.

Carla   . . . Okay . . . it says 'Many different suggestions for improvements . . . of Central . . . have recently been made.' . . .so . . . like . . . you mean just from students.

Martin   They are thinking about . . . um . . . giving money for . . . to make the school look a little better. And then . . . they've . . . they've got a big grant . . . state or federal or something . . . .to improve the curriculum . . . of the school.

Don   . . . and I don't know an . . . of any suggestions of . . . for improvement . . . that've been made recently.

Data from a Postwriting Interview

Katie   The way I interpreted that was just as an introduction..I figured they were just saying this so they could tell you to describe one problem . . . I didn't think that was important . . . The most important part was the beginning of the second sentence.

These excerpts show that some students did interpret the first sentence in a variety of ways. Certain students, Alice for example, indicated that they were aware of "suggestions" that had been made. The students who did have knowledge of "suggestions," however, attributed them to different sources—some to other students and some to school authorities. Carla, for example, attributed the "suggestions" to students. Martin, on the other hand, indicated that he knew of specific "suggestions" which fitted the temporal constraints specified in the first sentence by the phrase "recently made." These "suggestions" actually had been given detailed coverage in a school newspaper article discussing the tentative plans that school personnel were considering for using recently acquired California State Department of Education grants for School Improvement Projects (SIP).

In contrast to those students who claimed to have some knowledge of what the first sentence could refer to, other students, such as Don, indicated a lack of such knowledge. Don is also an example of a student who interpreted the first sentence as a statement about something he was expected to know about. Frustrated by his lack of knowledge, he spent a good deal of time in the interview trying to figure out what "those suggestions" could have been. Other students, however, ones who were perhaps more test-wise than Don, simply chose to ignore the first sentence. Katie, for example, who was interviewed after she wrote a particularly successful essay, characterized the first sentence as "just . . . an introduction" and said she didn't think it was "important."

The students interpreted not only the first sentence differently, but other segments of the topic as well. As one might expect, these divergent interpretations were reflected in the content of the essays. In some cases, these divergent interpretations resulted in very different kinds of essays. For example, when Martin responded to the phrase "giving reasons for your choice," he justified his choice of a problem in relation to other problems. In his interview, he said, ". . . that I would single that out (attitude) . . . and . . . and ah . . . the ah . . . grounds . . . the . . . landscaping and stuff,. . . that's not so important." In his essay, Martin employed these same ideas. He wrote:

Martin's Essay

The many suggestion for improvement have been made landscaping, the C.I.P. grant, and the additeud of the students. I feel the greatest problem that Central has is it's additude of the students. The student seem to have a large additude problem. They seem to think they are above normal thing, to go to put their garbage in the trash can, to good to give a little respect to the teacher or other students. I feel that this is a major problem at Central because if the student had a better additude tword their school it would be a better school. If the student gave so respect to the school It would do more than anything else could. Because after all, all a school is students. By bettering their out look on this school it would improve it. Improve it more than C.I.P. because no matter how good the currulem get's the student are what make a school.

And what is landscaping just a superficial cover that would be destroy by student with bad additude.

I think the only way that you are going to improve the additude or outlook of the average student is either to get him involved in his school or get this friends to tell him to shape up. First we would need to get a large group of people involved in wanting to get the outlook of the students changed. I think the way to acompilce this would be peer pressure. It would work by student ingoreing other student who don't care and telling them that they do care what happens to their school.

Then if you do this you would improve the school more than landscaping more than C.I.P. These other thing could only be fully appeacated by student who care about their school.

Because he constructed a reading of the task as requiring him to justify his choice of a problem to discuss, Martin never got around to doing an important part of the task intended by the topic authors—describing the problem—except in a superficial way.

In contrast to Martin, Katie, a student who chose to ignore the first sentence, fared much better. She described a single "problem," she provided a vivid illustration, explained why it was a problem, and suggested a solution.

Katie's Essay

Buzzz. The five minute bell rang. My fourth period teacher had finished his lecture and we had the rest of the period for ourselves. I scrawled out one last math problem before closing my books. "How much time, Kirsten?" I asked. "Two minutes." Kirsten said after looking at her watch. I put my homework paper into my binder, and stacked my books in my arms. Bzzz. I jumped up and raced out of the room emerging into the traffic of other students hurrying to lunch. I ran to my locker, shoved in my books and sprinted to the cafeteria. There I was met by a gigantic line. My stomach growling I waited in line for fifteen minutes. With a sigh of relief I got my lunch and went out side to eat. Half way through my lunch the bell rang signaling for the end of lunch. This time my stomach didn't growl, I did!

This situation is a slightly exaggerated example of one of the main problems at Central High.

At every school I suppose there are problems concerning the cafeteria. But at Central you not only face the lines but you also have to deal with the crowd of people who've gotten their lunch but don't know where to take it.

I think there is a simple solution to the line problems. I think that if Central only sold hot food in the cafeteria that would reduce the lines by one quarter at least. What could be done, is, have all the ice cream that is sold in the cafeteria, be put in machines. Another helpful change would be to get a machine that sold drinks besides coke or milk.

I think these suggestions are profitable to all. The students would benefit because they wouldn't have to wait so long for their food and the cafeteria would benefit because more people would buy instead of being discouraged and giving up the idea of getting any-thing.

Evidence in Questionnaire Data of a Range of Topic Interpretations

Ninety percent of the teachers surveyed by questionnaire in this study felt that a focus on a single problem would be a vital part of a response to this topic. But many of the students who took the test failed to recognize the significance of the cue "Describe one problem." Only 35% of the students who took the exam thought it was important to focus on a single problem.

Needless to say, Katie received a better score than Martin. What we are suggesting here is that the way a student construes a writing task can have an effect on the score he/she receives. Part of Martin's composing problem, of course, is that he has trouble with mechanics—spelling, verb tenses, and so on—but another part of Martin's composing problem has to do with the way he construed the task. Martin's predicament significantly underscores how success in a writing test is not just determined by whether or not a student can deal with the mechanics of writing, but also, at least partly, it is determined by how the student interprets the topic.

Other information from the study also supports this contention about the relation of score to topic interpretation. For example, in the questionnaire distributed after the test, students were asked to rate the importance of statements about the task. The statement, "It is important to explain why the subject chosen is a problem at the school," and the statement, "It is important to explain how the solution will improve the school," were significantly correlated with holistic scores. Students who agreed with these statements received higher scores. However, neither of these statements are precisely equivalent to what is stated explicitly in the topic. It appears that the real task for student writers is not simply just to read the words of the text and form plausible interpretations, but also to form interpretations that will anticipate the expectations of evaluators.

Implications of the Results

The strong degree of professional agreement among the teachers is not surprising. They commented on the need for a focus in the student essays, and they recognized that the phrase "Describe one problem," was an intentional cue to indicate that focus. The authors of the topic had expected the students to respond to the cue with a description of a single problem or a situation. Many of the students, however, including Martin, apparently failed either to notice the cue or to recognize its significance. The findings in this study call into question the practice of relying solely on expert review of items in field testing. Students and teachers, as groups, clearly had very different ideas about what an adequate response to the topic would entail. Further, the results of the study suggest that reading and writing are inseparable in writing assessment.

Clearly, if we wish to give students a fair chance to do their best, we need to acknowledge that the act of writing in a writing assessment begins with an act of reading for understanding, and we need to deal with the implications. We have described the data from this topic interpretation study in some detail, because they call into question the psychometric assumption underlying most large-scale assessments, the idea that students are getting the same message to direct their writing performance. Obviously, that is a questionable premise.

This study demonstrated that different students will interpret the same topic in a variety of ways; they read selectively, constructing in the process several different but arguably valid interpretations. Obviously, multiple constructions of meaning create a problem for the test maker, since to some degree the fairness of a test depends on students having an equal chance to do their best, to begin the race from the same starting line.

The Significance of Individual User Interviews

One way to address this problem is to attempt to reduce the potential for divergent interpretations of writing tasks. Thus, an important part of the evaluation process occurs at the stage of reviewing and editing when many ambiguities can be detected. But there are no guarantees that even the most careful "expert" review process will catch all of the potential problems with topics. For this reason, we strongly urge assessors to undertake field tests that include an examination of sample essays and user interviews.

The conventional procedures in field tryouts produce massed data which are insufficiently revealing of individual processes of interpretation. Statistics may tell us *when* some effects are occurring but not *what causes* them. It is not enough to know that some topics induce better scores than others; we need to know why. The standard approaches are quite unsuited to the detection of the sources of individual misunderstanding and the analyses of causes. So, the tryout procedure should be taken one step further to also include a sample of individual user interviews. Field testing that directly samples writers' and teacher-readers' interpretations of the language of topics is essential. We need to know how particular features of the task organize the discourse event of the test from the perspective of the writer-as-reader and the writer-as-composer. This further step is essential so that the constructive comprehension processes of reading and writing can be studied as sources of knowledge for improving the design of topics used for subsequent assessments.

Interestingly, several measurement specialists recognize a need for asking examinees directly in field trials about their experience with the item, sometimes through questionnaires, and sometimes in general discussions at the trial site. For example, Popham (1981) suggests that it would be a "serious error" to ignore examinee judgment in evaluating both selected-response and constructed-response item types: "A rich source of data is often overlooked because we typically fail to secure advice from examinees" (p. 293). He then proposes using an item-improvement questionnaire with examinees. An extremely valuable strategy for improving items, according to Osterlind (1989), is a "leading questions approach" (p. 272) which may be used as early as second grade, with questions asked of teachers and examinees in a discussion. Osterlind comments that "in fact, students of all ages frequently demonstrate remarkable insight into the reason for asking a particular question, and they can diagnose specific flaws in items and suggest improvements" (p. 273).

Osterlind acknowledges that an informal discussion of items with an appropriate group is not a widely practiced technique for analyzing items. Unfortunately, as both Popham and Osterlind indicate, these more direct methods of tracking the ways items or topics function tend to get short shrift because they are considered "problematic," "too time-consuming," or "too costly." Although Stalnaker (1951) made the following observation 40 years ago, there is little evidence in the literature to suggest that the situation today is any different: "Item analysis can be useful in improving essay examinations as well as objective examinations, although because of the time required and difficulties encountered, essay examinations are seldom analyzed by item response" (p. 521). In other fields, however, obtaining information from respondents to questions is considered standard practice.

Reducing the Various Types of Response "Errors"

User interviews as developed in survey research (Belson, 1981) are not employed frequently enough in the process of topic development. They can uncover many discrepancies between what the test maker intends, and what the test taker actually comprehends, discrepancies that may be difficult or impossible to predict in advance. The intentions of test makers can easily "misfire," to use Austin's (1965) apt metaphor for those occasions when the act of communication is "botched," when responses fail to meet expectations (pp. 17ff.).

In the field of survey research, misfires are called "response errors." In that literature, response errors are further categorized according to the source of error; hence, there are *instrument errors, respondent errors,* and *contextual errors* (Cannell & Robinson, 1971; Hawkins & Cobele, 1971). These concepts from survey research seem useful in considering the potential sources of error in writing assessment tasks. Given information provided from fields such as linguistics, we might thus analyze errors that derive from linguistic features of the *test instrument,* for example, the ambiguity in the phrase "giving reasons for your choice" in the topic from the writing episode study.

We might also thus analyze the *respondent errors,* that is, errors that derive from a *misreading* of the topic. There is a potential, of course, for students with reading disabilities to misinterpret a topic in ways that are quite different from the range of plausible alternate interpretations that a general community of readers might give it. The interpretations revealed by the excerpts from the student data are the kinds of interpretations we mean when we say *plausible*. They are not misreadings; they are simply alternate readings of the same text. In contrast to these, Greenberg (March, 1981, letter) supplied us with a striking example of misreading, when she wrote to us about a topic which had been developed for use at the City University of New York. This topic referred to vigilante groups that had been patrolling New York City's streets; to some New Yorkers these groups were known as the Guardian Angels. When Greenberg got back responses to the topic, some students had written about "vigorous" groups, others about "villain" groups, and so on (Ruth & Murphy, 1988, p.62).

Contextual errors, on the other hand, derive from the kinds of problems which we described at the beginning of this chapter—problems related to the ways social context can influence the interpretation of writing tasks. Those first "school" topics failed, not necessarily because of any deficiencies in wording, but because variation in social contexts of the school sites made a difference in how students reacted to the topic. We also provided an example of how social context influenced interpretations of a school topic in the research team's study of a writing assessment episode. In that case, suggestions actually had been made at their school that the teachers assumed everyone would know about. This assumption reflected a contextual error, a mistaken estimate of the extent of the students' prior knowledge about suggestions that had been made at their school.

Yet another kind of *contextual error* has to do with students' understanding of the tacit rules operating within the examination context in which they are writing. Contextual errors can occur when students fail to understand how rules of normal discourse may have to be suspended in a writing test. For example, the "friendly letter," when requested in a writing test, requires a different register than the casual style that one might adopt when writing a real letter to a friend. The student who confuses the function of the two types of letter writing will risk penalties for composing a casual letter in a test. In one study conducted by the Writing Assessment Project, students were asked to evaluate compositions framed as letters to friends. The results revealed that students tended to value the papers which sounded like "real" letters more than the papers which sounded like English themes in the guise of real letters (Keech & McNelly, 1982). The students considered the intrusion of "school writing" into letters as unnatural or as "showing off." Teachers, on the other hand, who evaluated the same set of papers, paid less attention to the conventions of friendly letters and looked for evidence of school writing. In some cases, teachers even penalized students for components of writing which could have been justified as plausible features of the friendly letter genre, for example, the lack of detail in a letter to parents who could be presumed to know the missing particulars. The data from that study suggest that when we specify a rhetorical context that conflicts with the purpose of a test, we may be misleading student writers.

STUDYING THE PROBLEM OF MAKING TRUSTWORTHY APPRAISALS OF INDIVIDUAL GROWTH IN WRITING PROFICIENCY

Constructivist Theory and Psychometric Reliability

Interaction with examinees may help the item writer avoid ambiguities, but we will not be able to eliminate variations in task interpretation. Ultimately, we need to acknowledge that no matter how careful we are about controlling the set of constraints and options expressed or implied in the text of a writing assignment, we cannot reliably predict how each student will construct the task. As early as 1982, Hoetker raised this issue in his review of research on essay examination topics, pointing out that "the 'mode' of writing called for by any essay topic is precisely that mode that any particular student interprets it as calling for" (p. 379). In our own work, we have found this to be true. Current literary theory tells us not only that variations in interpretation will occur among groups of individuals given the same topic, but also that students may construct very different interpretations at different points in time.

Contemporary literary theory and reading comprehension theory offer two streams of work flowing toward an overlapping transactional conception of reading as a complex, socially constructed, inferential process guided by the text. Thus, the reader's act of response to a test item or a writing task is invited and opened by the presented text, but not controlled by it as the response may expand into an internal dialogue between reader and text that was only vaguely anticipated by the author. The event of communication is only initiated by the author of a writing task. Ultimately, this initiation culminates uniquely in the transactional construction of meanings that occur as each individual writer recursively "reads-through" the given text of the task and "reads and writes-through" the text being created in writing (Rosenblatt, 1989). Variations in construction of meaning are not limitless or idiosyncratic; many can be recognized systematically as reasonable possibilities. Nevertheless, constructivist theories of language comprehension pose a strong threat to psychometric theory for they destabilize and subjectivize its positivistic theoretical underpinnings.

Consider for example the two papers written by Debbie (a fictitious name) which follow:

Debbie's First Construction
6th Grade Graduation

One of the most exciting things that happened to me was when I graduated from 6th grade. I was 12yrs old in Sequoia School on June 15, 1989.

I think it was around 10:00-12:30. The first thing that happened was that my group and I went up on stage and we began to say the poem "Desiderita." We have been practicing for a few months and we were sure we were going to do good. My turn came up and I was really nervous. Everybody was looking at me, but I said it and I thought I did good.

Next, some of the guys went up and said the poem "If." Then a girl named Sarah went up and played the piano. She played it very gracefully.

After that we sang songs. The audience was all parents and teachers. Pictures were taken every minute. The songs we sang were "that's what friends are for," "whatever will be, will be." A girl named Kuyler sang "The Greatest Love of All." then Monique and Amanda sang a duet together "Somewhere Out There."

Everybody was dressed nicely and beautifully. The guys were mostly all in suits and ties. The girls were in fancy dresses in white, black, etc.

Then the end came and we walked out the auditorium, we had to walk with a guy or girl out the auditorium.

When everybody was outside, we hugged each other. Then some of the people left to go home or to go to restaurants.

Graduation was a very happy day for all of us and we will never forget that wonderful day.

Debbie's Second Construction
The Tropical Rainforest

I feel angry because people are destroying the Tropical Rainforests. They are cutting too much trees. When they cut down trees they destroy an animal's home.

We get alot of our food and medicine from the rainforests! They are making the place smaller and smaller each day. They destroy the land for furniture, houses, ect. I am worried about the rainforests because I think that they are destroying too much things.

If we keep this up then soon enough there will be no place to get our food and no place for the animals to live in. The Tropical Rainforest is such a beautiful place and I don't want to see it destroyed.

Sometimes I feel angry because people are destroying such a beautiful place. We just have to save the Tropical Rainforests because its getting smaller and smaller each day and I don't want that to happen. We just have to save the Tropical Rainforests!

The Contexts of Debbie's Two Constructions of the "Autobiographical Incident" Topic

Debbie, a student at a junior high school in Northern California, wrote these two papers on two separate occasions for a school-wide pre/postassessment of student writing. The teachers had selected "autobiographical incident" as the type of writing to assess because it was part of the schools' writing curriculum, because it represented a designated type of writing included in the state-wide writing test, and because it drew on personal experience rather than specialized knowledge from students. Two versions of an autobiographical incident topic modeled closely on the format of the topics used in the state testing program were created by the teachers. This state format provides two sections: the first presents a writing situation; the second gives directions for writing. The writing samples were collected under normal classroom conditions over two class periods, allowing students time to prewrite, draft, revise, and edit.

Topics A and B follow:

Topic A
Writing Situation

Your English class is publishing a booklet about events in students' lives that have triggered strong emotions. This booklet will be shared with English students in another class at (name of school),

Directions for Writing

Write about an incident or event which resulted in your experiencing a strong feeling. It might have been a time when you were very happy, sad, or embarrassed. Include enough details so that your readers can understand what happened and how you felt. Try to make your readers understand why you felt such a strong emotion at this moment of your life.

Topic B
Writing Situation

Your English class is publishing a booklet about events in students' lives that have triggered strong emotions. This booklet will be shared with English students in another class at (name of school),

Directions for Writing

Write about an incident or event when you had a strong feeling. It might have been a time when you were very scared, angry, or excited. Include enough details so that your readers can understand what happened and how you felt. Try to make your readers understand why you felt such a strong emotion at this moment of your life.

Topic B was nearly identical to Topic A. Note that the emotions—scared, angry, or excited—in Topic B were substituted for the emotions — happy, sad, or embarrassed —in Topic A. There was also a slight variation in wording in the first sentences of the directions. The clause, "which resulted in your experiencing a strong feeling," in Topic A was worded, "when you had a strong feeling," in Topic B. While the topics were not entirely identical, we think they illustrate our point: How the student interprets the topic and construes the writing task is ultimately unpredictable. In one case Debbie wrote a narrative describing a personal experience; in the other, she wrote a persuasive essay about a controversial issue—the decimation of the world's rainforests. Debbie's essays were eliminated from the sample of papers scored for the pre/post test. But, in many assessments, no such steps are taken; the assumption is simply made that the kind of writing the test makers expect to be elicited has in fact been elicited by the topics they assign.

We are describing this assessment in some detail because it illustrates yet another difficulty arising from student variations in the constructions of the writing tasks they are given—the problem of assessing students' ability to compose a particular type of writing on demand.

Scoring procedures. In the pre/postassessment at the junior high school, teachers used a forced-choice method adapted from Haswell (1988) to see whether students were improving in certain dimensions of general writing ability: fluency, specificity (use of details), organization, and sentence development (sentence complexity and use of a variety of sentence structures). They also scored for a special rhetorical feature related to the particular type of writing they expected the topics to elicit: the narration and description of an event or incident. Their interest in this latter category stemmed from the use of rhetorical effectiveness scoring in the state-wide test, and they based their own scoring criteria on the criteria employed in the California Assessment Program test. Figure 1 contains a summary of the scoring criteria used in the state-wide test for the evaluation of autobiographical incident writing.

Commentary on the CAP Scoring Guide. The reader may note the emphasis on narration and the focus on a "well-told incident" in the CAP scoring guide. Debbie's paper on the rainforest would clearly not fare well in relation to this rubric. In fact, if her paper had been scored in relation to this particular guide, it probably would have been scored as off-topic. In Debbie's essay there is "no incident related," and it is clearly not autobiographical. But if we assess the piece as a persuasive essay, she does a fairly good job. We are not saying, of course, that Debbie's paper should be assessed as an example of autobiographical incident writing. Rather, the point we are making is that given all the possibilities for

Summary of Rhetorical Effectiveness Score
for AUTOBIOGRAPHICAL INCIDENT

Score
Point   Criteria

6   **Exceptional Achievement**

- *Incident:* Essay centers on one well-told incident narrated engagingly and coherently. The incident is realized dramatically. A 6 is notable for the effectiveness of its narrative strategies.
- *Context:* Writer orients readers, describing scene and people and providing context or background for the central incident. Details are well chosen and relevant. Context does not dominate the essay at the expense of the incident.
- *Significance:* Writer implies or states personal significance of the incident in a well integrated way. Significance is not tacked on.
- *Voice and Style:* Voice is authentic, revealing attitude toward the incident. Apt word choices and graceful, varied sentences. Immediately engages the reader and brings the incident to closure.

5   **Commendable Achievement**

- *Incident:* Well-told, coherent incident. Less interesting, more predictable or less focused than a 6. Uses fewer strategies and/or uses them less effectively than a 6.
- *Context:* Orients reader, as in a 6. Context does not dominate essay.
- *Significance:* Writer implies or states personal significance. Reflections may not be as insightful as in a 6 and/or not so well integrated into the essay.
- *Voice and Style:* Authentic voice. Essay may not have the sparkle of a 6. Expanded vocabulary, varied sentences.

4   **Adequate Achievement**

- *Incident:* Well-told incident. Limited use of strategies. May have momentary lapses in coherence or momentum.
- *Context:* Adequate to orient readers to the incident.
- *Significance:* Implied or stated. Usually not as insightful as a 5 or as well integrated. May be just added to the end.
- *Voice and Style:* Earnest storyteller. Predictable sentences and word choices.

Figure 1. Cap Direct Writing Assessment Grade 8

Figure 1 continued.

3   **Some Evidence of Achievement**

- *Incident:* Will tell a specific incident. Competently told but with limited use of narrative strategies. Usually briefer than a 4. Flat, loosely connected series of events.
- *Context:* Out of balance with narrative; either too much context while neglecting narrative or abrupt start with minimal orientation.
- *Significance:* Implied or stated in limited way. If the incident is complete, a paper may receive a 3 even with minimal reflection.
- *Voice and Style:* Writer fails to relate the incident with appropriate detail. Predictable sentences and word choice. Often uninvolved.

2   **Limited Evidence of Achievement**

- *Incident:* Incident may be presented in a general or fragmentary way. Often very brief.
- *Context:* Limited or missing.
- *Significance:* Reflection either superficial or missing.
- *Voice and Style:* Minimal evidence of personal involvement. Little or no detail. Sentences short or confusing.

1   **Minimal Achievement**

- *Incident:* Responds to prompt but usually briefly. Reader may have to infer incident. Focus may be on others rather than self.
- *Context:* Very limited or missing.
- *Significance:* Little or none.
- *Voice and Style:* Little or no evidence of personal involvement. Frequent lapses in sentence control. Possible garbled syntax interfering with sense.

0   **Inappropriate Achievement**

- Off Topic

"error"—and the resulting probability that there will be a range of interpretations on any given topic—it is questionable to assume that any given topic will elicit the task interpretation intended by the test maker. The CAP scoring guide recognizes this problem since it contains a category for off-topic papers, but other scoring guides may not. Recognizing that it is certainly a legitimate goal to assess a student's ability to employ particular rhetorical strategies or to compose particular modes of writing, we are suggesting that we need to be especially careful that we are, in fact, assessing what we intend to assess when we score for rhetorical features.

In large-scale assessments, it is impossible to insure in advance that students will, in fact, attempt to write what we want them to attempt to write. However, some steps can be taken to minimize the possibility that students will misunderstand what kind of writing they are expected to produce. The topic format adopted in California, for example, provides prewriting information and directives designed to help students think about the assignment. Students are given some information about the kind of writing that is expected, about the assignment's intent, subject, and audience. Not all assessments provide this kind of information for students. But ultimately, it may not matter how carefully we frame topics for writing since there is no way to guarantee that students will understand the task in the same way assessors do. Fair procedures for dealing with papers which do not exhibit the intended mode of writing should be adopted. Students should not be penalized for misunderstanding what they are asked to do.

SUMMARY AND RECOMMENDATIONS

The relationship between testing, teaching, learning, curriculum, and real-life writing behavior is not as direct, ordered, or uniform as traditional test makers might like it to be, because neither students nor teachers are standardized. To gain "control" of this messy reality, psychometricians have employed the strategies of a narrow positivist science to reduce the "confounding variables" of the curriculum and real-life writing behavior to meet the requirements of a mathematical model of testing. But item analysis strategies which yield only the distributions of scores fail to give adequate information. These numbers do not tell us, for example, whether the differences in scores reflect true differences in students' writing abilities or differences in the ways they have interpreted the test maker's intention. The fact that reader response and comprehension theories teach us to expect variations in interpretation has important implications for the ways we evaluate topics during field trials. Because writing behavior varies as a function of communicative context, traditional psychometric procedures have limited value.

In our discussion thus far, we have demonstrated ways in which social context can influence the usefulness of the practice of borrowing topics from other assessments, and we have argued that field testing is always advisable, especially when "high-stakes" decisions are involved, such as decisions about graduation, admission, or promotion. We have questioned the practice of assuming that different topics are necessarily equivalent simply because they draw on personal experience. The results of our early pilot study suggest that even within personal experience writing, the nature and difficulty of rhetorical demands vary and are related to the scores students receive. In considering field-testing options, we have pointed out the limitations of relying solely on mathematical models for evaluating topics for writing assessment; such methods, though useful for gross screening purposes, do not ensure that students will be given the chance to do their best. Calling into question the psychometric assumption that students are getting the same message to direct their writing performance, we have demonstrated that different students may produce a number of valid and plausible interpretations of the same topic, and that their interpretations can lead to very different kinds of writing. We have shown that the same student on different occasions, given nearly identical topics, may also produce very different kinds of writing.

We have argued that field testing needs to include a review of the papers produced in response to a topic in addition to the calculation of their scores in order to determine the full range of students' task interpretations. We have also pointed out that it is impossible to prevent divergent interpretations—that is, divergent in the sense that the students' interpretations differ from those of the test maker. At best, field-testing procedures can only attempt to decrease possibilities for misinterpretation.

New knowledge about a range of possible, valid constructions of the meaning of topics makes an extension and refinement of field-tryout procedures desirable. Pilot testing needs to move beyond the standard practice of conducting informal discussions or administering written questionnaires to representative sample groups of teachers and students. To this end, we advocate employing "user interviews," a practice common in survey research, but rarely found in assessments of writing.

Recommendation 1: Discover the Examinee's Perspective

One reason we advocate user interviews so strongly is that they give us information from the test takers' perspective. Concern over the way given tasks are interpreted has been a long-standing issue in both research and in assessment. For example, Haney and Scott (1987) review the history of this concern in relation to standardized tests, citing several authors who have advocated talking with children about why they answer test items in particular ways (Anastasi, 1976; Hoffman, 1962; Taylor, 1977). Haney and Scott question the utility of the mathematical model and expert review for evaluation of test items. They observe that these procedures do not necessarily get at the issue of test or item quality from the perspective of individual test-takers . . . what it is that a test or item measures—that is, its content validity—depends not on what adult experts or critics think it measures nor on what item statistics suggest about the item but rather on how individual test-takers perceive and react to the test or item. (p. 301)

The issue of considering the student's point of view is clearly not confined to standardized testing of the multiple-choice variety. As we have demonstrated here, it applies as well to traditional, standardized direct writing assessment programs. In assessment situations in which writing is collected under conditions which do not allow discussion, the issue is especially problematic because potential misunderstandings cannot be clarified. For this reason, we have suggested that test admini-strators consider foregoing such constraints to allow time for discussion. But this issue surfaces in yet another way, both in more traditional writing assessment situations and in "new" approaches to assessing writing in which writing is collected in normal classroom conditions, for example, portfolio assessment. In many such assessments, the classroom teacher as *the evaluator of the essay* may use only his/her own individual interpretation of what the task entails to gauge the student's response. It's not unreasonable to think that these readers might make the same assump-tion held by many test makers and researchers: namely, the student's interpretation is the same as one's own. But, whether they recognize diverse interpretations or not, they still must judge how well a student accomplishes the given task. The point is that in making this judgment it is useful to consider the relation between two sets of data: the evaluator's intentions as conveyed through the assignment, and information about what the student was trying to accomplish. Consider the following writing sample from the portfolio of a high school student in northern California, and imagine how difficult it would be to evaluate it without knowing anything about the assignment or the writer's intention.

The Horse

My totem, the horse, has somewhat similar qualities as me. For one thing, when I see a horse running freely across a field, it gives me a feeling that the horse is in a happy mood—as if nothing could penetrate the horse's good state of mind. this is the same for me. When I'm in a happy mood, nothing or no one can break that aura of happiness around me.

I've noticed that the horse is very slow to anger. I've tried to keep my temper cool no matter how difficult the situation called for anger. I learned, "What's the use in losing my temper when there's another rational way to solve the problem? One should already know that if the horse is slow to anger, then it is calm and peaceful, never causing any trouble or disturbance.

The horse can be frightened at times. For example, when a horse hears a loud noise, it goes off running scared. If I hear something unexpected, I jump, gasp, or scream to show that I was caught off guard. that's another characteristic that relates myself to the horse.

In my past experience, the horse is by far the one who stands out when it comes to taking orders without complaint. If they have to carry a heavy load down/up a hill, it's be without hesitation. The only time they won't be able to follow a command is when they're handled wrong. So, it's imperative to manage them correctly. As for me, I'm able to carry out commands without complaint only if the right word is asked—"please."

Finally, the last, but not the least, quality of a horse in relation to me is their eyes of compassion. Whenever I look into a horse's eyes, it's like looking at a reflection of me.

Without some idea of what the assignment was, and what the student was trying to accomplish, the reader may well struggle to make sense of the essay. But in the afterword which follows, the student explains:

Afterword

The characters in *The Clan of the Cave Bear* all had totems, protective spirits in the form of animals. I was to discover my own totem. This paper was a bit difficult to write due to the fact that I could not think of an animal that had similar qualities as me. First, I chose a cat, but after a few words, I decided that a cat didn't fit me. After several tries, I decided on the horse as my totem. My purpose was to relate how my totem and myself were alike to show why this was an appropriate totem for me. By the time you are finished reading this, you will gain insights into the connection between the horse and me.

We are providing this example to illustrate how useful it can be to obtain information from students about tests—especially about how they interpret the prompts they receive for writing. Although user interviews can be helpful during the initial stages of developing and field testing topics, it may be equally informative to gather information about the student's goals after they write their essays.

The process which includes the collection of information about student intention bears exploration with further research. In teaching, in assessments, and in research we would do well to listen to what students have to say, following the model of Donaldson (1978) who said,

When children fail, I wondered, why do they fail? What is it they cannot do? To try to find out I sat down with some children . . . and got them to tackle a selection of typical questions and talk to me about what they were doing. I asked them. (p. 78)

Recommendation 2:
Honor Unexpected But Plausible Constructions of Meaning

The static behaviorist model of reading is unable to account for different, but simultaneously valid, interpretations of a single text. We need to build a model of writing assessment that respects the range and complexity of individual responses to writing topics. The model needs to allow for alternative perspectives on meaning according to contextual factors. Rosenblatt's (1989) transactional model illuminates how plausible variant readings can happen in the reading of any text, whether it be a topic in writing assessment or the student essay written in response to the given task:

> Every reading act is an event, a transaction involving a particular reader and a particular configuration of marks on a page, and occurring at a particular time in a particular context. Certain organismic states, certain ranges of feeling, certain verbal or symbolic linkages, are stirred up in the linguistic reservoir. From these activated areas, selective attention— conditioned by multiple personal and social factors that enter into the situation—picks out elements that synthesize or blend into what constitutes "meaning." Meaning does not reside ready-made in the text or in the reader; it happens during the transaction between reader and text. (p. 157)

All achievement tests, including tests of writing proficiency, to some degree require the act of reading with comprehension. The outmoded behavioristic model of reading that governs the psychometric model of testing is out of alignment with contemporary research in literary theory and language comprehension. The study of writing and reading now draw information from fields in which interactional epistemologies are being articulated. For example, new theories of reading and writing are being constructed with converging ideas from linguistics, literary theory, cognitive science, reading comprehension, and ethnography of communication (Comprone, 1987; Cook-Gumperz & Gumperz, 1982; Johnson, 1983; Pearson, 1986; Rosenblatt, 1978, 1989; Squire, 1990). Theories of reading have shifted from behaviorist to constructivist orientations with cognitive and social dimensions. Reading is seen as a cognitive, context-dependent, psycholinguistic process, involving background knowledge, memory, discourse schemata, and so forth. The dominant formulations portray reading as a social, cognitive, aesthetic transaction in which the reading is a joint creation of the author and the reader. Just as the script for a play can evoke responsibly conceived variations in performances, so can any other bit of discourse such as a test item or writing task.

Recommendation 3:
Adopt Constructivist Models of Evaluation and Testing

Various scholars concerned with reductionist approaches in research, testing, and evaluation are challenging the overcommitment to the underlying scientific model (Connors, 1983; Guba & Lincoln, 1989). Within the framework of evaluation studies, Guba and Lincoln (1989) have produced a particularly thorough critique of the dominant positivist, scientific methodologies of investigation used in testing and evaluation research in general. They argue that this orientation places the investigator in a "managerial" position "outside" the evaluation process where he may determine the questions to be asked, what data are collected, and what interpretations are made of it all without due regard to the interests and participation of "stakeholders" (pp. 32-34). According to Guba and Lincoln, stakeholders are individuals or groups who have something at stake, at risk in an evaluation (p. 51). They define the process of evaluation in terms of an interpretive, hermeneutic inquiry paradigm "which unites the evaluator and the stakeholder in an interaction that *creates* the product of the evaluation" (p. 13). Stakeholders then are in a position to contribute to evaluative inquiry, broadening the benefits of the hermeneutic/dialectic process of inquiry. Guba and Lincoln maintain that giving stakeholders entree to the process enlarges the scope and meaningfulness of inquiry. The use of stakeholder contributions calls for an open-ended, "emergent" inquiry designed to allow for the interactions that will disclose issues and concerns beyond those contemplated by the evaluator. The process becomes mutually educative for all participants. Each stakeholder comes to understand his/her own evaluative constructions and those of others better. This open process takes participants beyond traditional methodologies in which deliberations are limited to a discussion of the technical adequacy of procedures (pp. 55-57). Guba and Lincoln's constructivist theories of evaluation seem to connect with constructivist theories of language cognition and transactional theories of literary understanding in ways that bear further exploration.

Recommendation 4: Adopt Models Which Honor Natural Approaches to Appraisal of Writing in Context

We need a model of writing assessment that respects the integrity of natural forms of written discourse and the psychological processes of composing them, for the practice of testing constructs the norms for what counts as skilled writing. Current psychometric theory encourages the construction of skills as independently observable results of instruction which are examinable through a sample of performance undertaken in a special testing context apart from the practice of teaching. It defines a universe of discourse, such as writing, into variables to be factored into psychometric grids of specification. This type of approach assumes that human behavior is composed of isolated reactions, each of which can be understood, explained, and appraised outside of teaching contexts. Meanwhile, on the pedagogical front, new conceptions of reading and writing (Willinsky, 1990) suggest that "literacy is best understood not as an isolated skill, as something one can do on demand, but a social process in the daily landscape" (p. 6). Willinsky proposes a definition characteristic of the "new literacy:"

> The New Literacy consists of those strategies in the teaching of reading and writing which attempt to shift the control of literacy from the teacher to the student; literacy is promoted in such programs as a social process with language that can from the very beginning extend the students' range of meaning and connection. (p. 8)

A truly holistic model of writing assessment would meet the following conditions: It would take an extended view of the composing process, allowing for the performance of various modes of writing as social processes under observation; it would take into account the intertextuality of oral and written events; and it would recognize that any individual piece of writing is situated in the ongoing life of a classroom and that it cannot be adequately understood without reference to that wider context. Under this model, writing would be undertaken and appraised in encouraging contexts, with appropriate time, reference materials, and opportunities for consultation with peers and teachers available during the process of composing and revising the necessary number of drafts needed to enable the writer to prepare a sample of his/her peak achievements. When the appraisal of writing occurs in natural contexts as part of an ongoing process of instruction, the need for field testing collapses into the process.

REFERENCES

Anastasi, A. (1976). *Principles of psychological testing.* New York: Collier Macmillan.

Anastasi, A. (1988). *Psychological testing* (6th ed.). New York: Macmillan.

Austin, J. L. (1965). *How to do things with words.* (J. O. Urmson, Ed.). New York: Oxford University Press.

Belson, W. A. (1981). *The design and understanding of survey questions.* London: Gower Publishing.

Cannell, C. F., & Robinson, S. (1971). Analysis of individual questions. In J. B. Lansing, S. B. Withey, & A. C. Wolfe (Eds.), *Working papers on survey research in poverty areas* (pp. 236–291). Ann Arbor: University of Michigan, Survey Research Center, Institute for Social Research.

Coffman, W. E. (1971). Essay examinations. In R. Thorndike (Ed.), *Educational measurement* (2nd ed., pp. 271-303). Washington, DC: American Council on Education.

Comprone, J. J. (1987). Literary theory and composition. In G. Tate (Ed.), *Teaching composition: 12 bibliographic essays* (pp. 291-331). Fort Worth, TX: Texas Christian University Press.

Connors, R. J. (1983, January). Composition studies and science. *College English, 45*, 1-20.

Cook-Gumperz, J., & Gumperz, J. J. (1982). Communicative competence in educational perspective. In L.C. Wilkinson (Ed.), *Communicating in the classroom* (pp. 13-23). New York: Academic Press.

Donaldson, M. (1978). *Children's minds.* London: Fontana, Collins.

Emig, J. (1982). Inquiry paradigms and writing. *College Composition and Communication, 33*, 64-75.

Greenberg, K. (1981, March). Letter. In L. Ruth & S. Murphy *Designing writing tasks for the assessment of writing* (p. 62). Norwood, NJ: Ablex Publishing.

Gronlund, N. E. (1985). *Measurement and evaluation in teaching* (5th ed.). New York: Macmillan.

Guba, E. G., & Lincoln, Y. S. (1989). *Fourth generation evaluation.* Newbury Park, CA: Sage.

Haney, W., & Scott, L. (1987). Talking with children about tests: An exploratory study of test item ambiguity. In R. O. Freedle & R. P. Duran (Eds.), *Cognitive and linguistic analysis of test performance* (Vol. XXII, pp. 298-369). Norwood, NJ: Ablex Publishing.

Haswell, W. (1988). *Contrasting ways to appraise improvement in writing courses: Paired comparison and holistic.* Unpublished manuscript, Washington State University, Department of English, Pullman.

Hawkins, L. & Cobele, J. (1971). The problem of response error in interviews. In J. B. Lansing, S. B. Withey, & A. C. Wolfe (Eds.), *Working papers on survey research in poverty areas* (pp. 60-97). Ann Arbor: University of Michigan, Survey Research Center, Institute for Social Research.

Hoetker, J. (1982). Essay examination topics and student's writing. *College Composition and Communication, 33*, pp. 377-392.

Hoffman, B. (1962). *The tyranny of testing.* New York: Crowell-Collier.

Hopkins, K. D., & Stanley, J. C. (1981). *Educational and psychological measurement and evaluation* (6th ed.). Englewood Cliffs, NJ: Prentice-Hall.

Johnson, P. H. (1983). *Reading comprehension assessment: A cognitive basis.*

Newark, DE: International Reading Association.

Keech, C. L. (1982). Practices in designing writing test prompts: Analysis and recommendations. In J. R. Gray, & L. P. Ruth (Eds.), *Properties of writing tasks: A study of alternative procedures for holistic writing assessment* (pp. 132-214). Berkeley: University of California, Graduate School of Education, Bay Area Writing Project. (ERIC No. ED 230 576)

Keech, C., & McNelly, M. E. (1982). Comparison and analysis of rater responses to the anchor papers in the writing prompt variation study. In J. R. Gray & L. P. Ruth (Eds.), *Properties of writing tasks: A study of alternative procedures for holistic writing assessment* (pp. 132-214). Berkeley: University of California, Graduate School of Education, Bay Area Writing Project. (ERIC No. ED 230 576)

Kinzer, C. (1987). Effects of topic and response variables on holistic score. *English Quarterly, 20,* 2, pp. 106-120.

Kinzer, C., & Murphy, S. (1982). The effects of assessment prompt and response variables on holistic score: A pilot study and validation of an analysis technique. In J. R. Gray & L. P. Ruth (Eds.), *Properties of writing tasks: A study of alternative procedures for holistic writing assessment* (pp. 132-214). Berkeley: University of California, Graduate School of Education, Bay Area Writing Project. (ERIC No. ED 230 576)

Kubiszyn, T., & Borich, G. (1987). *Educational testing and measurement: Classroom application and practice* (2nd ed.). Glenview, IL: Scott, Foresman.

Marascuilo, L., & McSweeney, M. (1977). *Nonparametric and distribution-free methods for the social sciences.* Monterey, CA: Brooks/Cole Publishing.

Messick, S. (1989). Validity. In R. Linn (Ed.), *Educational measurement* (3rd ed., pp. 13-103). New York: American Council on Education, Macmillan.

Millman, J., & Green, J. (1989). The specification and development of tests of achievement and ability. In R. Linn (Ed.), *Educational measurement* (3rd ed., pp. 335-366). New York: American Council on Education, Macmillan.

Murphy, S., Carroll, K., Kinzer, C., & Robyns, A. (1982). A study of the construction of the meanings of a writing prompt by its authors, the student writers, and the raters. In J. R. Gray & L. P. Ruth (Eds.), *Properties of writing tasks: A study of alternative procedures for holistic writing assessment* (pp. 336-471). Berkeley: University of California, Graduate School of Education, Bay Area Writing Project. (ERIC No. ED 230 576)

Osterlind, S. J. (1989). *Constructing test items.* Boston: Kluwer Academic Publishers.

Payne, D. A., & McMorris, R. F. (1967). *Educational and psychological measurement.* Waltham, MA: Blaisdell.

Pearson, P. D. (1986). Twenty years of research in reading comprehension. In T. E. Raphael (Ed.), *The contexts of school-based literacy* (pp. 43-61). New York: Random House.

Popham, W. J. (1981). *Modern educational measurement.* Englewood Cliffs, NJ: Prentice-Hall.

Rosenblatt, L. M. (1938). *Literature as exploration* (3rd ed.). New York: Modern Language Association.

Rosenblatt, L. M. (1978). *The reader, the text, and the poem.* Carbondale, IL: Southern Illinois University Press.

Rosenblatt, L. M. (1989). Writing and reading: The transactional theory. In J. M. Mason (Ed.), *Reading and writing connections.* Boston: Allyn and Bacon.

Ruth, L., & Murphy, S. (1984). Designing topics for writing assessment: Problems of meaning. *College Composition and Communication,* pp. 410-422.

Ruth, L., & Murphy, S. (1988). *Designing writing tasks for the assessment of writing.* Norwood, NJ: Ablex Publishing.

Squire, J. R. (1990). Research on reader response and the national literature initiative. In M. Hayhoe & S. Parker (Eds.), *Reading and response* (pp. 13-24). Philadelphia: Oxford University Press & Milton Keynes.

Stalnaker, J. M. (1951). The essay type of examination. In E. F. Lindquist (Ed.), *Educational measurement* (pp. 495-529). Washington, DC: American Council on Education.

Taylor, E. F. (1977). The looking glass world of testing. In *Standardized testing issues: Teachers' perspectives.* Washington, DC: National Education Association.

Wesman, A. G. (1971). Writing the test item. In R. Thorndike (Ed.), *Educational measurement* (2nd ed., pp. 81-128). Washington, DC: American Council on Education

Willinsky, J. (1990). *The new literacy: Redefining reading and writing in the schools.* New York: Routledge.

9

Comprehension, Communicative Competence, and Construct Validity: Holistic Scoring from an ESL Perspective

Michael Janopoulos
University of Northern Iowa

Where there is commitment and time to do the work required to achieve reliability of judgment, holistic evaluation remains the most valid and direct means of rank-ordering students by writing ability. (Cooper, 1977, p. 3)

[T]he validity of holistic scoring remains an open question . . . (Charney, 1984, p. 67)

[H]olistic scoring has the highest construct validity when overall attained writing proficiency is the construct to be assessed. (Perkins, 1983, p. 652)

At this point in the development of holistic scoring, there is no information which can guarantee its validity as a true measure of writing quality. (Huot, 1990, p. 206)

INTRODUCTION

It is an axiom of psychometrics that a "good" test allows us access to the construct we seek to measure. With the exception of Perkins, however, none of the researchers cited above refer directly to the *construct validity* of holistic scoring. Instead, they limit their comments to issues of either *content* or *criterion-referenced validity*. This is not surprising, as evidence of construct validity may be obtainable only through behavioral data that are inferential rather than direct (Ausubel, Novac, & Hanesian, 1978). Therefore, since in construct validation a test is validated against a theory, evidence of validity of *content* and *criteria* help "establish the credibility of a test of a construct" (Gay, 1981, p. 113), rather than provide direct evidence that the test provides access to the construct itself. Thus, evidence of content validity and criterion-referenced validity are, of themselves, not necessarily sufficient.

Moreover, such evidence is not easy to obtain. For example, claims of content validity are based on the assumption that a subset of tasks in a test-taking environment (the "tasks one normally performs in exhibiting the skill or ability that the task purports to measure" [Oller, 1979, p. 50]) "is representative of the larger set (universe) of tasks" (Palmer & Groot, 1981, p. 2). In its broadest terms, this means that tests of writing proficiency should require subjects to write. But the vast range of writing tasks makes selection of "representative" test assignments more difficult than it might appear at first glance.

Arguments for criterion-referenced validity (whose criteria are generally "tests that purport to measure the same skill, or component(s) of a skill" [Oller, 1979, p. 51] as the test against which they are compared) can be equally limited in providing "proof" of construct validity. For example, Palmer and Groot (1981) note that it is possible for "scores on tests of two distinct abilities to correlate highly with one another without any actual causal relation between them" (p. 3). It is also possible that tests may correlate highly with one another without correlating significantly with the construct they purport to measure. Finally, "even if there were a valid criterion, a high correlation between a test and a criterion would not . . . tell us much about what the scores on the test *mean*" (p. 4).

Despite such limitations, however, evidence of content and/or criterion-referenced validity—provided it is interpreted with caution—can provide useful insights into the construct validity of holistic scoring, as neither the content nor the criteria can ultimately be considered in isolation from the underlying construct of writing proficiency itself. Still, what emerges from an examination of the claims and counterclaims regarding the construct validity of holistic evaluation of writing proficiency represented either implicitly or explicitly in the quotes cited above is that no clear answer has emerged either for or against. Notwithstanding this lack of consensus, holistic scoring has come into common use because, as Huot and Williamson (1990) point out, "writing evaluation presented such pressing need (that) we were forced to adopt assessment procedures without testing them for their theoretic soundness" (p. 1). Today, both English and English as a Second/Foreign Language (ESL) composition teachers find themselves in a situation where they continue to rely on a scoring procedure that is, at best, imperfectly understood and insufficiently validated.

As was alluded to above, this situation exists, in large part, because construct validity is exceedingly difficult to establish under the best of conditions. In their classic paper, Cronbach and Meehl (1955) define a construct as "some postulated attribute of people assumed to be reflected in performance" (p. 283). Ausubel et al. (1978) point out that no suitable criterion may exist for the construct we wish to measure; therefore, "Construct validity is based on logical defensible inferences from experimental or other evidence" (p. 609). Thus, validation of theoretical constructs relies on instruments which "tend to be indirect and inferential rather than based on direct behavioral samples of the trait or ability in question" (p. 608).

CONSTRUCT VALIDITY:
AN ESL COMPOSITION PERSPECTIVE

For teachers of ESL composition, any measure of writing proficiency must possess three attributes. First, the writing task must be pragmatic in the sense that "[t]he writer must have something to say; there must be someone to say it to; and the task must require the sequential production of elements in the language that are temporally constrained and related . . . to the context of discourse defined by (or for) the writer" (Oller, 1979, p. 384). Second, the writing task must allow the subject to demonstrate his/her *communicative competence* in writing. According to Savignon (1984a), "the term has come to be used in language teaching contexts to refer to the ability to convey meaning, to successfully combine a knowledge of linguistic and sociolinguistic rules in communicative interactions" (p. v). Finally, the writing assessment procedure must allow for adequate time to access the second/foreign language (FL) writer's efforts, in keeping with a *process approach* to teaching writing that values interaction of author and audience through the medium of the text.

Proficiency and Pragmatic Language Tests

From the standpoint of the teacher of ESL composition, when considering the construct validity of holistic scoring, it is first necessary to ask the question, "Does the test (i.e., an actual sample of a subject's writing) allow the subject to demonstrate proficiency?" In ESL, we can answer this question in the affirmative if the writing task satisfies Oller's (1979) criteria for *pragmatic* language tests; namely, that "they relate to full-fledged contexts of discourse that are known to the writer and that the writer is attempting to make known to the reader" (p. 384). That is, if the FL writer is challenged with a task that requires him/her to manipulate written text so that meaning is conveyed through a medium which conforms to grammatical, semantic, and discourse constraints, then the said task is pragmatic in that it taps an underlying linguistic competency (see Oller, 1979, for a complete discussion of this issue).

Proficiency and Communicative Competence

Confidence that a writing task is *pragmatic* is essential, but it is not enough. ESL composition teachers must also have confidence that the method they use to *evaluate* that sample of writing allows them access to the construct they wish to measure, that is, *communicative competence.* To this end, they need to know that holistic scoring will allow them to judge FL writers primarily in terms of their ability to express ideas, since, as Raimes (1983) points out, writing "means expressing ideas, conveying ideas" (p. 83).

Proficiency and the Process Approach

Of central importance to the issue of whether holistic assessment of ESL writing proficiency allows the rater to evaluate the construct of *communicative competence* is the question of *time.* ESL practitioners have been profoundly influenced by the work of such colleagues in English composition as Emig (1971), Perl (1980), and Sommers (1982), whose insights into what is commonly termed the *process approach* have been strongly advocated for use in ESL by Raimes (1986) and Zamel (1986). Thus, ESL writing teachers share with their English composition colleagues a recognition that the *process approach* classroom is a place in which time and care are recognized as essential, not just in the *writing* of a text, but in its *reading* as well.

ESL practitioners are well aware of research into the text-processing strategies employed by both native English language (NL) (e.g., Rumelhart, 1980) and FL (e.g., Carrell, 1983) readers. This awareness has allowed ESL practitioners to recognize that meaning does not reside in the text, per se. Instead, they see the text, as Spiro (1980) describes it, as "a skeleton, a blueprint for the creation of meaning" through which reader and writer interact (p. 245).

Consequently, they, similar to NL composition teachers, need to be able to reconcile what they see as a fundamental conflict between teaching the writing *process* and evaluating the writing *product.* In other words, ESL composition teachers need reassurance that a procedure which emphasizes quick and general reading of a text truly measures what they are trying to teach; namely, a process in which success is measured in terms of the FL writer's ability to communicate his/her intended meaning.

To again cite Ausubel et al. (1978), "construct validity is based on logical defensible inferences from experimental or other evidence" (p. 609). Thus, it follows for ESL composition teachers that the instrument they use to score a test that purports to measure FL writing proficiency must also be based on similarly "logical defensible inferences," including the assumption that the holistic scoring procedure allows the NL reader sufficient time to access the FL writer's intended meaning, even if that meaning is obscured by the sort of errors FL writers typically commit.

PROCESS, PRODUCT, AND TIME

The author of a popular ESL composition textbook reminds teachers that "the novice writer needs instruction on the process which writers go through in order to produce texts: a process of exploration and generation of ideas on paper; of seeking out appropriate feedback; and of reworking and revising the presentation of ideas" (Leki, 1989, vii). Her audience represents a growing number of ESL practitioners who endorse and strive to implement the *process approach* to FL writing instruction. As it does with English composition, this approach values time, care, and interaction between reader and writer through the medium of the text. Moreover, ESL teachers are mindful that, for FL students, communicative competence "involves being able to use the language appropriate to a given social context" (Larsen-Freeman, 1986, p. 131) that is likely to be significantly different than the one to which the FL writer is accustomed.

Accordingly, process-approach-minded ESL writing teachers, like their colleagues in English composition, place a premium on evaluating a student's efforts in terms of how effectively that student is able to communicate. This view of the holistic reading process has been influenced by both Goodman (1967), who characterizes reading as a "psycholinguistic guessing game" (p. 2) in which the reader attempts to reconstruct the author's message, and Pearson and Tierney (1984), who assert that readers "must approach a text with the same deliberateness, time, and reflection that a good author employs as he revises his text" (p. 151). These related viewpoints are supported by research in both NL (e.g., Tierney, LaZansky, Raphael, & Cohen, 1973) and FL (e.g., Bernhardt, 1984) that reading is an *interactive* process between author and audience that is mediated *by* the text, in which meaning is a product of negotiation between author and audience *through* the text. In Tierney's view, this process involves the construction and analysis of an *implicit text* comprised of (a) what the writer *means* to convey in the text, (b) the text that is actually produced, and (c) what the reader *understands* from the text. Moreover, it is generally conceded that for the process to work well, the author must manipulate the text in such a way that the message is communicated to an audience capable of bringing to bear the appropriate conceptual abilities, process strategies, and background knowledge (Coady, 1979).

Such a view of the interactive relationship between reader and writer is, of course, not unique to the field of ESL. What sets ESL practitioners apart from their colleagues in English composition, however, is the fact that writing by ESL students is likely to contain a greater number of errors than is contained in the writing of NL students of comparable age and educational level. Moreover, unlike the errors in most NL student writers' texts, the errors in FL student writers' texts may be so different from the structure of Standard American English that the meaning of whole stretches of discourse may be seriously obscured. The practical manifestation of exposure to such writing is twofold: First, ESL composition teachers tend to focus more on content than on "correctness," especially when confronted with what Burt and Kiparsky (1974) term "local" errors of grammar, spelling, and punctuation, which may cause reader irritation but do not affect overall comprehension. However, they are not necessarily more tolerant of FL writing errors than instructors in other disciplines. Research by the author (1992), for example, has shown that professors generally judge sentence-level FL errors less severely than comparable NS errors, while a study by Santos (1988) has presented evidence that university faculty at large demonstrate a willingness to look beyond the language deficiencies of a FL text to its content. Nevertheless, given their linguistic background and training, ESL composition teachers may well be more predisposed to view writing errors as a normal, necessary, and integral part of the language learning process *as a whole* than are NL composition teachers whose orientation is more toward working with students who already possess linguistic competence in English.

Second, ESL writing instructors generally become quite adept at "reading through" the surface errors of a FL text to glean the writer's message, even when those errors seriously affect the reader's rate of processing. This skill results from several factors, including preservice training in such specialized areas in applied linguistics as error analysis, intuition borne out of experience in dealing with the kind of errors FL students typically make, and the sheer repetition of dealing with FL essays on an ongoing basis. In practice, then, reading a FL essay is more often than not likely to be a painstakingly slow process, since it will frequently contain errors severe enough to seriously obscure its author's intended meaning. Still, to an ESL composition teacher who sees evaluating the writing product and teaching the writing process as opposite sides of the same coin, taking the extra time is a reasonable price to pay.

Given such an orientation, it is not surprising that ESL composition teachers might approach the holistic scoring process with certain misgivings, despite findings by Coffman (1968), Freedman (1979), and Breland and Jones (1984) that holistic raters of NL writing proficiency seem to attend less to mechanics and sentence structure than they do to content features (see also Huot, this volume, and Pula & Huot, this volume). Instead, they may point to contradictory NL findings reported by Rafoth and Rubin (1984) as evidence that "college instructors' perceptions of composition quality are most influenced by mechanics" (p. 455), and so will be more inclined to agree with Charney's (1984) observation that the way holistic scorers read texts may create an unnatural reading environment in which scores might "only reflect agreement on salient but superficial features of writing, such as the quality of the handwriting or the presence of spelling errors" (p. 78). Moreover, specific misgivings about the effects of time constraints on comprehension during the holistic reading process may be intensified by findings in the field of NL reading comprehension. Researchers such as Kintsch, Mandel, and Kozminsky (1977), Baker and Anderson (1982), and Meyer (1982) have demonstrated that the presence of inconsistent information in a text coupled with time constraints imposed upon a reading task can severely impede the reader's ability to access meaning, thereby adversely affecting comprehension.

PROFICIENCY AND COMMUNICATIVE COMPETENCE

Writing proficiency has frequently been acknowledged as a multifaceted construct. Odell (1977), for example, notes the variety of dimensions necessary to define English language "writing proficiency," while Spandel and Stiggins (1980) point out the ephemeral nature of any definition. Thus, defining a construct for writing proficiency is complicated by the wide range of interrelated variables that must be considered when attempting to establish measurable parameters for NL writing proficiency, because the question of what constitutes "good writing" in one's own language is affected, on the one hand, by the interactive and subjective nature of the reader-writer relationship (see de Beaugrande, 1978; Pearson & Tierney, 1984), and on the other by the fact that standards of quality will vary with the context and purpose of the assessment, changing in response to what Spandel and Stiggins (1980) refer to as "the broad range of potentially relevant writing competencies and the difficulties in setting standards of acceptable performance" (pp. 5-6).

Defining the parameters of FL writing proficiency, on the other hand, is even more complicated because FL writing involves the additional dimension of coping with the need to bridge the gap between different languages, cultures, and rhetorical conventions. Thus, this factor must also be included in the equation along with the NL assessment variables of context and purpose.

Fortunately, our task in assessing FL writing skills can be simplified somewhat by returning to a notion alluded to earlier in this chapter: *communicative competence*. Communicative competence, in its simplest meaning, is the ability to communicate one's intended message to the appropriate audience. Stern (1983) observes that the term was first coined by Hymes in 1972 to articulate a more semantic and social view of language than was generally accepted by linguists at that time. According to Stern, this view in language learning theory (and with it, language teaching methodology) reflects a movement away from views of language that were either focused on structure and form (as exemplified by Skinner's 1957 work, *Verbal Behavior*), or were concerned with abstract "universals" thought to underlie all human languages (as articulated in Chomsky's 1965 book, *Aspects of the Theory of Syntax*).

For teachers of ESL composition, the result of using a communicative approach is that "correctness" is no longer seen as a primary goal of instruction as it had been when ESL was taught via an audiolingual methodology based upon behaviorist principles, including habit formation. As was noted earlier, teaching for communicative competence does not mean ignoring errors, except perhaps during the very early drafting stages of the composing process, but it does mean that teaching communicative competence obliges the ESL writing teacher to make a conscious effort to look beyond form to content.

Teachers of ESL composition agree with Savignon (1984b) that communicative competence is "an underlying construct"(p. 3) of FL proficiency. Implicit in this belief is the assumption that comprehension, which necessarily involves consideration of the entire range of variables that constitute the FL writer's communicative competence, plays an integral role in the assessment of FL writing proficiency. Thus, ESL composition teachers feel that the problem of establishing the construct validity of holistic assessment of FL writing proficiency can be reduced to a more manageable dimension: the measurement of FL writing proficiency in terms of how well-trained holistic raters comprehend the FL texts they read. First, however, it must be demonstrated that the more effective a FL text is, the more of its content a trained holistic scorer will understand, despite the fact that holistic scoring is done in an environment that obliges the scorer to read, in a relatively short time, a text that is likely to contain stretches of discourse in which meaning is obscured. The balance of this chapter will discuss two experiments designed to address this question.

EXPERIMENT 1[1]

Purpose

In order to investigate the degree to which trained holistic raters comprehend texts written by FL university students, the following research question was posed: *Will trained holistic raters of FL writing proficiency recall significantly more of the higher rated of two FL texts representing distinctly different proficiency levels?* In this experiment, Connor's (1984) operational definition of reading comprehension—the amount of content correctly recalled in an immediate written recall protocol—was used to measure how much readers understood the texts they read (see Bernhardt, 1983, for an overview of research employing the written recall protocol procedure to measure aspects of reading comprehension).

Subjects

Twelve university-level ESL composition instructors with prior holistic scoring experience participated.

Materials

Texts used in the study were selected from among approximately 250 timed in-class (1-hour) essays written by foreign graduate students placed into the ESL composition sequence at a large midwestern university. These essays, which were designed to verify initial placement decisions, addressed one of two contrast/comparison prompts. Essays were initially scored on a 4-point proficiency scale corresponding to the university's three-tiered ESL course sequence (106, 107, 108), plus "Q" (Qualified to bypass ESL Composition entirely). All texts used in the study were typed exactly as written, so that handwriting would not be a factor in the raters' judgments of writing quality (see Charney, 1984).

Procedures[2]

The recall task. Subjects were given four model compositions and a list of holistic criteria prior to the experimental session, so that they could

---

[1] The results of this study were originally reported in the April 1989 issue of *Written Communication* under the title "Reader Comprehension and Holistic Assessment of Second Language Writing Proficiency." Copyright by Sage Publications, 1989. Reprinted by permission.

[2] Due to the publisher's restrictions on length, appendices containing essay prompts, holistic scoring criteria, original and negotiated texts, and protocol scoring matrices were omitted from this chapter. The author will gladly provide them on request.

familiarize themselves in advance with the scoring standards used in the study. The session began with a general discussion of the holistic scoring criteria, followed by a practice session in which four texts were rated on a 4-point scale. After each text was read, results were discussed and scores were compared to assist subjects in reaching general agreement about the rating criteria being used. Next, subjects scored a series of nine randomly selected and ordered essays one by one, taking no more than the maximum allotted time of 2 minutes recommended by Cooper (1977) and White (1985). During this procedure, each subject was given the same essay to rate. After reading each essay, subjects recorded their scores on tally sheets.

This phase served two purposes. First, subjects were given additional practice in rating FL essays to help improve interrater reliability. Second, scoring several essays under a 2-minute time limit served to simulate the kind of environment typically found in a holistic rating session. Thus, subjects were conditioned to approach the rating task without being forewarned of the recall task to follow. This precaution proved to be necessary, as subsequent research reported by the author (1991) has demonstrated that awareness of a recall task alters the way in which subjects read FL texts during a holistic rating session to the extent that the amount of content recalled is significantly affected.

Once subjects read and rated the nine essays, the final phase of the experiment began. Subjects were instructed to rate a tenth essay immediately after the ninth. At this point, though, subjects were given different essays to rate.

Half of the subjects were given a higher quality (Level 108), while the other half received a lower quality (Level 107) text. Both texts were chosen from among papers that had been assigned, respectively, scores of "108" and "107" by independent raters during the initial placement procedure. As a further safeguard, the researcher and the ESL Composition Program Director independently verified that both texts were representative of the levels in which they had been placed. Texts were of approximately the same length (Level 107 = 274 words; Level 108 = 328 words) and were typed to give the appearance of being of essentially equal length to minimize the potentially confounding effects of composition length on assessment of writing quality noted by Rafoth and Rubin (1984).

Upon completion of the the rating task, subjects were instructed to put aside the essays and write a recall protocol of what they had just read. Specific instructions conformed to guidelines set down by Johnson (1970). Subjects were allowed unlimited time to write everything they recalled, although they were not allowed to refer to the essays they had just read. Paraphrasing was allowed when necessary (Frederiksen, 1977; Mandler, 1978).

The scoring task: Creation of "negotiated" texts. As the texts were produced by FL writers, each was rewritten to insure that the protocol scoring instruments used to measure raters' recall were based on its authors' intended meaning. Three readers independently rewrote each text to reflect what they felt was the author's intended meaning, and then met to resolve discrepancies of interpretation. In cases where disagreements persisted, the author of the text in question was also consulted. The resulting "negotiated" texts served as the basis on which a count of each essay's constituent "idea units" (defined by Bernhardt, 1983, as "primarily consisting of noun, verb, and prepositional phrases" [p. 29]) were tallied.

Creation of Protocol Scoring Matrices (PSMs). To obtain a quantifiable measure of the content recalled in the subjects' written protocols, a list of all possible idea units for each negotiated text was compiled by the researcher and independently verified by a colleague. Next, using a procedure first devised by Meyer (1973), the idea units were weighted according to their relative importance to the text in which they were contained (see Janopoulos, 1989, for a complete description of the procedure). Each PSM served as the rating scale for its respective text.

Scoring of Written Recall Protocols. Using the appropriate PSM as a guide, the researcher read each protocol and identified the number of correctly recalled idea units it contained. These figures were then compared with those of a colleague who had been extensively trained in the procedure. Interrater reliability (Pearson r) was computed in at 0.97. Next, the idea units appearing in each protocol were assigned their weighted values, which were then tallied to obtain an adjusted recall score for each protocol.

Data Analysis. Individual recall protocol scores for each text were added and then divided by the number of recall protocols for each text. In this way percentage scores that were amenable to comparison were obtained. A *t*-test was then computed to compare the mean recall scores of the two groups.

Results

The null hypothesis predicted that for trained holistic raters, there would be no significant difference between the amount of content recalled from the higher rated (Level 108) and lower rated (Level 107) FL texts.

Table 1 shows subjects' individual percentage recall scores, in addition to the holistic score each subject assigned to the texts. Examination of this table indicates that the subjects' ratings were generally consistent with one another's, as well as with the scores originally assigned the essays. Table 2 displays means and standard deviations for the two groups of subjects who read, rated, and wrote recall protocols based on the higher and lower rated FL essays. Table 3 provides the results of a t-test of the means of the two groups. Examination of Table 3 reveals a statistically significant difference in the mean recall scores of the two groups in favor of the group which read the higher quality text (t=2.26, p<.05). In other words, holistic raters who read the higher quality (Level 108) FL essay recalled significantly more content than did holistic raters who read the lower quality (Level 107) FL text. On the basis of these results, the null hypothesis is rejected.

Table 1. Individual Percentage Recall Scores and Holistic Ratings (Study #1)

Text	Subject	Rating	Recall %
	A	Q	58.74
	B	Q	41.26
108	C	108	58.17
	D	108	53.55
	E	108	35.06
	F	108	18.27
	G	108	36.34
	H	108	30.09
107	I	107	34.60
	J	107	30.09
	K	107	19.48
	L	107	13.08

Table 2. Means and Standard Deviations of Recall Scores, by Level of Proficiency Assessment (Study #1)

ASSESSED PROFICIENCY								
LOWER (107)			HIGHER (108)			OVERALL		
n	$\overline{x}$	S.D.	n	$\overline{x}$	S.D.	n	$\overline{x}$	S.D.
6	27.28	9.09	6	44.17	15.86	12	35.72	15.16

Table 3. T-Test for Mean Recall Scores of Readers of Lower and Higher Quality NNS Texts

$\overline{x}(lo)$	$\overline{x}(hi)$	$S(\overline{x}1-\overline{x}2)$	df	t-value
27.28	44.17	7.46	10	2.26[a]

[a]p<.05, n=12

EXPERIMENT 2

Purpose

The results obtained in Experiment 1 indicated that trained holistic raters of FL writing proficiency recall (comprehend) more of the better written of two qualitatively distinct texts. However, the relatively wide difference in quality between those texts leaves an incomplete picture of the extent to which holistic scorers are able to recall more of better written FL texts when rating texts representing a lesser difference in quality than those used in Experiment 1. To investigate this question, Experiment 2 addressed the following research question: *Will trained holistic raters of FL writing proficiency recall significantly more of the better written of two texts judged as equivalent on a 4-point scale of writing proficiency?*

Subjects

Fourteen subjects were used. Relative to the subjects in Experiment 2, this group was somewhat more heterogeneous with regard to the amount of experience in ESL composition and holistic scoring. Overall, however, most subjects had experience in both ESL composition and holistic scoring, while the remainder were either ESL composition teachers or were in training to become teachers and holistic scorers in the university's ESL composition program.

Materials

This experiment used the same corpus of texts that was used in Experiment 1. Placement essay prompts, holistic criteria, range-finder papers, and all samples of FL writing used during the training and scoring sessions prior to the recall protocol task were identical in both studies. All texts were typed.

Procedures

The recall task. Prior to the recall protocol phase of the experiment, the same procedure that was used in Experiment 1 was followed. This served the same function as it had in Experiment 1, in that it helped to create a realistic holistic scoring environment and provided additional practice in the scoring procedure, which was especially useful for those subjects who were relatively inexperienced.

As with Experiment 1, once subjects had rated the same nine essays, they were directed to rate one of two qualitatively distinct texts. In contrast to the texts used in Experiment 1, however, these texts were selected from a group of essays previously assessed as representing the same proficiency level (Level 108). In terms of relative quality, however, one (henceforth designated 108Hi) was judged to be better written than the other (henceforth designated 108Lo). This judgment was accomplished by having ESL composition teachers rank five texts, including 108Hi, 108Lo, and the 107 text from Experiment 1, in order from best to worst. In 4 out of 5 rankings, 108Hi was judged higher than 108Lo, and both were ranked higher than the 107 text in all five cases.

Once subjects had completed rating their tenth essay, they were directed to write recall protocols of what they had just read, following the same instructions given in Experiment 1.

The scoring task. The same procedures that were used in Experiment 1 to create negotiated texts and PSMs were followed. Scoring of recall protocols was also identical, with one exception. After later analysis showed that the weighted and raw scores of Experiment 1 yielded virtually identical results, the procedure was not used in this study. Instead, scores were based on the unweighted tally of correctly recalled idea units contained in each protocol. Data analysis involved computing mean recall scores for each group, and then performing a *t*-test to compare the mean recall scores of the 108Hi and 108Lo groups.

Results

Table 4 shows percentage recall scores and ratings individual subjects assigned to the texts they assessed. This table shows that, while both FL texts were rated as roughly equivalent, the 108Hi text was rated somewhat higher than 108Lo. Table 5 displays the means and standard deviations of the two groups. Table 6 reveals the results of a *t*-test of the means of the two groups, which show a statistically significant difference in recall between the 108Hi and 108Lo groups. Specifically, subjects who read the higher quality (108Hi) text recalled more of it than the second group recalled of the lower quality (108Lo) text ($t=3.60$, $p<.01$). Thus, the null hypothesis in this study must also be rejected.

Table 4. Individual Percentage Recall Scores and Holistic Ratings (Study #2)

Text	Subject	Rating	Recall %
	A	107	43.08
	B	Q	67.69
	C	108	73.85
108Hi	D	108	67.69
	E	108	53.85
	F	108	49.23
	G	108	44.62

Table 4. Individual Percentage Recall Scores and Holistic Ratings (Study #2) (continued)

Text	Subject	Rating	Recall %
	H	108	50.00
	I	108	32.26
	J	108	29.03
108Lo	K	108	24.19
	L	107	46.77
	M	107	37.09
	N	107	16.92

Table 5. Means and Standard Deviations of Recall Scores, by Level of Proficiency Assessment (Study #2)

ASSESSED PROFICIENCY								
LOWER (108Lo)			HIGHER (108Hi)			OVERALL		
n	$\overline{x}$	S.D.	n	$\overline{x}$	S.D.	n	$\overline{x}$	S.D.
7	33.75	11.86	7	57.14	12.45	14	45.44	16.84

Table 6. T-Test for Mean Recall Scores of Readers of Lower and Higher Quality NNS Texts

$\overline{x}(lo)$	$\overline{x}(hi)$	$S(\overline{x}1-\overline{x}2)$	df	t-value
33.75	57.14	6.49	12	3.60[a]

[a]$p<.01$, $n=14$

CONCLUSIONS

The purpose of these studies was to determine if—and to what degree—trained raters of FL writing proficiency are able to comprehend the texts they read during a holistic scoring session. Specifically, it was hypothesized that if such readers attend to meaning during the rating task, they should recall significantly more of a text written by a more proficient FL writer than they do of a text written by a less proficient FL writer. Results obtained in Experiment 1 showed that subjects recalled significantly more of the higher rated of two FL writing samples representing distinctly different proficiency levels. Experiment 2 showed that holistic raters demonstrated the same tendency when recalling FL essays representing a lesser difference in quality than those used in Experiment 1.

The results of these studies indicate that an apparent connection exists between a trained holistic rater's comprehension of a FL text and his/her assessment of its quality. In other words, it appears that the better written a FL text is, the better it is recalled by a holistic scorer of FL writing proficiency. Moreover, it seems that holistic raters tend to recall more of the better written FL papers, even when confronted by texts whose qualitative differences are comparatively subtle. These results support the position that holistic scoring of FL writing proficiency by trained raters possesses construct validity when the construct being measured is communicative competence.

DISCUSSION

The focus of these studies was on the construct validity of holistic assessment of FL writing proficiency, where communicative competence was the construct to be measured. Proceeding from the assumption that most ESL practitioners agree with Spandel and Stiggins (1980) that proficiency is best measured on a continuum where the narrower the gap between the message as sent and the message as received, the more proficient the writer, it was hypothesized that if trained holistic raters of FL writing proficiency attended to meaning, they would recall significantly more of a text written by a more proficient author than written by a less proficient author. Analysis of the data from these experiments leads to the conclusion that comprehension is facilitated by the level of quality of a text, even when it is read for the purpose of holistically assessing FL writing proficiency rather than for the purpose of comprehension per se.

There is abundant NL empirical support for this conclusion. For example, research (e.g., Kintsch & van Dijk, 1978; Meyer, 1973) has shown that readers recall more of a better organized essay than of an essay lacking in organizational cohesion. In addition, Baker and Anderson (1982) report that, even when engaged in a focused-reading task requiring attention to textual inconsistencies, their subjects were able to monitor their comprehension in order to determine if ideas expressed in a text were consistent. Two things are significant about this conclusion: (a) it applies to holistic scoring of texts, when one might expect a reader's depth of processing to be limited by the presence of time constraints; and (b) it applies to FL texts, which are likely to contain a considerable amount of textual inconsistencies. Again, NL research (e.g., Kintsch & van Dijk, 1978; Kintsch, Mandel, & Kozminsky, 1977) would seem to support these suppositions.

Interestingly, however, one of the more striking phenomena observed in these studies is that the time constraints under which subjects performed their holistic reading task did not appear to prevent them from reading with comprehension. While the reasons for this are not entirely clear, it may be that the holistic reading process itself promotes something analogous to what de Beaugrande (1978) calls a "sampling process," in which certain elements of presented textual input are accepted while others are rejected. In fact, the presence of such elements—provided they are recognized by the reader—may actually facilitate the process by which a holistic reader is able to access meaning from a text, in which case the reader can operate effectively within the time constraints of the holistic scoring task. Conversely, however, if they are not recognized, these elements may have the opposite effect.

Support for this hypothesis is given by Meyer (1982), who asserts that much of a reader's ability to comprehend a text can be attributed to the knowledge and experience (i.e., schema) a skilled holistic reader brings to the reader-text-writer equation. Her findings indicate that a skilled reader with the ability and desire to understand the author's logic will employ a comprehension process that entails the formation of a memorial representation of the text that parallels its content structure, thereby allowing recall of a significant portion of the text. In the context of the reading process of an experienced holistic rater of FL writing proficiency, such schema would presumably consist of not only prior knowledge about the *topic* addressed in the FL text, but also *experience* in reading FL texts, as well as specific knowledge of, for example, *contrastive rhetoric* (see Kaplan, 1966), which might provide him/her with clues of how to decode a text that did not conform to the rhetorical conventions of English.

The importance of a reader's goals in holistic scoring was also underscored by the results of these studies, as it was hypothesized that trained raters of FL writing proficiency read for the purpose of evaluating communicative competence. That subjects apparently read both for and with comprehension is consistent with the findings of Kintsch and van Dijk (1978) and Just and Carpenter (1980). Moreover, the possibility that ESL practitioners might somehow read a FL text differently than their English counterparts is supported by Kintsch and van Dijk (1978), who note that in the absence of a controlling schema, whether due to vague reader goals or unconventional text structure, the comprehension process becomes haphazard and inefficient. But when the task is undertaken by subjects "who read a text with a specific problem-solving set," the special purpose "overrides whatever text structure there is" (p. 373).

As we near the end of this chapter, it must be emphasized that key assumptions that were made regarding "a perceived need to teach for communication" (Savignon 1984b, p.7) are based on FL research that has consistently stressed the salience of meaning to judgments of writing proficiency (e.g., Raimes, 1983; Taylor, 1986). Thus, while it would not be unreasonable to predict that the findings reported here would be mirrored in comparable NL research, it cannot be assumed that they can be applied in their entirety to the NL domain, despite the fact that NL researchers such as Huot and Williamson (1990) acknowledge the need to base writing assessment on the author's ability to communicate. This is especially significant in light of the fact that reader *expectations* about the text and its author have been shown to play an important role in the degree to which readers tolerate FL, as opposed to NL, errors (see Ludwig, 1982, for an overview of research in this area). In particular, research by the author (1992) has indicated that university professors tend to judge NL errors more severely than they do comparable FL errors. Thus, it appears that when the reader's expectations concerning the author's ability to conform to the rules and conventions of Standard American English are higher (as they would plausibly be if the reader assumed the author were an educated NL student), she may not apply the same standards.

The possibility that shifting NL/FL expectations might influence a holistic rater's judgment could have an enormous impact on how we set our academic standards, particularly in those universities in which writing proficiency is a graduation requirement. It is true that research on how readers regard FL errors has shown that readers are more tolerant of errors *known to be FL in origin*. However, if FL and NL essays are holistically evaluated together, as they are during university-wide writing proficiency exams, it is by no means certain that raters either can (if they recognize authorship) or will (if they adhere strictly to scoring criteria) adjust their expectations when reading FL essays. Thus, tolerance of errors recognized as FL in origin may not (and probably should not) translate into a more lenient set of standards for FL students taking writing proficiency exams. In fact, evidence provided by Thompson (1990) suggests that FL student failure rates on such exams may be considerably higher than for NL students. It is not surprising that such a dichotomy of expectations may exist within classrooms in which teachers are sensitive to the difficulties a FL student may experience in mastering the art of communicating effectively in English. What is worrisome, however, is the possibility that such a dichotomy is not consistently applied, for Thompson has also noted that the majority of those FL students who failed writing proficiency exams were students of good academic standing who had successfully completed required writing courses. Granted, such issues go well beyond the scope of this chapter, but they do pose questions that must be addressed.

Taken together, the conclusions that emerge in this chapter lend support to the argument that ESL composition teachers are better equipped to assess the communicative competence of FL writers than their counterparts in English composition. Whether this ability is due to their linguistic training, experience in dealing with FL writing from creation of a draft to the evaluation of a finished product, or another factor or combination of factors is not clear. Certainly, however, a strong case can be made for the assertion that their ability to identify unconventional text organization while operating under time constraints, coupled with the likelihood that they approach a FL text with different goals and expectations than other readers, plays a significant role. Just how much experience is needed, or how long it takes to acquire such experience, is also uncertain. In Experiment 2, some subjects were relatively inexperienced in either ESL composition theory or practice. Still, even the relative novices had had some systematic exposure to FL writing prior to the rating task, and were oriented toward reading FL texts during the task as well.

What implications vis-á-vis holistic scoring can be drawn from all this? In terms of the question—"Who should assess FL writing proficiency?—it seems clear that if evaluating FL communicative competence is the goal of assessment, then ESL composition-experienced teachers trained in holistic scoring are the best choice. While on the surface this position may seem extreme, it is actually consistent with the generally accepted view that raters should share a common background and be trained in a mutually accepted and understood scoring system. But what if the goal of the assessment is to measure FL writers against institutional norms? The answer to this question is still uncertain, although the issue will no doubt be eventually addressed, in political if not pedagogical terms.

Equally uncertain is the opposite side of the issue: namely, whether ESL composition teachers (or for that matter, general faculty members without training or experience in assessing NL writing proficiency) should participate in such university-wide holistic scoring sessions, since they may be as lacking in the appropriate training and experience in English composition as English composition teachers may be in ESL. To a certain extent, thorough training in rating procedures, coupled with thorough familiarity with rating criteria, should allow for the process to work as intended, for it may well be that the only prerequisite raters need to assess NL writing proficiency is that they, themselves, possess reasonable competence in written English. Nevertheless, this is another question that needs to be addressed, lest responsibility (and blame?) for (not?) defining, developing, and evaluating academic writing proficiency once again resides exclusively with the English Department faculty.

Whatever the final disposition of the issues, questions, and conjectures posed above, we can draw the following conclusions about the construct validity of holistic scoring of FL texts: On the basis of the evidence presented, comprehension plays a significant role in holistic assessment of FL writing proficiency. However, as a reader's ability to access meaning from a text depends considerably on the form in which that meaning is expressed, the two should not (and probably cannot) be considered as either separate or mutually exclusive. Instead, the role of comprehension in FL holistic assessment should be viewed as part of an interactive process involving both text-based and reader-based variables.

Thus, at the present time it is at best premature and at worst simplistic to attempt to reduce the operational definition of FL writing proficiency to "comprehension." Similarly, it is an overstatement of the significance of these experimental findings to feel justified in reducing the criteria for gauging FL proficiency to the simple equation "comprehension equals quality." Nevertheless, these results can offer some reassurance to ESL composition teachers who measure success in terms of communicative competence that when they use holistic scoring to assess FL writing proficiency, the procedure they use allows them to access the construct they seek to measure.

REFERENCES

Ausubel, D., Novac, J., & Hanesian, H. (1978). *Educational psychology: A cognitive view* . New York: Holt, Rinehart & Winston.

Baker, L., & Anderson, R. (1982). Effects of inconsistent information on text processing: Evidence for comprehension monitoring. *Reading Research Quarterly, 17*(2),160-164.

Bernhardt, E. (1983). Testing foreign language reading comprehension: The immediate recall protocol. *Die Unterrichtspraxis, 16*(1), 27-33.

Bernhardt, E. (1984). Toward an information processing perspective in foreign language reading. *Modern Language Journal, 68*(4), 322-331.

Breland, H., & Jones, R. (1984). Perceptions of writing skills. *Written Communication, 1*(1), 101-119.

Burt, M., & Kiparsky, C. (1974). Global and local mistakes. In J. Schumann & N. Stenson (Eds.), *New frontiers in second language learning* (pp. 71-80). Rowley, MA: Newbury House.

Carrell, P. (1983). Three components of background knowledge in reading comprehension. *Language Learning, 33*, 183-207.

Charney, D. (1984). The validity of using holistic scoring to evaluate writing: A critical overview. *Research in the Teaching of English, 18*(1), 65-81.

Coady, J. (1979). A psycholinguistic model of the ESL reader. In R. Mackay, B. Barkman, & R. Jordan (Eds.), *Reading in a second language* (pp. 5-12). Rowley, MA: Newbury House.

Chomsky, N. (1965). *Aspects of the theory of syntax.* Cambridge, MA: MIT Press.

Coffman, W. (1968). A comparison of two methods of reading essay examinations. Cited by L. Cronbach in R. L. Thorndike (Ed.), *Educational measurement* (pp. 443-507). Washington, DC: American Council on Education.

Connor, U. (1984). Recall of text: Differences between first and second language learners. *TESOL Quarterly, 18*(2), 239-256.

Cooper, C. (1977). Holistic evaluation in writing. In C. Cooper & L. Odell (Eds), *Evaluating writing: Describing, measuring, judging* (pp. 3-31). Urbana, IL: National Council of Teachers of English.

Cronbach, L., & Meehl, P. (1955). Construct validity in psychological tests. *Psychological Bulletin, 27*, 281-302.

de Beaugrande, R. (1978). *Theoretical issues in the process-product controversy.* Gainesville, FL: University of Florida. (ERIC Document Reproduction Service No. ED 161 034).

Emig, J. (1971). *The composing processes of 12th graders.* Urbana, IL: National Council of Teachers of English.

Frederiksen, C. (1977). Semantic processing units in understanding text. In R. Freedle (Ed.), *Discourse production and comprehension* (Vol. 1, pp. 57-88). Norwood, NJ: Ablex Publishing.

Freedman, S. (1979). How characteristics of students' essays influence teachers' evaluation. *Journal of Educational Psychology, 71*, 328-338.

Gay, L. (1981). Educational research: *Competencies for analysis and application.* Columbus, OH: Charles E. Merrill.

Goodman, K. (1967). Reading: A psycholinguistic guessing game. *Journal of the Reading Specialist, 6*, 126-135.

Huot, B. (1990). Reliability, validity, and holistic scoring: What we know and what we need to know. *College Composition and Communication, 41*(2), 201-211.

Huot, B., & Williamson, M. (1990). *Toward a language-based theory of writing assessment.* Unpublished manuscript.

Janopoulos, M. (1989). Reader comprehension and holistic assessment of second language writing proficiency. *Written Communication, 6*, 218-237.

Janopoulos, M. (1991). Using written recall protocols to measure aspects of second language writing proficiency: The effect of task awareness. (Report). Cedar Falls, IA: University of Northern Iowa. (ERIC Document Reproduction Service No. ED 335 869).

Janopoulos, M. (1992). University faculty tolerance of NS and NNS writing errors: A comparison. *Journal of Second Language Writing, 1*(2), 109–121.

Johnson, R. (1970). Recall of prose as a function of the structural importance of the linguistic units. *Journal of Verbal Learning and Verbal Behavior, 9*, 12-20.

Just, M., & Carpenter, P. (1980). A theory of reading: From eye fixations to comprehension. *Psychological Review, 87*, 329-354.

Kaplan, R. (1966). Cultural thought patterns in inter-cultural education. *Language Learning, 16*(1), 1-20.

Kintsch, W., & van Dijk, T. (1978). Toward a model of discourse comprehension and production. *Psychological Review, 85*(1), 363-394.

Kintsch, W., Mandel, T., & Kozminsky, E. (1977). Summarizing scrambled stories. *Memory and Cognition, 5,* 547-552.

Larsen-Freeman, D. (1986).*Techniques and principles in language teaching.* Hong Kong: Oxford University Press.

Leki, I. (1989). *Academic writing.* New York: St. Martin's Press.

Ludwig, J. (1982). Native-speaker judgments of second-language learners' efforts at communication: A review. *Modern Language Journal, 66*(3), 274-283.

Mandler, J. (1978). A code in the node: The use of a story schema retrieval. *Discourse Processes, 1*(1): 14-35.

Meyer, B. (1973, May). *Identifying variables in prose.* Paper presented at the Annual Meeting of the Eastern Psychological Association, Washington, DC. (ERIC Document Reproduction Service No. ED 082 218).

Meyer, B. (1982). Reading research and the composition teacher: The importance of plans. *College Composition and Communication, 33*(1), 37-49.

Odell, L. (1977). Measuring changes in intellectual processes as one dimension of growth in writing. In C. Cooper & L. Odell (Eds.), *Evaluating writing* (pp. 107-132). Buffalo, NY: National Council of Teachers of English.

Oller, J. (1979). *Language tests at school.* London: Longman.

Palmer, A., & Groot, P. (1981). An introduction. In A. Palmer, P. Groot, & G. Trosper (Eds.), *The construct validation of tests of communicative competence* (pp. 1-11) . Washington, DC: TESOL.

Pearson, D., & Tierney, R. (1984). On becoming a thoughtful reader: Learning to read like a writer. In *Becoming readers in a complex society.* (83rd Yearbook of the National Society for the Study of Education). Chicago, IL: University of Chicago Press.

Perkins, K. (1983). On the use of composition scoring techniques, objective measures, and objective tests to evaluate ESL writing ability. *TESOL Quarterly, 17*(4), 651-671.

Perl, S. (1980). Understanding composing. *College Composition and Communication, 31*(4), 363-369.

Rafoth, B., & Rubin, D. (1984). The impact of content and mechanics on judgments of writing quality. *Written Communication, 1*(4), 446-458.

Raimes, A. (1983). Anguish as a second language? Remedies for composition teachers. In S. McKay (Ed.), *Composing in a second language* (pp. 81-96). Rowley, MA: Newbury House.

Raimes, A. (1986, March). *Practical considerations in teaching writing as a process.* Paper presented at the 20th annual meeting of TESOL, Anaheim, CA.

Rumelhart, D. (1980). Schemata: The building blocks of cognition. In R. Spiro, B. Bruce, & W. Brewer (Eds.), *Theoretical issues in reading comprehension* (pp. 33-58). Hillsdale, NJ: Erlbaum.

Santos, T. (1988). Professors' reactions to the academic writing of non-native speaking students. *TESOL Quarterly, 22*(1), 69-90.

Savignon, S. (1984a). *Communicative competence: Theory and classroom practice*. Reading, MA: Addison-Wesley.

Savignon, S. (1984b). *Evaluation of communicative competence: The ACTFL Provisional Proficiency Guidelines.* Paper presented at the ACTFL Annual Meeting, Chicago, IL.

Skinner, B. F. (1957). *Verbal behavior.* New York: Appleton-Century-Crofts.

Sommers, N. (1982). Responding to student writing. *College Composition and Communication, 33*(2), 378-388.

Spandel, V., & Stiggins, R. (1980). *Direct measures of writing skill: Issues and applications.* (Grant No. OB-NIE-G-78-0206). Northwest Regional Educational Laboratory, Portland, OR. (ERIC Document Reproduction Service No. ED 213 035).

Spiro, R. (1980). Constructive processes in prose comprehension and recall. In R. Spiro, B. Bruce, & W. Brewer (Eds.), *Theoretical issues in reading comprehension.* Hillsdale, NJ: Erlbaum.

Stern, H. (1983). *Fundamental concepts of language teaching.* New York: Oxford.

Taylor, B. (1986, March). *Some principal characteristics of the prose-oriented writing class.* Paper presented at the 20th annual meeting of TESOL, Anaheim, CA.

Thompson, R. (1990). Writing-proficiency tests and remediation: Some cultural differences. *TESOL Quarterly, 24*(1), 99-105.

Tierney, R., LaZansky, J., Raphael, T., & Cohen, P. (1973). *Author's intentions and reader's interpretations.* (NIE Contract No. 400-76-0116). (ERIC Document Reproduction Service No. ED 229 740).

White, W. (1985). *Teaching and assessing writing.* San Francisco, CA: Jossey-Bass.

Zamel, V. (1986, March). *From process to product.* Paper presented at the 20th annual meeting of TESOL, Anaheim, CA.

Author Index

A

Ackerman, J., 238, *262*
Adams, G., 66-67, *72*
Adelman, C., 99, *107*
Alexander, J., 148, 169, *204*
Algina, J., 128, *138*
Allal, L., 128, *138*
Anastasi, A., 4, 11, 13, 15, 22, *39*, 259, 262, 269, 294, *299*
Anderson, C. C., 118, *138*
Anderson, H. A., 128, *141*
Anderson, J. A., 95, *108*, 128, *139*, 160, *205*
Anderson, M., 210, *230*
Anderson, R. C., 207, *229*, 238, *262*, 309, 318, *322*
Anson, C., 238, *262*
Applebee, A. N., 25-26, 37, *39*, 45-46, *72*, *75*
Archbald, D. A., 66-68, *72*
Ascher, C., 67, *74*,
Ash, B.H., 126, *138*
Asher, J. W., 116, *140*
Austin, J. L., 285, *299*
Ausubel, D., 304-305, 307, *322*
Avner, R. A., 128, *139*

B

Baker, E. L., 63, 68, *76*, 148, 173, *205*

Baker, L., 309, 318, *322*
Ball, C., 142, 148, *205*
Ballard, P. B., 128, *139*
Barritt, L., 208, *229*, 238, *262*
Bartholomae, D., 38, *39*, 48, *72*, 144, 160, *204*
Bartko, J. J., 128, *138*
Baumgartner, V., 210, *230*
Bazerman, C., 245, *262*
Beebe, S. A., 255, *262*
Beaugrande, R. de, 48, *72*, 309, 319, *323*
Belanoff, P., 67, 70, *72*, 100-101, *107*
Belson, W. A., 285, *299*
Benne, K. D., 254, *262*
Bereiter, C., 47, 56, 58, *72*, 77
Berk, R. A., 119, 128, 132, 135, *138*
Berkenkotter, C., 238, *262*
Berlak, H., 66-67, *72*
Bernhardt, E., 307, 310, 313, *322*
Bertrand, C. V., 206, *229*
Binet, A., 23, *39*
Bishop, W, 238, *262*
Bixby, J., 65, *78*
Bizzell, P., 10, 38, *39*
Blair, H., 27, *39*
Bleich, D., 207, *229*
Bloom, A., 34, *39*
Bloom, B. S., 28, 33, *39*
Borich, G., 269, *301*

Subject Index